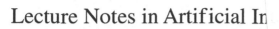

Lecture Notes in Artificial Intelligence

Edited by J. G. Carbonell and J. Siekman.

Subseries of Lecture Notes in Computer Science

Rafael H. Bordini   Mehdi Dastani
Jürgen Dix   Amal El Fallah Seghrouchni (Eds.)

Programming
Multi-Agent Systems

Third International Workshop, ProMAS 2005
Utrecht, The Netherlands, July 26, 2005
Revised and Invited Papers

 Springer

Volume Editors

Rafael H. Bordini
University of Durham, Department of Computer Science
Durham DH1 3LE, UK
E-mail: R.Bordini@durham.ac.uk

Mehdi Dastani
Utrecht University, Intelligent Systems Group
3508 TB Utrecht, The Netherlands
E-mail: mehdi@cs.uu.nl

Jürgen Dix
Clausthal University of Technology, Department of Computer Science
Julius-Albert-Str. 4, 38678 Clausthal-Zellerfeld, Germany
E-mail: dix@tu-clausthal.de

Amal El Fallah Seghrouchni
University of Paris 6, LIP6, Paris, France
E-mail: Amal.Elfallah@lip6.fr

Library of Congress Control Number: 2006921790

CR Subject Classification (1998): I.2.11, I.2, C.2.4, D.2, F.3, D.3

LNCS Sublibrary: SL 7 – Artificial Intelligence

ISSN   0302-9743
ISBN-10   3-540-32616-2 Springer Berlin Heidelberg New York
ISBN-13   978-3-540-32616-8 Springer Berlin Heidelberg New York

Springer is a part of Springer Science+Business Media

springer.com

© Springer-Verlag Berlin Heidelberg 2006
Printed in Germany

Typesetting: Camera-ready by author, data conversion by Scientific Publishing Services, Chennai, India
Printed on acid-free paper   SPIN: 11678823   06/3142   5 4 3 2 1 0

Preface

These are the proceedings of the Third International Workshop on Programming Multi-Agent Systems (ProMAS 2005), held in July 2005 in Utrecht (Netherlands) as an associated event of AAMAS 2005: the main international conference on autonomous agents and multi-agent systems. ProMAS 2005 was the third of a series of workshops that is attracting increasing attention of researchers and practitioners in multi-agent systems.

The idea of organizing the first workshop of the series was first discussed during the Dagstuhl seminar *Programming Multi-Agent Systems based on Logic* (see [4]), where the focus was on *logic-based approaches*. It was felt that the scope should be broadened beyond logic-based approaches, thus giving the current scope and aims of ProMAS; see [3] for the proceedings of the first event (ProMAS 2003) and [1] for the proceedings of the second workshop (ProMAS 2004). All three events of the series were held as AAMAS workshops.

Besides the ProMAS Steering Committee (Rafael Bordini, Mehdi Dastani, Jürgen Dix, and Amal El Fallah Seghrouchni), an AgentLink III Technical Forum Group on Programming Multi-Agent Systems has been very active in the last couple of years (see http://www.cs.uu.nl/~mehdi/al3promas.html for details on that group). Moreover, we have edited a book on *Multi-Agent Programming* [2], and ProMAS 2006 will be held with AAMAS 2006 on May, in Hakodate, Japan (see http://www.cs.uu.nl/ProMAS/ for up-to-date information about ProMAS).

One of the driving motivations behind this workshop series is the observation that the area of autonomous agents and multi-agent systems (MAS) has grown into a promising technology offering sensible alternatives for the design of distributed, intelligent systems. Several efforts have been made by researchers and practitioners, both in academia and industry, and by several standardization consortia in order to provide new languages, tools, methods, and frameworks so as to establish the necessary standards for a wide use of MAS technology.

However, until recently the main focus of the MAS research community has been on the development, sometimes by formal methods but often informally, of concepts (concerning both mental and social attitudes), architectures, coordination techniques, and general approaches to the analysis and specification of MAS. In particular, this contribution has been quite fragmented, without any clear way of "putting it all together," and thus completely inaccessible to practitioners.

We are convinced that the next step in furthering the achievement of the MAS project is irrevocably associated with the *development of programming languages and tools that can effectively support MAS programming* and the *implementation of key notions in MAS in a unified framework*. The success of MAS development can only be guaranteed if we can bridge the gap from analysis and design to effective implementation. This, in turn, requires the development of fully fledged and general purpose programming technology so that the concepts and techniques of MAS can be easily and directly implemented.

ProMAS 2005, as indeed ProMAS 2003 and ProMAS 2004, was an invaluable opportunity that brought together leading researchers from both academia and industry to discuss various issues on programming languages and tools for MAS. Showing the increasing importance of the ProMAS aims, the attendance in our workshop has been growing steadily: ProMAS 2005 was the most popular of all AMAAS workshops in terms of number of registered participants.

This volume of the LNAI series constitutes the official (post-)proceedings of ProMAS 2005. It presents the main contributions that featured in the latest ProMAS event. Besides the final 14 high-quality accepted papers, we also invited two additional papers. The structure of this volume is as follows:

Invited Papers: Michael Fisher, a leading researcher in the area, gave an invited talk at the ProMAS workshop. Subsequently, he wrote a paper based on his talk, which is featured in these proceedings. We also invited Peter McBurney and Mike Luck, who were at the time actively working on the AgentLink III "Agent Technology Roadmap," to summarize their findings from that exercise, highlighting the importance that the ProMAS topics will have in the efforts towards widespread uptake of agent technology.

  – The first invited paper, *MetaTem: The Story So Far*, by Michael Fisher, illustrates MetaTem, a programming language based on the direct execution of temporal statements. After a brief introduction to temporal logic and the notion of executing a formula, a concurrent version of MetaTem is introduced. This allows to model multiple, asynchronously executing agents. These agents can be organized into groups that allow for multicast message passing.
  – The second invited paper, *Agent-Based Computing and Programming of Agent Systems*, by Michael Luck, Peter McBurney and Jorge Gonzalez-Palacios, is partly based on the Agentlink III Roadmap, from which a nice classification of the development of MAS within the next decade is taken. The paper discusses several issues involved in multi-agent programming and open, distributed systems in general.

Multi-agent Techniques and Issues: The second part of this volume contains five papers. The first paper, *Dynamic Self-Control of Autonomous Agents* by Caroline Chopinaud, Amal El Fallah Seghrouchni and Patrick Taillibert, focuses on ensuring that a MAS behaves correspondingly to what its developers expect. As standard validation techniques still allow the occurrence of errors during execution, the paper proposes an additional approach of dynamic self-monitoring and self-regulation such that an agent can control its own behavior.

The second paper, *Bridging Agent Theory and Object Orientation: Importing Social Roles in Object-Oriented Languages* by Matteo Baldoni, Guido Boella and Leendert van der Torre focuses on describing how to introduce the notion of social role in programming languages. To limit the restrictions on their approach, the authors extended Java itself as it is the most commonly used language to develop software agents. This way they were not restricted by specific agent or MAS architectures or other characteristics.

The third paper, *Implementation Techniques for Solving POMDPs in Personal Assistant Domains* by Pradeep Varakantham, Rajiv Maheswaran and Milind Tambe, treats the problem of using POMDPs to build agents able to make decisions in an environment that includes human beings. As this is computationally very expensive, the authors propose two new solutions to reach decisions faster, one of them is optimal and the other approximated. To achieve this, they based their work on the notion of progress or dynamics in personal assistant domains and the density of policy vectors.

The fourth paper, *Using a Planner for Coordination Of Multiagent Team Behavior*, authored by Oliver Obst, concentrates on using HTN planners to achieve coordination between agents in a MAS. This paper also presents promising results obtained during the RoboCup.

Finally, Juan M. Serrano, Sascha Ossowski and Sergio Saugar's paper on *Reusability Issues in the Instrumentation of Agent Interactions* is about engineering component interactions in large-scale open systems. To advance this issue, the authors present the RICA-J programming framework which provides executable constructs for every organizational, ACL-based abstraction of the RICA theory. Their execution semantics is defined over the JADE platform. This paper also presents a systematic reuse approach for interactions engineering.

Multi-agent Programming: The third part comprises four papers on "Multi-Agent Programming." The first paper is entitled *An AgentSpeak Meta-Interpreter and its Applications* by Michael Winikoff. It presents a meta-interpreter for AgentSpeak (i.e., the interpreter itself is written in AgentSpeak) and gives a sketch of its correctness proof. Furthermore, the paper argues that using a meta-interpreter may facilitate certain aspects such as debugging, failure handling, making selection functions explicit, and extending the language.

The second paper, *Extending the Capability Concept for Flexible BDI Modularization* by Lars Braubach, Alexander Pokahr, and Winfried Lamersdorf, deals with the *capability* construct found in the literature, and discusses how to implement an extended notion within Jadex. Capabilities allow for the implementation of BDI agents to be carried out as a composition of configurable modules, very much in the spirit of software engineering principles.

The third paper, *A Model-Based Executive for Commanding Robot Teams* by Anthony Barrett, builds upon Milind Tambe's model of flexible teamwork and combines it with a high-level language that facilitates the task of giving commands to a robotic system. From the initial global model, a compiler handles the distribution of control functions to team members.

The final paper in this part, *Hermes: Implementing Goal-Oriented Agent Interactions,* by Christopher Cheong and Michael Winikoff, presents the Hermes methodology for designing agent interaction in terms of *interaction goals.* The paper also provides guidelines on how interaction goals can be mapped down to plans typical of BDI-like agents, therefore appropriate for many existing agent platforms.

Multi-agent Platforms and Organization: The first paper of the last part of this book is from Ichiro Satoh: *Organization and Mobility in Mobile Agent Computing.* It presents two mechanisms for dynamically organizing mobile agents distributed over several computers. In the first mechanism, a mobile agent may contain other mobile agents, while in the second mechanism a group of mobile agents are bound to one mobile agent. The migration of mobile agents is determined by the migration of the agents that contains/binds other agents.

The second paper, *Programming MAS with Artifacts*, is from Alessandro Ricci, Mirko Viroli and Andrea Omicini. It discusses the role of coordination artifacts as first-class entities in the development of MAS. In particular, there is a discussion on the implementation of MAS in terms of programming coordination artifact that coordinate the behavior of programmed individual cognitive agents.

The third paper, *Programming Deliberative Agents for Mobile Services: the 3APL-M Platform*, written by Fernando Koch, John-Jules C. Meyer, Frank Dignum, and Iyad Rahwan, presents a platform for building MAS where individual agents execute on handheld and embedded computational devices. Individual agents are implemented by a 3APL-inspired programming language.

The fourth paper, entitled *Implementing Multi-Agent Systems Organizations with INGENIAS*, is by Jorge J. Gomez-Sanz and Juan Pavon. This paper discusses some general requirements for organization modelling that can be used to analyze, design, and implement MAS. The discussion is accompanied with an example of a MAS developed with the INGENIAS methodology and implemented on the JADE platform.

Finally, the last paper of this book is by Mengqiu Wang, Mariusz Homeostasis and Martin Parvis: *Declarative Agent Programming Support for a FIPA-Compliant Agent Platform*. This paper focuses on the relation between high-level declarative agent models and low-level agent platforms that enable the communication between agents. In particular, it discusses how declarative agent programming support can be provided to develop MAS on the OPAL platform that supports FICA standards.

We would like to thank all the authors, the invited speaker, Programme Committee members, and reviewers for their outstanding contribution to the success of ProMAS 2005. We are particularly grateful to the AMAAS 2005 organizers for their technical support and for hosting ProMAS 2005.

November 2005   Rafael H. Bordini
                                                            Mehdi Dastani
                                                            Jürgen Dix
                                                Amal El Fallah Seghrouchni

                                                      Organizers ProMAS 2005

References

1. Rafael H. Bordini, Mehdi Dastani, Jürgen Dix, and Amal El Fallah Seghrouchni, editors. *Programming Multi-Agent Systems: Second International Workshop (ProMAS 2004), held with AAMAS-2004, 20th of July, New York City, NY (Revised Selected and Invited Papers)*, number 3346 in LNAI, Berlin, 2004. Springer-Verlag.
2. Rafael H. Bordini, Mehdi Dastani, Jürgen Dix, and Amal El Fallah Seghrouchni, editors. *Multi-Agent Programming: Languages, Platforms and Applications.* Number 15 in Multiagent Systems, Artificial Societies, and Simulated Organizations. Springer, 2005.
3. M. Dastani, J. Dix, and A. El Fallah Segrouchni, editors. *Programming Multi Agent Systems (ProMAS'03)*, LNCS 3067, Berlin, 2004. Springer.
4. Jürgen Dix, Michael Fisher, and Yingqian Zhang. Programming Multi Agent Systems based on Logic. Technical Report Dagstuhl Seminar Report 361, IBFI GmbH, Schloß Dagstuhl, 2002.

References

Organization

ProMAS 2005 was held as a workshop of the Fourth International Joint Conference on Autonomous Agents and Multi-Agent Systems, in Utrecht, The Netherlands, on July 2005.

Organizing Committee

Rafael H. Bordini (University of Durham, UK)
Mehdi Dastani (Utrecht University, Netherlands)
Jürgen Dix (Clausthal University of Technology, Germany)
Amal El Fallah Seghrouchni (University of Paris VI, France)

Programme Committee

Chris van Aart (Acklin, The Netherlands)
Jean-Pierre Briot (University of Paris VI, France)
Monique Calisti (Whitestein Technologies, Switzerland)
Yves Demazeau (Institut IMAG – Grenoble, France)
Frank Dignum (Utrecht University, Netherlands)
Michael Fisher (University of Liverpool, UK)
Vladimir Gorodetsky (Russian Academy of Sciences, Russia)
Jomi Hübner (Universidade Regional de Blumenau, Brazil)
Toru Ishida (Kyoto University, Japan)
David Kinny (CTO, Agentis Software, USA)
João Alexandre Leite (Universidade Nova de Lisboa, Portugal)
Jiming Liu (Hong Kong Baptist University, Hong Kong)
John-Jules Meyer (Utrecht University, Netherlands)
Jörg Müller (Clausthal University of Technology, Germany)
Oliver Obst (Koblenz-Landau University, Germany)
Gregory O'Hare (University College Dublin, Ireland)
Andrea Omicini (University of Bologna, Italy)
Julian Padget (University of Bath, UK)
Agostino Poggi (Università degli Studi di Parma, Italy)
Chris Reed (Calico Jack Ltd., UK)
Ichiro Satoh (National Institute of Informatics, Kyoto, Japan)
Onn Shehory (IBM Haifa Research Labs, Haifa University, Israel)
Kostas Stathis (City University London, UK)
Milind Tambe (University of Southern California, USA)
Leendert van der Torre (CWI, Netherlands)
Paolo Torroni (University of Bologna, Italy)

Table of Contents

IV   Multi-agent Platforms and Organisation

Part I

Invited Papers

METATEM: The Story so Far

Michael Fisher

Department of Computer Science, University of Liverpool, United Kingdom
http://www.csc.liv.ac.uk/~michael

1 Introduction

METATEM is a simple programming language based on the direct execution of temporal logic statements. It was introduced through a number of papers [35,2,3] culminating in a book collecting together work on the basic temporal language [5]. However, since that time, there has been a programme of research, carried out over a number of years, extending, adapting and applying the basic approach. In particular, much of the research has concerned the development of descendents of METATEM for describing and implementing complex multi-agent systems.

Thus, while there are a number of other approaches to executing temporal statements [32,18], we will concentrate on this one particular approach and will describe the developments over the last 15 years. The structure of this article mirrors the research developments in that the path through these developments is not linear. The diagram below gives a pictorial explanation of the sections that follow.

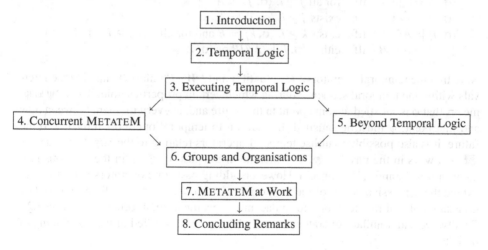

Thus, we begin with a brief review of temporal logic itself.

2 Temporal Logic

We will begin with a review of basic temporal logic. Rather than providing an in-depth account of temporal logic, we will just provide a simple description that can be used throughout this article. For a more thorough exposition of the formal properties of this

R.H. Bordini et al. (Eds.): ProMAS 2005, LNAI 3862, pp. 3–22, 2006.

logic, see [11], while for examples of the use of temporal logic in program specification in general, see [50].

Temporal logic is an extension of classical logic, whereby time becomes an extra parameter when considering the truth of logical statements. The variety of temporal logic we are concerned with is based upon a discrete, linear model of time, having both a finite past and infinite future, i.e.,

$$\sigma = s_0, s_1, s_2, s_3, \ldots$$

Here, a model (σ) for the logic is an infinite sequence of states which can be thought of as 'moments' or 'points' in time. Since we will only consider propositional temporal logic here, then, associated with each of these states is a valuation for all the propositions in the language.

The temporal language we use is that of classical logic extended with various modalities characterising different aspects of the temporal structure above. Examples of the key operators include '$\bigcirc\varphi$', which is satisfied if φ is satisfied at the *next* moment in time, '$\Diamond\varphi$', which is satisfied if φ is satisfied at *some* future moment in time, and '$\square\varphi$', which is satisfied if φ is satisfied at *all* future moments in time.

More formally, a semantics of the language can be defined with respect to the model (σ) in which the statement is to be interpreted, and the moment in time (i) at which it is to be interpreted. Thus, a semantics for the key temporal operators is given below.

$$\langle \sigma, i \rangle \models \bigcirc A \quad \text{iff} \quad \langle \sigma, i+1 \rangle \models A$$
$$\langle \sigma, i \rangle \models \square A \quad \text{iff} \quad \text{for all } j \geq i. \ \langle \sigma, j \rangle \models A$$
$$\langle \sigma, i \rangle \models \Diamond A \quad \text{iff} \quad \text{exists } j \geq i. \ \langle \sigma, j \rangle \models A$$
$$\langle \sigma, i \rangle \models A \, \mathcal{U} B \quad \text{iff} \quad \text{exists } k \geq i. \ \langle \sigma, k \rangle \models B \text{ and for all } k > j \geq i. \ \langle \sigma, j \rangle \models A$$
$$\langle \sigma, i \rangle \models A \, \mathcal{W} B \quad \text{iff} \quad \text{either } \langle \sigma, i \rangle \models A \, \mathcal{U} B \text{ or } \langle \sigma, i \rangle \models \square A$$

Note that the temporal operators '$\mathcal{U}$' ("until") and '$\mathcal{W}$' ("unless") characterise intervals within the temporal sequence during which certain properties hold. Thus, '$\psi \, \mathcal{U} \varphi$' means that φ is satisfied at some point in the future and, at every moment between now and that point, ψ must be satisfied. In addition to temporal operators referring to the future, it is also possible to utilise temporal operators relating to the *past* [49], such as '■' ("always in the past"), '◆' ("sometime in the past"), '●' ("in the previous moment in time"), and '$\mathcal{S}$' ("since"). However, adding past-time operators here does not extend the expressive power of the language and such operators can all be removed by translation of arbitrary temporal formulae into a specific normal form (see Section 3.2). Finally, we add a nullary operator '**start**', which is only satisfied at the "beginning of time":

$$\langle \sigma, i \rangle \models \textbf{start} \quad \text{iff} \quad i = 0$$

2.1 Why Temporal Logic?

But, why do we use temporal logic? One reason is that it allows the concise expression of useful dynamic properties of individual components. For example, the formula

$$request \ \Rightarrow \ reply \ \mathcal{U} \, acknowledgement$$

characterises a system where, once a *request* is received, a *reply* is continually sent up until the point where an *acknowledgement* is received. And, importantly, an acknowledgement is guaranteed to be received eventually. In addition, pre-conditions, such as

$$\blacksquare \neg started \;\Rightarrow\; \bigcirc \neg moving$$

can easily be described in this logic.

As the temporal model on which the logic is based comprises a linear sequence of moments, then the logic can also be used to express the *order* in which activities occur, for example

$$hungry \;\Rightarrow\; (buy\_food \wedge \bigcirc cook\_food \wedge \bigcirc\bigcirc eat).$$

While the logic is clearly useful for representing the dynamic activity of individual components, and this relates very closely to traditional applications of temporal logic in program specification [50], the formalism is also useful for characterising properties of the overall system. For example, the formula

$$broadcast(msg) \;\Rightarrow\; \forall a \in Group.\;\; \Diamond receive(msg,a)$$

describes the message-passing behaviour within a group of components (characterised by the finite set '*Group*'). Thus, temporal logic can be used to represent both the internal behaviour of a component and the macro-level behaviour of systems.

3   Executing Temporal Logic

3.1   What Is Execution?

But, what does it mean to execute a formula, φ, of logic, L? In general, this means constructing a model, $\mathcal{M}$, for φ, i.e.

$$\mathcal{M} \models_L \varphi.$$

Typically, this construction takes place under some external constraints on φ, and many different models might satisfy φ. However, we note that:

- as φ represents a declarative statement, then producing $\mathcal{M}$ can be seen as execution in the declarative language L; and
- if φ is a specification, then constructing $\mathcal{M}$ can also be seen as prototyping an implementation of that specification.

Languages such as Prolog effectively build a form of model by attempting to refute the negation of a goal.

We execute arbitrary formulae from the temporal logic using an execution mechanism which is complete for propositional, linear temporal logic. In order to simplify the execution algorithm, arbitrary formulae are transformed into a specific normal form, called SNF (see Section 3.2). Thus, the execution algorithm works on formulae in SNF; this algorithm will be described in more detail in Section 3.3.

Although deciding propositional temporal logic formulae is complex (PSPACE-complete), deciding first-order temporal logic (FOTL) formulae is *much* worse! FOTL is incomplete (i.e. not recursively enumerable) [56,1] and so, if we wish to use arbitrary FOTL in our specifications then we are left with a few options:

1. restrict the logic and provide a 'complete' execution mechanism; or
2. execute the full logic, treating execution as simply an *attempt* to build a model for the formula.

Fragments of FOTL with 'good' properties are difficult to find and, once found [53,44], turn out to be quite restrictive. Thus, we choose (2). In addition, completeness cannot be retained in general, especially as we wish to extend the basic execution mechanism to include not only constrained backtracking, but also a dynamic model of concurrent computation and communication. Thus, in summary, execution of temporal specifications is synonymous with *attempting* to build models for such specifications.

3.2   What Is SNF?

The specification of a component's behaviour is given as a temporal formula, then transformed into a simple normal form, called Separated Normal Form (SNF) [14,19]. In this normal form, the majority of the temporal operators are removed, and formulae are represented as

$$\Box \bigwedge_{i=1}^{n} R_i$$

where each R_i, termed a *rule*, is one of the following forms.

$$\textbf{start} \Rightarrow \bigvee_{b=1}^{r} l_b \qquad \text{(an \textit{initial} rule)}$$

$$\bigwedge_{a=1}^{g} k_a \Rightarrow \bigcirc \left[\bigvee_{b=1}^{r} l_b \right] \qquad \text{(a \textit{step} rule)}$$

$$\bigwedge_{a=1}^{g} k_a \Rightarrow \Diamond l \qquad \text{(a \textit{sometime} rule)}$$

Note, here, that each k_a, l_b, or l is a literal. This normal form gives a simple and intuitive description of what is true at the beginning of execution (via initial rules), what must be true during any execution step (via step rules), and what constraints exist on future execution states (via sometime rules). For example, the formulae below correspond to the three different types of SNF rules.

INITIAL:	$\textbf{start} \Rightarrow (sad \lor optimistic)$
STEP:	$(sad \land \neg optimistic) \Rightarrow \bigcirc sad$
SOMETIME:	$optimistic \Rightarrow \Diamond \neg sad$

3.3   Execution Algorithm

The basic execution algorithm of METATEM [2,3] attempts to build a model for the formula in a simple forward-chaining fashion. The basic approach, as defined in [31,3] is described below. Assuming we are executing a set of SNF rules, R:

1. By examining the *initial* rules in R, constraints on the possible start states for the temporal model can be generated. Call these choices, C. Let 'Ω', the list of outstanding eventualities, be an empty list.
2. Make a choice from C. If there are no unexplored choices, return to a choice point in a previous state. Note that this choice mechanism takes into account a number of elements, including Ω.
   For the choice taken, generate additional eventualities, *Evs*, by checking applicability of sometime rules. Append *Evs* to Ω.
3. Generate a new state, s, from the choice made in (2) and define s as being a successor to the current state. Note that, by default, if propositions are not constrained we choose to leave them unsatisfied.
   Remove from Ω all eventualities satisfied within s.
   If s is inconsistent, or if any member of Ω has been continuously outstanding for more than $2^{5|R|}$ states, then return to (2) and select a different alternative.
4. Generate constraints on *next* states by checking applicability in s of step rules in R. Set C to be these choices. Note that C here represents all the possible choices of valuations for the next state, while Ω gives the list of eventualities that remain to be satisfied.
5. With current state, s, the set of choices on next state, C, and the list of outstanding eventualities, Ω, go to (2).

The key result here is that, under certain constraints on the choice mechanism within (2), this execution algorithm represents a decision procedure.

Theorem 1 (See [3]). *If a set of SNF rules, R, is executed using the above algorithm, with the proviso that the choice in (3) ensures that the oldest outstanding eventualities are attempted first at each step, then a model for R will be generated if, and only if, R is satisfiable.*

The above proviso ensures that, if an eventuality is outstanding for an infinite number of steps, then it will be attempted an infinite number of times. Once the choice mechanism is extended to include arbitrary ordering functions, as in [20] (see Section 5.1), then a more general version of the above theorem can be given wherein we only require a form of *fairness* on the choice mechanism. While the above proviso effectively means that we *can* potentially explore every possibility, the incorporation in the algorithm of a bound on the number of states that eventualities can remain outstanding, together with the finite model property of the logic, ensures that all of the possible states in the model can be explored if necessary.

Example. Imagine a 'car' component which can *go*, *turn* and *stop*, but can also run out of fuel (*empty*) and *overheat*.

The internal definition might be given by a temporal logic specification in SNF, for example,

$$\textbf{start} \Rightarrow \neg moving$$
$$go \Rightarrow \Diamond moving$$
$$(moving \wedge go) \Rightarrow \bigcirc(overheat \vee empty)$$

The component's behaviour is implemented by *forward-chaining* through these formulae.

- Thus, *moving* is false at the beginning of time.
- Whenever *go* is true, a commitment to eventually make *moving* true is given.
- Whenever both *go* and *moving* are true, then either *overheat* or *empty* will be made true in the next moment in time.

4   Concurrent METATEM

4.1   From One to Many

Once we have a temporal description for a component, we can extend this to give its behaviour within an environment consisting of multiple other components. We do this simply by providing a definition of the component's interface with its environment [16]. Such an interface describes the messages that the reactive component can receive (i.e. those that come in) and send (i.e. those that go out). For example, let us consider the abstract specification of a 'car' with the behaviour given above. This car can be told to *go*, *turn* and *stop*, but can also notify other components that it has run out of fuel (*empty*) or has overheated (*overheat*). A (partial) definition is given below.

$$
\begin{aligned}
&\texttt{car()}\\
&\quad\texttt{in:}\ go,stop,turn\\
&\quad\texttt{out:}\ empty,overheat\\
&\texttt{rules:}\qquad \textbf{start} \Rightarrow \neg moving\\
&\qquad\qquad (moving \wedge go) \Rightarrow \bigcirc(overheat \vee empty)\\
&\qquad\qquad\qquad go \Rightarrow \Diamond moving
\end{aligned}
$$

This shows that the component recognises the messages 'go', 'stop' and 'turn', and can potentially send out '*empty*' and '*overheat*' messages. Its behaviour is then specified by the temporal formula

$$
\square \left[
\begin{array}{c}
\textbf{start} \Rightarrow \neg moving\\
\wedge\\
(moving \wedge go) \Rightarrow \bigcirc(overheat \vee empty)\\
\wedge\\
go \Rightarrow \Diamond moving
\end{array}
\right]
$$

Both the messages received and the messages sent are interpreted as propositions (or predicates) that can be used as part of the reactive component's specification. In addition, standard propositions (predicates) appear in the specification, for example '*moving*' in the description above. These atoms are essentially internal and do not directly correspond to communication activity by either the component or its environment.

4.2   Communication and Concurrency

Each component executes independently. However, execution may be either *synchronous*, whereby the steps in each component occur at exactly the same time (and thus the notion of *next* is common amongst the executing components), or *asynchronous*, whereby the steps in each component are distinct. The classification of a component's predicates as *environment* or *component* (or, indeed, *internal*) implements communication in a natural (and logical) way. Environment predicates are under the control of the component's environment, while the other categories of predicate can be made true or false by the component itself. Thus, when a component's execution mechanism makes an internal predicate true, it just records the fact in its internal memory, while when it makes a component predicate true, it also *broadcasts* a message corresponding to this predicate to all other components. Thus, in the above car example, when either *empty* or *overheat* is made true, then the message empty or overheat, respectively, is broadcast. If an appropriate message is received, the corresponding environment predicate set to true. In the example given above, if a go message is received, the proposition *go* is made true.

The use of broadcast message passing not only matches the logical view of computation but, as we will see later, also fits well with applications which concern open and dynamic systems (and where a component cannot know all the other components it might deal with).

4.3 Towards Semantics

If we consider a single METATEM component, then its semantics is effectively its temporal specification. However, once we move to a scenario with multiple components, the semantics of our system becomes more complex. If, as in [17,22], we consider '$[\![\ ]\!]$' to represent a function providing temporal semantics, then the behaviour of a system of multiple (in this case, two) components running in parallel ('$\|$'), is typically given by

$$[\![c_1 \| c_2]\!] \ = \ [\![c_1]\!] \wedge [\![c_2]\!].$$

However, we must also be careful to distinguish the information that c_1 deals with from that which c_2 deals with. Consequently, $[\![c_1]\!]$ is *not* just the temporal rules contained within the c_1's specification and so we must enhance these rules in some way in order to capture the different components.

An obvious way to ensure that, for example, proposition p in c_1 is distinguished from p in c_2, is to rename the propositions in the component's rules ensuring that each one is 'tagged' by the name of the component in which it occurs. Thus, we would have propositions such as p_{c_1} and p_{c_2}; this is exactly the approach used in [17]. A further important aspect of the semantics given in [17] is that it allows for *either* synchronous or asynchronous models of concurrency within the framework. In the case of synchronous execution, the semantics of each component is given as a (tagged) temporal formula in a discrete, linear temporal, as described above. However, once we consider asynchronous execution, the semantics is given as a formula in the Temporal Logic of the Reals (TLR) [6], which is a temporal logic based upon the Real, rather than Natural, Numbers. The density of this Real Number model is useful in representing the asynchronous nature of each component's execution.

A further complication is that, once communication is added to the synchronous case, we use

$$[\![c_1 \| c_2]\!] \ = \ [\![c_1]\!] \wedge [\![c_2]\!] \wedge comms(c_1, c_2).$$

where $comms(c_1, c_2)$ is a temporal specification of the communication properties, such as broadcast message-passing. However, since once a message is broadcast from a component, then the execution of that component can no longer backtrack past such a broadcast, the semantics of communicating components becomes much more complex [60].

5 Beyond Temporal Logics

So far, we have seen how specifications given in temporal logic can be *directly executed* in order to animate the component's behaviour. Thus, this approach provides a high-level programming notation, while maintaining a close link between the program and its specification. However, when moving towards the representation and execution of *agents* [61], particularly *rational agents* [62,58], we naturally want to represent more than an agent's basic temporal behaviour. Basic agents are just autonomous components and these can be modelled, at a simple level, by Concurrent METATEM as described above [16,15,33].

Although the central aspect of an agent is *autonomy*, rational agents are agents that have *reasonable* and *explainable* courses of action that they undertake. The key concept that rational agents have brought to the forefront of software design is that, as well as describing *what* an agent does, it is vital to describe *why* it does it. Hence the need to represent the reasons for certain autonomous behaviour within agents.

In line with the BDI framework [54], and with other rational agent theories [57], it is important to represent not only an agent's temporal behaviour, but also

- its informational aspects, such as what it *believes* or *knows*,
- its motivational aspects, such as its *goals* or *intentions*, and
- its deliberative aspects, such as *why* it makes the choices it does.

Thus, inspired by the success of the BDI framework [54] in representing deliberation, the basic METATEM system was extended, in [20], with information representation, in terms of *beliefs* and explicit mechanisms for ordering goals. The representation of belief was given by extending the temporal basis with a standard modal logic having Kripke semantics [40]. Thus, during execution, modal formulae related to belief were decided again by a forward chaining process. This allowed more complex (and mixed) formulae such as

$$happy \Rightarrow Bx$$
$$x \Rightarrow \bigcirc rich.$$

Goals, corresponding to both desires and intentions in the BDI model were, in turn, represented by temporal eventualities. This then allowed deliberation to be represented via user defined functions providing an ordering on the satisfaction of eventualities. This is best explained with an example.

5.1 Deliberation Via Goal Re-ordering

Recall that, in the basic METATEM execution above, outstanding eventualities are stored in an age-ordered (i.e. oldest-first) list that is passed on to the next execution state. For example, consider an agent that has the following eventualities it needs to satisfy

$$[\Diamond be\_famous, \Diamond sleep, \Diamond eat\_lunch, \Diamond make\_lunch].$$

Now, if these were passed on to the next execution state, the standard approach would be to execute these oldest-first, i.e attempt to make *be_famous* true, then attempt to make *sleep* true, and so on. In [20], the ability to *re-order* this list before it is passed on to the next execution state was provided. Now, in the example above, imagine the agent actually re-ordered the list in terms of what it considered to be most important, e.g.

$$[\Diamond be\_famous, \Diamond eat\_lunch, \Diamond sleep, \Diamond make\_lunch].$$

Indeed, the agent could re-order the list further if it had an idea about what it could actually achieve, e.g. what it knew *how* to make true. Thus, if the agent had no way (i.e. no plan) to make *be_famous* true, it might move it to the end of the list. If the agent knew how to make *eat_lunch* true, it might move it towards the front of the list. However, it might also be able to infer that a pre-condition of making *eat_lunch* true is to make *make_lunch* lunch true and so it might well move this to the front of the list. Thus, the list passed on to the next execution state is then

$$[\Diamond make\_lunch, \Diamond eat\_lunch, \Diamond sleep, \Diamond be\_famous].$$

5.2 Resource-Bounded Reasoning

While the above provides a simple and concise mechanism for representing and implementing deliberative agents, it does not deal with a further important aspect of 'real' agents, namely their resource-bounded nature [9]. In particular, the representation of belief was given by extending the temporal basis with a standard modal logic having Kripke semantics [40]. As is well known, this does not match the resource-bounded nature of 'real' reasoners [39]. Indeed modal logics generally model logically omniscient agents which are forced to believe (and compute) all the logical consequences of their own beliefs.

Thus, in [23], we modified the METATEM execution framework so that it was based on *multi-context* logics of belief [10,37,36] rather than traditional modal logics. Multi-context logics [38,7] allow much finer control of the reasoning processes. In using this basis for belief in METATEM, we then have much finer control over how beliefs are explored, executed and reasoned about. In particular, we can control how much reasoning an agent carried out during its execution, and this allows us to capture an element of resource-boundedness.

This work was applied, for example to parts of the RoboCup scenario [24,25], and was extended to incorporate bounds on the temporal resourced consumed, i.e. the agent can reason about what it might do in the future, but the distance it can reason into the future about is limited [34].

A final modification brought in the concepts of *ability* and *confidence* [26], giving us the ABC framework which incorporates:

- Ability — captured in a very simple modal extension, where $A_i\varphi$ intuitively means "*i* is able to do φ", for example,

$$A_{me}buy\_ticket \Rightarrow \bigcirc buy\_ticket$$

- **Belief** — captured by multi-context belief with potential resource-bounds, where B_i represents the beliefs of agent i, for example

$$buy\_ticket \Rightarrow B_{me} lottery\_winner$$

- **Confidence** — captured by the combination of B_i and $\Diamond$, where "agent i is confident of φ' is given by $B_i \Diamond \varphi$.

The idea of confidence replaces the use of just '$\Diamond$' to represent goals. Expressing confidence in terms of belief about the future not only keeps the logic simple, it allows us to express weaker motivational attitudes. This confidence can be used as an agent's reason for doing something. Importantly, confidence can come not only from the agent itself, but also from the agent's confidence *in other agents in this system*. This allows us to use the notion of confidence in a number of ways within both individual agents and multi-agent systems [26].

This also leads us on to considering more complex multi-agent systems.

6   Groups and Organisations

In Concurrent METATEM we introduced the idea of multiple, asynchronously executing, agents (let us call them this, rather than 'components' from now on) communicating through broadcast message-passing. Although this is a good model from a logical point of view it has two disadvantages: (1) in practice, broadcasting to large numbers of agents is costly, and (2) the multi-agent system is essentially flat and unstructured, and so it is difficult to represent more complex systems using this approach.

Thus, as Concurrent METATEM has developed, a range of structuring mechanisms for the agent space have been developed. All are based on the notion of *groups*, derived from both social constructs and ideas in distributed operating systems [8]. Thus all agents can occur in multiple groups [15], while groups themselves are dynamic and open, and may contain sub-groups and each agent may be a member of several groups. When an agent broadcasts a message it is restricted to being sent to members of (some of) the groups the agent occurs within. Hence, groups are useful both for restricting the extent of broadcast and structuring the agent space, effectively replacing full broadcast by a form of *multicast* message-passing.

However, a basic grouping mechanism is not enough. We often want to define different computational properties for the different groups the agent might be a member of. Thus, from initial ideas concerning additional logical properties that groups might have [21], we developed the view that agents and groups are *exactly* the same entities [30,28]. Thus, the notion of a group as essentially being a container, where agents have behaviour and groups contain agents, i.e.,

$$Agent \; ::= Behaviour : Spec$$

$$Group \; ::= Contents : \mathcal{P}(Agent)$$

became the notion that all agents have the potential to contain others, just as all have the potential to have behaviour, i.e.

$$Agent ::= Behaviour : Spec$$
$$Contents : \mathcal{P}(Agent)$$
$$Context : \mathcal{P}(Agent)$$

Thus, we can think of several varieties of agent:

- A simple agent: $Contents = \emptyset$.
- A simple group: $Behaviour = \emptyset$.
- A more complex group: $Contents \neq \emptyset$ and $Behaviour \neq \emptyset$.

Thus groups, rather than being mere *containers*, can now have behaviours, captured by their internal policies and rules. In particular, agents can control the communication policies, organisation policies, etc., within their Contents. Once agents and groups are the same entities, a number of aspects become clear. For example, since agents are opaque (i.e., their internal structure is hidden from other agents) it is not obvious whether agents have certain abilities natively, or merely make use of other (internal) agents. In addition, any agent has the potential to dynamically become a group! In particular, all agents respond to 'addToContent' and 'addToContext' messages (two primitive operations accessing the *Content* and *Context* aspects of an agent), and all agents can clone themselves (and perform a shallow copy of their contents), as well as terminate themselves or merge with another agent.

6.1 Building Organisations

With the structures in place to support more complex multi-agent systems, the question remains: how can we use the logical apparatus, such as the Ability, Belief and Confidence framework, in order to program agents to dynamically form complex structures. In a number of papers, mechanisms for describing and constructing such complex groups, teams and organisations have been described [27,28,29].

Let us give an outline using an example. Suppose that agent i wishes for φ to occur $(B_i \Diamond \varphi)$, but does not have the corresponding ability $(\neg A_i \varphi)$. Within the agent's behaviour we might have a rule such as

$$B_i \Diamond \varphi \wedge \neg A_i \varphi \Rightarrow \bigcirc send_i(A_? \varphi)$$

In this case the agent sends out a message asking for help from any agent that is able to achieve φ. Various agents, depending on their own goals, might choose to reply that they have the required ability (namely, the ability to achieve φ, i.e. $A\varphi$). Then the original (sending) agent has a choice about how to deal with these replies and, consequently, how to deal with the agents who might be of help. For example [27], the sender might

- invite relevant agents to join its *Content*,
- create a new "dedicated" agent to serve as a container for agents that share the relevant ability, or
- join a group that can help it solve its problem,

All of these can be supported through the flexible group structure and can be implemented using logical rules. Each gives a very different organisation structure.

7 METATEM at Work

Here we outline a number of examples showing how METATEM can be used. Note that we only provide an overview of each example — full details can usually be found in the cited papers.

7.1 Train Signalling

In [13], METATEM was used to model a simple railway signalling scenario. Here, the system was modelled as one large set of SNF rules. Thus there was not the separation one might expect with Concurrent METATEM. The SNF specification is then executed to animate the rail simulation. The specification consists of predicates relating to stations, trains and lines, and the key specifications concern each station's control of the trains that come into it and each trains request for entry to a station. Each of the stations 'knows' which lines it has connecting itself to other stations, what trains the station *has*, and which lines each train runs on. Consequently, there are rules such as[1]:

- $[station(S) \land moved(T, S)] \Rightarrow \bigcirc has(S, T)$
  i.e., the station (S) now has the train (T) if T moved to S in the last step;
- $[station(S) \land request(T, S)] \Rightarrow \Diamond permit(T, S)$
  i.e., if station S receives a request from train T to enter S, then the station guarantees to *permit* this move at some point in the future;
- $[station(S) \land has(S, T) \land \neg moved(T, New)] \Rightarrow \bigcirc has(S, T)$
  i.e., if station S has train T and T does not move, then S will still have T in the next step;
- $[station(S) \land permit(T1, S) \land permit(T2, S)] \Rightarrow (T1 == T2)$
  i.e., if a station permits two trains, $T1$ and $T2$, to enter, then $T1$ and $T2$ must actually be the same train.

7.2 Patient Monitoring

In [55], Reynolds applies METATEM to the modelling and animation of a patient monitoring system (PMS). Temporal formulae are used to specify, for example, under what conditions (i.e. what patient vital signs) an alarm should be sounded. Here, the specification is split into separate components, e.g.

```
nurse(alarm, display)[act, seen, req]
```

Here, for example, the message req is sent out by the nurse requesting information. SNF rules then characterise the internal behaviour of such components:

- $[wtr(P) \land \neg req(P)] \Rightarrow \bigcirc wtr(Q)$
  i.e., if the nurse is "waiting to request information" (*wtr*) about a patient, but does not request such information (*req*) then the nurse will continue to wait to request information in the next step;

---

[1] Assume, here, that all variables beginning with upper-case letters and all variables are universally quantified.

- $[wtr(P) \wedge req(P) \wedge next(P,Q)] \Rightarrow \bigcirc wtr(P)$
  i.e., if the nurse is "waiting to request information" about a patient, and does also request this information, then the nurse moves on to "waiting to request information" from the *next* patient;
- $alarm(P) \Rightarrow \bigcirc act$
  i.e., if an alarm sounds for a patient, the nurse will act.

7.3   Economic Games

We next outline a simple economic game, a simplified variation of the Nash [51] demand game. Here, two synchronous agents make bids to an arbiter who gives out rewards (in line with a specific matrix). Agents usually bid based on the best previous strategy, but sometimes (quite rarely) can choose a random value. In our case, the `arbiter` agent implements the reward matrix:

agent1 bid :	1	2	3	1	2	3	1	2	3
agent2 bid :	1	1	1	2	2	2	3	3	3
agent1 reward :	1	2	3	1	2	0	1	0	0
agent2 reward :	1	1	1	2	2	0	3	0	0

Thus, sample `arbiter` code includes (for brevity we replace *agent*1 by *a*1, and *agent*2 by *a*2, respectively)

$$[bid(a1,V1) \wedge bid(a2,V2) \wedge (4 < (V1+V2))] \Rightarrow \bigcirc reward(a1,V1,0)$$
$$[bid(a1,V1) \wedge bid(a2,V2) \wedge (4 < (V1+V2))] \Rightarrow \bigcirc reward(a2,V2,0)$$
$$[bid(a1,V1) \wedge bid(a2,V2) \wedge (4 \geq (V1+V2))] \Rightarrow \bigcirc reward(a1,V1,V1)$$
$$[bid(a1,V1) \wedge bid(a2,V2) \wedge (4 \geq (V1+V2))] \Rightarrow \bigcirc reward(a2,V2,V2)$$

The `arbiter` agent receives `bid` messages from each of the agents and then sends out `reward` messages. Note that the `reward` sent from the arbiter back to bidding agents contains the bid made in its second argument.

As we can see from the above, these rules make use of much more arithmetical operators. The rules within the bidding agents use even more. Bidding agents send out bids and receive rewards. Internally, they keep track of which bids (1, 2, or 3) have generated the most rewards. In addition, a small random element is introduced so that the bidding agent can choose a different bid, rather than just the most successful so far. Some sample rules for the bidding agents are[2]:

$$rand(V) \Rightarrow \bigcirc seed(V)$$
$$[seed(V) \wedge (V \leq 3072) \wedge (V1 == (V\%3+1))] \Rightarrow \bigcirc bid(agent1,V1)$$
$$[seed(V) \wedge (3072 < V) \wedge bestsofar(V1)] \Rightarrow \bigcirc bid(agent1,V1)$$

Once executing, even though small perturbations (i.e. random bids outside the optimal) are introduced, the bidding stabilises so that the agent's bid is based on the accumulated history and this isn't significantly distorted by small numbers of random bids. In the case of our reward matrix above, both bidding agent settle down to bidding '2'.

---

[2] Note that *rand*(V) binds V to a random number between 0 and 2^{16} and $V\%3+1$ is V modulo 3, with 1 then added (thus giving a result of either 1, 2 or 3).

7.4 Resource-Bounded Deliberation

In this example, taken from [24], we have a simple football scenario. Pictorially, we have the following situation.

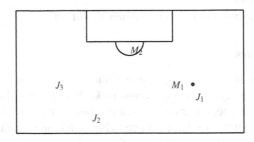

The 'J' team are attacking the goal, while the 'M' team are defending it. Agent J_1 has the ball but has two abilities: to shoot towards goal, or to pass to a team-mate. Motivated by the aim of scoring, J_1 has to decide what to do.

Now, rather than giving the program rules (which are quite complex), we outline the reasoning process that J_1 goes through.

– We again note that J_1 has two things it can do: pass or shoot. Initially, before any reasoning is carried out, J_1 has a slight (in-built) preference for shooting.
– However, J_1 begins to reason about its options, about its beliefs about its team-mates, about its beliefs about its team-mates beliefs, etc. Given sufficient reasoning time, J_1 can work out that the best approach is to pass to J_2 who, J_1 believes, will then pass on to J_3. This is based on the belief that J_3 has the best chance of scoring, and that J_2 believes this also.
  Thus, given sufficient reasoning time, J_1 will choose to pass rather than shoot.
– However, in time-constrained situations, such as near the end of the game, we can put a *bound* on the amount of reasoning concerning belief that J_1 is able to carry out. We do this by fixing a maximum depth of nested beliefs that J_1 is able to deal with.
  In such a scenario, J_1 does not have enough (reasoning) time to work out that passing is the best option.
  Consequently, in time-constrained situations, such as this, J_1 chooses to shoot.

It is important to note here that the program rules are exactly the same for both options. All that has happened is that a belief bound is changed, yet this has the significant effect of leading the agent to prefer one action over another.

7.5 Active Museum

In [42] a particular scenario from pervasive/ubiquitous computing was examined. This is the idea of an *Active Museum* [52]. Here, a museum provides visitors with electronic guides (such as PDAs) and these guides can be programmed with the visitor's preferences. As the visitor moves through the museum, the rooms, exhibits, etc., can all interact with the PDA and, in this way, the PDA can advise the visitor what to look at next.

We model this via three aspects:

– the organisational structure of rooms, exhibits, visitors, etc.;
– the organisational structure of the agent's interests; and
– the rule(s) within the visitor agent concerning deliberation.

Thus, the group structure, combining physical aspects and museum interests can be represented as

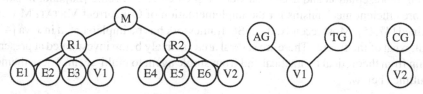

For example, visitor V1 is within the group representing room R1 but is also within the groups representing the two interest groups relating to a particular artist (AG) and to time (TG). Now, those groups provide the context for the visitor agent and broadcast important information to it.

Each visitor agent effectively only has one rule:

$$[canSee(Exhibit) \wedge \neg exclude(Exhibit)] \Rightarrow \Diamond lookAt(Exhibit)$$

Thus, if the visitor agent can see an exhibit and is not excluded (by one of its interest groups) from looking at it, it will eventually look at it. Note that canSee messages are broadcast by the agent's context, and so moving context changes what the agent does.

While visitor agents have one main rule, the important aspect concerns the deliberation of the visitor agent about what order to visit the exhibits in. In this, the agent utilises preferences to implement the deliberative re-ordering of eventualities seen earlier. Preferences are *very* simple, e.g. prefer(E3,E1). Pictorially, we have:

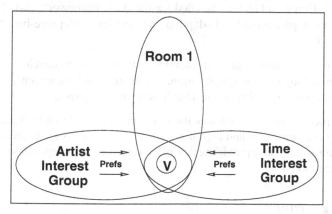

Some preferences are internal to the agent; most are obtained by the agent from its Context. Thus, the preferences help the visitor agent decide between eventualities. Moving between rooms changes what the agent can see, but it is moving between interest groups that changes what the agent prefers to look at first.

8 Concluding Remarks

This article has provided an overview of the work that has been carried out on executable temporal and modal logics based on the METATEM approach. This has led to several practical systems developed over the years. Initially, Owens developed a basic METATEM system in Prolog, while Fisher developed a Concurrent METATEM harness in C++; early implementation techniques were described in [31]. The developments on agent representation and execution were implemented in Prolog [20] and, in parallel, more efficient mechanisms for the implementation of Concurrent METATEM were examined [47,46]. Most recently, the ABC framework has be implemented in Java [43].

But, what of the future? There are several areas actively being investigated at present, ranging from theoretical to practical and from single agent to multi-agent. These themes are outlined below.

- The broader application, particularly of the ABC approach, to the modelling and simulating of various forms of organisations. In particular, the development of virtual organisations (along the lines of the Active Museum example) and applications in pervasive and ubiquitous computing.
  This mainly involves practical application, but also involves more work on ad-hoc team formation and on probabilistic ABC, some of which is already under way [12].
- The development of a lightweight implementation, based on J2ME[3] and use of the above approaches in resource constrained environments, e.g. mobile, wearable, devices.
- Extending the theoretical work on high-level semantics of the group approach, which was recently investigated in [43] where groups were shown to match Milner's bigraphs [45] in many ways, while adapting earlier work on the use of Concurrent METATEM as a high-level coordination language [48] for use in multi-agent and pervasive applications.
- Developing a more practical (and flexible) approach to meta-level programming in METATEM. Based on [4], but extended for the ABC framework, and allowing the use of both complex meta-level adaption and simpler, preference-based, deliberation (as in [42]).

Through previous and future work our intention is to continue to develop a framework that utilises formal logic in the specification, verification and implementation of reactive [41] and multi-agent [59] systems. This framework comprises

- a logic (typically based on a combination of simpler logics) in which the high-level behaviours (of both agent and organisation) can be concisely specified, and
- a programming language providing flexible and practical concepts close to the specification notation used.

Acknowledgements

Most of the work outlined in this article was carried out in collaboration with others, and so thanks go to Howard Barringer, Nivea de Carvalho Ferreira, Marcello Finger, Dov

---

[3] http://java.sun.com/j2me

Gabbay, Chiara Ghidini, Graham Gough, Benjamin Hirsch, Wiebe van der Hoek, Tony Kakoudakis, Adam Kellett, Richard Owens, Mark Reynolds, and Mike Wooldridge.

References

1. M. Abadi. The Power of Temporal Proofs. *Theoretical Computer Science*, 64:35–84, 1989.
2. H. Barringer, M. Fisher, D. Gabbay, G. Gough, and R. Owens. METATEM: A Framework for Programming in Temporal Logic. In *Proceedings of REX Workshop on Stepwise Refinement of Distributed Systems: Models, Formalisms, Correctness*, Mook, Netherlands, June 1989. (Published in *Lecture Notes in Computer Science*, volume 430, Springer Verlag).
3. H. Barringer, M. Fisher, D. Gabbay, G. Gough, and R. Owens. METATEM: An Introduction. *Formal Aspects of Computing*, 7(5):533–549, 1995.
4. H. Barringer, M. Fisher, D. Gabbay, and A. Hunter. Meta-Reasoning in Executable Temporal Logic. In J. Allen, R. Fikes, and E. Sandewall, editors, *Proceedings of the International Conference on Principles of Knowledge Representation and Reasoning (KR)*, Cambridge, Massachusetts, April 1991. Morgan Kaufmann.
5. H. Barringer, M. Fisher, D. Gabbay, R. Owens, and M. Reynolds, editors. *The Imperative Future: Principles of Executable Temporal Logics*. Research Studies Press, Chichester, United Kingdom, 1996.
6. H. Barringer, R. Kuiper, and A. Pnueli. A Really Abstract Concurrent Model and its Temporal Logic. In *Proceedings of the Thirteenth ACM Symposium on the Principles of Programming Languages*, St. Petersberg Beach, Florida, January 1986.
7. M. Benerecetti, A. Cimatti, E. Giunchiglia, F. Giunchiglia, and L. Serafini. Formal Specification of Beliefs in Multi-Agent Systems. In J. P. Müller, M. J. Wooldridge, and N. R. Jennings, editors, *Intelligent Agents III — Proceedings of the Third International Workshop on Agent Theories, Architectures, and Languages (ATAL-96)*, Lecture Notes in Artificial Intelligence. Springer-Verlag, Heidelberg, 1996.
8. K. P. Birman. The Process Group Approach to Reliable Distributed Computing. Techanical Report TR91-1216, Department of Computer Science, Cornell University, July 1991.
9. M. E. Bratman, D. J. Israel, and M. E. Pollack. Plans and Resource-Bounded Practical Reasoning. *Computational Intelligence*, 4:349–355, 1988.
10. A. Cimatti and L. Serafini. Multi-Agent Reasoning with Belief Contexts: the Approach and a Case Study. In M. Wooldridge and N. R. Jennings, editors, *Intelligent Agents: Theories, Architectures, and Languages (LNAI Volume 890)*, pages 71–85. Springer-Verlag: Heidelberg, Germany, January 1995.
11. E. A. Emerson. Temporal and Modal Logic. In J. van Leeuwen, editor, *Handbook of Theoretical Computer Science*, pages 996–1072. Elsevier, 1990.
12. N. de C. Ferreira, M. Fisher, and W. van der Hoek. A Logical Implementation of Uncertain Agents. In *Workshop on Multi-Agent Systems: Theory and Applications (MASTA)*, Lecture Notes in Artificial Intelligence. Springer-Verlag, 2005.
13. M. Finger, M. Fisher, and R. Owens. METATEM at Work: Modelling Reactive Systems Using Executable Temporal Logic. In *Sixth International Conference on Industrial and Engineering Applications of Artificial Intelligence and Expert Systems (IEA/AIE)*, Edinburgh, U.K., June 1993. Gordon and Breach Publishers.
14. M. Fisher. A Normal Form for First-Order Temporal Formulae. In *Proceedings of Eleventh International Conference on Automated Deduction (CADE)*, Saratoga Springs, New York, June 1992. (Published in *Lecture Notes in Computer Science*, volume 607, Springer-Verlag).
15. M. Fisher. A Survey of Concurrent METATEM — The Language and its Applications. In *First International Conference on Temporal Logic (ICTL)*, Bonn, Germany, July 1994. (Published in *Lecture Notes in Computer Science*, volume 827, Springer-Verlag).

16. M. Fisher. Representing and Executing Agent-Based Systems. In M. Wooldridge and N. R. Jennings, editors, *Intelligent Agents*. Springer-Verlag, 1995.
17. M. Fisher. A Temporal Semantics for Concurrent METATEM. *Journal of Symbolic Computation*, 22(5/6), November/December 1996.
18. M. Fisher. An Introduction to Executable Temporal Logics. *Knowledge Engineering Review*, 11(1):43–56, March 1996.
19. M. Fisher. A Normal Form for Temporal Logic and its Application in Theorem-Proving and Execution. *Journal of Logic and Computation*, 7(4), August 1997.
20. M. Fisher. Implementing BDI-like Systems by Direct Execution. In *Proceedings of International Joint Conference on Artificial Intelligence (IJCAI)*. Morgan-Kaufmann, 1997.
21. M. Fisher. Representing Abstract Agent Architectures. In J. P. Müller, M. P. Singh, and A. S. Rao, editors, *Intelligent Agents V — Proceedings of the Fifth International Workshop on Agent Theories, Architectures, and Languages (ATAL-98)*, Lecture Notes in Artificial Intelligence. Springer-Verlag, Heidelberg, 1999.
22. M. Fisher. Temporal Development Methods for Agent-Based Systems. *Journal of Autonomous Agents and Multi-Agent Systems*, 10(1):41–66, January 2005.
23. M. Fisher and C. Ghidini. Programming Resource-Bounded Deliberative Agents. In *Proceedings of International Joint Conference on Artificial Intelligence (IJCAI)*. Morgan Kaufmann, 1999.
24. M. Fisher and C. Ghidini. Agents Playing with Dynamic Resource Bounds. In *ECAI Workshop on Balancing Reactivity and Social Deliberation in Multi-Agent Systems*, Berlin, Germany, 2000.
25. M. Fisher and C. Ghidini. Specifying and Implementing Agents with Dynamic Resource Bounds. In *Proceedings of Second International Cognitive Robotics Workshop*, Berlin, Germany, 2000.
26. M. Fisher and C. Ghidini. The ABC of Rational Agent Programming. In *Proc. First International Conference on Autonomous Agents and Multi-Agent Systems (AAMAS)*, pages 849–856. ACM Press, July 2002.
27. M. Fisher, C. Ghidini, and B. Hirsch. Organising Logic-Based Agents. In M. Hinchey, J. Rash, W. Truszkowski, C. Rouff, and D. Gordon-Spears, editors, *Formal Approaches to Agent-Based Systems, Second International Workshop, FAABS 2002, Greenbelt, MD, USA, October 29-31, 2002, Revised Papers*, volume 2699 of *Lecture Notes in Computer Science*, pages 15–27. Springer, 2003.
28. M. Fisher, C. Ghidini, and B. Hirsch. Organising Computation through Dynamic Grouping. In *Objects, Agents and Features*, volume 2975 of *Lecture Notes in Computer Science*, pages 117–136. Springer-Verlag, 2004.
29. M. Fisher, C. Ghidini, and B. Hirsch. Programming Groups of Rational Agents. In *Computational Logic in Multi-Agent Systems (CLIMA-IV)*, volume 3259 of *849–856*. Springer-Verlag, November 2004.
30. M. Fisher and T. Kakoudakis. Flexible Agent Grouping in Executable Temporal Logic. In Gergatsoulis and Rondogiannis, editors, *Intensional Programming II*. World Scientific Publishing Co., March 2000.
31. M. Fisher and R. Owens. From the Past to the Future: Executing Temporal Logic Programs. In *Proceedings of Logic Programming and Automated Reasoning (LPAR)*, St. Petersberg, Russia, July 1992. (Published in *Lecture Notes in Computer Science*, volume 624, Springer-Verlag).
32. M. Fisher and R. Owens, editors. *Executable Modal and Temporal Logics*, volume 897 of *Lecture Notes in Artificial Intelligence*. Springer-Verlag, Heidelberg, Germany, February 1995.
33. M. Fisher and M. Wooldridge. A Logical Approach to the Representation of Societies of Agents. In N. Gilbert and R. Conte, editors, *Artificial Societies*. UCL Press, 1995.

34. M. Fisher and C. Ghidini. Agents with Bounded Temporal Resources. *Lecture Notes in Computer Science*, 2403:169–??, 2002.

35. D. Gabbay. Declarative Past and Imperative Future: Executable Temporal Logic for Interactive Systems. In B. Banieqbal, H. Barringer, and A. Pnueli, editors, *Proceedings of Colloquium on Temporal Logic in Specification*, pages 402–450, Altrincham, U.K., 1987. (Published in *Lecture Notes in Computer Science*, volume 398, Springer-Verlag).

36. C. Ghidini. Modelling (Un)Bounded Beliefs. In *Proc. Second International and Interdisciplinary Conf. on Modeling and Using Context (CONTEXT)*, Trento, Italy, 1999.

37. F. Giunchiglia and C. Ghidini. Local Models Semantics, or Contextual Reasoning = Locality + Compatibility. In *Proceedings of the Sixth International Conference on Principles of Knowledge Representation and Reasoning (KR'98)*, pages 282–289, Trento, 1998. Morgan Kaufmann. Long version forthcoming in "Artificial Intelligence".

38. F. Giunchiglia and L. Serafini. Multilanguage Hierarchical Logics (or: how we can do without modal logics). *Artificial Intelligence*, 65:29–70, 1994. Also IRST-Technical Report 9110-07, IRST, Trento, Italy.

39. F. Giunchiglia, L. Serafini, E. Giunchiglia, and M. Frixione. Non-Omniscient Belief as Context-Based Reasoning. In *Proceedings of the Thirteenth International Joint Conference on Artificial Intelligence (IJCAI)*, pages 548–554, Chambery, France, 1993. Also IRST-Technical Report 9206-03, IRST, Trento, Italy.

40. J. Y. Halpern and Y. Moses. A Guide to Completeness and Complexity for Modal Logics of Knowledge and Belief. *Artificial Intelligence*, 54:319–379, 1992.

41. D. Harel and A. Pnueli. On the Development of Reactive Systems. Technical Report CS85-02, Department of Applied Mathematics, The Weizmann Institute of Science, Revohot, Israel, January 1985.

42. B. Hirsch, M. Fisher, C. Ghidini, and P. Busetta. Organising Software in Active Environments. In *Computational Logic in Multi-Agent Systems (CLIMA-V)*, volume 3487 of *Lecture Notes in Computer Science*. Springer-Verlag, 2005.

43. B. Hirsch. *Programming Rational Agents*. PhD thesis, Department of Computer Science, University of Liverpool, United Kingdom, May 2005.

44. I. Hodkinson, F. Wolter, and M. Zakharyashev. Decidable Fragments of First-Order Temporal Logics. *Annals of Pure and Applied Logic*, 2000.

45. O. H. Jensen and R. Milner. Bigraphs and Mobile Processes (revised). Technical Report UCAM-CL-TR-580, Computer Lab, Cambridge University, U.K., 2004.

46. A. Kellett. *Implementation Techniques for Concurrent* METATEM. PhD thesis, Department of Computing and Mathematics, Manchester Metropolitan University, 2000.

47. A. Kellett and M. Fisher. Automata Representations for Concurrent METATEM. In *Proceedings of the Fourth International Workshop on Temporal Representation and Reasoning (TIME)*. IEEE Press, May 1997.

48. A. Kellett and M. Fisher. Coordinating Heterogeneous Components using Executable Temporal Logic. In Meyer and Treur, editors, *Agents, Reasoning and Dynamics*, Vol. 6 in Series of Handbooks in Defeasible Reasoning and Uncertainty Management Systems. Kluwer Academic publishers, 2001.

49. O. Lichtenstein, A. Pnueli, and L. Zuck. The Glory of the Past. *Lecture Notes in Computer Science*, 193:196–218, June 1985.

50. Z. Manna and A. Pnueli. *The Temporal Logic of Reactive and Concurrent Systems: Specification*. Springer-Verlag, New York, 1992.

51. J. F. Nash. Two-person Cooperative Games. *Econometrica*, 21:128–140, 1953.

52. O. Stock and M. Zancanaro. Intelligent Interactive Information Presentation for Cultural Tourism. In *Proceedings of the International CLASS Workshop on Natural Intell igent and Effective Interaction in Multimodal Dialogue Systems*, Copenhagen, Denmark, 28-29 June 2002.

53. R. Pliuskevicius. On the Completeness and Decidability of a Restricted First Order Linear Temporal Logic. In *LNCS 1289*, pages 241–254. Springer-Verlag, 1997.
54. A. S. Rao and M. P. Georgeff. Modeling Agents within a BDI-Architecture. In R. Fikes and E. Sandewall, editors, *International Conference on Principles of Knowledge Representation and Reasoning (KR)*, Cambridge, Massachusetts, April 1991. Morgan Kaufmann.
55. M. Reynolds. METATEM in Intensive Care. Technical Report tr-97-01, Kings College, London, 1997.
56. A. Szalas and L. Holenderski. Incompleteness of First-Order Temporal Logic with Until. *Theoretical Computer Science*, 57:317–325, 1988.
57. B. van Linder, W. van der Hoek, and J. J. Ch. Meyer. How to Motivate your Agents. In M. Wooldridge, J. P. Müller, and M. Tambe, editors, *Intelligent Agents II (LNAI 1037)*, pages 17–32. Springer-Verlag: Heidelberg, Germany, 1996.
58. M. Wooldridge. *Reasoning about Rational Agents*. MIT Press, 2000.
59. M. Wooldridge. *An Introduction to Multiagent Systems*. John Wiley & Sons, 2002.
60. M. Wooldridge, J. Bradfield, M. Fisher, and M. Pauly. Game-Theoretic Interpretations of Executable Logic. (Unpublished paper.).
61. M. Wooldridge and N. R. Jennings. Intelligent Agents: Theory and Practice. *The Knowledge Engineering Review*, 10(2):115–152, 1995.
62. M. Wooldridge and A. Rao, editors. *Foundations of Rational Agency*. Applied Logic Series. Kluwer Academic Publishers, March 1999.

Agent-Based Computing and Programming of Agent Systems

Michael Luck[1], Peter McBurney[2], and Jorge Gonzalez-Palacios[1]

[1] School of Electronics and Computer Science,
University of Southampton, United Kingdom
mml@ecs.soton.ac.uk, jlgp03r@ecs.soton.ac.uk
[2] Department of Computer Science,
University of Liverpool, United Kingdom
p.j.mcburney@csc.liv.ac.uk

Abstract. The concepts of autonomous agent and multi-agent system provide appropriate levels of abstraction for the design, implementation and simulation of many complex, distributed computational systems, particularly those systems open to external participants. Programming such agent systems presents many difficult challenges, both conceptually and practically, and addressing these challenges will be crucial for the development of agent technologies. We discuss, at a general level, some of the issues involved in programming multi-agent and open, distributed systems, drawing on the recently-published AgentLink III *Roadmap of Agent Based Computing Technologies*.

1 Introduction

Since Shoham's seminal paper [14] on agent-oriented programming in 1993, programming of agent systems has been a key focus of interest. Certainly, the issues surrounding the programming of agent systems had been considered earlier, but Shoham's work marked a key point in identifying agent-oriented programming as a distinct paradigm in a way that had not been done previously. Yet programming agent systems is in fact a broader area that is not restricted to programming paradigms, but includes a whole host of issues ranging from methodological concerns for developers to the specific agent architectures that are required for particular interpreters for agent systems. The purpose of this paper is neither to review the field of programming of agent systems, nor to provide an analysis of particular problems in the area, but more generally to examine the broader context for programming of agents systems in relation to the field of agent-based computing.

As we have argued previously [11], agent technologies can be considered from three perspectives: as a design metaphor; as a source of distinct technologies; and as a simulation tool. Interestingly, the programming of agent systems can be considered in relation to each of these perspectives. First, the programming of agent systems is clearly related to the design metaphor in the development of systems involving large numbers of interacting autonomous components. Second,

R.H. Bordini et al. (Eds.): ProMAS 2005, LNAI 3862, pp. 23–37, 2006.
© Springer-Verlag Berlin Heidelberg 2006

programming such systems requires the use of particular techniques to develop appropriate architectures and interaction mechanisms. And third, multi-agent systems may also be used as simulations of a system under construction or in operation, thereby assisting developers or controllers with programming of multi-agent systems.

As a design metaphor, agents provide designers and developers with a way of structuring an application around autonomous, communicative elements, and lead to the construction of software tools and infrastructure to support systems development. In this sense, they offer a new and often more appropriate route to the development of complex systems, especially in open and dynamic environments. In order to support this view of systems development, particular tools and techniques need to be introduced. For example, methodologies to guide analysis and design are required; agent architectures are needed for the design of individual components, and supporting infrastructure (including more general, current technologies, such as Web Services) must be integrated.

As a source of technologies, agent-based computing spans a range of specific techniques and algorithms for dealing with interactions with others in dynamic and open environments. These include issues such as balancing reaction and deliberation in individual agent architectures, learning from and about other agents in the environment and user preferences, finding ways to negotiate and cooperate with agents and developing appropriate means of forming and managing coalitions. Moreover, the adoption of agent-based approaches is increasingly influential in other domains. For example, multi-agent systems can provide faster and more effective methods of resource allocation in complex environments, such as the management of utility networks, than any human-centred approach.

As a simulation tool, multi-agent systems can also play a role in programming MAS. One common means to develop a complex, computational system is to proceed through construction of a sequence of prototypes, in a Rapid Applications Development (RAD)-style approach. In such an approach, the successive prototypes effectively act as simulations of the final system under construction; they may be used by the system designers and developers as means to understand system properties under differing conditions or parameter values, and to learn about the system dynamics as agents enter, interact and leave the system. If adequate formal verification methods for multi-agent systems existed, such simulations would not be necessary, but most systems are too complex for the current state-of-the-art in formal verification. For example, the development of online auction systems relies on mathematical game theory for the design of the precise rules of auctions (what economists call *mechanism design*). However, with any more than just a handful of participants, many common auction institutions result in mathematics that is not tractable, and for which analytic solutions may not be known to exist. Thus, auction designers are forced to make assumptions about the participants (for example, that they are utility-maximisers with unbounded processing capabilities) or the mechanism (for example, that communication between participants is instantaneous) that do not apply in the real world. Moreover, designers of *computational* auction systems face problems not envisioned by game theory pioneers, such as malicious participants or participants with buggy code. Accordingly, designers and developers of complex computational systems often build prototypes in which to simulate system performance.[1] Similarly, system controllers may use a simulation of a system in order to diagnose and manage system performance; this is common practice, for example, in utility networks, where a controller may have end-to-end responsibility for quality of service levels provided over physical infrastructures that are not all within the same network. As with the designers' use of MAS systems for simulation, both the end-system being simulated and the system used for simulation are multi-agent systems.

Although this paper does not delve deeply into such distinctions, these are a useful means of drawing out the relevant current and future issues that must be addressed for agent-based computing to see more general application, and for programming and development frameworks to consider if they are to move out of the laboratory, or even provide an alternative to the current *de facto* use of object technologies for building agents systems.

Instead, however, the paper is structured as follows. First, in Section 2, we present in outline form a structure of different levels of abstraction of multi-agent system, which provides a framework through which research and development in agent technologies may be viewed. Then, in Section 3, we discuss agent programming languages and methods, while in Section 4, we consider infrastructure and supporting technologies. Specific aspects of programming open multi-agent systems are then discussed in Section 5, and the paper concludes in Section 6.

2   Levels of Abstraction

There are several distinct high-level trends and drivers, such as Grid computing, ambient intelligence and service-oriented computing, for example, which have led to a heightened interest in agent technologies, and in the low-level computing infrastructures that make them practically feasible. In this context, we consider the key technologies and techniques required to design and implement agent systems that are the focus of current research and development. Because agent technologies are mission-critical for engineering and for managing certain types of information systems, such as Grid systems and systems for ambient intelligence, the technologies and techniques discussed below will be important for many applications, even those not labeled as agent systems. These technologies can be grouped into three categories, according to the scale at which they apply.

- Organisation-level: at the top level are technologies and techniques related to agent societies as a whole. Here, issues of organisational structure, trust, norms and obligations, and self-organisation in open agent societies are

---

[1] For example, Guala [5] describes the simulation activities — both computational and human — used by economists who advised the US Federal Communications Commission on the development of online mobile spectrum auctions, undertaken since 1994.

paramount. Once again, many of these questions have been studied in other disciplines — for example, in sociology, anthropology and biology. Drawing on this related work, research and development is currently focused on technologies for designing, evolving and managing complex agent societies.

- Interaction-level: these are technologies and techniques that concern communications between agents — for example, technologies related to communication languages, interaction protocols and resource allocation mechanisms. Many of the problems that these technologies aim to solve have been studied in other disciplines, including economics, political science, philosophy and linguistics. Accordingly, research and development is drawing on this prior work to develop computational theories and technologies for agent interaction, communication and decision-making.
- Agent-level: these are technologies and techniques concerned only with individual agents — for example, procedures for agent reasoning and learning. Problems at this level have been the primary focus of artificial intelligence since its inception, aiming to build machines that can reason and operate autonomously in the world. Agent research and development has drawn extensively on this prior work, and most attention in the field of agent-based computing now focuses at the previous two higher levels.

This analysis parallels the abstraction of Zambonelli and Omicini [17] in referring to the macro, meso and micro levels of agent-oriented software engineering, respectively. Within these levels of abstraction, we can consider technologies providing infrastructure and supporting tools for agent systems, such as agent programming languages and software engineering methodologies. These supporting technologies and techniques provide the basis for both the theoretical understanding and the practical implementation of agent systems, and are considered in more detail in the next section. In particular, we outline key issues, and consider likely and important challenges to move forward the technology, in research, development and application.

3   Agent Programming

3.1   Agent Programming Languages

Most research in agent-oriented programming languages is based on declarative approaches, mostly logic based. Imperative languages are in essence inappropriate for expressing the high-level abstractions associated with agent systems design; however, agent-oriented programming languages should (and indeed tend to) allow for easy integration with (legacy) code written in imperative languages. From the technological perspective, the design and development of agent-based languages is also important.

Currently, real agent-oriented languages (such as BDI-style ones) are limited, and used largely for research purposes; apart from some niche applications, they remain unused in practice. However, recent years have seen a significant increase in the degree of maturity of such languages, and major improvements in the development platforms and tools that support them [1]. Current research emphasises the role of multi-agent systems development environments to assist in the development of complex multi-agent systems, new programming principles to model and realise agent features, and formal semantics for agent programming languages to implement specific agent behaviours.

A programming language for multi-agent systems should respect the principle of separation of concerns and provide dedicated programming constructs for implementing individual agents, their organisation, their coordination, and their environment. However, due to the lack of dedicated agent programming languages and development tools (as well as more fundamental concerns relating to the lack of clear semantics for agents, coordination, etc), the construction of multi-agent systems is still a time-consuming and demanding activity.

One key challenge in agent-oriented programming is to define and implement some truly agent-oriented languages that integrate concepts from both declarative and object-oriented programming, to allow the definition of agents in a declarative way, yet supported by serious monitoring and debugging facilities. These languages should be highly efficient, and provide interfaces to existing mainstream languages for easy integration with code and legacy packages. While existing agent languages already address some of these issues, further progress is expected in the short term, but thorough practical experimentation in real-world settings (particularly large-scale systems) will be required before such languages can be adopted by industry, in the medium to long term.

In addition to languages for single agents, we also need languages for high-level programming of multi-agent systems. In particular, the need for expressive, easy-to-use, and efficient languages for coordinating and orchestrating intelligent heterogeneous components is already pressing and, although much research is already being done, the development of an effective programming language for coordinating huge, open, scalable and dynamic multi-agent systems composed of heterogeneous components is a longer term goal.

3.2   Formal Methods

While agent-oriented programming ultimately seeks practical application, the development of appropriate languages demands an associated formal analysis. While the notion of an agent acting autonomously in the world is intuitively simple, formal analysis of systems containing multiple agents is inherently complex. In particular, to understand the properties of systems containing multiple actors, powerful modelling and reasoning techniques are needed to capture possible trajectories of the system. Such techniques are required if agents and agent systems are to be modelled and analysed computationally.

Research in the area of formal models for agent systems attempts to represent and understand properties of the systems through the use of logical formalisms describing both the mental states of individual agents and the possible interactions in the system. The logics used are often logics of belief or other modalities, along with temporal modalities, and such logics require efficient theorem-proving or model-checking algorithms when applied to problems of significant scale.

Recent efforts have used logical formalisms to represent social properties, such as coalitions of agents, preferences and game-type properties.

It is clear that formal techniques such as model checking are needed to test, debug and verify properties of implemented multi-agent systems. Despite progress, there is still a real need to address the issues that arise from differences in agent systems, in relation to the paradigm, the programming languages used, and especially the design of self-organising and emergent behaviour. For the latter, a programming paradigm that supports automated checking of both functional and non-functional system properties may be needed. This would lead to the need to certify agent components for correctness with respect to their specifications. Such a certification could be obtained either by selecting components that have already been verified and validated off-line using traditional techniques such as inspection, testing and model checking or by generating code automatically from specifications. Furthermore, techniques are needed to ensure that the system still executes in an acceptable, or safe, manner during the adaptation process, for example using techniques such as dependency analysis or high level contracts and invariants to monitor system correctness before, during and after adaptation.

4   Infrastructure and Supporting Technologies

Any infrastructure deployed to support the execution of agent applications, such as those found in ambient and ubiquitous computing must, by definition, be long lived and robust. In the context of self-organising systems, this is further complicated, and new approaches supporting the evolution of the infrastructures, and facilitating their upgrade and update at runtime, will be required. Given the potentially vast collection of devices, sensors, and personalised applications for which agent systems and self-organisation may be applicable, this update problem is significantly more complex than so far encountered. More generally, middleware, or platforms for agent interoperability, as well as standards, will be crucial for the medium term development of agent systems.

4.1   Interoperability

At present, the majority of agent applications exist in academic and commercial laboratories, but are not widely available in the real world. The move out of the laboratory is likely to happen over the next ten years, but far greater automation than is currently available in dealing with knowledge management is needed for information agents. In particular, this demands new web standards that enable structural and semantic description of information; and services that make use of these semantic representations for information access at a higher level. The creation of common ontologies, thesauri or knowledge bases plays a central role here, and merits further work on the formal descriptions of information and actions, and, potentially, a reference architecture to support the higher level services mentioned above.

Distributed agent systems that adapt to their environment must both adapt individual agent components and coordinate adaptation across system layers (i.e. application, presentation and middleware) and platforms. In other words interoperability must be maintained across possibly heterogeneous agent components during and after self-organisation actions and outcomes. Furthermore, agent components are likely to come from different vendors and hence the developer may need to integrate different self-organisation mechanisms to meet application requirements. The problem is further complicated by the diversity of self-organisation approaches applicable at different system layers. In many cases, even solutions within the same layer are often not compatible. Consequently, developers need tools and methods to integrate the operation of agent components across the layers of a single system, among multiple computing systems, as well as between different self-organisation frameworks.

4.2 Agent Oriented Software Engineering Methodologies

Despite a number of languages, frameworks, development environments, and platforms that have appeared in the literature, implementing multi-agent systems is still a challenging task. To manage the complexity of multi-agent systems design and implementation, the research community has produced a number of methodologies that aim to structure agent development. However, even if practitioners follow such methodologies during the design phase, there are difficulties in the implementation phase, partly due to the lack of maturity in both methodologies and programming tools. There are also difficulties in implementation due to: a lack of specialised debugging tools; skills needed to move from analysis and design to code; the problems associated with awareness of the specifics of different agent platforms; and in understanding the nature of what is a new and distinct approach to systems development.

In relation to open and dynamic systems, new methodologies for systematically considering self-organisation are required. These methodologies should be able to provide support for all phases of the agent-based software engineering lifecycle, allowing the developer to start from requirements analysis, identify the aspects of the problem that should be addressed using self-organisation and design and implement the self-organisation mechanisms in the behaviour of the agent components. Such methodologies should also encompass techniques for monitoring and controlling the self-organising application or system once deployed.

4.3 Integrated Development Environments

In general, integrated development environment (IDE) support for developing agent systems is rather weak, and existing agent tools do not offer the same level of usability as state-of-the-art object oriented IDEs. One main reason for this is the previous unavoidable tight coupling of agent IDEs and agent platforms, which results from the variety of agent models, platforms and programming languages.

This is now changing, however, with an increased trend towards modelling rather than programming.

With existing tools, multi-agent systems often generate a huge amount of information related to the internal state of agents, messages sent and actions taken, but there are not yet adequate methods for managing this information in the context of the development process. This has impacts both for dealing with the information generated in the system and for obtaining this information without altering the design of the agents within it.

Platforms like JADE provide general introspection facilities for the state of agents and for messages, but they enforce a concrete agent architecture that may not be appropriate for all applications. Thus, tools for inspecting any agent architecture, analogous to the remote debugging tools in current object-oriented IDEs, are needed, and some are now starting to appear [2]. Extending this to address other issues related to debugging for organisational features, and for considering issues arising from emergence in self-organising systems will also be important in the longer term. The challenge is relevant now, but will grow in importance as the complexity of installed systems increases further.

The inherent complexity of agent applications also demands a new generation of CASE tools to assist application designers in harnessing the large amount of information involved. This requires providing reasoning at appropriate levels of abstraction, automating the design and implementation process as much as possible, and allowing for the calibration of deployed multi-agent systems by simulation and run-time verification and control.

More generally, there is a need to integrate existing tools into IDEs rather than starting from scratch. At present there are many research tools, but little that integrates with generic development environments, such as Eclipse; such advances would boost agent development and reduce implementation costs. Indeed, developing multi-agent systems currently involves higher costs than using conventional paradigms due to the lack of supporting methods and tools.

The next generation of computing system is likely to demand large numbers of interacting components, be they services, agents or otherwise. Current tools work well with limited numbers of agents, but are generally not yet suitable for the development of large-scale (and efficient) agent systems, nor do they offer development, management or monitoring facilities able to deal with large amounts of information or tune the behaviour of the system in such cases.

4.4   Metrics

Metrics for agent-oriented software are also needed: engineering always implies some activity of measurement, and traditional software engineering already uses widely applied measuring methods to quantify aspects of software such as complexity, robustness and mean time between failures. However, the dynamic nature of agent systems, and the generally non-deterministic behaviour of self-organising agent applications deem traditional techniques for measurement and evaluation inappropriate. Consequently, new measures and techniques for both quantitatively and qualitatively assessing and classifying multi-agent systems applications (be they self-organising or not) are needed.

5 Open Systems

5.1 Introduction

The advent of low-cost computation has driven the proliferation of computers and computational devices over the last two decades, and with them, a proliferation of physical networks. With the interconnections provided by physical networks come requirements for computational societies — means of distributing data gathering, processing intelligence, resource allocation and system control, as in ambient intelligence, pervasive computing, Grid computing, etc. These computational societies increasingly require applications which are large-scale, decentralised, proactive, situated and open.

However, traditional approaches (for example, object-oriented and component-based computing) have fallen short in engineering these types of application because they utilise too low a level of abstraction, focusing on the *"physical distribution of data, resources and processes,"* rather than on the *"logical distribution of responsibility, control and regulation,"* to quote Pitt's apt distinction [13, p. 140]. As a consequence, alternative approaches have been proposed, with a consensus emerging that the concept of autonomous agency provides the appropriate level of abstraction to successfully develop these types of systems [8]. As mentioned above, this has led to the appearance of several agent-oriented software methodologies, which aim to support development of open systems.

More specifically, an open system is a one that allows run-time incorporation of components that may not be known at design time. In addition, the components of an open system are typically not designed and developed by the same design team or for the same stakeholders, and different teams may use different development tools or adopt different policies or objectives, leading to the appearance of self-interested components. In whatever way or for whom the components are developed, they will normally have the right to access the corresponding facilities provided by the system, as well as having an obligation to adhere to the system's rules.

5.2 Specification of Open Systems

Even though several methodologies exist to support the development of open systems, these present drawbacks when dealing with the incorporation of new components to an existing system. In fact, the phase of operation of a system is generally not considered in methodologies. For example, despite the importance of providing developers with a description of system properties, the problem of *what* must be present in such a description and *how* it must be described has been scarcely addressed.

Although each system can have its own form of specification (comprising a list of the features provided by the system, as well as the requirements to join it), a common *model* of specification would bring multiple benefits. First, by using pre-defined models, the time spent on creating specifications can be reduced. Second, using common models would promote the creation of standards, of which much has already been written, and much work undertaken. Finally, by defining and structuring the description of a system, the model of specification is valuable in defining the inputs of run-time components that check system properties, for example that new agents comply with required characteristics, and do not violate operating principles.

In particular, because of the autonomous and pro-active nature of the components (agents) of multi-agent systems, such specifications are likely to be vital in appropriately enabling and regulating self-interested behaviour in open system. This suggests that tools and techniques for the development of open systems (including the above discussed methodologies, design tools, monitoring tools, debuggers, platforms, and so on) will be required if the requirements of large-scale open systems that underlie visions of Grid computing and similar paradigms are to be satisfied. In addition, a focus on standardisation of abstractions, operating models, interaction protocols and other *patterns* of activity will be needed.

In relation to these issues, we outline below some further concerns in the context of the current situation that require further research and development.

5.3   Methodologies

Current methodologies are not complete or detailed enough. Even if we restrict our attention only to the analysis and design phases of the development cycle, very few methodologies cover all the corresponding activities. For example, SODA does not address intra-agent issues, Gaia does not consider how the services an agent provides are realised [15], Gaia extended with organisational abstractions is not sufficiently elaborated [16], the models of MAS-CommonKADS require further improvement, as recognised by its developers [7], and the evaluation of MESSAGE reports that it is not complete nor mature [9].

5.4   Agent Architectures

Despite the focus on development and programming, it is impossible not to consider specific agent architectures during the design and programming of individual agents. Different approaches are taken by different methodologies, with three significant styles as follows.

- For some methodologies, architectures are outside their scope since they were designed only for analysis and high-level design, for example, Gaia [15].
- Some methodologies and languages are tied to a specific architecture. For example the methodological work of Kinny, Georgeff and Rao [10] is tied to the BDI architecture.
- Some other methodologies are tied to a specific architecture but it is suggested that the same principles can be applied to other architectures, or that other architectures can be adapted to fit. For example, MESSAGE [9] uses the generic Layer Architecture for this purpose.

While there are clearly efforts to incorporate architectures into methodologies, no methodology satisfactorily incorporates even a subset of the most popular agent architectures. Conversely, the development of programming languages seems to require commitment to particular architectures (see, for example, 3APL [6], AgentSpeak(L) [3], and AGENT-0[14]), yet mapping from one to another is problematic. The variety of domains of application of agent-based computing, especially in open systems, requires programming languages such as these to be broadly applicable; for this to be the case, some solution, technical or consensual, is needed.

5.5   Interactions in Open Systems

Interactions are a key element in both the modelling and operation of multi-agent systems, since agents achieve their goals by interacting with other agents. In the case of open systems, interaction mechanisms should be flexible enough to allow new agents to be incorporated into the system. However, most methodologies neither facilitate nor obstruct the development of open systems, and some effort is required to explicitly consider this issue. For example, enriching the analysis and upper design phases of MESSAGE [9] with the organisational abstractions recommended by Zambonelli et al. [16] could lead to a methodology suitable for tackling open systems.

6   Conclusions

In any high-technology domain, the systems deployed in commercial or industrial applications tend to embody research findings somewhat behind the leading edge of academic and industrial research. Multi-agent systems are no exception to this, with currently-deployed systems having features found in published research and prototypes of three to five years ago. By looking at current research interests and areas of focus, we were therefore able in [12] to extrapolate future trends in deployed systems, which we classified into four broad phases of development of multi-agent system technology over the next decade; we summarise these phases here.

The four phases are, of necessity, only indicative, since there will always be some companies and organisations which are leading users of agent technologies, pushing applications ahead of these phases, while many other organisations will not be as advanced in their use of the technology. We aim to describe the majority of research challenges at each time period.

6.1   Phase 1: Current

Multi-agent systems are currently typically designed by one design team for one corporate environment, with participating agents sharing common high-level goals in a single domain. These systems may be characterised as closed. (Of course, there is also work on individual competitive agents for automated negotiation, trading agents, and so forth, but typically also constrained by closed environments.) The communication languages and interaction protocols are typically in-house protocols, defined by the design team prior to any agent interactions. Systems are usually only scalable under controlled, or simulated, conditions. Design approaches, as well as development platforms, tend to be ad hoc, inspired by the agent paradigm rather than using principled methodologies, tools or languages. Although this is still largely true, there is now an increased focus on, for example, taking methodologies out of the laboratory and into development environments, with commercial work being done on establishing industrial-strength development techniques and notations. As part of this effort, some platforms now come with their own protocol libraries and force the use of standardised messages, taking one step towards the short-term agenda.

6.2   Phase 2: Short-Term Future

In the next phase of development, systems will increasingly be designed to cross corporate boundaries, so that the participating agents have fewer goals in common, although their interactions will still concern a common domain, and the agents will be designed by the same team, and will share common domain knowledge. Increasingly, standard agent communication languages, such as FIPA ACL [4], will be used, but interaction protocols will be mixed between standard and non-standard ones. These systems will be able to handle large numbers of agents in pre-determined environments, such as those of Grid applications. Development methodologies, languages and tools will have reached a degree of maturity, and systems will be designed on top of standard infrastructures such as web services or Grid services, for example.

6.3   Phase 3: Medium-Term Future

In the third phase, multi-agent systems will permit participation by heterogeneous agents, designed by different designers or teams. Any agent will be able to participate in these systems, provided their (observable) behaviour conforms to publicly-stated requirements and standards. However, these open systems will typically be specific to particular application domains, such as B2B eCommerce or bioinformatics. The languages and protocols used in these systems will be agreed and standardised, perhaps drawn from public libraries of alternative protocols that will, nevertheless, likely differ by domain. In particular, it will be important for agents and systems to master this semantic heterogeneity. Supporting this will be the increased use of new, commonly agreed modelling languages (such as Agent-UML, an extension of UML 2.0), which will promote the use of IDEs and, hopefully, start a harmonisation process as was the case for objects with UML.

Systems will scale to large numbers of participants, although typically only within the domains concerned, and with particular techniques (such as domain-bridging agents), to translate between separate domains. System development will proceed by standard agent-specific methodologies, including templates and patterns for different types of agents and organisations. Agent-specific programming languages and tools will be increasingly used, making the use of formal verification techniques possible to some extent. Semantic issues related to, for example, coordination between heterogeneous agents, access control and trust, are of particular importance here. Also, because these systems will typically be open, issues such as robustness against malicious or faulty agents, and finding an appropriate trade-off between system adaptability and system predictability, will become increasingly important.

6.4   Phase 4: Long-Term Future

The fourth phase in this projected future will see the development of open multi-agent systems spanning multiple application domains, and involving heterogeneous participants developed by diverse design teams. Agents seeking to participate in these systems will be able to learn the appropriate behaviour for participation in the course of interacting, rather than having to prove adherence before entry. Selection of communications protocols and mechanisms, and of participant strategies, will be undertaken automatically, without human intervention. Similarly, *ad hoc* coalitions of agents will be formed, managed and dissolved automatically. Although standard communication languages and interaction protocols will have been available for some time, systems in this phase will enable these mechanisms to emerge by evolutionary means from actual participant interactions, rather than being imposed at design time. In addition, agents will be able to form and re-form dynamic coalitions and virtual organisations on-the-fly and pursue ever-changing goals through appropriate interaction mechanisms for distributed cognition and joint action. In these environments, emergent phenomena will likely appear, with systems having properties (both good and bad) not imagined by the initial design team. Multi-agent systems will be able, adaptable and adept in the face of such dynamic, indeed turbulent, environments, and they will exhibit many of the self-aware characteristics described in the autonomic computing vision.

By this phase, systems will be fully scalable in the sense that they will not be restricted to arbitrary limits (on agents, users, interaction mechanisms, agent relationships, complexity, etc). As previously, systems development will proceed by use of rigorous agent-specification design methodologies, in conjunction with programming and verification techniques.

6.5   Realization

Of course, achieving the ambitious future vision outlined in these four phases of development will not proceed without obstacles. Significant research, development and deployment challenges exist for both academic researchers and for commercial developers of agent computing technologies. Languages and methodologies for programming autonomous agents and multi-agent systems are among the most important of these, and will remain at the centre of agent-based computing for at least the next decade.

Acknowledgements

This paper is in part based on, and borrows heavily from, the AgentLink III Roadmap [12] which, in turn, drew on inputs and contributions from the PROMAS Technical Forum Group (as well as others) during the lifetime of AgentLink III.

References

1. R. H. Bordini, M. Dastani, J. Dix, and A. El Fallah Seghrouchni, editors. *Multi-Agent Programming: Languages, Platforms and Applications.* Springer, 2005.
2. J. Botia, A. Lopez-Acosta, and A. Gomez-Skarmeta. Aclanalyser: A tool for debugging multi-agent systems. In *Proceedings of the Sixteenth European Conference on Artificial Intelligence*, pages 967–968, 2004.
3. M. d'Inverno and M. Luck. Engineering AgentSpeak(L): A formal computational model. *Journal of Logic and Computation*, 8(3):233–260, 1998.
4. FIPA. Communicative Act Library Specification. Standard SC00037J, Foundation for Intelligent Physical Agents, 3 December 2002.
5. F. Guala. Building economic machines: The FCC Auctions. *Studies in the History and Philosophy of Science*, 32(3):453–477, 2001.
6. K. V. Hindriks, F. S. de Boer, W. van der Hoek, , and J-J. Ch. Meyer. Formal semantics for an abstract agent programming language. In *Intelligent Agents IV: Proceedings of the Fourth International Workshop on Agent Theories, Architectures and Languages*, Lecture Notes in Artificial Intelligence, Volume 1365, pages 215–229. Springer-Verlag, 1998.
7. C. A. Iglesias, M. Garijo, J. C. Gonzalez, and J. R. Velasco. Analysis and design of multiagent systems using mas-commonkads. In M. P. Singh, A. Rao, and M. J. Wooldridge, editors, *Intelligent Agents IV: Proceedings of the Fourth International Workshop on Agent Theories, Architectures, and Languages*, Lecture Notes in Artificial Intelligence, Volume 1365, pages 313–326. Springer-Verlag, 1998.
8. N. R. Jennings. An agent-based approach for building complex software systems. *Communications of the ACM*, 44(4):35–41, 2001.
9. P. Kearney, J. Stark, G. Caire, F. J. Garijo, J. J. Gomez Sanz, J. Pavon, F. Leal, P. Chainho, and P. Massonet. Message: Methodology for engineering systems of software agents. Technical Report EDIN 0223-0907, Eurescom, 2001.
10. D. Kinny, M. Georgeff, and A. Rao. A methodology and modelling technique for systems of bdi agents. In W. van der Velde and J. Perram, editors, *Agents Breaking Away: Proceedings of the Seventh European Workshop on Modelling Autonomous Agents in a Multi-Agent World*, Lecture Notes in Artificial Intelligence, Volume 1038, pages 56–71. Springer-Verlag, 1996.
11. M. Luck, P. McBurney, and C. Preist. A manifesto for agent technology: Towards next generation computing. *Autonomous Agents and Multi-Agent Systems*, 9(3):203–252, 2004.
12. M. Luck, P. McBurney, O. Shehory, and S. Willmott. *Agent Technology: Computing as Interaction. A Roadmap for Agent Based Computing.* AgentLink III, 2005.

13. J. Pitt. The open agent society as a platform for the user-friendly information society. *AI and Society*, 19:123–158, 2005.
14. Y. Shoham. Agent-oriented programming. *Artificial Intelligence*, 60(1):51–92, 1993.
15. M. Wooldridge, N. Jennings, and D. Kinny. The Gaia methodology for agent-oriented analysis and design. *Autonomous Agents and Multi-Agent Systems*, 3(3):285–312, 2000.
16. F. Zambonelli, N. R. Jennings, and M. Wooldridge. Organisational rules as an abstraction for the analysis and design of multi-agent systems. *International Journal of Software Engineering and Knowledge Engineering*, 11(3):303–328, 2001.
17. F. Zambonelli and A. Omicini. Challenges and research directions in agent-oriented software engineering. *Autonomous Agents and Multi-Agent Systems*, 9(3):253–283, 2004.

Part II

Multi-agent Techniques and Issues

Dynamic Self-control of Autonomous Agents

Caroline Chopinaud[1,2], Amal El Fallah Seghrouchni[2], and Patrick Taillibert[1]

[1] Thales Airborne Systems, 2 avenue Gay Lussac 78851 Elancourt, France
{caroline.chopinaud, patrick.taillibert}@fr.thalesgroup.com
[2] LIP6, 8 rue du Capitaine Scott 75015 Paris, France
amal.elfallah@lip6.fr

Abstract. Being able to trust in a system behavior is of prime importance, particularly within the context of critical applications as embedded or real-time systems. We want to ensure that a multiagent system
has a behavior corresponding to what its developers expect. The use of
standard techniques to validate a system does not guarantee it against
the occurence of errors in real condition of execution. So, we propose
an additional approach of dynamic self-monitoring and self-regulation
such that an agent might control, in real condition, its own behavior.
Our approach consists in providing the agents with a set of laws that
they have to respect throughout their execution. This paper presents a
framework which generates agents capable of self-control from an agent
model, a behavior description and laws. For that, the framework modifies
the agents program by injecting, some checkpoints allowing the detection of particular events. The laws are represented in the agents by Petri
nets connected to the checkpoints in order to verify the agreement between their behavior and the laws. The principles of the framework are
illustrated on an example.

1 Introduction

Autonomy is an essential feature of cognitive agents. We will consider the autonomy as the ability of an agent to take its decisions without the help of another
entity [1]. From the developer's point of view, it means that the implementation
of an agent requires to take into account that the behavior of the other agents
cannot be predicted with certainty. This perspective brings up the problem of
the confidence that we can have in a system behavior. When critical applications
are concerned, the use of such system might raise objections because of this un-
predictability. So, it is essential to ensure that MAS and its agents respect some
behavioral requirements which are essential for the application.

The aim of our research is to ensure that a MAS behavior will fulfill with these
requirements. A first approach could be the use of classical methods of validation,
such as tests, Model Checking [2] and automatic demonstration to validate a
multiagent system. But, these techniques are never in the position to detect all
possible errors and let situations in which errors may occur at runtime. That is
the reason why we will consider an on-line verification of the system behavior.

R.H. Bordini et al. (Eds.): ProMAS 2005, LNAI 3862, pp. 41–56, 2006.
© Springer-Verlag Berlin Heidelberg 2006

This verification consists in monitoring and regulating the system behavior to prevent its failure. We call this verification the **agent control**.

Moreover, we think that the agents are better placed to make themselves the control of their behavior. So, we provide the agents with the means to monitor their behavior and, thanks to their capabilities of reasoning, they can regulate their behavior in order to avoid **undesirable behaviors**.

Although it is possible for a developer to insert the control code into the agents, a manual instrumentation of a system program, to insert probes, is hard, time-consuming and prone to error [12]. When several agents are concerned, it is worst. So, upgrading the agents behavior and control becomes hard, if we consider that the monitoring code is fragmented in the agent program and also distributed among the agents. On the basis of automatic instrumentation for monitoring distributed systems, a possible solution could be to automatically modify the agent program in order to introduce the control and so, facilitate the work of the developer. We are particularly interested in monitoring software which consists in inserting software probes into the program to detect events [3]. The automation of the insertion can take two forms : (1) the developer uses a metalanguage [10] or a routines library [6] allowing the insertion of probes in a transparent way; (2) the insertion will be made by compiler from the speci-fication of the interested events [9]. We focus on the last form and we propose a generator which creates agents being able to check their own behavior from a description of the requirements associated with the agents and their behavior program.

In the section 2 we will present the principles of the control of autonomous agent. An example will be described in the section 3 to illustrate during the rest of the paper the operation of the generator. In the section 4, we will de-scribe the SCAAR framework allowing the generation of self-controlled agents. In this part we will focus on laws concepts and generation of the control from these laws.

2   Control of Autonomous Agent

We consider controlling MAS relies on the monitoring of agents behavior during the MAS execution and also the regulation when an error occurs. The idea it to make an automatic insertion into the agents of the necessary means of control, allowing agents to monitor themselves and detect undesirable behaviors.

2.1   Behavior Verification

Making a model of a whole MAS and its agents is not conceivable because of its complexity (indeterminism, state explosion, distributed nature). So, we propose to use norms to express properties about the agents behavior. In general, norms [15] define constraints on the agents behavior in order to guarantee a social order. An agent decide to respect or not a norm by restricting its set of possible actions. We use **laws** to describe desired or dreaded behaviors or situations. Laws are norms that don't be taken into account by the agents at the decision process (*i.e.* the agents can act as they want and our approach consists in verifying if the chosen action respects the laws afterwards) because we want to distinguish the agent implementation and the laws/control description. The laws represents signification or critical requirements of the system execution. An agent capable of self-control checks that laws are respected throughout its execution. But monitoring is not enough, when an agent detects the transgression of a law, it must regulate its behavior from transgression information.

In oder that the agent can deduce their behavior when they are informed of a law transgression, we suppose that the laws are known by the agents. Either the developer constructs the agents from requirements, consequently he verifies that the agents respect the laws by construction, or the agents have a representation of this laws that they attempt to respect throughout their execution. So our approach consists in adding a dynamic verification to make sure that the developer correctly implements the agents and the latter always respect the laws once running in multiagent context.

2.2 Level of Laws

We wish that the person who decides of the laws does not be necessarily the developer. In general the customers define the requirements and the developers implement the system form these requirements. Also, the customer is in position to know what is important to verify without to know the agents implementation. So, we suppose that the laws are expressed in natural language by the customer and translated by an expert in a description language. Therefore, it is necessary to express the laws at an abstraction level understandable by the customer and allowing an easy translation.

Moreover, for a sake of generality, we would provide a control mechanism for several agent models. The level of law must permit to include several kinds of agent models. So, the laws must state general **concepts** representing the agent model and the application. The model designer provides a set of concepts representing the model specificities and the system designer/developer provides typical application concepts. From this set of concepts, the expert can describe the laws expressed by the customer by using the description language.

2.3 Control Enforcement

The control enforcement is divided in five steps (Fig.1):

1. The model developer must provide a description of the concepts and their hooks with the model implementation.
2. The customer provides the set of laws that he wants to be verified throughout the system execution. These laws can concern one or several agents.
3. The system designer/developer describes the concepts representing the application. The system developer implements the agents form the set of laws or/and the agents use the laws to deduce their behavior at runtime. He provides the agents with strategies of regulation associated with each laws.

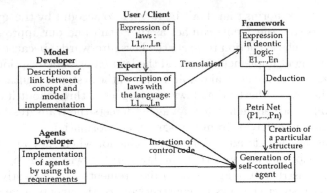

Fig. 1. Aspects of agent control

4. An expert translates the laws expressed in (2) by using a description language. The laws state concepts describes in (1) and (3).
5. The generator translates laws, written in a particular language, into expressions using deontic logic. From these expressions, the generator deduces the Petri nets representing the laws. Also, the generator inserts control points into the agents program to allow the detection of the expected events defined in the laws. The generator provides the agents with a particular structure to obtain self-controlled agents.

3   An Example

3.1   The Multiagent System

We introduce a simple multiagent system of problem resolution. MAS is constituted of three kinds of agent : an agent A, used as an interface between the user and the system; an agent B, assuming the management of the problems forwarded by A; an agent C, resolving the problems sent by B. The agent model used is a Petri net. The behavior of each agent is described in figure 2.

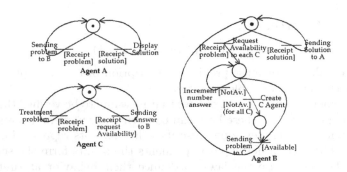

Fig. 2. The behavior of each agents

3.2   Laws of the System

The customer expresses the laws of the system in English. We will take the example of three laws which can be associated with the previous MAS :

L1: "an A agent must not send message to a B agent at a rate greater than one message per second". For instance, this law ensures that the agent B can follow the requests sent by the agent A and C can answer in a reasonable time.

L2: "a B agent must not create a C agent if another C agent is available in the system". This law prevents the agent B to create too many agents and consequently prevents the application overload.

L3: "a C agent must receive consecutively a message about the waiting time, a message of identification, the data of the problem without any other interleaved messages". This law allows the verification of communication protocols used between the agents. In this case, the law concerns the receiver agent which must receive three messages in a particular order without another message between them.

4   SCAAR: A Framework for the Generation of Self-controlled Autonomous Agents

SCAAR (Self-Controlled Autonomous Agent geneRator) is a framework allowing the generation of agents capable of self-control. The generator uses the set of laws associated to the agents, the set of concepts used in laws and injects the control code into the agents program. The figure 3 represents the framework architecture which consists of :

- **Ontology:** The set of concepts representing the agents models and the application.
- **Laws:** The set of properties that the agents must respect.
- **Agent Model:** The hooks between the model description (the concepts) and the model implementation.
- **Agent Program:** The code of agent behavior.
- **Generator:** The creator of the final agent from the previous elements.
- **Self-controlled agent:** The executable final agent. It monitors its own behavior in order to verify if the laws are respected and regulate it if a law is transgressed.

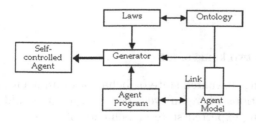

Fig. 3. The SCAAR Framework

4.1   Ontology

We saw that the laws are based on high-level concepts allowing the description of agents and system specificity. So, we construct a basic ontology representing known models used to construct agents. A set of agent concepts is provided by D.N. Lam and K.S. Barber [8] for agent verification. The concepts proposed are: *Goal, Belief, Intention, Action, Event, Message*. We take a part of this concepts (*Goal, Action, Message*) and we add other ones which are more typical of agent models from our point of view (BDI, CLAIM, personal agent models): *Agent, Object, Knowledge, Plan, Agent Creation, Message Sending, Message Receipt, Migration*). We propose to divide the concepts up into three categories: AGENT, textscFeature and AC-TION. The figure 4 represents the distribution of the concepts.

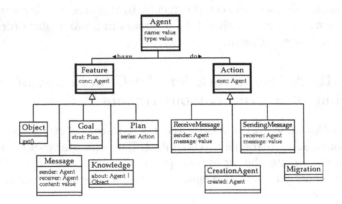

Fig. 4. Agent Ontology

This set of basic concepts can be extended by the model designer to refine the model description with sub-concepts or instances. The system designer can extend the set of concepts defining the model with instances. In our example, the agent model can be described with the basic concept of: `ReceiptMessage`, `SendingMessage`, `CreationAgent`, `Action`, `Agent`. The refinement of the description is done with the concepts of: `State` which is a sub-concept of `Knowledge` and has a parameter : available or not, and `ReceivedMessage` which is a sub-concept of `Message`.

4.2   The Laws

We can distinguish two kinds of law :

- One representing unwanted state or behavior of an agent. It allows the detection of situations where an event occurs while it should not.
- One representing expected state or behavior of an agent. It allows the detection of situations where an expected event does not occurs.

We propose that our laws are expressed by using deontic operators, which are widely used in the context of norms. So, we provide a language of law description allowing the expression of prohibition and obligation to represent the two previous kinds of law. The language applies to events and states about the agents, corresponding to the general basic concepts of FEATURES and ACTION introduced previously. An **event** can be the execution of an action or the change of a feature value. A **state** represents the resulting state of an event. The expression of time or temporal relation between the events and states is possible. We can divide a law in three parts:

- **CONCERNED_AGENTS (CA)**: The statement of the agents concerned by the law. These are the agents that can be subject to the law and agents used to describe the laws application context.
- **DEONTIC_ASSERTION (DA)**: The description of what is obligatory and forbidden. It is a set of relationship between an agent and an event or a state.
- **APPLICATION_CONDITIONS (APC)**: The description of the law context. It is an expression describing when the DA must be respected relatively to a set of events or states.

So, the language syntax is as follows:

```
LAW      := (CA)(DA ⟨APC⟩)
CA       := (agent : AGENT ⟨ and PROP⟩)+
DA       := DEONTIC EXP | DA AND EXP |
            DA THEN EXP
APC      := QUA1 EVENT ⟨ AND EVENT⟩ |
            QUA1 EVENT ⟨ THEN EVENT⟩ |
            QUA2 STATE ⟨ AND STATE⟩ |
            QUA1 seconde | APC APC
DEONTIC:= FORBIDDEN | OBLIGED
EXP      := (EVENT) | NOT EXP
EVENT    := agent do SMTH ⟨ and PROP⟩
STATE    := agent be SMTH ⟨ and PROP⟩
QUA1     := AFTER | BEFORE
QUA2     := IF
PROP     := funct(concept.argument)
AGENT    := Concept : Agent
SMTH     := Concept : Action | Concept : Feature
```

The semantic of our language is based on the dynamic deontic logic [13]. This logic is a variant of the deontic logic [16] and allows the expression of relation of time between actions and states. The table 1 represents the correspondence between the language of laws description and the dynamic deontic logic.

To explain the language we will express the law given in section 3[1].

---

[1] An agent of type X will be denoted agX.

Table 1. Relation between our language and the Dynamic Deontic logic (not exhaustive)

LANGUAGE	LOGIC
FORBIDDEN (EV)	F(EV)
OBLIGED (EV)	O (EV)
FORBIDDEN (EV1) AND (EV2)	F(EV1 & EV2)
FORBIDDEN (EV1) THEN (EV2)	F(EV1 ; EV2)
FORBIDDEN (EV2) AFTER (EV1)	[EV1]F(EV2)
FORBIDDEN (EV1) BEFORE (EV2)	F(EV1)[EV2]
... AFTER (EV1) AND (EV2)	[EV1 & EV2]...
... AFTER (EV1) THEN (EV2)	[EV1 ; EV2]...
FORBIDDEN (EV1) IF (STATE)	STATE ⊃ F(EV1)
NOT(EVENT)	*EVENT*
EV1 EV2 BEFORE(Sec)	EV1 EV2[time(Sec)]
EV1 EV2 AFTER(Sec)	EV1[time(Sec)]EV2

L1 : "an A agent must not send message to a B agent at a rate greater than one message per second" could be expressed as a prohibition:

(CA)   For each agA.
(DA)   It is forbidden for agA to send a message to agB,
(APC) After agA send a message to agB and before one second.

By using the language and the concepts defined for the system, we can write the law as:

(L1) (agA : Agent and agA.type = A)(agB : Agent and agB.type= B)
        FORBIDDEN(agA **do** SendingMessage **and** receiver = agB)
        AFTER(agA **do** SendingMessage **and** receiver = agB)
        BEFORE(1).

L2 : "a B agent must not create a C agent if another C agent is available in the system" could be expressed as a prohibition:

(CA)   For each agB and for each agC.
(DA)   It is forbidden for agB to create a new C agent,
(APC) If agC is in an available state.

By using the language:

(L2) (agB : Agent **and** agB.type = B)(agC : Agent **and** agC.type = C)
        FORBIDDEN(agB **do** CreationAgent **and** created.type = C)
        IF(agC **be** State **and** value = available).

L3 : "a C agent must receive consecutively a message about the waiting time (M1), a message of identification (M2), the data of the problem (M3) without any another interleaved message" could be expressed as an obligation:

(CA)   For each agC.

(DA)   It is obligatory for agC to receive M1 then M2 then M3 without any other interleaved message,

(CAP)   nothing.

By using the language:

(L3)(agC : Agent **and** agC.type = C)

 OBLIGED(agC **be** ReceivedMessage **and** content = M1)

 THEN (agC **do** ReceivedMessage **and** content = M2)

 AND NOT (agC **do** ReceivedMessage **and** content <> M2)

 THEN (agC **do** ReceivedMessage **and** content = M3)

 AND NOT(agC **do** ReceivedMessage **and** content <> M3).

4.3 Hooks Between Concepts and the Implementation of the Agent Model

The generation of self-controlled agents required the agents program instrumentation in order to insert control points for verifying the respect of the laws. The concepts used in laws must have a representation in the agents programs. The designer of the model provides the hooks between the abstract concepts and the implementation of the agent model. From this hooks the generator inserts the control code in the implementation of the agent model and consequently in the agents.

```
hook('SendingMessage', predicate(sendMessage, 2),
     [MESSAGE, RECEIVER], [argument(1), argument(2)]).

hook('ReceivedMessage', argument(predicate(setIncomingMessage,2),1),
     [CONTENT, SENDER],
     [call(predicate(getContent,1),1), call(predicate(getSender,1),1)]).
```

Fig. 5. Example of hooks between concepts and model program

Let's see on the example the necessary hooks to insert control in the agents. The agents are programmed in Prolog, we focus on two concepts: SendingMessage and ReceivedMessage. The first concept corresponds, in the implementation of agent model, to the *sendMessage* clause. The message can be found in the first argument and the receiver in the second argument of *sendMessage*. Received-Message concept is linked in the program with a certain variable. We get its value in argument of the clause *SetIncomingMessage*. The message content and the sender can also be get by a call of a method. The figure 5 shows the code to describe the hooks between the concepts and the program.

4.4   Structure of Generated Agents

A generated agent is obtained directly from :

- The agent behavior program
- The set of laws associated with the agent
- The links between the concepts used in the laws and the model implementation

To allow the agent to control their own behavior, we propose the use of the **observer approach** [4].

The Observer Approach. The observer approach consists in executing a program and a model of property, about the program execution, in parallel. The model and the program are connected with control points. A controller checks on the model and the program execution are consistent.

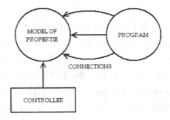

Fig. 6. The observer approach

For instance, the properties can be modeled in the form of Petri net whose transitions are bound to the program with the control points. When the program execution finds a control point, the controller makes sure the tokens are in the right place at the right time in the corresponding nets, and brings about some change in the model, accordingly. If the system execution does not match to the models, the verification fails.

So, we propose to put this approach in place into the agents in order to provide them the means of controlling their own behavior. Firstly, the laws are modeled by Petri nets. In order to simplify this stage of modeling, we propose to generate automatically the Petri nets representing the laws. Secondly, we insert into the agent behavior program the control points linked to the transitions of the Petri nets and we generate a runnable agent with a specific architecture, using the observer approach.

The Architecture. A generated agent has a specific architecture allowing the monitoring of the agent behavior and the detection of the transgression of the laws associated with an agent. The architecture is divided in two parts, the behavior part and the control part. The figure 7 represents the agent architecture.

The behavior part matches the program under surveillance in the observer approach. It includes the real agent behavior and strategies of regulation defined

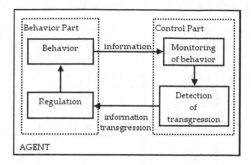

Fig. 7. The architecture of a self-controlled agent

by the developer. Indeed, we would not like only that the verification fails when an inconsistence is detected but that the agent can regulate its behavior when a law is transgressed. The control part matches the controller which is an integral part of the agent. The control part includes the set of Petri nets representing the laws associated with the agent and makes sure of the detection of the laws violation. The connections between the program and the models are simulated by a sending of information from the behavior part to the control part. To allow this sending of information, we instrument the behavior part by inserting automatically some control points associated with the events and states contained in the laws. The control part receives the information and verifies the respect of the laws.

4.5   The Generator

The generation of a self-controlled agent comes down to the generation of the Petri net representing each law concerning the agent and the instrumentation of the agent behavior to detect the occurrence of events and states expressed in the laws.

The Instrumentation. To monitor a system execution, it is essential to insert probes into the program to detect the occurrence of events. We propose an automatic instrumentation of the agent behavior program to monitor the occurrence of the events and states expressed in the laws by inserting **control points**. This instrumentation is done thanks to the hooks defined by the developer, between the concepts describing the model and its implementation. In order to do that, we draw ours inspiration from the principle of weaving. The **weaving** is an important part of the aspect programming [17]. The latter consists in modularizing crosscutting structure. The aspect programming uses the weaving to inject aspects in classes of an application, at methods level, to modify the system execution after the compilation. An aspect is a module representing crosscutting concerns. The interest of the aspect programming to integrate the monitoring in an application was demonstrated in another light by [11]. So, our approach consists in:

Table 2. Translation of logic expression in Petri Net (not exhaustive)

LOGIC	PETRI NET	LOGIC	PETRI NET
F(EVENT)		O(EVENT)	
F(EV1 & EV2)		O(EV1 & EV2)	
F(EV1 ; EV2)		[EV1]F(EV2)	
F(EV1)[EV2]		[EV1 & EV2]	
[EV1 ; EV2]		STATE ⊃ F(EV1)	
EV1 EV2 [Sec]		EV1 [Sec] EV2	

1. Extracting the events to be detected.
2. For each event, searching for the provided hook to the implementation.
3. Injecting, before or after the provided hook, the code allowing the sending of information to the control part and the recovery of possible information of transgression to enable the agent to begin a strategy of regulation.

The Generation of Petri Nets. The generation of a Petri net representing a law is divided in three stages :

- The translation of the law in a logic expression L, by using the table 1, in order to point out a set of elementary logic expressions, $\{l_1, ..., l_n\}$.
- The deduction of a set of Petri net, $\{p_1, ..., p_n\}$ representative of each expression in $\{l_1, ..., l_n\}$, by using the table 2.
- The fusion of all the nets in $\{p_1, ..., p_n\}$ from the relations between $l_1, ..., l_n$ expressed in L, by using the table 2 to obtain a final Petri net, P, representing the law.

The final Petri net P, is embedded into the control part of each agent submitted to the law. This Petri net includes two parts: the **conditional part** with states and transitions associated with the events and states described in the APC of the law; the **deontic part** with states and transitions associated with the events or states described in the DA of the law. For example, from the law L1:

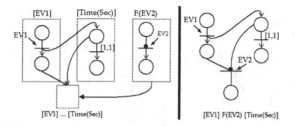

Fig. 8. The generation of the Petri net for L1

(L1) (agA : Agent and agA.type = A)(agB : Agent and agB.type= B)
    FORBIDDEN(agA **do** SendingMessage **and** receiver = agB)
    AFTER(agA **do** SendingMessage **and** receiver = agB)
    BEFORE(1).

We can deduce the following logic expression:

$$[SendingMessage(agA, agB, M1) \wedge agent(agA, A) \wedge agent(agB, B)]$$
$$F(SendingMessage(agA, agB, M2) \wedge agent(agA, A) \wedge agent(agB, B))[time(1)]$$

From this expression, the generator deduces the Petri net representing the law. To represent a prohibition we use an inhibitor hyperarc:

Inhibitor hyperarc: *A branch inhibitor hyperarc between places* $P_1, ..., P_k$ *and a transition* T, *means that* T *is not firable if all the places are marked* [7].

To express a real time, we use a timed Petri net. The figure 8 represents the generation of a Petri net representing the law **L1** with inhibitor hyperarc and time.

4.6 Multiagent Laws

For a law applied to several agents, our aim is to distribute as much as possible the control into each agent affected by the law. We would like to avoid a centralized solution. So the Petri net representing the "multiagent law" is deduces as in a single agent context. Then, the net is distributed into the control parts of the agents concerned by the law. For example, the figure 9 represents the distribution of the Petri net representing the multiagent law L2 :

(L2) (agB : Agent **and** agB.type = B)(agC : Agent **and** agC.type = C)
    FORBIDDEN(agB **do** CreationAgent **and** created.type = C)
    IF(agC **be** State **and** value = available).

Let us note that the control parts of each agents are only linked through the arcs between places and transitions (themselves distributed over the control parts of agents). These links represent the information flow between the control parts (*i.e.* the flow of the token).

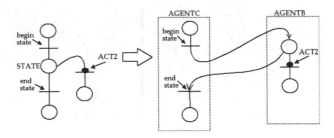

Fig. 9. Distribution between two agents

So, when a control part, C_A, receives an information from its agent, if this information is associated with a transition T whose the next place is in the control part of another agent, C_B, then C_A sends information about the firing of this transition, (actually, it sends the token) to the control part C_B and waits for an acknowledgment of receipt. During this waiting, the behavior of the agent is temporarily stopped and the information associated with T is considered as always available. The control part C_B receives the information, sends the acknowledgment to the control part C_A and verifies the respect of its part of the law. When C_A receives the acknowledgment, the transition can be really fired, the information associated with T is consumed and the agent behavior can continue.

5 Related Work

M.S. Feather *and al.* [5] treat also the agreement between a system and its requirements. In their approach, an external monitor collects events sent by the agents and a reconciler is going, when a requirement violation is detected, not to hand the system in a state that respected requirements, but to modify requirements so that they are in agreement with the new behavior. The authors do not consider essential requirements for the system execution, they do not seek to prevent inconsistent behavior. They try that a system and its requirements adapt themselves to stay in agreement during the system execution.

D.N. Lam and K.S. Barber [8] propose a methodology, the Tracing Method, to test and explain the agents behavior. The aim of this method is to ensure that an agent performs actions for the right reasons, and if an unexpected action occurred, to help explain why an agent decided to perform the action. We have in common an agent ontology to compare specifications (state-chart diagrams, communication protocol diagrams) and agents real behavior. But in our approach we propose an automation of the code instrumentation and the detection of inconsistencies between the expected and the observed behaviors. Finally, our control is embedded into agents to allow an on-line detection of errors. The Tracing Method allows an off-line analysis of the program traces generated during the system execution.

Finally, we cite the recent work of R. Paes [14]. In the context of open multi-agent systems, the authors propose the use of laws to control the emergence of wrong behaviors. If the idea is similar, the authors apply their control only to the messages passing between the agents and not to the whole behavior. They propose the use of a mediator which receives the messages, applies the laws on these messages and forwards them to the addressed agent. Here, it is about the surveillance of the agents interaction thanks to an external entity.

6 Conclusion

We have presented in this paper a framework, SCAAR, allowing the generation of agents being able to verify their own behavior. This verification consists in making sure that a set of laws associated with an agent is respected throughout the MAS execution. These laws represent requirements about agents behavior and state. The interest of our approach is principally to permit the description of laws by someone not involved in the MAS development. Another important point lies in the fact that the control can be applied to agents implemented with different kinds of agent model, in condition that the model used can be described from our agent concepts. With our framework, we provide a language to describe laws. We propose a mechanism for automatic generation of Petri nets representing the laws and insertion of control points to detect expected events. The Petri nets are used to monitor the agent behavior and detect when laws are transgressed, by using the observer approach. Finally, we propose a first solution for the enforcement of laws at the multiagent level.

References

1. K.S. Barber and C.E. Martin. Agent autonomy : Specification, measurement and dynamic adjustment. In *Proc. of the Autonomy Control Software workshop at Autonomous Agents'99*, pages 8–15, May 1999.
2. E.M. Clarke, O. Grumberg, and D.A. Peled. *Model Checking*. MIT Press, 2000.
3. M. de Sousa Dias and D.J. Richardson. Issues on software monitoring. Technical report, Department of Information and Computer Science, University of California, July 2002.
4. M. Diaz, G. Juanole, and J-P. Courtiat. Observer-a concept for formal on-line validation of distributed systems. *IEEE Trans. Softw. Eng.*, 20(12):900–913, 1994.
5. M.S. Feather, S. Fickas, A. van Lamsweerde, and C. Ponsard. Reconciling System Requirements and Runtime Behavior. In *Proceedings of IWSSD9*, Isobe, Japan, 1998.
6. Y. Huang and C. Kintala. Software fault tolerance in the application layer. In *Software Fault Tolerance*, 1995.
7. R. Janicki and M. Koutny. On causality semantics of nets with priorities. *Fundamenta Informaticae*, (38):223–255, 1999.
8. D.N. Lam and K.S. Barber. Debugging agent behavior in an implemented agent system. In *Proceedings of PROMAS'04*, pages 45–56, New York City, July 20 2004.
9. Y. Liao and D. Cohen. A specificational approach to high level program monitoring and measuring. *IEEE Trans. Software Engineering*, 18(11), November 1992.

10. J.E. Lumpp, T.L. Casavant, H.J. Siegle, and D.C. Marinescu. Specification and identification of events for debugging and performance monitoring of distributed multiprocessor systems. In *Proceedings of the 10th International Conference on Distributed Systems*, pages 476–483, June 1990.
11. D. Mahrenholz, O. Spinczyk, and W. Schröder-Preikschat. Program instrumentation for debugging and monitoring with AspectC++. In *Proc. of the 5th IEEE International symposium on Object-Oriented Real-time Distributed Computing*, Washington DC, USA, April 29 – May 1 2002.
12. M. Mansouri-Samani. *Monitoring of Distributed Sytems*. PhD thesis, University of London, London, UK, 1995.
13. JJCH. Meyer. A different approach to deontic logic: Deontic logic viewed as a variant of dynamic logic. *Notre Dame Journal of Formal Logic*, 29(1), 1988.
14. R. Paes, G. Carvalho, C. Lucena, P. Alencar, H. Almeida, and V. Silva. Specifying laws in open multi-agent systems. In *ANIREM*, Utrecht, July 2005.
15. J. Vázquez-Salceda, H. Aldewerld, and F. Dignum. Implementing norms in multi-agent systems. In *Proceedings of MATES'04*, Erfurt, Germany, September, 29–30 2004.
16. G.H. von Wright. Deontic logic. *Mind*, 60(237):1–15, 1951.
17. Dean Wampler. The future of aspect oriented programming, 2003. White Paper, available on *http://www.aspectprogramming.com*.

Bridging Agent Theory and Object Orientation: Importing Social Roles in Object Oriented Languages

Matteo Baldoni[1], Guido Boella[1], and Leendert van der Torre[2]

[1] Dipartimento di Informatica, Università degli Studi di Torino, Torino, Italy
{baldoni, guido}@di.unito.it
[2] CWI Amsterdam and Delft University of Technology, The Netherlands
torre@cwi.nl

Abstract. Social roles structure social institutions like organizations in Multi-Agent Systems (MAS). In this paper we describe how to introduce the notion of social role in programming languages. To avoid the commitment to a particular agent model, architecture or language, we decided to extend Java, the most prominent object oriented programming language, by adding social roles. The obtained language allows an easier implementation of MAS's w.r.t. the Java language. We also show that many important properties of social roles, studied in the MAS field, can be applied to objects. Two are the essential features of social roles according to an analysis reported in the paper: social roles are defined by other entities (called institutions), and when an agent plays a role it is endowed with powers by the institution that defines it. We interpret these two features into the object oriented paradigm as the fact that social roles are objects, which are defined in and exist only inside other objects (corresponding to institutions), and that, through a role, external objects playing the role can access to the object (institution) the role belongs to.

1 Introduction

Social roles are central in MAS since they are the basis for coordinating agents by means of organizations [1]. Roles are central also in object oriented modelling and programming (OO), where they are used to dynamically add behaviors to objects, to factorize features of objects like methods or access rights, and to separate the interactional properties of objects from their core behavior, thus achieving a separation of concerns.

Although it would surely be useful to find a unified notion of role, in both agent oriented (AO) and object oriented systems, the existence of many distinct notions of role (as well as of agent) makes this task a difficult challenge. Starting from the analysis of Boella and van der Torre [2], in this paper we describe how to introduce the notion of social role in programming languages. Since it is difficult to choose among the different agent systems and languages proposed by the MAS community, because each of them has its own idiosyncrasies (many types of agents are used, from reactive to cognitive ones; many architectures are used, from mobile to robotic ones; different definitions of organizations with social roles are used, from groups [4] to set of rules [5]), we propose an implementation that is set in the more traditional OO framework, whilst using the

R.H. Bordini et al. (Eds.): ProMAS 2005, LNAI 3862, pp. 57–75, 2006.

analysis developed in MAS research. More specifically, the research question of this paper is: How to extend Java by introducing the notion of social role? To answer this question we first analyze the relevant properties of social roles and, then, we map them to programming constructs in the OO context.

The choice of the Java language is due to the fact that it is one of the prototypical OO programming languages; moreover, MAS systems are often implemented in Java and some agent programming languages are extensions of Java, e.g., see the Jade framework [6]. In this way we can directly use roles offered by our extension of Java when building MAS systems or extending agent programming languages.

Furthermore, we believe that to contribute to the success of the Autonomous Agents and Multiagent Systems research, the theories and concepts developed in this area should be applicable also to more traditional views. It is a challenge for the agent community to apply its concepts outside strictly agent based applications, and the object oriented paradigm is central in Computer Science. As suggested also by Juan and Sterling [7], before AO can be widely used in industry, its attractive theoretical properties must be first translated to simple, concrete constructs and mechanisms that are of similar granularity as objects.

The methodology that we use in this paper is to map the properties of social roles to roles in objects. To provide a semantics for the new programming language, called powerJava, we use a mapping to pure Java by means of a precompilation phase.

In Section 2 we discuss how social roles can fit the ontology of OO. In Section 3 we provide our definition of social roles and in Section 4 we map it to the OO domain. In Section 5 we introduce powerJava and in Section 7 we describe how it is translated to Java. Conclusions end the paper.

2   Social Roles Among Objects

Why should it be useful for the OO paradigm to introduce a notion of social role, as developed in MAS? Even if the utility of roles is widely recognized in OO for organizing software programs, the diversity of conflicting approaches witnesses some difficulties, as the survey of Steimann [8] shows.

The success of the OO paradigm in many disciplines (KR, SE, DB, programming languages) is due also to the large conceptual modelling work behind it. The object orientation paradigm is inspired to the ontology used by humans to conceptualize material reality, in particular the fact that objects are composed of other objects, that they can be classified in classes, and that each class offers a different distinct behavior. These features find straightforward counterparts in programming languages. In particular, the abstraction and encapsulation principles, polymorphism, modularity and software reuse can be realized by means of the notion of object with its methods, and of class hierarchy.

The likely reason why the object oriented paradigm cannot accommodate easily the notion of role is that the notion of role does not belong to the fragment of ontology to which object orientation refers.

In this paper we extend the domain of the reference ontology of OO to the domain of social reality, which social roles belong to. The ontology of *social reality* represents the conceptual model of the social life of humans. Researches in this domain mostly stem from the agent oriented paradigm as a way to solve coordination problems among agents in multiagent systems. But it is also an area of interest of ontological research, like in [9,10].

The notion of social role refers to the structure of social entities like institutions, organizations, normative systems, or even groups. These social entities are organized in roles [1,4,5]. Roles are usually considered as a means to distribute the responsibilities necessary for the functioning of the institution or organization. Moreover, roles allow the uncoupling of the features of the individuals from those of their roles. Finally, roles are used to define common interaction patterns, and embed information and capabilities needed to communication and coordination [11]. E.g., the roles of auctioneer and bidder are defined in an auction, each with their possible moves.

We call our extension of Java powerJava, since the powers given by institutions to roles are a key feature of roles in our model. An example is the role of director of a department: a buying order, signed by the agent playing the role of director, is considered as a commitment of the institution, that will pay for the delivered goods.

3   Properties of Social Roles

We consider as characteristic of roles two properties highlighted respectively in the knowledge representation area [10] and in the multiagent system area [12].

Definitional dependence: The definition of the role must be given inside the definition of the institution it belongs to. This property is related to the foundation property of roles [13]: a role instance is always associated with an instance of the institution it belongs to.

Powers: When an agent starts playing a role in an institution, it is empowered by the institution: the actions which it performs in its role "count as" [14] actions of the institution itself. This is possible only because of the definitional dependence: since the role is defined by the institution it is the institution itself which gives it some powers.

Institutions like groups, organizations, normative systems are not material entities, since they belong to the *social* reality, which exists only as a construction of human beings. According to the model of Boella and van der Torre [15,16], social entities can be modelled as agents, albeit of a special kind since they act in the world via the actions of other agents. In [2,12], also *roles* are considered as (description of) agents.

In this work, agents - like their players and institutions are - are modelled as objects, and, thus, by the previous observation, roles are modelled as objects too. In order to work at the level of objects we do not consider typical properties of agents like autonomy or proactiveness.

To understand these issues we propose a running example. Consider the role "student". A student is always a student of some school. Without the school the role does not exist anymore: e.g., if the school goes bankrupt, the actor (e.g. a person) of the role cannot be called a student anymore. The institution (the school) also specifies which are the properties of the student which extend the properties of the person playing the role of student: the school specifies the role's enrollment number, its email address in the school intranet, its scores at past examinations. Most importantly the school also specifies how the student can behave. For example, the student can give an exam by submitting some written examination; this action is clearly defined by the school since it is the school which specifies how an examination is valued and it is the school which maintains the official records of the examinations which is updated with the new mark. Finally, the student can contact the secretary who is obliged to provide it with an enrollment certificate; also this action depends on the definition the school gives both to the student role and to the secretary role, otherwise the student could not have an effect on the her.

But in defining such actions the school *empowers* the person who is playing the role of student.

4   Modelling Roles as Objects

To translate the notion of social role in OO we need to find a suitable mapping between the agent domain and the object domain. The basic idea is that agents are mapped to objects. Their behaviors are mapped in methods invoked on the objects. We have to distinguish at least three different kinds of agents:

- Players of roles: their basic feature is that they can exercise the powers given by their roles when they act in a role, since their actions "count as" actions of their roles [14].
- Institutions: their basic feature is to have parts (roles) which are not independent, but which are defined by themselves. They must give to the defined roles access to their private fields and methods.
- Roles: they describe how the player of the role is connected to the institution via its powers. They do not exist without the institution defining them and they do not act without the agent playing the role.

The mapping between agents and objects must preserve this classification, so we need three kinds of objects.

- Objects playing roles: when they play a role, it is possible to invoke on them the methods representing the powers given by the role.
- Institutions: their definition must contain the definition they give to the roles belonging to them.
- Roles: they must specify which object can play the role and which powers are added to it. They must be connected both to the institution, since the powers have effect on it, and to the player of the role.

In OO terms, the player of the role can determine the behavior of the object, in which the role is defined, without having either a reference to it or access to its private fields and methods. In this way, it is possible to exogenously coordinate its behavior, as requested by Arbab [17].

In the next sections we will address in details the three different kinds of objects we need to model in `powerJava`.

4.1 Playing a Role

An object has different (or additional) properties when it plays a certain role, and it can perform new activities, as specified by the role definition. Moreover, a role represents a specific state which is different from the player's one, which can evolve with time by invoking methods on the roles (or on other roles of the same institution, as we have seen in the running example). The relation between the object and the role must be transparent to the programmer: it is the object which has to maintain a reference to its roles. For example, if a person is a student and a student can be asked to return its enrollment number, then, we want to be able to invoke the method on the person as a student without referring to the role instance. A role is not an independent object, it is a facet of the player.

Since an agent can play multiple roles, the same method will have a different behavior, depending on the role which the object is playing when it is invoked. It must be sufficient to specify with is the role of a given object we are referring to. On the other hand, methods of a role can exhibit different behaviors according to whom is playing a role. So a method returning the name of the student together with the name of the school returns not only a different school name according to the school, but also a different value for the name according to whom is playing the role of student.

Note that roles are always roles in an institution. Hence an object can play at the same moment a role more than once, albeit in different institutions. For example, one can be a student at the high school, a student of foreign languages in another school, *etc.* We do not consider in this paper the case of an object playing the same role more than once in the same institution. However, an object can play several roles in the same institution. For example, a person can be an MP and a minister at the same time (even if it is not required to be an MP to become minister).

In order to specify the role under which an object is referred to, we evocatively use the same terminology used for casting by Java. For example, if a person is playing the role of student and we want to invoke a method on it as a student, we say that there is a casting from the object to the role. Recall that to make this casting we do not only have to specify which role we are referring to, but also the institution where the object is playing the role, too. Otherwise, if an object plays the same role in more than one institution, the cast would be ambiguous.

We call this *role casting*. Type casting in Java allows to see the same object under different perspectives while maintaining the same structure and identity. In contrast, role casting conceals a *delegation* mechanism: the delegated object can only act as allowed by the powers of the role; it can access the state of the institution and, by exploiting a construct that will be introduced shortly (that) can also refer to the delegating object.

4.2 Institutions Defining Roles

The basic feature of institutions, as intended in our framework, is to define roles inside themselves. If roles are defined inside an institution, they can have access to the private variables and methods of the institution. The "definition" of an object must be read as the definition of the class the object is an instance of, thus, we have that the class defining an institution includes the class definition of the roles belonging to the institution.

The fact that the role class definition is included inside the institution class definition determines some special properties of the methods that can be invoked on a role. In fact, for the notion of role to be meaningful, these methods should go beyond standard methods, whose implementation can access the private state of the role only. Roles add powers to objects playing the roles. Power means the capability of modifying also the *state of the institution* which defines the role and the *state of the other roles* defined in the same institution. This capability seems to violate the standard encapsulation principle, where the private variables and methods are visible only to the class they belong to: however, here, the role definition is itself inside the class definition, so encapsulation is not violated. This means also that the role must have a reference to the institution, in order to refer to its private or public methods and fields.

In our example, the method by which a student takes an examination must modify the private state of the school. If the exam is successful, the mark will be added to the registry of exams in the school. Similarly, if the method of asking the secretary a certificate should be able to access the private method of the secretary to print a certificate.

In MAS, roles can be played by different agents, it is sufficient that they have the suitable capabilities. This is translated in OO as the fact that to play a role an object must implement the suitable methods. In Java this corresponds to implementing an interface, i.e., a collection of method signatures. To specify who can play it, a role specifies an interface representing the requirements to play a role. Thus, an object to play a role must implements an interface.

The objects which can play the role can be of different classes, so that roles can be specified independently of the particular classes playing the role. This possibility is a form of polymorphism which allows to achieve a flexible external coordination and to make roles reusable.

At the same time a role expresses the powers which can be exercised by its player. Again, since powers are mapped into methods, a role is related to another interface definition. In summary, a role has two faces (see also Figure 1):

– It describes the methods that an object must show in order to play/enact the role. We call them *requirements*.
– It describes the methods that are offered by the role to an object that might enact it. We call them *powers*.

For Steimann and Mayer [18] roles define a certain behavior or protocol demanded in a context independently of how or by whom this behavior is to be delivered. In our model this translates to the fact that a role defines both the behavior required by the player of the role and the behavior offered by playing the role. However, the implementation of both the requested and offered behavior is not specified in the role.

The implementation of the requirements is obviously given inside the class of the object playing the role. The implementation of the powers must be necessarily given in the definition of the institution, which the role belongs to; the reason is that only in this way such methods can really be powers: they can have access to the state of the institution and change it.

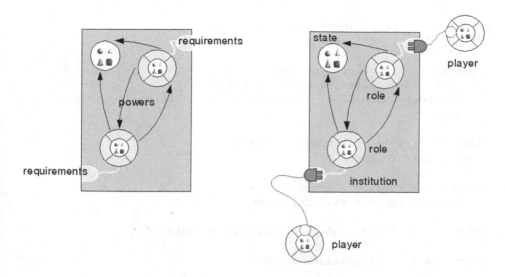

Fig. 1. The players will interact according to the acquired powers (they will follow the *protocol* implemented by the institution and its roles)

5   Introducing Roles in Java: `powerJava`

We now have all the elements to introduce roles as the new construct in `powerJava`.

5.1   The Syntax of `powerJava`

To introduce roles in `powerJava` we need very limited modifications of the Java syntax (see sketch in Figure 2):

1. A construct specifying the role with its name, requirements and powers (non-terminal symbol `rolespec`).
2. A construct that allows the implementation of a role, inside an institution and according to the specification of its powers (non-terminal symbol `roledef`).
3. A role casting construct, together with the specification of the institution to which the role belongs (non-terminal symbol `rcast`).

Note that nothing is required for an object to become the player of a role, apart from having the appropriate behavior required by the role specified by the keyword `enacts`.

The definition of a role using the keyword `role` is similar to the definition of an interface: it is in fact the specification of the powers acquired by the role in the form of methods signatures. The only difference is that the role specification refers also to another interface (e.g., `StudentRequirements` in Figure 3), that in turn gives the requirements to which an object, willing to play the role, must conform. This is implemented by the keyword `playedby`. This mechanism mirrors the idea, discussed in the previous section, that roles have two faces: the requirements and the powers. In the example, `role` specifies the powers of `Student`, whilst `StudentRequirements` - trivially - specifies its requirements.

```
rolespec := "role" identifier "playedby"
  identifier interfacebody

classdef ::= ["public"|"private"|...]
  "class" identifier ["enacts" identifier*]
  ["extends" identifier] ["implements" identifier*]
  classbody

classbody ::= "{" fielddef* constructors*
  methoddef* roledef* "}"

roledef ::= "definerole" identifier
  ["enacts" identifier*] rolebody

rolebody ::= "{" fielddef* methoddef* roledef* "}"

rcast ::= (expr.identifier) expr
```

Fig. 2. Syntax

```
role Student playedby StudentRequirements {
  public String getName ();
  public void takeExam (int examCode, String text);
  public int getMark (int examCode);
}

interface StudentRequirements {
  public String getName ();
  public int getSocSecNum ();
}
```

Fig. 3. Specification of the powers and requirements

Roles must be implemented inside an institution; the keyword definerole has been added to implement a role inside another class. A role implementation is like an inner-class definition. It is not possible, however, to define constructors; only the pre-defined one is available, having as a parameter the player of the role. Moreover, the definition of a role can contain other roles in turn (in this case the role itself becomes an institution). Finally, it is worth noting that the definition of institution is a class which can be extended by means of the normal Java constructs but the roles cannot be overridden.

Since the behavior of a role instance depends on the player of the role, in the method implementation the player instance can be retrieved via a new reserved keyword: that. So this keyword refers to *that* object which is playing the role at issue, and it is used only in the role implementation. The value of that is initialized when the constructor of the role is invoked. Notice that the type of the referred object is the type defined by the role requirements or a subtype of it.

The greatest conceptual change in powerJava is the introduction of role casting expressions with the original Java syntax for casting. A rcast specifies both the role and the instance of the institution the role belongs to (or no object in case of a single institution). Note that the casting of an object returns an object which can be manipulated as any other object invoking methods and accessing variables on it.

We do not need a special expression for creating roles since we use the notation of Java for inner classes: starting from an institution instance the keyword "new" allows the creation of an instance of the role as if the role were an inner class of the institution. For example, let us suppose that harvard is a instance of School and that chris is a person who wants to become a student of harvard. This is expressed by the instruction harvard.new Student(chris), using the predefined parameter having the role requirements StudentRequirements as type.

5.2 How to Use powerJava

In Figures 3-5 we present our running example in powerJava. In Figure 3, the name of the role Student is introduced as well as the prototypes of the methods that constitute the powers and requirements. For example, returning the name of the Student, submitting a text as an examination, and so forth. As in an interface, no non-static variables

```
class School {
  private int[][] marks;
  private String schoolName;
  public School (String name) {
    this.schoolName = name;
  }
  definerole Student {
    private int studentID;
    public void setStudentID (int studentID) {
      this.studentID = studentID;
    }
    public int getStudentID () {
      return studentID;
    }
    public void takeExam (int examCode, String text) {
      marks[studentID][examCode] = eval(text);
    }
    public int getMark (int examCode) {
      return mark[studentID][examCode];
    }
    public int getName () {
      return that.getName() + " at " + schoolName;
    }
  }
  public int eval (String text){...}
}
```

Fig. 4. Defining the institution and implementing a role specification

```
class Person enacts Student {
  private String name;
  private int SSNumber;
  public Person (String name) { this.name = name; }
  public String getName () { return name; }
  public int getSocSecNum () { return SSnumber; }
}

class TestRole {
  public static void main(String[] args) {
    Person   chris = new Person("Christine");
    School   harvard = new School("Harvard");
    School   mit = new School("MIT");
    harvard.new Student(chris);
    mit.new Student(chris);
    String x=((harvard.Student)chris).getName();
    String y=((mit.Student)chris).getName();
  }
}
```

Fig. 5. Palying a role

can be declared. Differently from a Java interface, we couple a role with the specification of its requirements. This specification is given by means of the name of a Java interface, in this case, StudentRequirements, imposing the presence of methods getName and getSocSecNum (the person's social security number).

As explained, roles must be implemented inside some institution. In our running example (Figure 4), the role Student is implemented in a class School. The implementation must respect the method signature of the role powers. As for an inner class in Java, a role implementation has access to the private fields and methods of the outer class and of the other roles defined in the outer class; this possibility does not disrupt the encapsulation principle since all roles of an institutions are defined by who defines the institution itself. In other words, an object that has assumed a given role, by means of it, has access and can change the state of the corresponding institution and of the sibling roles. In this way, we achieve what envisaged by the analysis of the notion of role.

The object playing a role can be accessed by means of the special construct that, which refers to the object that enacts the role. In the example such an object has type StudentRequirements; the that construct is used in the method getName() in order to combine the player's name with the name of the school it attends. Like an instance of a class, a role instance can have a state, specified by its private fields, in this example, studentID.

In order for an object to play a role it is sufficient that it conforms to the role requirements. Since the role requirements are implemented as a Java interface, it is sufficient that the class of the object implements the methods of such an interface. In Figure 4, the class Person can play the role Student, because it conforms to the interface StudentRequirements by implementing the methods getName and getSocSecNum.

A role is created by means of the construct new as well as it is done in Java for inner class instance creation. For example, (see Figure 5, method main of class TestRole), the object referred by chris can play the part of the student of the school harvard by executing the following instruction: harvard.new Student(chris). In this context, i.e. within the role definition, that will refer to chris. Moreover, note that the same person can play the same role in more than one school. In the example chris is also a student of mit: mit.new Student(chris).

Differently than other objects, role instances do not exist by themselves and are always associated to their players: when it is necessary to invoke a method of the student it is sufficient to have a referent to its player object. Methods can be invoked from the players of the role, given that the player is seen in its role (e.g. Student). This is done in powerJava by casting the player of the role to the role we want to refer to.

We use the Java cast syntax with a difference: the object is not casted to a type, but to a *role*. However, since roles do not exist out of the institution defining them, in order to specify a role, it is necessary to specify the institution it belongs to. In the syntax of powerJava the structure of a role casting is captured by rcast (see Figure 2). For instance, ((harvard.Student) chris).getName() takes chris in the role of student in the institution harvard. As a result, if getName applied to chris initially returned only the person's name, after the cast, the same invocation will return "Christine at Harvard". Obviously, if we cast chris to the role of student at mit ((mit.Student) chris).getName(), we obtain "Christine at MIT".

With respect to type casting, role casting does not only selects the methods available for the object, but it changes also the state of the object and the meaning of the methods: here, the name returned by the role is different from the name of the player since the method has a different behavior. As it is done in Java for the interfaces, roles can be viewed as types, and, as such, they can be used also in variable declarations, parameter declarations, and as method return types. Thus, roles allow programmers to conform to Gamma *et al.* [19]'s principle of "programming to an interface".

powerJava allows the definition of roles which can be further articulated into other roles. For example, a school can be articulated in school classes (another social entity) which are, in turn, articulated into student roles. This is possible because, as we discuss in next section, roles are implemented by means of classes, which can be nested one into the other. In this way, it is possible to create a hierarchy of social entities, where each entity defines the social entities it contains. As described by [12], this hierarchy recalls the composition hierarchy of objects, which have other objects as their parts.

6   An Example About Protocols

Hereafter, we report an example set in the framework of interaction protocols, describing an implementation of well-known *contract net* protocol [3] in our language. Contract net is used in electronic commerce and in robotics for allowing object of the class Agent which are unable to do some task to have them done. The protocol is only concerned with the realization of a specific pattern of interaction, in which the manager sends a call for proposal to a set of bidders. Each bidder can either accept and send a proposal or refuse. The manager collects all the proposals and selects one of them.

The powerJava implementation comprises the roles of Manager and that of Bidder. A Manager has the power of of starting a negotiation. Bidders have the power of taking part to a negotiation. The contract net protocol is the institution inside which the two roles are defined. Notice that the capability of the Bidder of defining a proposal as well as that of the Manager of evaluating the proposals depend on the specific task that is the object of the negotiation and on the business logics of the two role players. The requirements of the two roles express the need of having this capabilities in the role players.

```
role Manager {
  public void startNegotiation(Task task);
}
interface ManagerReq {
  public int evaluateProposal(Proposal[] proposal);
  public void receiveResult(Object result);
}

interface Bidder {
  public void partecipateNegotiation();
}
interface BidderReq {
  public boolean evaluateTask(Task task);
  public Proposal getProposal(Task task);
  public void removeProposal(Task task, Proposal proposal);
  public ResultTask performTask(Task task);
}

class ContractNetProtocol {
  Task task;
  Manager manager;
  Bidders[] bidders;
  Proposal[] proposals;
  int i; int count;
  public ContractNetProtocol() {
      // initializes the state
  }

  definerole Manager {
    public void startNegotiation(Task task) {
      ContractNetProtocol.this.manager = that;
      ContractNetProrocol.this.task = task;
      for (int i=0; i < count; i++)
        bidders[i].cfp(task);
      }
      private void refuse(Bidder bidder) {
        i = i + 1;
        if (i >= count) notifyBidders();
      }
      private void propose(Proposal proposal, Bidder bidder) {
```

```
        i = i + 1;
        proposals[bidder.getID()] = proposal;
        if (i >= count) notifyBidders();
      }
      private void failure(TaskExecException err, Bidder bidder){
        that.receiveResult(err);
      }
      private void inform(ResultTask result, Bidder bidder) {
        that.receiveResult(result);
      }
      private void notifyBidders() (
        int selectedProposal =
          that.evaluateProposals(proposals);
        bidders[selectedProposal].acceptProposal(
          proposals[selectedProposal]);
          for (int j=0; j<count; J++)
            if (selectedProposals != j)
              bidders[j].refuseProposal(
                proposals[selectedProposal]);
      }
  }
  definerole Bidder {
    int ID;
    public void partecipateNegotiation() {
      // add this new bidder to the array of bidders
      // assign an ID and increments count
    }
    private void cfp() {
      if (that.evaluateTask(task))
        manager.propose(that.getProposal(task));
      else
        manager.refuse(this);
    }
    private void refusePoposal(Proposal proposal) {
      that.removeProposal(proposal);
    }
    private void acceptProposal(Proposal proposal) {
      try {
        manager.inform(that.performTask(proposal, task)), this);
      } catch(TaskExecException err) {
        manager.failure(err, this);
      }
    }
  }
}
```

Notice that in LifeTimeManager, which is the part of the code in which three "agents" are created and used to play a Manager and two Bidders, to carry on the negotiation it is sufficient that the players respectively invoke the power for initiating and the power for partecipating to the negation itself. The interaction at this level is "hidden" because it is carried on within the institution corresponding to the protocol. For the sake of simplicity the code does not contain references to threads, which are indeed necessary for a correct execution. An object of class Agent that shows a complete set of requirements could play different roles even at the same time even in the same instance of protocol.

```
class LifeTimeManager {
  public static void main(String[] args) {
    Agent initiator = new Agent(...);
    Agent partecipant1 = new Agent(...);
    Agent partecipant2 = new Agent(...);
    ContractNetProtocol cnp = new ContractNetProtocol();
    cnp.new Manager(initiator, task);
    cnp.new Bidder(partecipant1);
    ((cnp.Bidder)partecipant1).partecipateNegotiation();
    cnp.new Bidder(partecipant2);
    ((cnp.Bidder)partecipant1).partecipateNegotiation();
    ((cnp.Manager)initiator).startNegotiation();
  }
}
```

7   Translating Roles in Java

In this section we provide a translation of the role construct into Java, for giving a semantics to powerJava and to validate our proposal. This is done by means of a

```
interface Student {
  public String getName();
  public void giveExam(int examCode, String text);
  public int getMark(int examCode);
}
```

```
class Person enacts StudentRequirements {
  private java.util.Hashtable studentList =
    new java.util.Hashtable();
  public void setStudent (Student sp, Object inst) {
    studentList.put(inst, sp);
  }
  public Student getStudent (Object inst) {
    return studentList.get(inst);
  }
  private String name;
  private int SSNumber;
  public Person (String name) { this.name = name; }
  public String getName() { return name; }
  public int getSocSecNum () { return SSNumber; }
}
```

Fig. 6. Translation of a role and its player

precompilation phase, as, e.g., [17] proposes for introducing components and channels in Java, or in the way inner classes are implemented in Java. The precompiler has been implemented by means of the tool javaCC, provided by Sun Microsystems [20].

The role definition is simply an interface (see Figure 6) to be implemented by the inner class defining the role. So the role powers and its requirements form a pair of interfaces used to match the player of the role and the institution the role belongs to. The relation between the role interface and the requirement interface is used to constrain the creation of role instances relatively to players that conform to the requirements.

While a role definition is precompiled into a Java interface, a specific role implementation is precompiled into a Java inner class which implements such an interface. The inner class resides in the class that implements the institution. For example, the implementation of the role Student in the class School is precompiled into an inner class of School, named automatically StudentPower. StudentPower implements the interface into which the role is translated, Student. The that construct, which keeps the relation between the player instance and the role instance, is precompiled into a field of StudentPower of type StudentRequirements. This field is automatically initialized by means of an *ad hoc* constructor School. This predefined constructor is introduced by the precompiler in the inner class and it takes the player as a parameter which must have the type required by the role definition. In this case StudentRequirements.

All the constructor does is to initialize the that parameter with the player instance and to manipulate the player instance in order to let it have a referent to the role instance. This is necessary for establishing a correspondence between the instance of the player class and the instance of the inner class. The remaining link between the instance of the inner class and the outer class defining it (the institution) is provided automatically by Java (e.g., School.this).

Since every object can play many roles simultaneously, it is necessary to keep, related to the object at hand, the set of its roles. This is obtained by adding, at precompilation time, to every class for each different kind of role that it can play, a structure for book-keeping its role instances. As an example, Person enacts the role Student. So

```
class School {
  public School (String schoolName) {
    this.schoolName = schoolName;
  }
  class StudentPower implements Student {
    StudentRequirements that;
    public Student (StudentRequirements that) {
      this.that = that;
      (this.that).setStudent(this, School.this);
    //role's fields and methods ...
  }
  //institution's fields and methods ...
}
```

Fig. 7. Translation of institution

its instances will have a hash-table that keeps the many student roles played by them in different institutions. In the case of `chris` there will be an instance corresponding to the fact that she is a student of `harvard` and one for her being a student of `mit`. Methods for accessing to this structure are supplied. In the example they allow setting and getting the Student role: `setStudent` and `getStudent`. Notice that book-keeping could be implemented in a more general way, using just one hash table and indexing w.r.t. the institution and the role.

Finally, we describe how role casting is precompiled. The expression referring to an object in its role (a `Person` as a `Student`, e.g., `(harvard.Student)chris`) is translated into the selector returning the reference to the inner class instance, representing the desired role w.r.t. the specified institution. The translation will be `chris.getStudent(harvard)` (see Figure 7).

A summary of all this translation is shown in Figure 9 as an UML class diagram, where dashed lines represent the newly introduced concepts.

```
class TestRole {
  public static void main(String[] args) {
    Person  chris = new Person("Christine");
    School  harvard = new School("harvard");
    School  mit = new School("MIT");
    harvard.new StudentPower(chris);
    mit.new StudentPower(chris);
    String x = chris.getStudent(harvard).getName();
    String y = chris.getStudent(mit).getName();
  }
}
```

Fig. 8. Translation of main

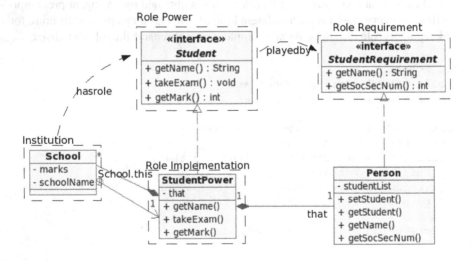

Fig. 9. The UML class diagram

8 Conclusion

In this paper, we extend Java by introducing the notion of social role developed in MAS. The basic features of roles in our model are that they are definitionally dependent on the institution they belong to, and they offer powers to the entities playing them. We map agents, institutions and roles to objects, and powers to methods, that are offered by roles to the objects playing those roles. The characteristic feature of powers is that they can access the private fields and methods of the institution they belong to and those of the sibling roles defined in the same institution. In order to allow an object to be seen in the role it plays we extend the notion of casting offered by Java: type casting in Java allows to see the same object under different perspectives while maintaining the same structure and identity; in contrast, role casting allows to see the object as having a different state and different methods, as specified by the role powers.

We are currently working at an extension of powerJava some preliminary results can be found in [24]. In particular, in this work powerJava is compared to proposals coming from the Object-Oriented community.

Our approach shares the idea of gathering roles inside wider entities with languages like Object Teams [21] and Ceasar [22]. These languages emerge as refinements of aspect oriented languages aiming at resolving practical limitations of other languages. In contrast, our language starts from a conceptual modelling of roles and then it implements the model as language constructs. Differently than these languages we do not model aspects. The motivation is that we want to stick as much as possible to the Java language. However, aspects can be included in our conceptual model as well, under the idea that actions of an agent playing a role "count as" actions executed by the role itself. In the same way, the execution of methods of an object can give raise by advice weaving to the execution of a method of a role. On the other hand, these languages do not provide the notion of role casting we introduce in powerJava. Roles as double face interfaces have some similarities with Traits [23] and Mixins. However, they are distinguished because roles are used to extend instances and not classes.

By implementing roles in an OO programming language, we gain in simplicity in the language development, importing concepts that have been developed by the agent community inside the Java language itself. This language is, undoubtedly, one of the most successful currently existing programming languages, which is also used to implement agents even though it does not supply specific features for doing it. The language extension that we propose is a step towards the overcoming of these limits.

At the same time, introducing theoretically attractive agent concepts in a widely used language can contribute to the success of the Autonomous Agents and Multiagent Systems research in other fields. Developers not interested in the complexity of agent systems can anyway benefit from the advances in this area by using simple and concrete constructs in a traditional programming language.

Future work concerns, on one hand, the provision of a formal semantics to powerJava and the extension of the Java type system with roles; on the other hand, the role construct of powerJava can be extended, for example, by allowing roles playing roles (e.g., a student can play the role of representative in the school), and we also study how our definition of social roles can directly be used in Java based agent programming languages, in frameworks like Jade [6].

In this paper we present a "lite" version of the powerJava language. We are currently developing a full fledged version that allows more natural programming for the Java expert, in which the role implementation does not require a specific construct (definerole), but it entirely relies upon the inner class definition mechanism. Such inner classes must implement the role specifications. The advantages are many: on a hand, one can have more implementations of a role inside the same institution, inner classes can enact other roles, they can be institutions themselves, and use extensions.

References

1. Bauer, B., Muller, J., Odell, J.: Agent UML: A formalism for specifying multiagent software systems. Int. Journal of Software Engineering and Knowledge Engineering **11(3)** (2001) 207–230
2. Boella, G., van der Torre, L.: Attributing mental attitudes to roles: The agent metaphor applied to organizational design. In: Procs. of ICEC'04, IEEE Press (2004)
3. Davis, R., and Smith, R. G.: Negotiation as a metaphor for distributed problem-solving. In Artificial Intelligence, 20, 1983.
4. Ferber, J., Gutknecht, O., Michel, F.: From agents to organizations: an organizational view of multiagent systems. In: LNCS n. 2935: Procs. of AOSE'03, Springer Verlag (2003) 214–230
5. Zambonelli, F., Jennings, N., Wooldridge, M.: Developing multiagent systems: The Gaia methodology. IEEE Transactions of Software Engineering and Methodology **12(3)** (2003) 317–370
6. Bellifemine, F., Poggi, A., Rimassa, G.: Developing multi-agent systems with a FIPA-compliant agent framework. (Software - Practice And Experience) 103–128
7. Juan, T., Sterling, L.: Achieving dynamic interfaces with agents concepts. In: Procs. of AAMAS'04. (2004)
8. Steimann, F.: On the representation of roles in object-oriented and conceptual modelling. Data and Knowledge Engineering **35** (2000) 83–848
9. Boella, G., van der Torre, L.: An agent oriented ontology of social reality. In: Procs. of FOIS'04, Torino (2004) 199–209
10. Masolo, C., Vieu, L., Bottazzi, E., Catenacci, C., Ferrario, R., Gangemi, A., Guarino, N.: Social roles and their descriptions. In: Procs. of KR'04. (2004)
11. Cabri, G., Ferrari, L., Leonardi, L.: Agent role-based collaboration and coordination: a survey about existing approaches. In: IEEE Systems, Man and Cybernetics Conference. (2004)
12. Boella, G., van der Torre, L.: Organizations as socially constructed agents in the agent oriented paradigm. In: Procs. of ESAW'04, Berlin, Springer Verlag (2004)
13. Guarino, N., Welty, C.: Evaluating ontological decisions with ontoclean. Communications of ACM **45(2)** (2002) 61–65
14. Searle, J.: The Construction of Social Reality. The Free Press, New York (1995)
15. Boella, G., van der Torre, L.: Groups as agents with mental attitudes. In: Procs. of AAMAS'04, ACM Press (2004) 964–971
16. Boella, G., van der Torre, L.: Regulative and constitutive norms in normative multiagent systems. In: Procs. of KR'04, AAAI Press (2004) 255–265
17. Arbab, F.: Abstract behavior types: A foundation model for components and their composition. In: Formal Methods for Components and Objects, LNCS 2852. Springer Verlag, Berlin (2003) 33–70
18. Steimann, F., Mayer, P.: Patterns of interface-based programming. Journal of Object Technology (2005)

19. Gamma, E., Helm, R., Johnson, R., Vlissides, J.: Design Patterns: Elements of Reusable Software. Addison-Wesley (1995)
20. Java compiler compiler [tm] (javaCC [tm]) - the java parser generator. (Sun Microsystems) https://javacc.dev.java.net/.
21. Herrmann, S.: Object teams: Improving modularity for crosscutting collaborations. In: Procs. of Net.ObjectDays. (2002)
22. Mezini, M., K.Ostermann: Conquering aspects with caesar. In: Procs. of the 2nd International Conference on Aspect-Oriented Software Development (AOSD), ACM Press (2004) 90–100
23. N. Scharli, S. Ducasse, O.N., Black, A.: Traits: Composable units of behavior. In Verlag, S., ed.: LNCS, vol. 2743: Procs. of ECOOP'03, Berlin (2003) 248–274
24. Baldoni, M., Boella, G., and van der Torre, L.: powerJava : Ontologically Founded Roles in Object Oriented Programming Languages. In D. Ancona and M. Viroli, editors, Proc. of 21st ACM Symposium on Applied Computing, SAC 2006, Special Track on Object-Oriented Programming Languages and Systems (OOPS 2006), Dijon, France, April 2006. ACM. To appear.

Implementation Techniques for Solving POMDPs in Personal Assistant Agents

Pradeep Varakantham, Rajiv Maheswaran, and Milind Tambe

Department of Computer Science,
University of Southern California,
Los Angeles, CA, 90089
{varakant, maheswar, tambe}@usc.edu

Abstract. Agents or agent teams deployed to assist humans often face the challenges of monitoring the state of key processes in their environment (including the state of their human users themselves) and making periodic decisions based on such monitoring. POMDPs appear well suited to enable agents to address these challenges, given the uncertain environment and cost of actions, but optimal policy generation for POMDPs is computationally expensive. This paper introduces two key implementation techniques (one exact and one approximate) to speedup POMDP policy generation that exploit the notion of progress or dynamics in personal assistant domains and the density of policy vectors. Policy computation is restricted to the belief space polytope that remains reachable given the progress structure of a domain. One is based on applying Lagrangian methods to compute a bounded belief space support in polynomial time and other based on approximating policy vectors in the bounded belief polytope. We illustrate this by enhancing two of the fastest existing algorithms for exact POMDP policy generation. The order of magnitude speedups demonstrate the utility of our implementation techniques in facilitating the deployment of POMDPs within agents assisting human users.

1 Introduction

Recent research has focused on individual agents or agent teams that assist humans in offices, at home, in medical care and in many other spheres of daily activities [13,9,4,12,6,8]. Such agents must often monitor the evolution of some process or state over time (including that of the human, the agents are deployed to assist) and make periodic decisions based on such monitoring. For example, in office environments, agent assistants may monitor the location of users in transit and make decisions such as delaying, canceling meetings or asking users for more information [12]. Similarly, in assisting with caring for the elderly [9] and therapy planning [6,8], agents may monitor users' states/plans and make periodic decisions such as sending reminders.

Unfortunately, such agents (henceforth referred to as personal assistant agents (PAAs)) must monitor and make decisions despite significant uncertainty in their observations (as the true state of the world may not be known explicitly) and

R.H. Bordini et al. (Eds.): ProMAS 2005, LNAI 3862, pp. 76–89, 2006.

actions (outcome of agents' actions may be non-deterministic). Furthermore, actions have costs, e.g., delaying a meeting has repercussions on attendees. Researchers have turned to decision-theoretic frameworks to reason about costs and benefits under uncertainty. However, this research has mostly focused on Markov decision processes (MDPs) [12, 6, 8], ignoring the observational uncertainty in these domains, and thus potentially degrading agent performance significantly and/or requiring unrealistic assumptions about PAAs' observational abilities. POMDPs (Partially Observable Markov Decision Processes) address such uncertainty, but the long run-times for generating optimal policies for POMDPs remains a significant hurdle in their use in PAAs.

Recognizing the run-time barrier to POMDP usage, previous work on POMDPs has made encouraging progress using two approaches. The first is an exact approach, where one tries to find the optimal solution [1, 2]. However, despite advances, exact algorithms remain computationally expensive and currently do not scale to problems of interest in PAA domains. The second is an approximate approach, where one sacrifices solution quality for speed [14,5,3,15]. Unfortunately, current approximate algorithms often provide loose (or no) quality guarantees on the solutions, even though such guarantees are crucial for PAAs to inhabit human environments.

This paper aims to practically apply POMDPs to PAA domains by introducing novel implementation techniques that are particularly suitable for such settings. One key insight is that when monitoring users or processes over time, large but shifting parts of the belief space in POMDPs (i.e., regions or states of uncertainty) remain unreachable. Thus, we can focus policy computation on the reachable belief-space polytope, which changes dynamically due to progress in the domain. For instance, consider a PAA monitoring a user driving to a meeting. Given knowledge of the user's current location, the reachable belief region is bounded by the maximum probability of the user's being in different locations at the next time step as defined by the transition function. Similarly, in a POMDP where decisions are made every 5 minutes, an agent can exploit the fact that there is zero probability of going from a world state with $Time = $ 1:00 PM to a world state with $Time = $ 1:30 PM. Current POMDP algorithms typically fail to exploit such belief region reachability properties. POMDP algorithms that restrict belief regions fail to do so dynamically [11,7]. The other key contribution of this paper is an approximation technique, that considers all policies which have expected values seperated by ϵ(the parameter of approximation) as one single policy. As shown in later sections, this method provides an error bound, which depends on the exact structure of the value function, rather than depending on upper and lower bounds for expected value. This fact in itself can help provide tighter bounds. We enhance two state-of-the-art exact POMDP algorithms [1,2] delivering over an order of magnitude speedup for two different PAA domains.

2   Motivating PAA Domains

We present two motivating examples, where teams of software PAAs are deployed in office environments to assist human users [12,4]. The first is a meeting rescheduling problem (MRP), as implemented in the Electric-Elves system [12]. In this large-scale operationalized system, agents monitored the location of users and made decisions such as: (i) delaying the meeting if the user is projected to be late; (ii) asking the user for information if he/she plans to attend the meeting; (iii) canceling the meeting; (iv) waiting. The agent relied on MDPs to arrive at decisions, as its actions such as asking had non-deterministic outcomes (e.g. a user may or may not respond) and decisions such as delaying had costs. The MDP state represented user location, meeting location and time to the meeting (e.g., user@home, meeting@USC, 10 minutes) and a policy mapped such states to actions. Unfortunately, observational uncertainty about user location was ignored while computing the policy.

A second key example is a task management problem (TMP) domain [4]. In this domain, a set of dependent tasks (e.g. T1, T2, T3 in Figure 1) is to be performed by human users (e.g. users U1, U2, U3 in Figure 1). Agents (e.g. A1, A2, A3 in Figure 1) monitor the progress of humans and make reallocation decisions. The lines connecting agents and users indicate the lines of communication. An illustration of reallocation is the following scenario: suppose T1, T2 and T3 are assigned to U1, U2 and U3 respectively based on their initial capabilities. However, if U1 is observed to be progressing too slowly on T1, e.g., U1 may be unwell, then A1 may need to reallocate T1 to ensure that the three tasks finish before a given deadline. A1 may reallocate T1 to U2, if U2's original task T2 is nearing completion and U2 is known to be more capable than U3 for T1. However, if U2 is also progressing slowly, then T1 may have to be reallocated to U3 despite the potential loss in capability. POMDPs provide a framework to analyze and obtain policies in domains such as MRP and TMP. In a TMP, a POMDP policy can take into account the possibly uneven progress of different users, e.g., some users may make most of their progress well before the deadline, while others do the bulk of their work closer to the deadline. In contrast, an instantaneous decision-maker cannot take into account such dynamics of progress. For instance, consider a TMP scenario where there are five levels of task progress $x \in \{0.00, 0.25, 0.50, 0.75, 1.00\}$ and five decision points before the deadline $t \in \{1, 2, 3, 4, 5\}$. Observations are the five levels of task progress $\{0.00, 0.25, 0.50, 0.75, 1.00\}$ and time moves forward in single steps, i.e. $T([x, t], a, [\tilde{x}, \tilde{t}]) = 0$ if $\tilde{t} \neq t + 1$. While transition uncertainty implies irregular task progress, observation uncertainty implies agent may observe progress x as for instance x or $x + 0.25$ (unless $x = 1.00$). Despite this uncertainty in observ-

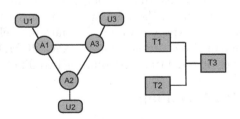

Fig. 1. Comm. Structure and Task Dependency

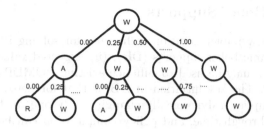

Fig. 2. Partial Sample Policy for a TMP

ing task progress, a PAA needs to choose among waiting (W), asking user for info (A), or reallocate (R). A POMDP policy tree that takes into account both the uncertainty of observations and future costs of decisions, and maps observations to actions, for the above scenario is shown in Figure 2 (nodes=actions, links=observations). In more complex domains with additional actions such as delaying deadlines, the cascading effects of actions will require even more careful planning afforded by POMDP policy generation. Such scenarios in TMP and MRPs are investigated and discussed in Section 5.

3 POMDPs and Incremental Pruning

A POMDP can be represented using the tuple $\{S, A, T, O, \Omega, R\}$, where S is a finite set of states; A is a finite set of actions; Ω is a finite set of observations; $T(s, a, s')$ provides the probability of transitioning from state s to s' when taking action a; $O(s', a, o)$ is probability of observing o after taking an action a and reaching s'; $R(s, a)$ is the reward function. A belief state b, is a probability distribution over the set of states S. A value function over a belief state is defined as: $V(b) = \max_{a \in A} \{R(b, a) + \beta \, \Sigma_{b' \in B} T(b, a, b') V(b')\}$. Currently, the most efficient exact algorithms for POMDPs are value iteration algorithms, specifically GIP [1] and RBIP [2]. These are dynamic programming algorithms, where at each iteration the value function is represented with a minimal set of dominant vectors called the parsimonious set. Given a parsimonious set at time t, $\mathcal{V}_t$, we generate the parsimonious set at time $t - 1$, $\mathcal{V}_{t-1}$ as follows (notation similar to the one used in [1] and [2]):

1. $\left\{ v_{t-1}^{a,o,i}(s) = r(s,a)/|\Omega| + \beta \, \Sigma_{s' \in S} Pr(o, s'|s, a) v_t^i(s') \right\} =: \hat{\mathcal{V}}_{t-1}^{a,o}$ where $v_t^i \in \mathcal{V}_t$.
2. $\mathcal{V}_{t-1}^{a,o} = PRUNE(\hat{\mathcal{V}}_{t-1}^{a,o})$
3. $\mathcal{V}_{t-1}^{a} = PRUNE(\cdots (PRUNE(\mathcal{V}_{t-1}^{a,o_1} \oplus \mathcal{V}_{t-1}^{a,o_2}) \cdots \oplus \mathcal{V}_{t-1}^{a,o_{|\Omega|}})$
4. $\mathcal{V}_{t-1} = PRUNE(\bigcup_{a \in A} \mathcal{V}_{t-1}^{a})$

Each *PRUNE* call executes a linear program (LP) which is recognized as a computationally expensive phase in the generation of parsimonious sets in exact algorithm [1,2]. Our approach effectively translates into obtaining speedups by reducing the quantity of these calls.

4 Dynamic Belief Supports

We propose two new implementation techniques for solving POMDPs in PAA domains: (i) dynamic belief supports (DB); (ii) expected value approximation (EVA). These ideas may be used to enhance existing POMDP algorithms such as GIP and RBIP. The key intuition in DB, is that for personal assistant domains, *progress* implies a dynamically changing polytope (of belief states) remains reachable through time, and policy computation can be speeded up by computing the parsimonious set over just this polytope. The speedups with (i) are due to the elimination of policies dominant in regions outside this polytope, which reduces the number of LP calls. On the other hand, EVA exploits the density of policy vectors in the belief polytope calculated using DB. EVA works by using a lesser density set to represent the optimal set, thus sacrificing on quality of the solution.

4.1 Dynamic Belief Spaces (DB)

Before introducing the general belief support technique, we introduce a special case of it called as DBSimple. In this only states that are reachable (given the transitional dynamics) at each epoch are considered. This is a special case of the general belief restriction in that the belief support is bounded by only 0.00, rather than any number less than 1.00. By introducing DBSimple, we are attempting to more accurately model the support on which reachable beliefs will occur. We can make this process more precise by using information about the initial belief distribution, the transition and observation probabilities to bound belief dimensions with positive support. For example, if we know that our initial belief regarding task progress can have at most 0.10 probability of being at 0.25 with the rest of the probability mass on being at 0.00, we can find the maximum probability of being at 0.00 or 0.25 or 0.50 at the next stage, given a dynamic transition matrix. Below we outline a polynomial-time procedure by which we can obtain such bounds on belief support.

Let $B_t \subset [0\ 1]^{|S_t|}$ be a space such that $P(b_t \notin B_t) = 0$. That is, there exists no initial belief vector and action/observation sequence of length t such that by applying the standard belief update rule, one would get a belief vector b_t not captured in the set B_t. Then, we have

$$b_{t+1}(s_{t+1}) \geq \min_{a \in A, o \in O_t, b_t \in B_t} F(s_{t+1}, a, o, b_t) =: b_{t+1}^{\min}(s_{t+1})$$

$$b_{t+1}(s_{t+1}) \leq \max_{a \in A, o \in O_t, b_t \in B_t} F(s_{t+1}, a, o, b_t) =: b_{t+1}^{\max}(s_{t+1})$$

where $F(s_{t+1}, a, o, b_t) :=$

$$\frac{O_t(s_{t+1}, a, o) \sum_{s_t \in S_t} T_t(s_t, a, s_{t+1}) b_t(s_t)}{\sum_{\tilde{s}_{t+1} \in S_{t+1}} O_t(\tilde{s}_{t+1}, a, o) \sum_{s_t \in S_t} T_t(s_t, a, \tilde{s}_{t+1}) b_t(s_t)}$$

Thus, if we have the belief polytope

$$B_{t+1} = [b_{t+1}^{\min}(s_1) b_{t+1}^{\max}(s_1)] \times \cdots \times [b_{t+1}^{\min}(s_{|S_{t+1}|}) b_{t+1}^{\max}(s_{|S_{t+1}|})],$$

Algorithm 1. DB + GIP

Func POMDP-SOLVE $(L, S, A, T, \Omega, O, R)$

1: $(\{S_t\}, \{O_t\}, \{B_t^{max}\}) = $ DSDODB-GIP $(L, S, A, T, \Omega, O, R)$
2: $t \leftarrow L; V_t \leftarrow 0$
3: **for** $t = L$ to 1 **do**
4:     $\mathcal{V}_{t-1} = $ DP-UPDATE$(\mathcal{V}_t, t)$

Func DP-UPDATE $(\mathcal{V}, t)$

1: **for all** $a \in A$ **do**
2:     $\mathcal{V}_{t-1}^a \leftarrow \phi$
3:     **for all** $\omega_t \in O_t$ **do**
4:         **for all** $v_t^i \in V$ **do**
5:             **for all** $s_{t-1} \in S_{t-1}$ **do**
6:                 $v_{t-1}^{a,\omega_t,i}(s_{t-1}) = r_{t-1}(s_{t-1}, a)/|O_t| + \gamma \Sigma_{s_t \in S_t} Pr(\omega_t, s_t | s_{t-1}, a) v_t^i(s_t)$
7:         $\mathcal{V}_{t-1}^{a,\omega_t} \leftarrow PRUNE(\{v_{t-1}^{a,\omega_t,i}\}, t)$
8:     $\mathcal{V}_{t-1}^a \leftarrow PRUNE(\mathcal{V}_{t-1}^a \oplus \mathcal{V}_{t-1}^{a,\omega_t}, t)$
9: $\mathcal{V}_{t-1} \leftarrow PRUNE(\bigcup_{a \in A} \mathcal{V}_{t-1}^a, t)$
10: return $\mathcal{V}_{t-1}$

Func POINT-DOMINATE(w, U, t)

1: **for all** $u \in U$ **do**
2:     **if** $w(s_t) \leq u(s_t), \forall s_t \in S_t$ **then** return true
3: return false

Func LP-DOMINATE(w, U, t)

1: LP vars: $d, b(s_t)[\forall s_t \in S_t]$
2: LP max d subject to:
3:     $b \cdot (w - u) \geq d, \forall u \in U$
4:     $\Sigma_{s_t \in S_t} b(s_t) \leftarrow 1$
5:     $b(s_t) <= b_t^{max}(s_t); b(s_t) >= 0$
6: **if** $d \geq 0$ return b else return nil

Func BEST(b, U)

1: $max \leftarrow Inf$
2: **for all** $u \in U$ **do**
3:     **if** $(b \cdot u > max)$ or $((b \cdot u = max)$ and $(u <_{lex} w))$ **then**
4:         $w \leftarrow u; max \leftarrow b \cdot u$
5: return w

Func PRUNE(U, t)

1: $W \leftarrow \phi$
2: while $U \neq \phi$
3: $u \leftarrow$ any element in U
4: **if** POINT-DOMINATE$(u, W, t) = $ true **then**
5:     $U \leftarrow U - u$
6: **else**
7:     $b \leftarrow$ LP-DOMINATE(u, W, t)
8:     **if** $b = nil$ **then** $U \leftarrow U - u$
9:     **else** $w \leftarrow BEST(b, U); W \leftarrow W \bigcup w; U \leftarrow U - w$
10: return W

Func DB-GIP(L, S, A, T, Ω, O, R)

1: $t \leftarrow 1$; $S_t =$ Set of starting states
2: **for all** $s_t \in S_t$ **do**
3:     $b_t^{max}(s_t) = 1$
4: **for** $t = 1$ to $L - 1$ **do**
5:     **for all** $s \in S_t$ **do**
6:        ADD-TO(S_{t+1},REACHABLE-STATES(s, T))
7:        $\Omega_{t+1} =$ GET-RELEVANT-OBS(S_{t+1}, O)
8:        C = GET-CONSTRAINTS (s_t)
9:        $b_{t+1}^{max}(s_{t+1}) = \text{MAX}_{c \in C}$(GET-BOUND($s_{t+1}, c$))
10: return ($\{S_t\}, \{\Omega_t\}, \{b_t^{max}\}$)

Func GET-BOUND($s_t, constraint$)

1: $y_{min} = \text{MIN}_{s \in S_{t-1}}(constraint.c[s]/constraint.d[s])$
2: $y_{max} = \text{MAX}_{s \in S_{t-1}}(constraint.c[s]/constraint.d[s])$
3: INT = GET-INTERSECT-SORTED($constraint, y_{min}, y_{max}$)
4: **for all** $i \in$ INT **do**
5:     $Z = \text{SORT}(((i + \epsilon) * constraint.d[s] - constraint.c[s]), \forall s \in S_{t-1}$
6:     $sumBound = 1, numer = 0, denom = 0$
7:     /* IN ASCENDING ORDER */
8:     **for all** $z \in Z$ **do**
9:        $s =$ FIND-CORRESPONDING-STATE(z)
10:        **if** $sumBound - bound[s_{t-1}] > 0$ **then**
11:           $sumBound - = bound[s_{t-1}]$
12:           $numer + = bound[s_{t-1}] * constraint.c[s_{t-1}]$
13:           $denom + = bound[s_{t-1}] * constraint.d[s_{t-1}]$
14:        **if** $sumBound - bound[s_{t-1}] <= 0$ **then**
15:           $numer + = sumBound * constraint.c[s_{t-1}]$
16:           $denom + = sumBound * constraint.d[s_{t-1}]$
17:        BREAK-FOR
18:     **if** $numer/denom > i$ and $numer/denom < max$ **then**
19:        return $numer/denom$

then we have $P(b_{t+1} \notin B_{t+1}) = 0$. The proof of optimality preservation for dynamic beliefs is omitted due to lack of space.

We now show how $b_{t+1}^{max}(s_{t+1})$ (and similarly $b_{t+1}^{min}(s_{t+1})$) can be generated through a polynomial-time procedure deduced from Lagrangian methods. The method involves iterating over all a and ω, where for a given action a and observation ω, we can express the problem as

$$\max_{b_t \in B_t} b_{t+1}^{a,\omega}(s_{t+1}) \quad \text{s.t.} \quad b_{t+1}^{a,\omega}(s_{t+1}) = c^T b_t / d^T b_t$$

where $c(s_t) = O_t(s_{t+1}, a, \omega) T_t(s_t, a, s_{t+1})$ and $d(s_t) = \sum_{s_{t+1} \in S_{t+1}} O_t(s_{t+1}, a, \omega) T_t(s_t, a, s_{t+1})$. We rewrite the problem in terms of the new variables as follows:

$$\min_x \left(-c^T x / d^T x\right) \quad \text{s.t.} \quad \sum_i x_i = 1, \; 0 \le x_i \le b_t^{max}(s_i) =: \bar{x}_i$$

where $\sum_i b_t^{\max}(s_i) \geq 1$ to ensure existence of a feasible solution. Expressing this problem as a Lagrangian, we have

$$\mathcal{L} = \left(-c^T x/d^T x\right) + \lambda\left(1 - \sum_i x_i\right) + \sum_i \bar{\mu}_i(x_i - \bar{x}_i) - \sum_i \mu_i x_i$$

from which the KKT conditions imply

$$x_k = \bar{x}_k \qquad \lambda = [(c^T x)d_k - (d^T x)c_k]/(d^T x)^2 + \bar{\mu}_k$$
$$0 < x_k < \bar{x}_k \qquad \lambda = [(c^T x)d_k - (d^T x)c_k]/(d^T x)^2$$
$$x_k = 0 \qquad \lambda = [(c^T x)d_k - (d^T x)c_k]/(d^T x)^2 - \mu_k.$$

Because λ is identical in all three conditions and $\bar{\mu}_k$ and μ_k are non-negative for all k, the component x_k associated with the lowest value of $[(c^T x)/(d^T x)]d_k - c_k$ must receive a maximal allocation (assuming $\bar{x}_k < 1$) or the entire allocation otherwise. Using this reasoning recursively, we see that if x^* is an extremal point (i.e. a candidate solution), then the values of its components $\{x_k\}$ must be constructed by giving as much weight possible to components in the order prescribed by $z_k = yd_k - c_k$, where $y = (c^T x^*)/(d^T x^*)$. Given a value of y, one can construct a solution by iteratively giving as much weight as possible (without violating the equality constraint) to the component not already at its bound with the lowest z_k.

The question then becomes finding the maximum value of y which yields a consistent solution. We note that y is the value we are attempting to maximize, which we can bound with $y_{\max} = \max_i c_i/d_i$ and $y_{\min} = \min_i c_i/d_i$. We also note that for each component k, z_k describes a line over the support $[y_{\min}, y_{\max}]$. We can then find the set of all points where the set of lines described by $\{z_k\}$ intersect. There can be at most $(|s_t| - 1)|s_t|/2$ intersections points. We can then partition the support $[y_{\min}, y_{\max}]$ into disjoint intervals using these intersection points yielding at most $(|s_t| - 1)|s_t|/2 + 1$ regions. In each region, there is a consistent ordering of $\{z_k\}$ which can be obtained in polynomial time. An illustration of this can be seen in Figure 3. Beginning with the region furthest to the right on the real line, we can create the candidate solution implied by the ordering of $\{z_k\}$ in that region and then calculate the value of y for that candidate solution. If the obtained value of y does not fall within region, then the solution is inconsistent and we move to the region immediately to the left. If the obtained value of y does fall within the region, then we have the candidate extremal point which yields the highest possible value of y, which is the solution to the problem.

By using this technique we can dynamically propagate forward bounds on feasible belief states. Line 8 and 9 of the DSDODB-GIP function in Algorithm 1 provide the procedure for DB. The GET-CONSTRAINTS function on Line 8 gives the set of c and d vectors for each state at time t for each action and observation. By using dynamic beliefs, we increase the costs of pruning by adding some constraints on maximum probability $b^{max}(s_t)$ as shown in line 5 of LP-dominate. However, there is an overall gain because we are looking for dominant

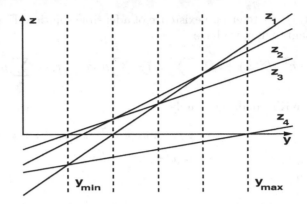

Fig. 3. Partition Procedure for Solving Belief Maximization Lagrangian

vectors over a smaller belief polytope. Thus, reducing the cardinality of the parsimonious set, leaving fewer vectors/policies to consider at the next iteration.

4.2 Expected Value Approximation (EVA)

Expected Value Approximation (EVA) is an approximate approach for solving POMDPs. Most of the approximate algorithms for solving POMDPs [5,15] discretize the belief space to obtain, however here we provide an algorithm that discretizes the expected value space. As is known from the literature, the value function in a POMDP can be expressed using a finite set of linear vectors. EVA approximates the parsimonious set of the linear vectors (in the "CUP") using lesser number of vectors given the approximation parameter α, which indicates the maximumm error allowed in expected value at any belief point.

Algorithm 2 provides the procedure used for checking whether a vector is dominated by a set of vectors in algorithms such as GIP and RBIP. EVA uses the same procedure except for $d + \epsilon$ instead of d in RHS of line 5. This extra

---

Algorithm 2. LP-DOMINATE(w, U, t, ϵ)

1: solve the following linear program
2: **variables:** $d, b(s_t)[\forall s_t \in S_t]$
3: **maximize** d
4: **subject to the constraints**
5:      $b \cdot (w - u) \geq d + \epsilon, \forall u \in U$
6:      $\Sigma_{s_t \in S_t} b(s_t) \leftarrow 1$
7:      $b(s_t) <= b_t^{max}(s_t)$
8:      $b(s_t) >= 0$
9: **if** $d \geq 0$ **then**
10:      return b
11: **else**
12:      return nil

ϵ (in line 5) implies that for a vector to dominate a set of vectors, it should dominate each of the vectors by at least ϵ. That is to say, all vectors which don't dominate all the vectors in the set by at least ϵ are pruned out, hence decreasing the size of the parsimonious set. Savings provided by EVA are in the number of vectors in the parsimonious set (vectors after pruning) at each epoch. Reduced number of vectors after pruning has a chain effect, since it leads to less number of projections (or vectors before pruning) at the next epoch, which in turn might lead to reduced number of vectors after pruning in that epoch.

The main difference between some of the existing methods (like the point based or grid based approaches) and EVA is the space in which approximation is done. In point-based or grid-based, the approximation is in the belief space, while in our approach it is in the value space. EVA can provide better bounds because it is based on value space based approximation that approximates based on the exact structure of the value function rather than take worst case bounds on the value function. This is studied extensively in [10].

Proposition 1. *Error of the EVA algorithm can be bounded by $2 * \epsilon * |\Omega|$ for GIP type cross sum pruning.*

Proof. EVA algorithm introduces an error whenever a pruning operation is performed. Since there are three stages where pruning operations are performed, this proof proceeds by summing the error introduced at each of these stages.

1. $\mathcal{V}^{a,o} = PRUNE(\mathcal{V}^{a,o,i})$
   After this pruning step, each of $\mathcal{V}^{a,o}$'s ($\forall a, \forall o$) are away from the optimal by at-most ϵ.
2. $\mathcal{V}^a = PRUNE(\cdots(PRUNE(\mathcal{V}^{a,o_1} \oplus \mathcal{V}^{a,o_2})\cdots \oplus \mathcal{V}^{a,o_{|\Omega|}})$ To calculate the error bound after this pruning step, we start from the innermost cross-sum PRUNE. The innermost prune would give a set of vectors which in the worst case is $\epsilon + \epsilon + \epsilon$ away from the optimal set. In the above bound, first and second epsilon follow from the fact that there is a cross sum and that each term is away from optimal by ϵ in the worst case, while the third epsilon is because of the PRUNE on this cross sum. Each subsequent prune adds a further $2 * \epsilon$ to the bound. Thus each $\mathcal{V}^{a,o}$ is away from the optimal by at-most $2 * \epsilon * (|\Omega| - 1) + \epsilon$.
3. $\mathcal{V}' = PRUNE(\bigcup_{a \in A} \mathcal{V}^a)$ Now since this step does a PRUNE over UNION of $\mathcal{V}^a, \forall a$, it further adds an ϵ to the bound. Hence making the final error bound to be $2 * \epsilon * |\Omega|$.

Thus proved. ∎

5   Experimental Results

Experiments were conducted on the TMPs and MRPs explained in Section 2. Each agent uses a POMDP for decision making in both domains. Our enhancements, DBSimple (Dynamic States), and DB (Dynamic Beliefs), were implemented over both GIP and RBIP [2] (RBIP is itself a recent enhancement to

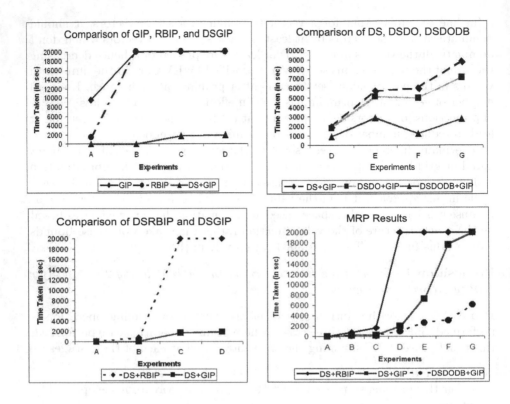

Fig. 4. TMP: (a) DBSimple+GIP gives orders of magnitude speedup over GIP and RBIP (b) DB+GIP dominates DBSimple+GIP (c) DBSimple+GIP dominates DB-Simple+RBIP; MRP: (d) DB+GIP dominates

GIP). All the experiments compare the performance (run-time) of GIP, RBIP and our enhancements over GIP and RBIP. For both domains, we ran 6 problems over all methods (GIP, RBIP, DBSimple+GIP, DB+GIP, DB+GIP, DB-Simple+RBIP, DB+RBIP). Each problem had pre-specified upper limit of 20000 seconds, after which it was terminated.

Figure 4(a)-(c) present results for the TMP domain. Experimental setup in TMP consisted of a set of seven problems of increasing complexity (A through G). In all the graphs, the x-axis denotes the problem name, and the y-axis denotes the run-time for a problem. GIP and RBIP finished before the time limit in only Problem A, as shown in Figure 4(a). DBSimple+GIP provides 100-fold speedup in Problem B, and 10-fold speedup in Problems C and D (however, the actual speedup which we expect to be even larger cannot be seen due to our cutoff).

DB+GIP finished in almost the same time as DS in Problems A-C. Figure 4(b) provides comparisons between the three of our enhancements on GIP. For Problems D-G that are even more complex than A-C, DB dominates the other enhancements providing approximately 5-fold speedup over DBSimple.

GIP and RBIP did not terminate within time limit and hence not shown. The key point of Figure 4(c) is to show that DBSimple+GIP provides 10-fold speedup (with cut-off) over DBSimple+RBIP, even though RBIP is faster than GIP. This is also the reason for providing the results of enhancements on GIP instead of RBIP in Figure 4(b).

Figure 4(d) presents results for the MRP domain. Experimental setup for MRP consisted of a set of seven problems(A through G). The figure does not show results for GIP and RBIP, because they did not finish before our cutoff for any of the 7 problems. DB+GIP provides approximately 6-fold speedups over DBSimple+GIP. DBSimple+RBIP seems comparable with the other three methods in Problems A-C, but for Problems D-G, it fails to even finish before the cutoff. Both domains provide similar conclusions: DB+GIP dominates other techniques (with around 100 fold speedup over GIP and RBIP in some cases) and this dominance becomes more significant in larger problems.

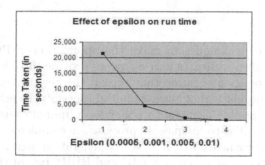

Fig. 5. Effect of epsilon on run times

Figure 5 presents results for the EVA approximation algorithm. x-axis shows different values of ϵ, approximation parameter and y-axis shows the run times. To clearly show the capacity of EVA, we present these results on a bigger problem than A-G. As can be seen, EVA provides orders of magnitude speedup as ϵ is decreased from 0.0001 - 0.01. The error bound in the 0.01 case was 2*36*0.01.

6   Related Work

We have already discussed some related work in Section 1. As discussed there, techniques for solving POMDPs can be categorized as exact and approximate. GIP [1] and RBIP [2] are exact algorithms, which we have enhanced. Other exact algorithms attempt to exploit domain-specific properties to speedup POMDPs. For instance, [7] presents a hybrid framework that combines MDPs with POMDPs to take advantage of perfectly and partially observable components of the model. They also focus on reachable belief spaces, but: (i) their analysis does not capture dynamic changes in belief space reachability; (ii) their analysis is limited to factored POMDPs; (iii) no speedup measurements are shown.

This contrasts with this work which focuses on dynamic changes in belief space reachability and its application to both flat and factored state POMDPs.

Approximate algorithms are faster than exact algorithms, but at the cost of solution quality. There has been a significant amount of work in this area, but point-based [14, 5], grid [3, 15], and policy search approaches dominate other algorithms. Though these approaches can solve larger problems, most of them provide loose (or no) quality guarantees on the solution. It is critical to have good quality guarantees in PAA domains, for an agent to gain the trust of a human user. Another recently developed technique uses state space dimensionality reduction using E-PCA, but it does not provide any guarantee on quality of the solution [11]. Point Based Value Iteration (PBVI) [5] provides the best quality guarantees, but to obtain good results it needs to increase sampling, consequently increasing the run-time. As explained earlier, EVA approach can provide tighter bounds because of its approximation in the expected value space.

7   Summary

This paper provides techniques to make the application of POMDPs in personal assistant agents a reality. In particular, we provide three key techniques to speedup POMDP policy generation that exploit the key properties of the PAA domains. One key insight is that given an initial (possibly uncertain) starting set of states, the agent needs to generate a policy for a limited range of dynamically shifting belief states. The techniques we propose are complementary to most existing exact and approximate POMDP policy generation algorithms. Indeed, we illustrate our technique by enhancing GIP and RBIP, two of the most efficient exact algorithms for POMDP policy generation and obtain orders of magnitude speedup in policy generation. Another key insight is to exploit the high density of value vectors, to speedup policy generation, while sacrificing very little in terms of the quality of solution. We provide a detailed algorithm illustrating our enhancements in Algorithm 1, and present proofs of correctness of our techniques. The techniques presented here facilitate agents' utilizing POMDPs for policies when assisting human users.

References

1. M. L. Littman A. R. Cassandra and N. L. Zhang. Incremental pruning: A simple, fast, exact method for partially observable markov decision processes. In *UAI*, 1997.
2. Z. Feng and S. Zilberstein. Region based incremental pruning for POMDPs. In *UAI*, 2004.
3. M. Hauskrecht. Value-function approximations for POMDPs. *JAIR*, 13:33–94, 2000.
4. http://www.ai.sri.com/project/CALO, http://calo.sri.com. *CALO: Cognitive Agent that Learns and Organizes*, 2003.
5. G. Gordon J. Pineau and S. Thrun. PBVI: An anytime algorithm for POMDPs. In *IJCAI*, 2003.

6. T. Y. Leong and C. Cao. Modeling medical decisions in DynaMoL: A new general framework of dynamic decision analysis. In *World Congress on Medical Informatics (MEDINFO)*, pages 483–487, 1998.
7. H. Fraser M. Hauskrecht. Planning treatment of ischemic heart disease with partially observable markov decision processes. *AI in Medicine*, 18:221–244, 2000.
8. F. Locatelli: P. Magni, R. Bellazzi. Using uncertainty management techniques in medical therapy planning: A decision-theoretic approach. In *Applications of Uncertainty Formalisms*, pages 38–57, 1998.
9. M. E. Pollack, L. Brown, D. Colbry, C. E. McCarthy, C. Orosz, B. Peintner, S. Ramakrishnan, and I. Tsamardinos. Autominder: An intelligent cognitive orthotic system for people with memory impairment. *Robotics and Autonomous Systems*, 44:273–282, 2003.
10. P. Poulpart and Craig Boutilier. Bounded finite state controllers. In *NIPS*, 2003.
11. N. Roy and G. Gordon. Exponential family PCA for belief compression in POMDPs. In *NIPS*, 2002.
12. P. Scerri, D. Pynadath, and M. Tambe. Towards adjustable autonomy for the real-world. *JAIR*, 17:171–228, 2002.
13. D. Schreckenghost, C. Martin, P. Bonasso, D. Kortenkamp, T.Milam, and C.Thronesbery. Supporting group interaction among humans and autonomous agents. In *AAAI*, 2002.
14. N. L. Zhang and W. Zhang. Speeding up convergence of value iteration in partially observable markov decision processes. *JAIR*, 14:29–51, 2001.
15. R. Zhou and E. Hansen. An improved grid-based approximation algorithm for POMDPs. In *IJCAI*, 2001.

Using a Planner for Coordination of Multiagent Team Behavior

Oliver Obst

Universität Koblenz-Landau, AI Research Group,
56070 Koblenz, Germany
fruit@uni-koblenz.de

Abstract. We present an approach to coordinate the behavior of a multiagent team using an HTN planning procedure. To coordinate teams, high level tasks have to be broken down into subtasks which is a basic operation in HTN planners. We are using planners in each of the agents to incorporate domain knowledge and to make agents follow a specified team strategy. With our approach, agents coordinate deliberatively and still maintain a high degree of reactivity. In our implementation for use in RoboCup Simulation League, first results were already very promising. Using a planner leads to better separation of agent code and expert knowledge.

1   Introduction

Coordination among different agents and the specification of strategies for multiagent systems (MAS) is a challenging task. For a human domain expert it is often very difficult to change the behavior of a multiagent system. This is especially true when not only general tasks should be specified, but also the way in which tasks are to be executed. Due to interdependencies simple changes in one place of the code may easily affect more than one situation during execution.

In this work, we suggest to use Hierarchical Task Network (HTN) planners in each of the agents in order to achieve coordinated team behavior which is in accordance with the strategy given by the human expert. The expert knowledge should be separated from the rest of the agent code in a way that it can easily be specified and changed. While pursuing the given strategy, agents should keep as much of their reactiveness as possible. HTN planning explicitly supports the use of domain specific strategies. To coordinate groups of agents, tasks usually have to be broken down into subtasks, which is one of the basic operations of HTN planning. Different levels of detail in the description of strategies further facilitate the generation of useful information for debugging or synchronization.

In classical planning, operators are deterministic and the single planning agent is the only reason for changes in the environment under consideration. We show how it is possible to use an HTN planner in the domain of robotic soccer, even though the robotic soccer environment is very different from classical planning domains. For our approach, we have chosen a team of agents using the RoboCup 3D Soccer Simulator [17] that was introduced at RoboCup-2004 in Lisbon [11].

R.H. Bordini et al. (Eds.): ProMAS 2005, LNAI 3862, pp. 90–100, 2006.

The following section describes our approach to coordinate the behavior of a multiagent team using an HTN planner. Section 3 contains the description of an implemented example. We present and discuss the results of our first tests, and a review of relevant related work. Finally, Sect. 6 concludes the paper.

2 HTN Planning for Multiagent Teams

The usual assumptions for HTN planning, like for classical planning approaches, are that we plan for a single agent who is the only cause for changes in the domain. When the plan is executed, all actions succeed as planned. Executing an action in a classical planning framework is instantaneous, it takes no time, and therefore the world is always in a defined state.

To plan for agents in a team and in a real-world domain, we have to relax some of these assumptions and find a way to deal with the new setting. Definition 1 is a way commonly used to define nondeterministic planning domains. An approach to deal with these kinds of domains is to use model checking (see for instance [3]). Depending on the problem and the desired properties of the results, the planner tries to compute solution plans that have a chance to succeed or solution plans that succeed no matter what the results of the non-deterministic actions of an agent are.

Definition 1. A *nondeterministic planning domain* is a triple $\Sigma = \langle S, A, \gamma \rangle$, where:

- S is a finite set of states.
- A is a finite set of actions.
- $\gamma \subseteq S \times A \times S$ is the state-transition relation. □

When the number of different possible results of γ is high, computing a plan can easily become intractable for domains where decisions have to be made quickly. Nevertheless, using a planner could still be useful to achieve high-level coordination for a team of several agents in a dynamic environment without using communication and without a centralized planning facility. For our approach, all planning should be done in a distributed fashion in each of the autonomous agents. The goal is that team behavior can easily be specified and extended, the task of the system is to automatically generate individual actions for the agents in accordance with those plans during execution. Despite using plans, agents should still be able to react to unforeseen changes in the environment.

2.1 Multiagent Team Behavior with HTN Plans

In Hierarchical Task Network (HTN, see also Definition 2) planning, the objective is to perform tasks. Tasks can be complex or primitive. HTN planners use *methods* to expand complex tasks into subtasks, until the tasks are primitive. Primitive tasks can be performed directly by using planning operators.

Definition 2. A *task network* is an acyclic directed graph $w = \langle N, A \rangle$, where N is the set of nodes, and A is the set of directed edges. Each node in N contains a task t_n. A task network is *primitive*, if all of its tasks are primitive, otherwise it is *nonprimitive*.   □

Our approach of interleaving planning and acting and also of handling non-deterministic actions is similar to the one described in [1], where a HTN planner is used for navigation planning of a single robot. Here, like in most realistic environments, it is not enough to initially create a plan and blindly execute it, but after execution of each action the state of the world needs to be sensed in order to monitor progress. As a consequence, for generating HTN plans it is not absolutely necessary to generate a primitive task network from the beginning. Instead a HTN where the first tasks are primitive is sufficient, if we interleave planning and acting. Future tasks are left unexpanded or partially expanded until the present tasks are done and there is no other task in front. In dynamic and complex environments, creating a detailed plan can be considered as wasted time, because it is virtually impossible to predict the state of the world after only a few actions.

Rather than expanding complex tasks completely, our planner generates what is called *plan stub* in [1], a task network with a primitive task as the first task. As soon as a plan stub has been found, an agent can start executing its task. The algorithm in Fig. 1 expands a list of tasks to a plan stub, if it is not already in that form.

Function: $\mathrm{plan}(s_{now}, \langle t_1, ..., t_k \rangle, O, M)$
Returns: (w, s), with w an ordered set of tasks, s a state; or *failure*

---

if $k = 0$ **then return** $(\emptyset, s_{now})$ // i.e. the empty plan
if t_1 *is a pending primitive task* **then**
    $active \leftarrow \{(a, \sigma)|a$ is a ground instance of an operator in O,
                    σ is a substitution such that a is relevant for $\sigma(t_1)$,
                    and a is applicable to $s_{now}\}$;
    if $active = \emptyset$ **then return** *failure*;
    nondeterministically choose any $(a, \sigma) \in active$;
    return $(\sigma(\langle t_1, ..., t_k \rangle), \gamma(s_{now}, a))$;
else if t_1 *is a pending complex task* **then**
    $active \leftarrow \{m|m$ is a ground instance of a method in M,
                    σ is a substitution such that m is relevant for $\sigma(t_1)$,
                    and m is applicable to $s_{now}\}$;
    if $active = \emptyset$ **then return** *failure*;
    nondeterministically choose any $(m, \sigma) \in active$;
    $w \leftarrow \mathrm{subtasks}(m).\sigma(\langle t_1, ..., t_k \rangle)$;
    set all tasks in front of t_1 to *pending*, set t_1 to *expanded*;
    return $\mathrm{plan}(s_{now}, w, O, M)$;
else
    // t_1 is an already executed expanded task and can be removed
    return $\mathrm{plan}(s_{now}, \langle t_2, ..., t_k \rangle, O, M)$;

Fig. 1. Creating an initial plan stub (Notation according to [7])

In classical planning, executing an action takes no time. That means immediately after executing a planning operator, the world is in the successor state. In our approach we have to consider that actions are not instantaneous and might not even yield the desired result. The first problem is when to regard operators as finally executed: Depending on the actual domain agents are acting in, actions can be regarded as finished after a given amount of time or when a specified condition holds. This domain specific solution to this problem is not part of the algorithms in this paper.

A second problem is the computation of the successor state: as defined above, for non-deterministic environments γ is a relation with possibly several results for the same state-action pair. For our algorithms, we expect γ to be a function returning the *desired* successor state. Likewise, the effects of an operator describe the desired effects. The underlying assumption is that operators have a single purpose so that the desired successor state can be uniquely described. The desired effects can be used by the operators to coordinate actions of teammates during the same plan step. For this, we introduce multiagent operators in Definition 3, which is effectively a shortcut for defining a set of combinations of operators. Actions that are executed simultaneously but which do not contribute to the desired effects of the multiagent operator are simply not included. This makes it easy for the developer of a multiagent team to create team operators, but the disadvantage is that agents not part of the multiagent team cannot be regarded with our approach.

Definition 3 (Multiagent Operator). Let $o_1, ..., o_n$ be operators, and $\text{effects}^-(o_j) \cap \text{effects}^+(o_k) = \emptyset$ for all $j, k \in \{1, ..., n\}$. p is a new operator with $\text{name}(p) = \text{name}(o_1)$ while $\langle \text{name}(o_2), ..., \text{name}(o_n) \rangle$. The preconditions and effects of p are defined as unions over the preconditions and effects of all o_i, respectively:

$$\text{pre}(p) = \bigcup_{i=1,...,n} \text{pre}(o_i), \quad \text{and} \quad \text{effects}(p) = \bigcup_{i=1,...,n} \text{effects}(o_i) \qquad \square$$

At the same time, the desired successor state is used to check the success of the last operator application in the second algorithm (see Fig. 2). Here, the executed tasks are removed from the plan and the first algorithm is used again to create an updated plan stub.

2.2 Handling Non-determinism

To handle non-determinism, we treat a plan as a stack. Tasks on this stack are marked as either *pending* or as *expanded*. Pending tasks are either about to be executed, if they are primitive, or waiting to be further expanded, if they are complex. Tasks marked as expanded are complex tasks which already have been expanded into subtasks. If a subtask of a complex task fails, all the remaining subtasks of that complex task are removed from the stack and it is checked if the complex task can be tried again. If a task was finished successfully, it is simply removed from the stack.

Function: step($s_{expected}, s_{now}, \langle t_1, ..., t_k \rangle, O, M$)
Returns: (w, s), with w a set of ordered tasks, s a state; or *failure*

---

if $k = 0$ then return $(\emptyset, s_{now})$ // i.e., the empty plan
if t_1 is a *pending task* then
    if $s_{expected}$ *is valid in* s_{now} then
        $i \leftarrow$ the position of the first non-primitive task in the list;
        return *plan*($s_{now}, \langle t_i, ..., t_k \rangle, O, M$);
    else
        // t_1 was unsuccessful; remove all pending children of our
           parent task
        return *step*($s_{expected}, s_{now}, \langle t_2, ..., t_k \rangle, O, M$);
else
    // t_1 is an unsuccessfully terminated expanded task, try to
      re-apply it
    $active \leftarrow \{m|m$ is a ground instance of a method in M,
               σ is a substitution such that m is relevant for $\sigma(t_1)$,
               and m is applicable to $s_{now}\}$;
    if $active = \emptyset$ then
        // t_1 cannot be re-applied, remove it from the list and recurse
        return step($s_{expected}, s_{now}, \langle t_2, ..., t_k \rangle, O, M$);
    else
        nondeterministically choose any $(m, \sigma) \in active$;
        $w \leftarrow$ subtasks(m).$\sigma(\langle t_1, ..., t_k \rangle)$;
        set all tasks in front of t_1 to *pending*, set t_1 to *expanded*;
        return plan(s_{now}, w, O, M);

Fig. 2. Remove the top primitive tasks and create a new plan stub

3   Robotic Soccer Sample Implementation

To give an example, we take an example from the simulated soccer domain
[10, 11] and the complex top level task play_soccer has already been partially
expanded as shown in Fig. 3. All the pending tasks in Fig. 3 are still complex
tasks. To create a plan stub, the planner needs to further expand the top pending
task. At this level of expansion, the plan still represents a team plan, as seen from
a global perspective. When team tasks – like pass(2,9) – get further expanded
to agent tasks, each agent has to find its role in the team task. In the soccer
domain, agents usually have predefined roles which can be used to describe roles
in specific tasks. An alternative possibility is a distance based role selection.

Agent #2 will expand pass(2,9) to do_pass(9), agent #9 has to do a
do_receive_pass for the same team task. The other agents position themselves
relatively to the current ball position with do_positioning at the same time.
The desired effect of pass(2,9) is the same for all the agents, even if the derived
primitive task is different depending on the role of the agent. That means each
agent has to execute a different action, which is realized as C++ function call in our
case, and at the same time an operator has to update the desired successor state
independently. To express that an agent should execute the do_positioning

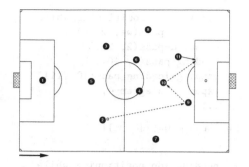

```
pending-pass(2,9)
pending-pass(9,10)
pending-leading-pass(10,11)
expanded-diagram-4
expanded-build_up_long_pass
expanded-build_up_play
pending-final_touch
pending-shooting
expanded-offensive_phase
expanded-play_soccer
```

Fig. 3. Soccer Example Situation (left) and plan stack during planning (right)

```
method pass(A,B)
pre [my_number(A)]
subtasks [do_pass(B) while pass(we,A,B),
do_positioning].

method pass(A,B)
pre [my_number(B)]
subtasks [do_receive_pass while pass(we,A,B)].

method pass(A,B)
pre [my_number(C),#\=(A,C),#\=(B,C)]
subtasks [do_positioning while pass(we,A,B)].
```

Fig. 4. Different methods to reduce the team task pass(A,B) to agent tasks

behavior while taking the effect of a simultaneous pass between two teammates into account, we are using terms like do_positioning while pass(we,2,9) in our planner. Figure 4 shows methods reducing the team task pass(A,B) to different primitive player tasks.

In different agents, the applicable methods for the top team task pass(2,9) lead to different plan stubs. This is an important difference to the work presented in [1]. The plan stubs created as first step for agent 9 and agent 11 are shown in Fig. 5. When a plan stub is found, the top primitive tasks are passed to the C++ module of our agent and executed. A 'step' for a plan in our agents can consist of more than a single action, for example, we do not want the agent who passes the ball to stop acting while the ball is already moving to a teammate, but instead after the kick the agent should adjust its position relative to the ball until the ball reached its destination and the step is finished. If possible, the agent has to execute all pending primitive tasks until the next step in the plan starts. If there are pending primitive tasks after one step is finished, these agent tasks are simply removed from the plan stack and the next team task can be expanded. Figure 6 shows the plan stub for the second step from the diagram in Fig. 3. For player 9, the expansion leads to a plan stub with two primitive tasks in a plan step while for player 11 there is only one task to be executed.

```
pending-(do_receive_pass while      pending-(do_positioning while
        pass(we, 2, 9)),                    pass(we, 2, 9)),
expanded-pass(2, 9),                expanded-pass(2, 9),
pending-pass(9, 10),                pending-pass(9, 10),
pending-leading_pass(10, 11),       pending-leading_pass(10, 11),
expanded-diagram-4,                 expanded-diagram-4,
...                                 ...
```

Fig. 5. Step 1: Plan Stubs for player 9 and player 11

```
pending-(do_pass(10) while          pending-(do_positioning while
        pass(we, 9, 10)),                   pass(we, 9, 10)),
pending-do_positioning,             expanded-pass(9, 10),
expanded-pass(9, 10),               pending-leading_pass(10, 11),
pending-leading_pass(10, 11),       expanded-diagram_4,
expanded-diagram_4,                 ...
...
```

Fig. 6. Step 2: Plan Stubs for player 9 and player 11

What we did not address so far was the point in time when the transition from one plan step to the next step takes place. Here, the basic idea is the following: each step in plans for our team stops or starts with an agent being in ball possession. If any of the agents on the field is in ball possession, we can check for the desired effect of our previous action. If the action succeeded, the right agent possesses the ball and the planner can continue planning by generating the next plan stub. If an adversarial agent intercepted the ball, the last action failed and the planner needs to backtrack. For dribbling, the planner needs to check if the dribbling agent still possesses the ball and arrived at the desired destination in order to start with the next step.

4   Results and Discussion

For our approach of generating coordinated actions in a team we implemented an HTN planner in Prolog which supports interleaving of planning and acting. Our planner supports team actions by explicitly taking the effects of operators simultaneously used by teammates into account. The planner ensures that the agents follow the strategy specified by the user of the system by generating individual actions for each of the agents that are in accordance with it. The *lazy evaluation* in the expansion of subtasks which generates plan stubs rather than a full plan, makes the planning process very fast and enables the agents to stay reactive to unexpected changes in the environment. The reactiveness could, however, be increased by adding a situation evaluation mechanism that is used prior to invoking the planner. This would improve the ability to exploit sudden, short-lived opportunities during the game.

We implemented a distributed planning system in the sense that each of the agents uses its own planner. This was, however, somewhat facilitated by the fact that agents in the RoboCup 3D Simulation League are equipped with sensors that provide them with a full (though possibly inaccurate) view of the world, similar to Middle-size League robots using omni-vision cameras.

To truly evaluate the approach we presented, it would be necessary to measure the effort it takes to create a team and compare it to other approaches to create a team exhibiting the same behavior. We strongly believe that our approach leads to a modular behavior design and facilitates rapid specification of team behavior for *users* of our agents, but we cannot present numbers here. Our plans can describe plays as introduced in [2], which have shown to be useful for synchronization in a team. There are some important differences to plays, however. First, our approach supports different levels of abstraction in plans. That means there are different levels of detail available to describe what our team and each single agent is actually doing, from very abstract tasks down to the agent level tasks. A second important difference is that the planner can find alternative ways to achieve tasks. This is possible if plays are specified in terms of player roles or properties rather than fixed player numbers. The approach in [2] was used for Small Size League, where the numbers of players and the number of alternative ways of doing plays is low. That means in Small Size League, a plan is either applicable or not. For Simulation League or larger teams in general, more opportunities are possible for which an approach using fixed teammates seems to restrictive. On the other hand, the approach in [2] supports adaptation by changing weights for the selection of successful plays. In our approach, the corresponding functionality could be achieved by changing the order in which HTN methods are used to reduce tasks. At this point in time, our approach does not support this yet. As soon as we do have an adaptive component in our approach, it makes sense to compare results of our team with and without adaptation.

The way our plans are created and executed, we assume synchronous actions for all our agents. Our team actions are geared to actions of the player in ball possession, so this simplification can be made. There are a few situations in soccer, where more detailed reasoning over the time actions take would be useful. This includes for instance all situations where a ball receiver should appear at the receiving position *just in time* to surprise the opponent. In our approach, we make this possible by synchronizing the behavior of two agents in the *current step* by using both ball and agent velocity to estimate interception times, in the operator implementations outside of the planning procedure. Inside our planning procedure, we do not reason about durations, which would be useful to make asynchronous actions possible.

Although more detailed evaluations have to be carried out, the first tests using the planner seem very promising and indicate that our approach provides a flexible, easily extendable method for coordinating a team of agents in dynamic domains like the RoboCup 3D Simulation League.

5 Related Work

Several approaches that use a planning component in a MAS can be found in the literature.

In [6], the authors describe a formalism to integrate the HTN planning system SHOP [16] with the IMPACT [21] multiagent environment (A-SHOP). The preconditions and effects used in SHOP are modified so that preconditions are evaluated using the code-call mechanism of the framework, and effects change the state of agents. While the environment of this work clearly is a multiagent system, the planning is carried out centralized by a single agent. This is a contrast to our approach, which uses a planner in each of the agents to coordinate the agents actions.

A general HTN planning framework for agents in dynamic environments has been presented in [9]. The authors show how to integrate task decomposition of HTN planning, action execution, program updates, and plan modifications. The planning process is done via abstract task decomposition and is augmented to include additional information such as the history of action execution for the plans to enable their incremental modification. Rules are given for plan modifications after having executed certain actions or after program updates. In the robotic soccer domain, however, the results of actions like e.g. kicking the ball cannot be undone. Thus, the plan modification mechanism given in [9] does not apply and could not easily be used for our purposes.

HTN planning has also been studied in the context of creating intelligent, cooperating Non-Player Characters in computer games. In [13], an HTN planner is used to enable agents in the highly dynamic environment of the Unreal Tournament game to pursue a grand strategy designed for the team of agents.

Bowling et al. [2] presents a strategy system that makes use of plays (essentially being multiagent plans) to coordinate team behavior of robots in the RoboCup Small Size League. Multiple plays are managed in a playbook which is responsible to choose appropriate plays, and evaluate them for adaption purposes. The plays are specified using a special language designed with ease of readability and extensibility in mind. Preconditions can be specified that determine when a play can be executed. Furthermore, plays contain termination conditions, role assignments and sequences of individual behaviors. While the use of preconditions resembles a classical planning approach, the effects of individual plays are not specified due to the difficulties in predicting the outcome of operators in the dynamic environment. This is in contrast to our approach, as we use desired effects of the operators in our plans. Another difference is that in [2] the planning component is also centralized.

Other approaches towards multiagent collaboration like [5, 8] are based on negotiations between the agents in a multiagent system. However, as pointed out in [20], this kind of complex communication might take too much time or might even be infeasible in highly dynamic real-time domains like robotic soccer.

The work in [15, 14] describes the approach to creating our agents so far: We used UML statecharts to specify behaviors for agents in a multiagent system. The agents were designed in a top-down manner with a layered architecture. At the highest level global patterns of behavior are specified in an abstract way, representing the different states the agent can be in. For each of these states, an agent has a repertoire of skeleton plans in the next layer. These are applicable as long as the state does not change. Explicit specification of cooperation and multiagent behaviors can be realized. The third and lowest level of the architecture encompasses the descriptions for the simple and complex actions the agents can execute, which are used by the scripts in the level above.

This hierarchical decomposition of agent behaviors is similar to the HTN plans described in this work. However, the separation of domain description knowledge and the reasoning formalism accomplished through the use of the HTN planner within our agents provides us with much greater flexibility in respect to the extensibility of methods and operators, compared to the amount of work needed to change the state machine description.

6 Conclusion and Future Work

We presented a novel approach that uses an HTN planning component to coordinate the behavior of multiple agents in a dynamic MAS. We formalized expert domain knowledge and used it in the planning methods to subdivide the given tasks. The hierarchical structure of the plans speeds up the planning and also helps to generate useful debugging output for development. Furthermore, the system is easily extensible as the planning logic and the domain knowledge are separated.

In order to use the system in the RoboCup competitions, we plan to integrate a lot more subdivision strategies for the different tasks as described in the diagrams in [12]. A desirable enhancement to our work would be the integration of an adaption mechanism. Monitoring the success of different strategies against a certain opponent, and using this information in the choice of several applicable action possibilities, as e.g. outlined in [2], should be explored. The introduction of *durative actions* into the planner (see for instance [4]) would give a more fine grained control over the parallelism in the multiagent plans. *Simple Temporal Networks* as used in [19] seem to be well suited for this purpose. Furthermore, a situation assessment will be added to the agents to be able to exploit unforeseen situations in a more reactive manner. Finally, we want to restrict the sensors of the agents to receive only partial information about the current world state, and address the issues that result for the distributed planning process.

References

1. Thorsten Belker, Martin Hammel, and Joachim Hertzberg. Learning to optimize mobile robot navigation based on HTN plans. In *Proceedings of the IEEE International Conference on Robotics and Automation (ICRA 2003)*, pages 4136–4141, Taipei, Taiwan, September 2003.
2. Michael Bowling, Brett Browning, and Manuela Veloso. Plays as team plans for coordination and adaptation. In *Proceedings of the 14th International Conference on Automated Planning and Scheduling (ICAPS-04)*, Vancouver, June 2004.
3. Alessandro Cimatti, Marco Pistore, Marco Roveri, and Paolo Traverso. Weak, strong, and strong cyclic planning via symbolic model checking. *Artificial Intelligence*, 147(1-2):35–84, 2003.

4. Alex M. Coddington, Maria Fox, and Derek Long. Handling durative actions in classical planning frameworks. In John Levine, editor, *Proceedings of the 20th Workshop of the UK Planning and Scheduling Special Interest Group*, pages 44–58. University of Edinburgh, December 2001.

5. Philip R. Cohen, Hector J. Levesque, and Ira Smith. On team formation. *Contemporary Action Theory*, 1998.

6. Jürgen Dix, Héctor Muñoz-Avila, and Dana Nau. IMPACTing SHOP: Planning in a Multi-Agent Environment. In Fariba Sadri and Ken Satoh, editors, *Proceedings of CLIMA 2000, Workshop at CL 2000*, pages 30–42. Imperial College, 2000.

7. Malik Ghallab, Dana Nau, and Paolo Traverso. *Automated Planning Theory and Practice*. Morgan Kaufmann, San Francisco, CA, USA, 2004.

8. Barbara J. Grosz. AAAI-94 presidential address: Collaborative systems. *AI Magazine*, 17(2):67–85, 1996.

9. Hisashi Hayashi, Kenta Cho, and Akihiko Ohsuga. A new HTN planning framework for agents in dynamic environments. In Jürgen Dix and João Leite, editors, *CLIMA IV 2004*, number 3259 in Lecture Notes in Computer Science, pages 108–133. Springer, Berlin, Heidelberg, New York, 2004.

10. Marco Kögler and Oliver Obst. Simulation league: The next generation. In Polani et al. [18], pages 458–469.

11. Pedro Lima, Luís Custódio, Levent Akin, Adam Jacoff, Gerhard Kraezschmar, Beng Kiat Ng, Oliver Obst, Thomas Röfer, Yasutake Takahashi, and Changjiu Zhou. Robocup 2004 competitions and symposium: A small kick for robots, a giant score for science. *AI Magazine*, 2005. To appear.

12. Massimo Lucchesi. *Coaching the 3-4-1-2 and 4-2-3-1*. Reedswain Publishing, 2001.

13. Héctor Muñoz-Avila and Todd Fisher. Strategic planning for Unreal Tournament bots. In *Proceedings of AAAI-04 Workshop on Challenges on Game AI*. AAAI Press, 2004.

14. Jan Murray. Specifying agent behaviors with UML statecharts and StatEdit. In Polani et al. [18], pages 145–156.

15. Jan Murray, Oliver Obst, and Frieder Stolzenburg. RoboLog Koblenz 2001. In Andreas Birk, Silvia Coradeschi, and Satoshi Tadokoro, editors, *RoboCup 2001: Robot Soccer World Cup V*, volume 2377 of *Lecture Notes in Artificial Intelligence*, pages 526–530. Springer, Berlin, Heidelberg, New York, 2002. Team description.

16. Dana S. Nau, Yue Cao, Amnon Lotem, and Héctor Muñoz-Avila. Shop: Simple hierarchical ordered planner. In *Proceedings of IJCAI-99*, pages 968–975, 1999.

17. Oliver Obst and Markus Rollmann. SPARK – A Generic Simulator for Physical Multiagent Simulations. *Engineering Intelligent Systems*, 13, 2005. To appear.

18. Daniel Polani, Brett Browning, Andrea Bonarini, and Kazuo Yoshida, editors. volume 3020 of *Lecture Notes in Artificial Intelligence*. Springer, 2004.

19. Patrick Riley and Manuela Veloso. Planning for distributed execution through use of probabilistic opponent models. In *Proceedings of the Sixth International Conference on Artificial Intelligence Planning Systems*, Toulouse, France, April 2002.

20. Peter Stone and Manuela Veloso. Task decomposition, dynamic role assignment, and low-bandwidth communication for real-time strategic teamwork. *Artificial Intelligence*, 1999.

21. V. S. Subrahmanian, Piero Bonatti, Jürgen Dix, Thomas Eiter, Sarit Kraus, Fatma Ozcan, and Robert Ross. *Heterogeneous Agent Systems*. MIT Press/AAAI Press, Cambridge, MA, USA, 2000.

Reusable Components for Implementing Agent Interactions*

Juan M. Serrano, Sascha Ossowski, and Sergio Saugar

University Rey Juan Carlos, Department of Computing
{JuanManuel.Serrano, Sascha.Ossowski, Sergio.Saugar}@urjc.es

Abstract. Engineering component interactions is a major challenge in the development of large-scale, open systems. In the realm of multiagent system research, organizational abstractions have been proposed to overcome the complexity of this task. However, the gap between these modeling abstractions, and the constructs provided by todays agent-oriented software frameworks is still rather big. This paper reports on the $\mathcal{RICA}$–$\mathcal{J}$ multiagent programming framework, which provides executable constructs for each of the organizational, ACL-based modeling abstractions of the $\mathcal{RICA}$ theory. Setting out from a components and connectors perspective on the elements of the $\mathcal{RICA}$ metamodel, their executions semantics is defined and instrumented on top of the JADE platform. Moreover, a systematic reuse approach to the engineering of interactions is put forward.

1 Introduction

In the past few years, multi-agent systems (MAS) have been proposed as a suitable software engineering paradigm to face the challenges posed by the development of large-scale, open systems [1, 2]. Two major characteristics of MAS are commonly put forward to justify this claim. Firstly, agents are excellent candidates to occupy the place of autonomous, heterogeneous and dynamic components that open systems require [2]. Secondly, the organizational stance advocated in various degrees by most MAS methodologies, provides an excellent basis to deal with the complexity and dynamism of the interactions among system components [1]. In particular, organization-oriented abstractions such as roles, social interactions, groups, organizations, institutions, etc., have proved to be an effective means to model the interaction space of complex MAS [1, 3–5].

However, the gap between these modeling abstractions, and the constructs provided by todays agent-oriented software frameworks is still huge. A way to bridge this gap is to include organization-oriented abstractions as first-class constructs into a multiagent programming language. For this purpose, it is essential to define the execution semantics of the new programming constructs, in a way that is independent from any technological basis [6]. In addition, from a mainstream software

---

* Research sponsored by the Spanish Ministry of Science and Education (MEC), project TIC2003-08763-C02-02.

R.H. Bordini et al. (Eds.): ProMAS 2005, LNAI 3862, pp. 101–119, 2006.

engineering perspective, it is of foremost importance that the new abstractions foster a systematic reuse approach, specially in the context of large-scale software systems [7]. A similar concern has been put forward in the field of MAS engineering regarding the reuse of organizational structures [8] and agents [9].

This paper reports on the $\mathcal{RICA}$–$\mathcal{J}$ multiagent programming framework, which provides executable constructs for each of the modeling abstractions of the *Role/Interaction/Communicative Action* ($\mathcal{RICA}$) theory [4]. For this purpose, the execution semantics of the different elements of the $\mathcal{RICA}$ metamodel is specified, drawing inspiration from component and connector (C&C) architectures [10]. With regard to reusability matters, the $\mathcal{RICA}$–$\mathcal{J}$ software framework exploits the organizational stance on ACLs postulated by the $\mathcal{RICA}$ theory, which results in the identification of generic application-independent social interactions.

The remainder of the paper is organized as follows. Section 2 shows how a C&C perspective on the $\mathcal{RICA}$ theory can be used to define an execution semantics for its elements. Section 3 analyzes communicative roles and interactions from the point of view of generic software components [7], so as to identify policies for their reuse. Section 4 provides a survey of the $\mathcal{RICA}$–$\mathcal{J}$ framework, emphasizing the mapping of the C&C-based execution semantics to the JADE platform, and the architecture of a $\mathcal{RICA}$–$\mathcal{J}$ application. The paper is concluded with a discussion on the lessons learned as well as pointers to current and future work.

2   MAS as a C&C Style

From a software architecture point of view an application structure is described as a collection of interacting components [10]. Components represent the computational elements or processing units of the system (the locus of control and computation), while connectors represent interactions among components. Different types of connectors represent different forms of interaction: pipes, procedure call, SQL link, event-broadcast, etc. This section will first show how this general view of software architecture fits the multiagent social architecture endorsed by the $\mathcal{RICA}$ theory. Then, based upon this view, and as a previous step to the instrumentation of the theory, the execution semantics of the $\mathcal{RICA}$ theory will be outlined.

2.1   Components and Connectors in the $\mathcal{RICA}$ Theory

The metamodel of the $\mathcal{RICA}$ theory provides a modeling language of the *organizational* and *communicative* features of MAS [4]. In this section we will focus on the key organizational abstraction, namely social interactions. Moreover, we introduce *group meetings* as the context in which social interactions take place, thus extending the basic set of abstractions of the theory[1]. The next section deals with the communicative layer of the metamodel.

---

[1] The metamodel may be further extended with other kinds of abstractions such as *Organization Types* and *Norms*. However, given the purpose of this paper, they are not needed.

Here, and throughout the rest of this paper, we will refer for illustration purposes to a common application domain in the organization literature: the management of scientific conferences [1][11]. *Authors, Reviewers, Program Committee Members* and *Program Committee Chairs* (PC chairs) would be common roles played by agents within an organization designed to support this process. Interactions among these agents will take place in the context of several group meetings, such as the *submission* and the *reviewing* group types. Figure 1 shows a partial $\mathcal{RICA}$ model of the submission group expressed in terms of a UML class diagram, which makes use of several stereotypes that refer to the kind of meta-entities and -relationships of the $\mathcal{RICA}$ metamodel (the <<C>> stereotype stands for the capabilities of interactive role types).

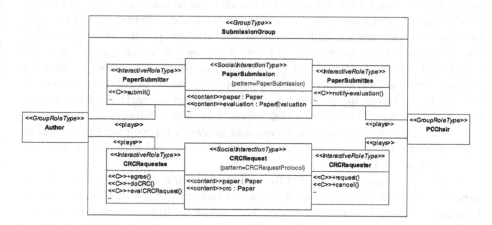

Fig. 1. $\mathcal{RICA}$ model of the *Submission* group

The specification of a group type establishes the kinds of agents which may participate in groups of that kind by identifying several *Group Role* types. Authors and PC Chairs, for example, represent the agents that may participate in a submission group. Moreover, the different kinds of interactions held in some group meeting must be specified as well. For instance, in the context of the submission group, *Paper Submission* and *Camera Ready Copy (CRC) Request* interactions will happen. An agent participates in a social interaction by taking on certain *Interactive Role* types. For instance, an author will participate in a paper submission interaction as the *Paper Submitter*, whereas the PC chair will take part in these interactions as a *Paper Submittee*. The *plays* association in the $\mathcal{RICA}$ metamodel among a group role and an interactive role establishes that agents occupying the former position may take part in some kind of interaction by playing the latter interactive role. Interactive role types characterize the behaviours that agents may show when they engage in the interaction, in terms of the communicative actions (CA) (e.g. *submit, agree*) and other types of social actions (e.g. *doCRC*, performed by authors in order to generate the CRC of an accepted paper) that they *can* perform. Besides the participant roles, other components may form part of the definition of a kind of social interaction. Firstly, a collection of parameter types which specify the *content* of the interaction, such as the *paper* to be submitted and its *evaluation*. Input/output parameters of communicative and social actions must refer to the parameters declared for the interaction type. Secondly, a collection of interaction protocol types representing different *patterns* along which the interaction is supposed to develop (e.g. the *submissionProcedure*).

From an organizational point of view on MAS [1, 11, 12], and without discarding the autonomy of agents, it is possible to abstract from the agents' internal architecture, and focus on the roles that an agent may play within the organization. So, agents can be conceived as a particular type of *software component*. Furthermore, social interactions can be considered as different kinds of *connectors*[2], since they establish the interaction rules among agents, and thus mediate their communication and coordination activities: paper submission, CRC requests, and so on, specify the particular manner in which authors and PC Chairs interact in the context of the submission group. Moreover, pushing the analogy even further, connector types declare a number of roles and protocols [13] which directly map onto the interactive roles and interaction protocols that the $\mathcal{RICA}$ theory associates to social interactions. For instance, *caller* and *callee* in a RPC connector interaction, *reader* and *writer* in a pipe interaction, and so forth, are analogues of *PaperSubmitter* and *PaperSubmittee* as declared by the paper submission interaction.

Social interactions mainly differ from pipes, SQL links, and other types of connectors in their characteristic interaction mechanism: the Agent Communication Language (ACL). Firstly, ACLs allow for a more anthropomorphic description of the interactive roles and protocols than connectors. Secondly, they allow for more flexibility, as the equivalent to connector protocols *may* be derived from the communicative action semantics [14].

2.2   An Execution Semantics for $\mathcal{RICA}$ Models

As a first step towards defining programming abstractions that correspond to the $\mathcal{RICA}$ modeling entities, the execution semantics of the later needs to be defined: we have to show how social social interactions are enacted by agents at run-time in the context of group meetings[3]. In this section we will sketch this execution semantics based on a run-time instance of the previous conference management model (see Figure 2). As we focus on the dynamics of social interactions, we will assume that an instance of the submission group has already been set up by some PC Chair. Moreover, we will consider that three authors, a_3, a_4 and a_5, and two PC chairs, a_1 and a_2, has joined this group meeting.

The behaviour of agents within a group meeting is given by the group role instances and the interactive role instances that they play. Hence, an agent

---

[2] Group types may also be conceptualised as a special kind of connector.

[3] Here, agents, social roles, interactions, and so forth, denote *instances* of the corresponding $\mathcal{RICA}$ metamodel abstractions.

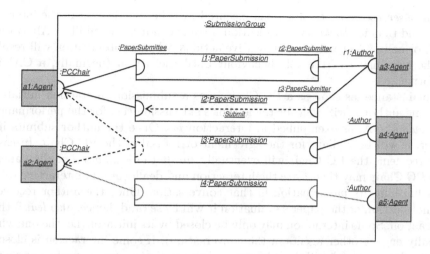

Fig. 2. Run-time instance of the e-commerce model

comprises a set of role instances: each of them encapsulates an action selection strategy that is compliant with the restrictions put forward by the role type. Role instances are run in parallel by the agent and may be active or suspended.

If some agent has activated a given group role instance, it may *engage* other agent(s) of the same group in social interaction. Submission interactions, for example, will be started by authors. The execution of an *engage* action results in the creation of a new interaction. Once the interaction has been created, the agent will instantiate the corresponding interactive role type to carry out its activity within that particular interaction. Thus, a given agent has as many interactive role instances as interactions in which it is participating. For instance, in figure 2, the participation of author agent a_3 in paper submission interactions i_1 and i_2 is carried out by its role instances r_2 and r_3, respectively.

The *engage* action specifies a collection of addressees which will be notified of the new interaction. In our example, authors will normally engage *any* PC Chair in paper submission. Interaction i_3, shown in the example, represents the result of the engagement performed by agent a_4. Once some agent is notified of a new interaction addressed to it, it may *join* that interaction and instantiate its corresponding interactive role type. Only the addressees of some interaction may join it. However, it may happen that some agent who received the engagement notification can not join the interaction because the role's position is already occupied by other agent who was faster in joining it[4]. Note that the *engage* action automatically involves a *join* action performed by the initiator agent.

The interactive role behaviour determines which types of actions will be *executed* by the agent in the course of the interaction. It also makes sure that the

---

[4] This essentially depends on the cardinality feature declared by the interactive role type. For instance, in multi-party conversations such as auctions multiple bidders may join the interaction.

agent *observes* the types of actions executed by other participant in the interaction, and that it *aborts* action execution if some condition is fulfilled. Abortions will normally affect non-communicative actions, whereas observation will result in the suspension of the role behaviour until the action (normally, a CA) is performed.

For instance, as soon as a PC Chair joins a submission interaction initiated by some author it will wait for the author's submission (i.e. for the performance of a *submit* CA, as exemplified in interaction i_2). Once the author submits its paper, it will be vigilant for the agreement or refusal of the PC Chair. In case of agreement, the PC Chair will eventually *notify* the *evaluation* of the paper. The PC Chair may then *leave* the interaction and deallocate its interactive role, thus finishing its participation in that conversation. Once the author receives the notification of the paper's evaluation it will *close* (and, hence, also *leave*) the interaction. Some interaction may only be closed by its initiator (i.e. the one who initially engage other agents in the conversation). If some interaction is closed the pending agent(s) will be only able to leave it (i.e. no action performing will be allowed). Interaction i_4 represents an interaction between agents a_5 and a_2, closed by the initiator agent a_5.

Interaction behaviour need not be explicitly declared by role types, but can also be inferred from the protocol which regulate the social interaction. Thus, protocol *instances* in $\mathcal{RICA}$ provide all the aforementioned services: action execution, observation, abortion, etc. Still, the particular way in which these services are provided depends on the execution semantics of the technique in which the interaction protocol is specified (FSMs, Petri nets, etc.).

3   ACLs and Component-Based Development

This section will evaluate the potential for reusability of the $\mathcal{RICA}$ theory in the context of the above execution semantics. Specifically, we look for reusable software artifacts (i.e. components[5] [7]), which may support a systematic reuse approach. First, we will show how ACL dialects serve to identify these reusable components. Then, we will discuss their associated customization mechanisms.

3.1   Reusable Components in the $\mathcal{RICA}$ Theory

As the *CRCRequest* interaction model shows (see figure 1), a social interaction type must specify the communicative actions that participating agents can perform. Protocols that regulate their behaviours may be defined as well. Still, PC Chairs are not the only kind of agents that will issue requests or cancellations. Similarly, a CRC request protocol may essentially be modeled after a generic "request protocol" (e.g. as the FIPA Request Protocol [15]). The $\mathcal{RICA}$ theory

---

[5] This sense of the word "component" should not be confused with the meaning of the term in the context of C&C architectures. The context will provide the right interpretation.

abstracts these pragmatic features (CAs and protocols) away from the definition of interactive roles and social interactions, and encapsulates them in their characteristic *communicative roles* and *communicative interactions*, particular types of interactive roles and social interactions defined from a set of performatives and protocols, i.e. an ACL dialect. For instance, the *requester* role type is the unique type of role characterized by *request* and *cancel* CAs. Communicative roles may also include non-communicative actions. For instance, *requestee* agents will need to determine if the requested action can be performed or not, which may be accomplished by the *evalRequest* action. We call the characteristic interaction in which requester and requestee agents participate *action performing*. This communicative interaction type, shown in figure 3, encapsulates the request protocol, besides generic content parameters such as the action to be requested, the agreement conditions, etc.

Thanks to the cross-domain features of CAs and protocols, ACL-based interactions are generic first-order reusable components[6]. Indeed, communicative interactions provide the pragmatic features of application-dependent social interactions, which basically differ at the semantic level. However, dynamic features of interactive role types are not completely defined at this level of abstraction. Particularly, a communicative interaction type says nothing about the rules to be followed in order to set up or close an interaction of that kind: the *engagement* and *closing* rules. Similarly, the *joining* and *leaving* rules for each kind of communicative role type are not declared either, so that these kinds of roles will be *abstract*. Note that these rules complements the static features of the $\mathcal{RICA}$ metamodel described in the last section.

3.2   Customization Mechanism

There are two major customization mechanisms to reuse communicative interaction components in a given application domain: *delegation* and *specialization*. Due to lack of space, the discussion is constrained to the latter mechanism, which relies in a recursive definition model by which some type (the derived type) is defined in terms of a super-type (or base type), by *extending, overriding* and/or *inheriting* some of its definition components[7].

For instance, figure 3 shows the recursive specification of the CRC Request social interaction, by customizing the action performing communicative interaction. Different characteristics are *inherited*: the content parameters and the request protocol. Similarly, CRC Requester and Requestees inherit the CAs. Some features of the action performing interaction are not inherited, but *overridden* by specializing components. For instance, the *evalRequest* action that CRC Requestees perform as a special kind of requestee, is overriden by the *evalCRCRequest* action, which represents the particular way in which a request will

---

[6] Note that these reusable components are actually *connectors*, in the C&C perspective.

[7] This recursive model applies not only to interactive roles and social interactions, but also to any kind of meta-entity of the $\mathcal{RICA}$ metamodel: group types, protocol types, and so forth.

be evaluated in this context. In general, social actions may either declare a default *execution* method, or be *abstract*, so that particular agents must provide the actual implementation. In the case of the *evalCRCRequest* action, a default implementation may be provided whereby the request will be accepted if the requestee is actually the author of the paper. Overriding declarations of role actions introduces a *dynamic binding* feature in the execution semantics of $\mathcal{RICA}$ models. For instance, when CRC Requestee agents are required to perform the *evalRequest* action (which is legal, since they are requestee agents), the action that is actually executed at run-time is *evalCRCRequest*[8].

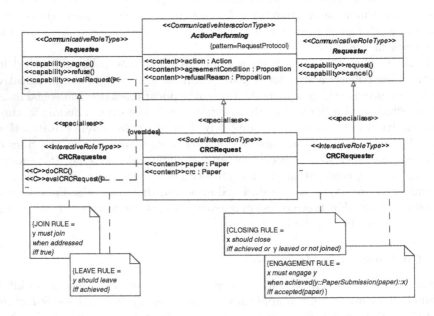

Fig. 3. Recursive definition of *CRCRequest* interactions

The model of figure 3 also illustrates the case of *extensions*: e.g. the *doCRC* action extends the inherited and overridden set of actions that CRC Requestee agents can perform. As another example of extension (involving abstract features of the parent type), the social interaction type also declares the engagement, closing, joining and leaving rules. These rules are represented in figure 3 as tagged values inside notes. Engagement and closing rules are defined for CRC Requesters, while joining and leaving are defined for CRC Requestees:

– *Engagement rule*: The set up may be established when a paper submission interaction finishes successfully and the paper was accepted. If so happens,

---

[8] This mechanism allows for a direct reuse of interaction protocols, fully specified in the scope of communicative interactions. For instance, the *Interaction State Machine* (ISM) specification of the request protocol [16] may be reused "as-is" by the CRC request interaction.

the paper submittee (a PC Chair, as declared in figure 1), must engage the paper submitter (an author) to play the requester role and obtain the CRC of the accepted paper[9].

- *Joining rule*: An author must join the interaction as a requestee when it is addressed by the PC Chair.
- *Leaving rule*: An author should leave the interaction when the CRC is provided (i.e. the interaction's purpose is achieved).
- *Closing rule*: A PC Chair should close the interaction if and only if the CRC has been provided, the author leaves the interaction before finishing its job, or the addressed author does not join before the established deadline for the delivery of the CRC.

Finally, it should be noted that communicative interactions may be reused to specify other communicative interactions as well. For example, the *Submission* communicative interaction may be defined as an specialisation of *Action Performing* interactions. Moreover, taking into account that a *submit* CA is a special kind of *request*, the generic *RequestProtocol* may be used in place of particular submission protocols.

4   The $\mathcal{RICA}$–$\mathcal{J}$ Framework

The $\mathcal{RICA}$ theory, given its metamodel and execution semantics, can be conceived as a programming language with close links to Architectural Description Languages (ADLs) [13]. For instance, the CRC Requestee role type may be declared as shown in figure 4. Unlike its UML representation (see figure 3), the grammatical form also conveys the full declaration of social actions (parameters and execution blocks). Dotted lines should be replaced by actual code, possibly object-oriented (e.g. Java). The reserved words `player` and `interaction` play a similar role to the reserved word `this` in Java: the first one denotes the agent which is playing that role instance (an *Author* agent, in the example); the second one, the interaction to which the agent is connected as a player of the interactive role type (an instance of *CRCRequest*, in the example). Finally, the functions `achieved` and `addressedFor` denote predefined operations of social interaction and agent instances, respectively.

As a more pragmatic alternative to the direct instrumentation of the "$\mathcal{RICA}$ programming language", the $\mathcal{RICA}$–$\mathcal{J}$ ($\mathcal{RICA}$-JADE [17]) framework instruments the $\mathcal{RICA}$ theory on top of the FIPA-compliant JADE platform [18], which is used as the underlying middleware and programming environment. This section will first describe the $\mathcal{RICA}$–$\mathcal{J}$ architecture and general features based on the execution semantics described in section 2. Then, we outline how the the reusability concern described in section 3 is captured in the framework.

---

[9] In general, the engagement rule may not specify a particular agent as the addressee but a definite description representing a collection of agents. The engagement rules for paper submission interactions, as suggested previously, may establish that the author must engage *any* agent playing the *PC Chair* role in the submission group.

```
interactive role type CRCRequestee specialises Requestee
must be joined by Author when player.addressedFor(CRCRequest)
should be leaved iff interaction.achieved()
performs{
        social action type evalCRCRequest(in paper)
        overrides evalRequest
        executes{ ... }

        social action type doCRC(in paper, out crc)
        executes{ ... }
}
```

Fig. 4. Grammatical declaration of the *Seller* role

4.1 $\mathcal{RICA{-}J}$ Architecture

The $\mathcal{RICA{-}J}$ framework extends the JADE platform with a layer that provides a virtual machine based on the $\mathcal{RICA}$ abstractions. This layer is decomposed into two major modules, implemented by the `rica.reflect` and `rica.core` Java packages, which instrument the $\mathcal{RICA}$ metamodel and execution semantics, respectively. Thus, the former package includes the classes `InteractiveRoleType`, `SocialInteractionType`, etc., while the latter contains abstract types, such as `Agent`, `InteractiveRole` and `SocialInteraction`. The `rica.reflect` classes are functional analogues of the reflective classes of the standard `java.lang.reflect` package. Moreover, they ensure the consistency of the programmed $\mathcal{RICA}$ model (e.g. that any social role specializes a communicative role). On the other hand, `rica.core` classes may be seen as analogues of the `java.lang.Object` class since, for instance, all particular agent types must be programmed by extending the `rica.core.Agent` class.

The `rica.core` classes map the common behaviour and structure of agents, roles, etc., as defined by the $\mathcal{RICA}$ execution semantics, to the supported abstractions of the JADE framework: basically, agents, behaviours and ACL messages. The resulting architecture of a $\mathcal{RICA{-}J}$ agent is exemplified in figure 5. This figure's object model depicts the run-time structure of the a_3 author agent previously shown in figure 2.

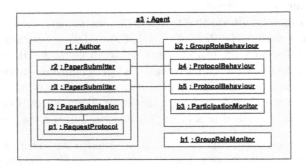

Fig. 5. $\mathcal{RICA{-}J}$ agent architecture

Any `rica.core.Agent` (a kind of JADE agent) schedules an `GroupRoleMonitor` (a JADE cyclic behaviour), in charge of creating and deallocating the group role instances in which its functionality is decomposed. The activation of a given group role has two major consequences: firstly, the agent makes public in a role-based Directory Facilitator (actually, a wrapper of the `jade.domain.DFService`) that it currently plays that role; secondly, the `GroupRoleBehaviour` (a JADE parallel behaviour) managed by the `rica.core.GroupRole` instance is scheduled. This parallel behaviour contains a `ParticipationMonitor` behaviour[10], in charge of enacting new interactions (through engagement) or joining the agent to interactions initiated by other agents. When some agent initiates its participation in a new interaction, it will instantiate the corresponding `rica.core.InteractiveRole` subclass, together with the JADE behaviour which manages its participation in the interaction. This behaviour will be part of the group role's parallel behaviour.

According to the execution semantics, the interactive role behaviour determines the actions that will be executed, observed or interrupted by the agent in the course of the interaction. As far as CAs are concerned, their execution will result in the automatic creation and sending of the corresponding `jade.lang.acl.ACLMessage`. Conversely, the observation of CAs results in receiving an `ACLMessage` and automatically translating it back to a `rica.core.CommAction` object. These conversions can be performed automatically by relying on the content parameters, the JADE ontology, and the addressee language that the interaction instance holds. The `ProtocolBehaviour` class models a generic interactive role behaviour which determines the agent's activity according to the rules established by a protocol which regulates the interaction. This behaviour is decoupled from the particular formalism used to specify the given protocol, since it only depends on the `rica.core.Protocol` interface (which declares the protocol services specified by the execution semantics). Particular formalisms may be integrated into the framework by instrumenting their execution semantics in a `Protocol` subclass.

4.2   Programming in $\mathcal{RICA-J}$

The architecture of a MAS in the $\mathcal{RICA-J}$ framework, shown in figure 6, is structured around two major types of modules: the first one refers to the implementation of the different agents participating in the MAS; the second one, to the implementation of the MAS organization. This composite module closely follows the structure of its $\mathcal{RICA}$ model: in essence, we may identify an optional *protocol formalism* module, one mandatory *communication* module, and the implementation of the *application-dependent* social interactions and non-interactive roles.

As we argued in section 3, communicative components are highly reusable components, so that they will be likely reused from an application-independent

---

[10] This cyclic behaviour acts as an *interaction factory*: since $\mathcal{RICA-J}$ interactions are instrumented *subjectively*, each participant (initiator or not) holds a `rica.core.SocialInteraction` instance representing the interaction from its own perspective.

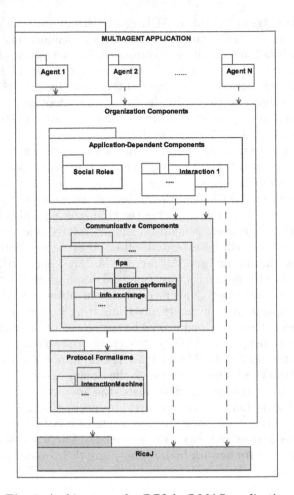

Fig. 6. Architecture of a $\mathcal{RICA}$–$\mathcal{J}$ MAS application

library of communicative interactions. This library, implemented under the `acl` package, currently contains some of the FIPA ACL underlying interactions [4], and other "non-standard" interactions such as submission and advisement interactions. On the other hand, protocol formalisms are highly reusable as well. The `protocol.ism` package instruments the *Interaction State Machine* specification technique [16]. Therefore, the protocol and communication module will be likely implemented by *component developers*, whereas the application-dependent social module would be in charge of *organization developers*. Finally, *independent users* would be in charged of implementing their agents. These programmers rely on the components available in the organizational library, possibly customizing the roles types to be played by overriding their default functionality or implementing their abstract actions. The following paragraphs will briefly describe some general guidelines in the implementation of communicative and social interaction components.

Communicative Components. Above all, communicative roles and interactions encapsulate the CAs and protocols of their characteristic ACL dialect. However, the Java classes which instrument these components also provide basic support functionality for the execution semantics of these components. Firstly, the constructors of the social interaction classes may provide the required initialization of the content parameters and participant addresses. Secondly, the generic vocabulary of the communicative interaction (including the performatives), will be implemented as a JADE ontology. Finally, generic social actions defined by communicative roles may be provided with default implementations.

For instance, figure 7 partially shows the implementation of the *Requestee* communicative role type. The $\mathcal{RICA}$ type information is embedded in the Java class by means of `public static final` fields, following the established implementation scheme for communicative roles types: a field of type `CommInteractionType` declares the type of communicative interaction to which the role type belongs, whereas role capabilities are declared by fields whose types are assignable from the `SocialActionType` class (so, `CommActType` fields will contribute to the role capabilities, since this class extends the former one). Furthermore, the class constructor allows the player agent to register the JADE ontology defined for action performing interactions. This ontology declares the performatives (e.g. *agree, refuse*, etc.) and other generic concepts and predicates (e.g. the predicate `CanNotPerform`, useful when the kind of requested action is not among the capabilities of the requestee agent). Note that the java class is declared `abstract`, since the rules for joining and leaving this kind of roles are not declared.

Figure 7 also shows a partial implementation of the *EvalRequest* social action. Similarly to the *Requestee* role type, the static features of the action type are declared by `static` fields: e.g. the `input` and `output` fields declares the input and output parameters of the action, which are initialised with the corresponding parameter types declared by the *ActionPerforming* communicative interaction. For each kind of *parameter*, a private field `parameterValue` of the corresponding type is declared, together with a pair of `get/set` methods to access and set the value of the parameter. The implementation of accessor methods for output parameters provide default values which may be overriden by specialisations of this action type. Thus, according to the `getRefusalReason` method, the request will be refused if the requested action can not be performed by the requestee agent (the method `getPerformer()` will return the role instance which is actually executing the action). A default value is also provided for the *notificationRequired* parameter, indicating that the agreement to perform the action should be notified (in particular requests, this default value might be overriden to *false* if the performance of the requested action is imminent). Finally, a default implementation of the `Action`'s `execute()` method is also provided: the action will be considered *successfully executed* if a refusal reason or the agreement condition has been set; otherwise, the method returns in a *suspended* state.

Social Components. Interactive roles and social interactions extend communicative roles and interaction classes, thus inheriting the general interaction management mechanism. Typically, they will provide the engagement, joining,

```java
public abstract class Requestee extends InteractiveRole{

    /** Type info. */
    public static final CommRoleType type = new CommRoleType(Requestee.class);
    public static final CommInteractionType interaction = ActionPerforming.type;
    public static final SocialActionType evalRequest = EvalRequest.type;
    public static final CommActType agree = Agree.type;
    public static final CommActType refuse = Refuse.type;
    ...

    /** Creates a requestee role for the specified agent. */
    public Requestee(Agent agent){
        super(agent);
        updateDomainOntology(ActionPerformingOntology.getInstance());
        ...
    }
}

public class EvalRequest extends SingleSocialAction{

    /** Type info. */
    public static final SingleSocialActionType type =
        new SingleSocialActionType(EvalRequest.class);
    public static final ParameterType[] input =
        new ParameterType[]{ActionPerforming.action};
    public static final ParameterType[] output =
        new ParameterType[]{ActionPerforming.notificationRequired,
                            ActionPerforming.agreementCondition,
                            ActionPerforming.refusalReason};

    /** Auxiliary methods for input/output parameters */
    private SocialAction actionValue;
    public void setAction(SocialAction newValue){...}
    public SocialAction getAction(){return actionValue;}

    private Predicate refusalReasonValue;
    public void setRefusalReason(Predicate newValue){...}
    public Predicate getRefusalReason(){
        if (refusalReasonValue == null &&
            !getAction().getType().canBePerformedBy(getPerformer().getType())){
            setRefusalReason(new CanNotPerform());
        }
        return refusalReasonValue;
    }

    private Predicate agreementConditionValue;
    public void setAgreementCondition(Predicate newValue){...}
    public Predicate getAgreementCondition(){return agreementConditionValue;}

    private Boolean notificationRequiredValue;
    public void setNotificationRequired(Boolean newValue) {...}
    public Predicate getNotificationRequired(){
        if (notificationRequired==null){
            setNotificationRequired(new Boolean.TRUE)
        }
        return notificationRequired;
    }

    /** Overriden SocialAction interface */
    public ExecutionState execute(){
        if (getRefusalReason()!=null || getAgreementCondition()!=null){
            return ExecutionState.SUCCESSFUL;
        }else{
            return ExecutionState.SUSPENDED;
        }
    }
}
```

Fig. 7. Implementation of the *Requestee* communicative role type

leaving and closing rules by overriding/declaring the corresponding methods: mustBeJoinedBy, shouldBeLeft, etc. Moreover, the Java classes will also provide the social interaction ontology, application-specific implementations of general

```
public class CRCRequestee extends Requestee{

    /** Type info. */
    public static final InteractiveRoleType type =
        new InteractiveRoleType(CRCRequestee.class);
    public static final SocialInteractionType interaction = CRCRequest.type;
    public static final SocialActionType evalCRCRequest = EvalCRCRequest.type;
    public static final SocialActionType doCRC = DoCRC.type;
    ...

    /** Overriden Interactive Role interface. */
    public static SocialInteraction mustBeJoinedBy(GroupRole role){
        if (role.getType()!=Author.type){
            return null;
        }else{
            return role.addressedFor(CRCRequest.type);
        }
    }

    public boolean shouldBeLeft(){
        return getInteraction().hasBeenSuccessful();
    }

    /** Creates a CRCRequestee role for the specified agent. */
    public CRCRequestee(Agent agent){
        super(agent);
        updateDomainOntology(CRCRequestOntology.getInstance());
    }

}

public class EvalCRCRequest extends EvalRequest{

    /** Type info */
    public static final SingleSocialActionType type =
        new SingleSocialActionType(EvalCRCRequest.class);
    public static final ParameterType[] input =
        new ParameterType[]{CRCRequest.paper};

    /** Auxiliary methods for input/output parameters */
    private Paper paperValue;
    public void setPaper(Paper newValue){...};
    public Paper getPaper(){ return paperValue; }

    /** Overriden Requestee interface */
    public Predicate getRefusalReason(){
        if (refusalReasonValue == null &&
            !getPaper().isAuthor(getPlayer().getAID())){
            setRefusalReason(new NotAuthor());
        }
        return refusalReasonValue;
    }

    public Predicate getAgreementCondition(){
        if (agreementConditionValue == null && getRefusalReason()==null){
            setAgreementCondition(new TrueProposition());
        }
        return agreementConditionValue;
    }

}
```

Fig. 8. Implementation of the *CRCRequestee* interactive role type

communicative role methods, and all other code concerning the actual environment in which the application is deployed (database connection, web servers, etc.).

As figure 8 shows, the implementation of the *CRCRequestee* role type firstly includes the declaration of the static features of the $\mathcal{RICA}$ type: essentially, the set of capabilities, which is extended with the *DoCRC* action; moreover, the

EvalRequest action is overriden by its specialisation *EvalCRCRequest*[11]. The method `mustBeJoined` declares the joining rule for *CRCRequestee* roles according to the specification discussed in section 3.2. This method is invoked by the group role playing the interactive role, i.e. an *Author* instance, in this particular case. If the return value is not `null`, the author agent will join the specified interaction and will instantiate the `CRCRequestee` class to carry out its activity within that interaction. The leaving rule is implemented by overriding the `shouldBeLeft` method, declared by the `rica.core.InteractiveRole` class. It returns `true` if, and only if, the interaction has finished successfully. Finally, the `CRCRequestee` constructor ensures that the specific ontology for this kind of interactions is registered in the agent's content manager. This ontology declares, for example, the proposition `NotAuthor`, which stands for the fact that the requestee is not the author of the paper specified in the interaction.

Figure 8 also shows a partial implementation of the *EvalCRCRequest* social action. The `EvalCRCRequest` class overrides some of the default methods specified by the `EvalRequest` class. Specifically, the request will be refused if the player agent is not the author of the input paper. Moreover, the agreement condition is automatically set to *true* if the condition for refusal is not satisfied. Thus, according to the generic implementation of the inherited `execute` method, the action will succeed the first time is performed.

5   Conclusion

This paper has shown how agent interactions can be modeled and instrumented by customizing generic communicative interactions identified from ACL-dialects. Communicative interactions serve as micro-organizational modeling patterns that structure the interaction space of specific MAS, complementing similar reuse-approaches based on macro-organizational structures [8] or agent components [9]. Communicative interactions are also the key computational abstraction in the $\mathcal{RICA}$–$\mathcal{J}$ programming framework, as their execution semantics determines a substantial part of the logic required to manage agent interactions. The encapsulation of these interactions around software component libraries significantly simplifies the implementation of the multi-agent organization. Moreover, the $\mathcal{RICA}$–$\mathcal{J}$ framework also relieves agent programmers from the implementation of low-level issues concerning the dynamics of agents within the organization. On the other hand, it should be stressed that the proposed approach does not endanger the autonomy of agents, since the social roles available in the organization library may be fully customized to account for the particular requirements of each agent.

The currently implemented library of communicative interactions may be extended to cover dialects proposed for other specific domains (e.g. negotiation [19, 20]), or the dialogue types put forward by argumentation theorists [21–24].

---

[11] If some action of the super-role is specialised by a new action of the derived role type, the super-action is implicitly overriden. This is a limitation of the current implementation.

Note that the implementation of communicative interactions by means of the $\mathcal{RICA{-}J}$ framework is independent of any semantic paradigm, be it intentional [25], social [26], or protocol-based [27]. In fact, BDI or commitment-based agent architectures may be instrumented as refinements of the general C&C agent architecture, thus complementing the protocol-based semantics that the $\mathcal{RICA{-}J}$ framework currently instruments.

Another contribution of this paper refers to the C&C perspective on MAS by defining the execution semantics of the $\mathcal{RICA}$ theory. This specification, albeit informal, shares the motivations of the formal operational semantics of groups and role dynamics established by Ferber & Gutknecht [6], and Dastani et al. [28]. Furthermore, the C&C-based perspective that we have put forward may well be extended to specify the execution semantics of this and related larger-grained organizational abstractions, such as scenes [5]. Since these abstractions can be ultimately reduced to different types of social interactions, they may be conceived as composite connectors [29]. Moreover, modeling social interactions in terms of software connectors has as a major consequence the identification of the characteristic roles that their participant agents may play within it. This feature of the $\mathcal{RICA}$ metamodel allows to distinguish it from other organizational approaches, and makes possible the reuse approach to social interactions put forward by this conceptual framework.

We have shown how the $\mathcal{RICA{-}J}$ framework instruments the $\mathcal{RICA}$ execution semantics on top of the JADE platform, but other agent infrastructures (e.g. tuple-based [9]), or technologies (e.g. web services), may provide the required underlying middleware services and basic abstractions as well. On the other hand, the programming language perspective on the $\mathcal{RICA}$ theory complements the results on the field of agent-oriented programming languages, currently geared towards deliberative or cognitive capabilities of agents [30,31]. Moreover, by placing MAS in the broader spectrum of software architectures, this paper motivates the transfer of research from this field (e.g. on ADLs [13]).

Future work will concentrate on further validation of the $\mathcal{RICA{-}J}$ framework with the final intention to get a JADE add-on release. The extension of the underlying metamodel with coarse-grained organizational abstractions, and the instrumentation of the interaction monitoring and compliance capabilities that any open-driven framework must offer [2], will be considered as well.

References

1. Zambonelli, F., Jennings, N.R., Wooldridge, M.: Developing multiagent systems: The Gaia methodology. ACM Transactions on Software Engineering and Methodology **12** (2003) 317–370
2. Singh, M.P.: Agent-based abstractions for software development. In Bergenti, F., Gleizes, M.P., Zambonelli, F., eds.: Methodologies and Software Engineering for Agent Systems. Kluwer (2004) 5–18
3. Ferber, J., Gutknecht, O.: A meta-model for the analysis of organizations in multi-agent systems. In Demazeau, Y., ed.: Proceedings of the Third International Conference on Multi-Agent Systems (ICMAS'98), Paris, France, IEEE Press (1998) 128–135

4. Serrano, J.M., Ossowski, S., Fernández, A.: The pragmatics of software agents - analysis and design of agent communication languages. Intelligent Information Agents - An AgentLink Perspective (Klusch, Bergamaschi, Edwards & Petta, ed.), Lecture Notes in Computer Science **2586** (2003) 234–274
5. Esteva, M., Rodriguez, J.A., Sierra, C., Garcia, P., Arcos, J.L.: On the formal specifications of electronic institutions. In Dignum, F., Sierra, C., eds.: Agent-mediated Electronic Commerce (The European AgentLink Perspective). Volume 1191 of LNAI., Berlin, Springer (2001) 126–147
6. Ferber, J., Gutknecht, O.: Operational semantics of a role-based agent architecture. In Jennings, N.R., Lesperance, Y., eds.: Intelligent Agents VI. Proceedings of the 6th Int. Workshop on Agent Theories, Architectures and Languages. Volume 1757 of LNAI., Springer (1999)
7. Jacobson, I., Griss, M., Jonsson, P.: Software Reuse. Architecture, Process and Organization for Business Success. Addison-Wesley (1997)
8. Zambonelli, F., Jennings, N.R., Wooldridge, M.: Organizational abstractions for the analysis and design of multi-agent systems. In Ciancarini, P., Wooldridge, M.J., eds.: AOSE. Volume 1957 of LNCS. Springer (2000) 235–252
9. Bergenti, F., Huhns, M.N.: On the use of agents as components of software systems. In Bergenti, F., Gleizes, M.P., Zambonelli, F., eds.: Methodologies and Software Engineering for Agent Systems. Kluwer (2004) 19–31
10. Allen, R., Garlan, D.: A Formal Basis for Architectural Connection. ACM Transactions on Software Engineering and Methodology **6** (1997) 213–249
11. Dignum, V., Vázquez-Salceda, J., Dignum, F.: Omni: Introducing social structure, norms and ontologies into agent organizations. In Bordini, R., Dastani, M., Dix, J., Seghrouchni, A., eds.: Programming Multi-Agent Systems Second International Workshop ProMAS 2004. Volume 3346 of LNAI., Springer (2005) 181–198
12. Ferber, J., Gutknecht, O., Michel, F.: From agents to organizations: An organizational view of multi-agent systems. In: AOSE. (2003)
13. Garlan, D., Monroe, R.T., Wile, D.: Acme: Architectural description of component-based systems. In Leavens, G.T., Sitaraman, M., eds.: Foundations of Component-Based Systems. Cambridge University Press (2000) 47–68
14. Bretier, P., Sadek, D.: A rational agent as the Kernel of a cooperative spoken dialogue system: Implementing a logical theory of interaction. In Müller, J.P., Wooldridge, M.J., Jennings, N.R., eds.: Proceedings of the ECAI'96 Workshop on Agent Theories, Architectures, and Languages: Intelligent Agents III. Volume 1193 of LNAI., Berlin, Springer (1997) 189–204
15. Foundation for Intelligent Physical Agents: FIPA Interaction Protocol Library Specification. http://www.fipa.org/repository/ips.html (2003)
16. Serrano, J.M., Ossowski, S.: A semantic framework for the recursive specification of interaction protocols. In: Coordination Models, Languages and Applications. Special Track of the 19th ACM Symposium on Applied Computing (SAC 2004). (2005)
17. Serrano, J.M.: The RICAJ framework. http://platon.escet.urjc.es/~jserrano (2005)
18. JADE: The JADE project home page. http://jade.cselt.it (2005)
19. Wooldridge, M., Parsons, S.: Languages for negotiation. In Horn, W., ed.: Proceedings of the Fourteenth European Conference on Artificial Intelligence (ECAI-2000), Berlin, IOS Press (2000) 393–397

20. Sierra, C., Jennings, N.R., Noriega, P., Parsons, S.:   A framework for argumentation-based negotiation. In Singh, M.P., Rao, A., Wooldridge, M.J., eds.: Proceedings of the 4th International Workshop on Agent Theories, Architectures, and Languages (ATAL-97. Volume 1365 of LNAI., Berlin, Springer (1998) 177–192

21. McBurney, P., Parsons, S.: A formal framework for inter-agent dialogues. In Müller, J.P., Andre, E., Sen, S., Frasson, C., eds.: Proceedings of the Fifth International Conference on Autonomous Agents, Montreal, Canada, ACM Press (2001) 178–179

22. Lebbink, H., Witteman, C., Meyer, J.J.: A dialogue game to offer an agreement to disagree. In Bordini, R., Dastani, M., Dix, J., Seghrouchni, A., eds.: Programming Multi-Agent Systems Second International Workshop ProMAS 2004. Volume 3346 of LNAI., Springer (2005)

23. Amgoud, L., Maudet, N., Parsons, S.: Modelling dialogues using argumentation. In: E. Durfee, editor, Proceedings of the 4th International Conference on Multi-Agent Systems (ICMAS-2000), Boston, MA, USA, IEEE Press (2000) 31–38

24. Walton, D.N., Krabbe, E.C.W.: Commitment in Dialogue. State University of New York Press (1995)

25. Cohen, P.R., Levesque, H.J.: Communicative actions for artificial agents. In Lesser, V., ed.: Proceedings of the First International Conference on Multi–Agent Systems, San Francisco, CA, MIT Press (1995) 65–72

26. Singh, M.P.: A social semantics for agent communication languages. In Dignum, F., Greaves, M., eds.: Issues in Agent Communication. LNAI, vol. 1916. Springer (2000) 31–45

27. Pitt, J., Mamdani, A.: A protocol-based semantics for an agent communication language. In Thomas, D., ed.: Proceedings of the 16th International Joint Conference on Artificial Intelligence (IJCAI-99-Vol1), S.F., Morgan Kaufmann Publishers (1999) 486–491

28. Dastani, M., van Riemsdijk, B., Hulstijn, J., Dignum, F., Meyer, J.J.: Enacting and deacting roles in agent programming. In Odell, J., Giorgini, P., Müller, J.P., eds.: Agent-Oriented Software Engineering V, 5th International Workshop, AOSE 2004,. Volume 3382 of Lecture Notes in Computer Science., Springer (2004)

29. Mehta, N.R., Medvidovic, N., Phadke, S.: Towards a taxonomy of software connectors. In: Proceedings of the 22nd International Conference on Software Engineering, ACM Press (2000) 178–187

30. Hindriks, K.V., Boer, F.S.D., der Hoek, W.V., Meyer, J.J.C.: Agent programming in 3APL. Autonomous Agents and Multi-Agent Systems **2** (1999) 357–401

31. Shoham, Y.: Agent-oriented programming. Artificial Intelligence **60** (1993) 51–92

Part III

Multi-agent Programming

An AgentSpeak Meta-interpreter and Its Applications

Michael Winikoff

RMIT University, Melbourne, Australia
winikoff@cs.rmit.edu.au

Abstract. A *meta-interpreter* for a language can provide an easy way of experimenting with modifications or extensions to a language. We give a meta-interpreter for the AgentSpeak language, prove its correctness, and show how the meta-interpreter can be used to extend the AgentSpeak language and to add features to the implementation.

1 Introduction

A *meta-interpreter* for a given programming language is an interpreter for that language which is written in the same language. For example, a program written in LISP that interprets LISP programs. A distinguishing feature of meta-interpreters (sometimes described as "meta-circular interpreters") is that certain details of the implementation are not handled directly by the meta-interpreter, but are delegated to the underlying implementation. For example, the original LISP meta-interpreter [1] defines the meaning of the symbol CAR (in code being interpreted by the meta-interpreter) in terms of the function car provided by the underlying implementation.

Although meta-interpreters can help in understanding a programming language, they do not give complete formal semantics, because certain aspects are delegated to the underlying language. For example, defining CAR in terms of car allows the meta-interpreter to correctly interpret programs (assuming that the underlying LISP implementation provides a suitable implementation of car), but does not shed any light on the meaning of the symbol CAR.

Meta-interpreters are useful as a way of easily prototyping extensions or changes to a language. For example, the Erlang language began life as a Prolog meta-interpreter which was then extended [2], and the interpreter for Concurrent Prolog can be seen as an extended Prolog meta-interpreter [3]. Being able to modify the semantics of an agent platform is often essential to researchers experimenting with extensions to agent platforms (e.g. [4,5]), and we argue that meta-interpreters can provide a much easier way of doing so than modifying the agent platform itself.

A drawback of meta-interpreters is the efficiency overhead of the additional layer of interpretation. However, this may not be significant in a prototype if the aim is to explore language design, rather than develop software of any significant size. It has also been suggested that *partial evaluation* could be used to "evaluate away" the meta-interpreter given a meta-interpreter and a program that it is to interpret [6].

In this paper we present a meta-interpreter for the *AgentSpeak*[1] agent-oriented programming language [7]. Although meta-interpreters exist for a range of programming

---

[1] Properly the language is called "AgentSpeak(L)", but in the remainder of the paper we shall refer to it as "AgentSpeak".

R.H. Bordini et al. (Eds.): ProMAS 2005, LNAI 3862, pp. 123–138, 2006.

languages, to the best of our knowledge this is the first meta-interpreter for an agent-oriented programming language.

Given the meta-interpreter for AgentSpeak, we then show a number of ways in which it can be modified for various purposes such as extending the language or adding functionality. The extensions that we present are very simple to implement: most involve the addition or change of a very small number of lines of code, and the code is written in AgentSpeak itself. By contrast, other approaches for making agent platforms extensible, such as PARADIGMA [8] and the Java Agent Framework[2], require the user to change languages to the implementation language and to delve into the implementation which includes both high-level control issues (what is the sequence of events), and lower-level representation issues (e.g. how are beliefs represented in terms of Java objects). Another approach, that is closer to the use of meta-interpreters, is that of Dastani et. al. [9] where the essential control cycle of an agent is broken down into primitives such as executing a goal, selecting a rule, etc. and a customised agent deliberation cycle is programmed in terms of these primitives using a meta-language. Compared with our approach, a disadvantage is the need to introduce a distinct meta-language with its own semantics. An interesting direction for future work would be to add similar primitives to the AgentSpeak language: this would extend the range of modifications that could be easily done using a meta-interpreter, and would avoid the need for a distinct meta-language by using AgentSpeak as its own meta-language.

The remainder of this paper is structured as follows. In section 2 we briefly summarise AgentSpeak's syntax, present (another) formal operational semantics for the language, and discuss a number of issues with the language. In section 3 we present a meta-interpreter for AgentSpeak and in section 4 show a number of modifications to the meta-interpreter. The implementation and performance of the meta-interpreter are briefly examined in section 5 and we then conclude in section 6.

2   AgentSpeak

Agent programming languages in the BDI tradition define an agent's behaviour by providing a library of recipes ("plans"), each indicating (i) the goal that it aims to achieve (modelled as a triggering event), (ii) the situations in which the plan should be used (defined using a logical condition, the "context condition"), and (iii) a plan body. Given a collection of plans, the following execution cycle is used:

1. An event is posted (which can be used to model a new goal being adopted by the agent, as well as new information ("percepts"), or a significant change that needs to be responded to).
2. The plans that handle that event are collected and form the *relevant* plan set.
3. A plan with a true context condition is *applicable*. An applicable plan is selected and its body is run.
4. If the plan fails, then an alternative applicable plan is found and its body is run. This repeats until either a plan succeeds, or there are no more applicable plans, in which case failure is propagated.

---

[2]   http://dis.cs.umass.edu/research/jaf/

There are a number of agent programming languages in the BDI tradition, such as dMARS [10], JAM [11], PRS [12,13], UM-PRS [14], and JACK [15]. The language AgentSpeak [7] was proposed by Anand Rao in an attempt to capture the common essence of existing BDI programming languages whilst having precisely defined semantics. Although Rao's formal semantics are incomplete, the work has inspired a number of implementations of AgentSpeak such as AgentTalk[3], an implementation based on SIM_AGENT [16], an implementation in Java that is designed to run on hand-held devices [17], and the Java-based Jason[4].

2.1 Syntax

An agent program (denoted by Π) consists of a collection of plan clauses of the form[5] $e : c \leftarrow P$ where e is an event[6], c is a context condition (a logical formula over the agent's beliefs) which must be true in order for the plan to be applicable and P is the plan body. A condition, C, is a logical formula over belief terms[7] (where b is a belief atom). The plan body P is built up the following constructs. We have primitive actions (act), operations to add ($+b$) and delete ($-b$) beliefs, a test for a condition ($?c$), and posting an event ($!e$). These can be sequenced ($P_1; P_2$). These cases are summarised below.

$$C ::= b \mid C \wedge C \mid C \vee C \mid \neg C \mid \exists x.C$$

$$P ::= act \mid +b \mid -b \mid ?c \mid !e \mid P; P$$

In addition to these constructs which can be used by the programmer, we define a number of constructs that are used in the formal semantics. These are:

- $true$ which is the empty step which always succeeds.
- $fail$ which is a step which always fails.
- $P_1 \rhd P_2$ is sequential disjunction: P_1 is run, and if it succeeds then P_2 is discarded and $P_1 \rhd P_2$ has succeeded. Otherwise, P_2 is executed.
- $(\!|\Delta|\!)$, where Δ is a set of plan bodies ($P_1 \ldots P_n$) which is used to represent a set of possible alternatives. It is executed by selecting a P_i from Δ and executing it (with the remainder of Δ being kept as possible alternatives in case P_i fails).

2.2 Semantics

In the years since Rao introduced AgentSpeak a number of authors have published (complete) formal semantics for the language. The specification language Z ("Zed")

---

[3] http://www.cs.rmit.edu.au/~winikoff/agenttalk

[4] http://jason.sourceforge.net/

[5] An omitted c is equivalent to $true$, i.e. $e \leftarrow P \equiv e : true \leftarrow P$.

[6] In Rao's original formulation, e is one of $+!g$, $+?g$, $-!g$, $-?g$, $+b$, $-b$ corresponding respectively to the addition of an achievement or query goal, the deletion of an achievement or query goal, the addition of a belief, and the deletion of a belief. In practice it is rare for any other than the $+!g$ form to be used. Indeed, Rao's semantics only address this event form, and so in the remainder of this paper we write e in the heads of clauses as shorthand for $+!e$. Similarly, we write e as shorthand for $!e$ in the bodies of clauses.

[7] In Rao's formulation only conjunctions of literals were permitted.

was used to formally specify the essential execution cycle of AgentSpeak [18], and an operational semantics for AgentSpeak was given by Moreira and Bordini [19]. The operational semantics that we give here is in the style of Plotkin's Structural Operational Semantics [20], and is based on the semantics of the CAN notation [21], which is a superset of AgentSpeak. Unlike the previous semantics, it includes failure handling: if a plan fails, then alternative plans are tried (step 4 of the execution cycle at the start of this section).

The semantics assume that operations exist that check whether a condition follows from a belief set ($B \models c$), that add a belief to a belief set ($B \cup \{b\}$), and that delete a belief from a belief set ($B \setminus \{b\}$). In the case of beliefs being a set of ground atoms these operations are respectively consequence checking, and set addition/deletion. Traditionally, agent systems have represented beliefs as a set of ground atoms, but there is no reason why more sophisticated representations and reasoning mechanisms (such as belief revision, Bayesian reasoning etc.) could not be used.

We define a basic configuration $S = \langle B, P \rangle$ where B is the beliefs of the agent and P is the plan body being executed (i.e. the intention). A transition $S_0 \longrightarrow S_1$ specifies that executing S_0 a single step yields S_1. We define $S_0 \overset{*}{\longrightarrow} S_n$ in the usual way: S_n is the result of zero or more single step transitions. The transition relation is defined using rules of the form $S \longrightarrow S'$ or of the form $\dfrac{S' \longrightarrow S_r}{S \longrightarrow S'_r}$; the latter are conditional with the top (numerator) being the premise and the bottom (denominator) being the conclusion. In order to make the presentation more readable we use the convention that where a component of S isn't mentioned it is the same in S and S' (and in S_r and S'_r). We also assume that B refers to the agent's beliefs, and elide angle brackets. Thus each of the following rules on the left is shorthand for the corresponding right rule.

$$\frac{B \models c}{?c \longrightarrow true} \ ?c \qquad \frac{B \models c}{\langle B, ?c \rangle \longrightarrow \langle B, true \rangle} \ ?c$$

$$\frac{P_1 \longrightarrow P'}{P_1; P_2 \longrightarrow P'; P_2} \ ; \qquad \frac{\langle B, P_1 \rangle \longrightarrow \langle B', P' \rangle}{\langle B, P_1; P_2 \rangle \longrightarrow \langle B', P'; P_2 \rangle} \ ;$$

The first rule above specifies that the condition test $?c$ transitions to true if the condition c is a consequence of the agent's beliefs ($B \models c$). The second rule specifies that $P_1; P_2$ transitions to $P'; P_2$ where P' is the result of a single execution step of P_1. The full set of rules are given in figure 1.

We extend simple configurations (which correspond to a single thread of execution within an agent) to agent configurations $S_A = \langle N, B, Ps \rangle$ which consist of a name, a single (shared) belief set, and a *set* of intentions (executing plans). The following rule defines the operational semantics over agent configurations in terms of the operational semantics over simple configurations.

$$\frac{P = \mathcal{S}_\mathcal{I}(\Gamma) \quad \langle B, P \rangle \longrightarrow \langle B', P' \rangle}{\langle N, B, \Gamma \rangle \longrightarrow \langle N, B', (\Gamma \setminus \{P\}) \cup \{P'\} \rangle} \ Agent$$

Note that there is non-determinism in AgentSpeak and in these semantics, e.g. the choice of plan to execute from a set of applicable plans. In addition, the *Agent* rule

$$\frac{B \models c}{?c \longrightarrow true} \ ?c_t \qquad \frac{B \not\models c}{?c \longrightarrow fail} \ ?c_f \qquad \frac{}{act \longrightarrow true} \ act$$

$$\frac{}{B, +b \longrightarrow B \cup \{b\}, true} \ {+b} \qquad \frac{}{B, -b \longrightarrow B \setminus \{b\}, true} \ {-b}$$

$$\frac{\Delta = \{P_i\theta | (t_i : c_i \leftarrow P_i) \in \Pi \wedge t_i = +!e \wedge B \models c_i\theta\}}{!e \longrightarrow (\!|\Delta|\!)} \ Ev$$

$$\frac{P_1 \longrightarrow P'}{P_1; P_2 \longrightarrow P'; P_2} \ ; \qquad \frac{}{true; P \longrightarrow P} \ ;t \qquad \frac{}{fail; P \longrightarrow fail} \ ;f$$

$$\frac{}{(\!|\,|\!) \longrightarrow fail} \ Sel_f \qquad \frac{P_i = \mathcal{S}_O(\Delta)}{(\!|\Delta|\!) \longrightarrow P_i \rhd (\!|\Delta \setminus \{P_i\}|\!)} \ Sel$$

$$\frac{P_1 \longrightarrow P'}{P_1 \rhd P_2 \longrightarrow P' \rhd P_2} \ \rhd \qquad \frac{}{true \rhd P \longrightarrow true} \ \rhd t \qquad \frac{}{fail \rhd P \longrightarrow P} \ \rhd f$$

$$\frac{P = \mathcal{S}_I(\Gamma) \quad \langle B, P \rangle \longrightarrow \langle B', P' \rangle}{\langle N, B, \Gamma \rangle \longrightarrow \langle N, B', (\Gamma \setminus \{P\}) \cup \{P'\} \rangle} \ Agent$$

$$\frac{P = \mathcal{S}_I(\Gamma) \quad P \in \{true, fail\}}{\langle N, B, \Gamma \rangle \longrightarrow \langle N, B, (\Gamma \setminus \{P\}) \rangle} \ Agent_{tf}$$

$$\frac{e \text{ is a new external event}}{\langle N, B, \Gamma \rangle \longrightarrow \langle N, B, \Gamma \cup \{!e\} \rangle} \ Agent_{ext}$$

Fig. 1. Operational Semantics for AgentSpeak

non-deterministically selects an executing plan. Instead of resolving these non-deterministic choices with an arbitrary policy, AgentSpeak defines selection functions $\mathcal{S}_I$, $\mathcal{S}_O$, and $\mathcal{S}_\mathcal{E}$ which respectively select a plan from the set of executing plans, an option from the set of applicable plans, and an event from the set of events. These are assumed to be provided by an AgentSpeak implementation and could also be replaced by the programmer.

Two of these selection functions ($\mathcal{S}_I$ and $\mathcal{S}_O$) are used in our formal semantics. The third selection function ($\mathcal{S}_\mathcal{E}$) is not used. The reason is that AgentSpeak splits event processing into two steps: adding the event to a set of events, and then selecting an event from the set and adding an intention corresponding to the applicable plans for that event. Since neither of these steps results in any changes to the agent's beliefs or to its environment, these two steps can be merged into a single atomic step without any loss of generality, i.e. events in AgentSpeak are eliminable (which has been formally proven by Hindriks et. al. [22]), and eliminating events simplifies the formal semantics.

2.3   Issues with AgentSpeak

The semantics of AgentSpeak as presented by Rao [7] are incomplete in a number of ways.

One area of incompleteness is failure recovery. All of the platforms that AgentSpeak was intended to model provide failure handling by trying alternative plans if a plan fails. This form of failure handling is based on the idea that for a given goal the relevant plans offer alternative means of achieving the goal, and that if one way of achieving a goal fails, alternative ways should be considered[8]. However, because AgentSpeak [7] focuses on describing the execution cycle around plan selection, it does not explicitly specify what should be done when a plan fails. This omission has led to certain implementations (such as Jason) not providing this form of failure handling[9]. We regard the omission of failure handling from Rao's semantics as unfortunate, since it has allowed implementations of AgentSpeak to be consistent with the original AgentSpeak paper, but to be incompatible with each other, and with other BDI-platforms. For example, although the semantics of Jason [19] are consistent with Rao's semantics [7], Jason's failure handling is quite different from that of other BDI-platforms such as dMARS [10], JAM [11], PRS [12,13], UM-PRS [14] and JACK [15].

A more subtle issue concerns the context condition of plans, specifically when are they evaluated? There are two possibilities: one can either evaluate the context conditions of all relevant plans at once giving a set of applicable plans, or one can evaluate relevant plans one at a time. The former – "eager" evaluation – is simpler semantically, but the latter – "lazy" evaluation – has the advantage that when a plan is considered for execution, its context condition is evaluated in the current state of the world, not in the state of the world that held when the event was first posted. The execution cycle at the start of this section is deliberately ambiguous about when context conditions are evaluated because BDI platforms differ in their handling of this issue. For example, JAM is eager whereas JACK is lazy, and in the CAN notation [21] each plan has an eager context condition *and* a lazy context condition. Since Rao's semantics for AgentSpeak specify eager evaluation [7, Figure 1], this is what our rule for Ev specifies.

Another issue concerns multiple solutions to context conditions. Suppose that we have a program clause $e : c \leftarrow P$ and that given the agent's current beliefs there are two different ways of satisfying c which give different substitutions θ_1 and θ_2. Should there be a single applicable plan $P\theta_i$ (where i is arbitrarily either 1 or 2), or should there be two applicable plan (instances), $P\theta_1$ and $P\theta_2$? Again, there is no consensus among BDI platforms, for example, JAM doesn't support multiple solutions to context conditions whereas JACK does. The semantics of AgentSpeak specifies multiple substitutions[10]: [7, Figure 1] computes the applicable plans O_e as $O_e = \{p\theta | \theta$ is an applicable unifier for event e and plan $p\}$. Our semantics therefore allows multiple substitutions, providing an applicable plan instance for each substitution.

Finally, a very minor syntactical issue that is nonetheless worth mentioning, is that having to write !e in the bodies of plans is error-prone: it is too easy to write e by mistake.

---

[8] This is not backtracking in the logic programming sense because there is no attempt to undo the actions of a failed plan.

[9] Jason provides an alternative form of failure handling where failure of a plan posts a failure event of the form $-!g$ and this event can be handled by an "exception handling" plan.

[10] But note that AgentSpeak's semantics are inconsistent as to whether θ is unique: although Figure 1 says that θ is "an" applicable unifier, Definition 10 says that θ is "**the** *correct answer substitution*" (emphasis added).

3 An AgentSpeak Meta Interpreter

Logic programming languages have particularly elegant meta-interpreters. For example, the meta-interpreter for Prolog is only a few lines long [23, section 17.2] and follows the pattern of interpreting connectives and primitives in terms of themselves (lines 1 & 2) and interpreting an atom by non-deterministically selecting a program clause and solving it (line 3).

1. solve(true) ← true.
2. solve((A,B)) ← solve(A) , solve(B).
3. solve(A) ← clause(A,B) , solve(B).

Meta-interpreters for other logic programming languages can be developed along similar lines, for example the logic programming language *Lygon*, which is based on linear logic, has a meta-interpreter along similar lines [24, section 5.6].

A meta-interpreter for AgentSpeak can also be defined similarly:

1. solve(Act) : isAction(Act) ← do(Act).
2. solve(true) ← true.
3. solve(fail) ← fail.
4. solve($-B$) ← $-B$.
5. solve($+B$) ← $+B$.
6. solve($?C$) ← $?C$.
7. solve(P_1 ; P_2) ← solve(P_1) ; solve(P_2).
8. solve(!E) : clause(+!E,G,P) $\wedge$ isTrue(G) ← solve(P).

We assume that the agent has a collection of beliefs of the form *clause(H,G,P)* which represent the program being interpreted.

In order for this meta-interpreter to work the underlying AgentSpeak implementation needs to support multiple solutions for context conditions. This is needed because the meta-interpreter's last clause, where alternative plans are retrieved, needs to have multiple instances corresponding to different solutions to *clause*.

Lemma 1. *If* $P \xrightarrow{*} X$ *and* $X \notin \{true, fail\}$ *then there exists* Y *such that* $X \longrightarrow Y$.

Theorem 1. *The above meta-interpreter is correct. Formally, given an AgentSpeak program* Π *and its translation into a collection of* clause *beliefs (denoted by* $\widehat{\Pi}$ *), the execution of an intention P with program* Π *is mirrored*[11] *by the execution of the intention* $solve(P)$ *with program* $\widehat{\Pi} \cup \mathcal{M}$, *where* $\mathcal{M}$ *denotes the above meta-interpreter. By "mirrored" we mean that* $\langle B, P \rangle \xrightarrow{*} \langle B', R \rangle$ *with* $R \in \{true, fail\}$ *and with a given sequence of actions A, if and only if* $\langle B, solve(P) \rangle \xrightarrow{*} \langle B', R \rangle$ *with the same sequence of actions A. We use* $S \Rightarrow S'$ *where* $S' = \langle A, B, R \rangle$ *as shorthand for "$S \xrightarrow{*} \langle B, R \rangle$ with the sequence of actions A". In the following proof we use* [] *to denote the empty sequence and* $\oplus$ *to denote sequence concatenation.*

Proof (sketch): *Proof by induction on the length of the derivation, we consider three cases since the other base cases are analogous to the first base case.*

---

[11] We don't precisely define this due to lack of space. The formal concept corresponding to this is bisimulation.

- *Firstly, consider a base case, $\langle B, +b \rangle \rightarrow \langle B \cup \{b\}, true \rangle$. Given the meta-interpreter clause* solve(+B) $\leftarrow$ +B *we have* $\langle B, solve(+b) \rangle \longrightarrow \langle B, (\!|+b|\!) \rangle \longrightarrow \langle B, +b \triangleright (\!|)\rangle \longrightarrow \langle B \cup \{b\}, true \triangleright (\!|)\rangle \longrightarrow \langle B \cup \{b\}, true \rangle$. *Since both sequences of transitions involve no actions we have that* $\langle B, +b \rangle \Rightarrow \langle [], B \cup \{b\}, true \rangle$ *and* $\langle B, solve(+b) \rangle \Rightarrow \langle [], B \cup \{b\}, true \rangle$. *Since both sequences of transitions are deterministic (no other transitions are possible) we have that* $\langle B, +b \rangle \Rightarrow S$ *iff* $\langle B, solve(+b) \rangle \Rightarrow S$ *as required.*

- *Now consider the case of* $P_1; P_2$. *We assume by the inductive hypothesis that* $\langle B, P_1 \rangle \Rightarrow S_1$ *iff* $\langle B, solve(P_1) \rangle \Rightarrow S_1$ *(where* $S_1 = \langle A_1, B_1, R_1 \rangle$) *and similarly for* P_2. *There are then two cases:* $P_1 \xrightarrow{*} true$ *and* $P_1 \xrightarrow{*} fail$. *In the first case we have that* $\langle B, P_1; P_2 \rangle \Rightarrow \langle A_1, B_1, true; P_2 \rangle$ *and then* $\langle B_1, true; P_2 \rangle \longrightarrow \langle B_1, P_2 \rangle \Rightarrow \langle A_2, B_2, R_2 \rangle$. *We also have that* $solve(P_1; P_2) \longrightarrow (\!|solve(P_1); solve(P_2)|\!) \longrightarrow solve(P_1); solve(P_2) \triangleright (\!|)$, *that* $\langle B, solve(P_1); solve(P_2) \triangleright (\!|) \rangle \Rightarrow \langle A_1, B_1, true; solve(P_2) \triangleright (\!|) \rangle$, *and that* $\langle B_1, true; solve(P_2) \triangleright (\!|) \rangle \longrightarrow \langle B_1, solve(P_2) \triangleright (\!|) \rangle \Rightarrow \langle A_2, B_2, R_2 \triangleright (\!|) \rangle$. *Now, regardless of whether* R_2 *is true or fail this transitions to* R_2 *since* $true \triangleright (\!|) \longrightarrow true$ *and* $fail \triangleright (\!|) \longrightarrow (\!|) \longrightarrow fail$. *Hence, in the first case, where* $P_1 \xrightarrow{*} true$, *we have that* $\langle B, P_1; P_2 \rangle \Rightarrow \langle A_1 \oplus A_2, B_2, R_2 \rangle$ *and that* $\langle B, solve(P_1; P_2) \rangle \Rightarrow \langle A_1 \oplus A_2, B_2, R_2 \rangle$. *In the second case,* $P_1 \xrightarrow{*} fail$, *we have that* $\langle B, P_1; P_2 \rangle \Rightarrow \langle A_1, B_1, fail; P_2 \rangle$. *We then have from the semantics that* $fail; P_2 \longrightarrow fail$ *and hence that* $\langle B, P_1; P_2 \rangle \Rightarrow \langle A_1, B_1, fail \rangle$. *We also have that* $solve(P_1; P_2) \longrightarrow (\!|solve(P_1); solve(P_2)|\!) \longrightarrow solve(P_1); solve(P_2) \triangleright (\!|)$, *that* $\langle B, solve(P_1); solve(P_2) \triangleright (\!|) \rangle \Rightarrow \langle A_1, B_1, fail; solve(P_2) \triangleright (\!|) \rangle$, *and that this then transitions to* $fail \triangleright (\!|) \longrightarrow (\!|) \longrightarrow fail$, *i.e. that* $\langle B, solve(P_1; P_2) \rangle \Rightarrow \langle A_1, B_1, fail \rangle$. *Thus, in both cases the execution of* $P_1; P_2$ *and* $solve(P_1; P_2)$ *mirror each other.*

- *We now consider the clause* solve(!E) : clause(+!E,G,P) $\wedge$ isTrue(G) $\leftarrow$ solve(P). *We have that if* Π *contains a program clause* +!e : $c \leftarrow p$ *then* !e $\longrightarrow (\!|\Delta|\!)$ *where* $\Delta = \{P_i\theta | (t_i : c_i \leftarrow P_i) \in \Pi \wedge t_i = +!e \wedge B \models c_i\theta\}$. *We also have* solve(!e) $\longrightarrow (\!|\Omega|\!)$ *where* Ω *is the instances of the clause in the meta-interpreter (since this is the only clause applicable to solving* !e*), i.e.* $\Omega = \{solve(P)\theta \mid B \models (clause(+!e, c_i, P) \wedge isTrue(c_i))\theta\}$. *Since for each clause* $t_i : c_i \leftarrow P_i$ *in* Π *there is an equivalent clause* (t_i, c_i, P_i) *in* $\widehat{\Pi}$ *we have that* $(t_i : c_i \leftarrow P_i) \in \Pi \wedge t_i = +!e$ *whenever* $B \models clause(+!e, c_i, P)$. *We also have that* $B \models c_i\theta$ *whenever* $B \models isTrue(c_i)\theta$ *(assuming a correct implementation of* isTrue*), thus* Ω *has the same alternatives as* Δ, *more precisely* $\Omega = \{solve(P) | P \in \Delta\}$. *Hence* !e $\longrightarrow (\!|\Delta|\!)$ *and* solve(!e) $\xrightarrow{*} (\!|\{solve(P) | P \in \Delta\}|\!)$. *Once a given* P_i *is selected from* Δ *(respectively* Ω*) we have by the induction hypothesis that* $\langle B, P_i \rangle \Rightarrow R_i$ *iff* $\langle B, solve(P_i) \rangle \Rightarrow R_i$ *which is easily extended to show that* $\langle B, P_i \triangleright (\!|\Delta \setminus \{P_i\}|\!) \rangle \Rightarrow R$ *iff* $\langle B, solve(P_i) \triangleright (\!|\Omega \setminus \{solve(P_i)\}|\!) \rangle \Rightarrow R$, *and hence, provided that* $S_{\mathcal{O}}(\Omega) = solve(S_{\mathcal{O}}(\Delta))$, *that* $\langle B, !e \rangle \Rightarrow R$ *iff* $\langle B, solve(!e) \rangle \Rightarrow R$ *as desired.* ∎

4   Variations on a Theme

In this section we present a number of variations of the meta-interpreter which extend the AgentSpeak language in various ways or add functionality to the implementation.

The key point here is that these modifications are very easy to implement by changing the meta-interpreter. We invite the reader to consider how much work would be involved in making each of these modifications to their favourite agent platform by modifying the underlying implementation.

4.1 Debugging

Just as with any form of software, agent systems need to be debugged. Unlike debugging logic programs, multi-agent systems offer additional challenges to debugging due to their concurrency, and due to the use of interaction between agents, i.e. debugging a MAS involves debugging multiple agents, not just a single agent.

One approach to debugging agent interaction is to use interaction protocols that have been produced as part of the design process. An additional "monitoring" agent is added to the system. This agent eavesdrops on conversations in the system and checks that the agents in the system are following the interaction protocols that they are supposed to follow [25,5].

In order for the monitoring agent to be able to eavesdrop on conversations all agents in the system need to send the monitoring agent copies of all messages that they send. This can be done manually, by changing the code of each agent. However, it is better (and more reliable) to do this by modifying the behaviour of the *send* primitive. Modifying the behaviour of a primitive using a meta-interpreter is quite simple: one merely modifies the existing clause that executes actions to exclude the primitive in question and adds an additional clause that provides the desired behaviour:

1a. solve(Act) : Act $\neq$ send(R,M) $\leftarrow$ do(Act).
1b. solve(send(R,M)) $\leftarrow$?myID(I) ; send(monitor,msg(I,R,M)) ; send(R,M).

Debugging the internals of agents can be done by enhancing the meta-interpreter in the same ways that one would enhance a Prolog meta-interpreter to aid in debugging [23, Section 17.2 & 17.3]. For example, it is easy to modify a meta-interpreter to trace through the computation. Another possibility is to modify the meta-interpreter to build up a data structure that captures the computation being performed. Once the computation has been completed the resulting data structure can be manipulated in various ways. Finally, another possible modification, suggested by one of the reviewers, is that the interpreter could be modified to send messages to a monitoring agent whenever the agent changes its beliefs:

4. solve($-B$) $\leftarrow$ $-B$; send(monitor,delbelief(B)).
5. solve($+B$) $\leftarrow$ $+B$; send(monitor,addbelief(B)).

4.2 Failure Handling

The meta-interpreter presented in the previous section delegates the handling of failure to the underlying implementation. However, if we want to change the way in which failure is handled, then we need to "take control" of failure handling. This involves extending the meta-interpreter to handle failure explicitly, which can be done by adding the following clause:

9. solve(!E) $\leftarrow$ fail.

This additional clause applies the default failure handling rule which simply fails, but it does provide a "hook" where we can insert code to deal with failure. For example, the code could call a planner to generate alternative plans. Note that this clause applies to any intention, and so it must be selected after the other clauses have been tried and failed. For example, if the selection function (S_O) selects clauses in the order in which they are listed in the program text then this clause should come last.

Another possible response to failure is to consider that perhaps the agent lacks the know-how to achieve the goal in question. One possible source for additional plans that might allow the agent to achieve its goal is other (trusted) agents [26]. Adding additional plans at run-time is difficult to do in compiled implementations, but is very easy to do using a meta-interpreter: since the program is stored as a belief set one simply adds to this belief set. Clause 9 below is intended as a replacement for the failure handling clause above. Once a plan is received it is stored, and then used immediately (*useClause*).

9. solve(!E) ← !getPlan(E,H,G,B) ; +clause(H,G,B) ; !useClause(G,B).
10. getPlan(E,H,G,B) :trust(Agent) ← send(Agent,getPlan(E)) ; receive(plan(H,G,B)).
11. useClause(G,B) : isTrue(G) ← solve(B).

4.3   Making Selection Explicit

AgentSpeak defines a number of selection functions that are used to select which event to process ($S_\mathcal{E}$), which intention to execute next ($S_\mathcal{I}$), and which plan (option) to use (S_O). In some implementations, such as Jason, these selection functions can be replaced with user-provided functions. However, other implementations may not allow easy replacement of the provided default selection functions. Even if the underlying implementation does allow for the selection functions to be replaced, using a meta-interpreter might be easier since it allows the selection functions to be written in AgentSpeak rather than in the underlying implementation language (for example in Jason user-provided selection functions are written in Java). By extending the meta-interpreter to make the selection of plans explicit we can override the provided defaults regardless of whether the implementation provides for this.

Extending the meta-interpreter to do plan selection (i.e. selecting the option, S_O), explicitly is done as follows. The key idea is that we add an additional argument to *solve* which holds the alternative options. Then instead of *solve(!E)* having multiple instances corresponding to different options, it collects all of the options into a set of alternatives (using *options*), selects an option (using the user-provided *select*), and solves it. The set of alternatives is ignored by solve, except where failure occurs, in which case we explicitly handle it (lines 9 and 10) by selecting an alternative from the set of remaining alternatives and trying it. If there are no alternatives remaining then fail (line 10).

0. solve(P) ← solve(P,[]).
1. solve(Act,_) : isAction(Act) ← do(Act).
... *Similarly, add an extra argument to solve for the other clauses*
7. solve((P_1; P_2), Os) ← solve(P_1, Os) ; solve(P_2, Os).
8. solve(!E,_) ← ?options(E,Os) ; ?select(I,Is,Os) ; solve(I,Is).

9. solve(B,Os) : Os ≠ [] ← ?select(I,Is,Os) ; solve(I,Is).
10. solve(B,Os) : Os = [] ← fail.
11. options(E,Os) ← find all solutions to *clause(+!E,G,P)* ∧ *isTrue(G)* and return the
    values of *P* in *Os*. In Prolog this could be written as *findall(P, appClause(E,P),Os)*
    where *appClause(E,B)* ← *clause(+!E,G,B)* ∧ *isTrue(G)*.
12. select(I,Is,Os) ← select an intention *I* from *Os* (*Is* is the remaining options, i.e.
    $Is = Os \setminus \{I\}$)

4.4 A Richer Plan Language

The bodies of plans in AgentSpeak are sequences of primitives (actions, belief manipulation etc.). This is fairly limited, and it can be useful to extend the language with
additional constructs such as disjunction and iteration:

9. solve(if(C,P_1,P_2)) : isTrue(C) ← solve(P_1).
10. solve(if(C,P_1,P_2)) : ¬ isTrue(C) ← solve(P_2).
11. solve(while(C,P)) : isTrue(C) ← solve(P) ; solve(while(C,P)).
12. solve(while(C,P)) : ¬ isTrue(C) ← true.

5 Implementation

The meta-interpreter described in section 3 has been implemented and tested. Since
Jason doesn't support failure handling and AgentTalk doesn't support multiple solutions
to a context condition, we have implemented a simple AgentSpeak interpreter in order
to be able to test the meta-interpreter. This simple interpreter runs under Prolog and can
be found at http://www.cs.rmit.edu.au/~winikoff/AS.

In addition to enabling the meta-interpreter to be tested, not just proven correct[12],
the implementation allowed us to quantify the efficiency overhead associated with the
additional layer of interpretation introduced by the meta-interpreter.

In order to measure the efficiency overhead incurred by the meta-interpreter we use
a simple benchmark program. This program controls a hypothetical robot who is travel-
ling along a one-dimensional track (perhaps a train track?) containing obstacles which
need to be cleared. The robot is given a list of obstacle locations which need to be
cleared, and it in turn travels to each obstacle, picks up the obstacle, returns to its starting point and disposes of the obstacle. Since we are interested in the relative efficiency
of the program running with and without the meta-interpreter, the details of the program
(given below) are not particularly important.

1. move ← message('moving towards obstacle').
2. moveback ← message('moving back towards base').
3. return(0) ← true.
4. return(N) : $N > 0 \wedge N1 = N - 1$ ← !moveback ; !return(N1).
5. get(0) ← true.

---

[12] *"Beware of bugs in the above code; I have only proved it correct, not tried it"* (Donald Knuth,
http://www-cs-faculty.stanford.edu/~knuth/faq.html)

6. get(N) : $N > 0 \wedge N1 = N - 1 \leftarrow$!move ; !get(N1).
7. collect([]) $\leftarrow$ true.
8. collect([$X|Xs$]) $\leftarrow$!get(X) ; message('pickup') ; !return(X) ; message('dispose')
   ; !collect(Xs).
9. collect30 $\leftarrow$!collect([1,2,3,4,5,6,7 . . . ,28,29,30]).

Handling the event *collect30* with the AgentSpeak interpreter (i.e. without the meta-interpreter) took 169 milliseconds[13] whereas the same program run with the meta-interpreter took 403 milliseconds. The graph below depicts the slow-down factor (403/169 = 2.42) compared with the slow-down factor for various Prolog meta-interpreters reported by O'Keefe [27, Page 273]. The comparison between our slow-down factor and O'Keefe's should be taken only as a rough indication that the overhead incurred by the AgentSpeak meta-interpreter is comparable to that of a carefully-engineered Prolog meta-interpreter. There are too many differences between our measurement and O'Keefe's measurements to allow much significance to be read into the results, e.g. the Prolog implementations are different, the underlying hardware is different, and O'Keefe measured the time to run a naïve reverse benchmark under the (Prolog) meta-interpreter and under the meta-interpreter interpreting itself interpreting the benchmark.

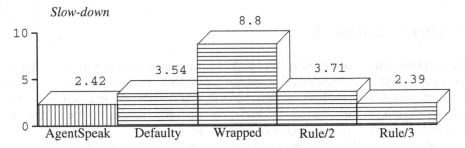

6   Conclusion

We presented an AgentSpeak meta-interpreter, proved its correctness, and then showed a number of ways in which it could be used to extend the AgentSpeak language and add facilities, such as debugging, to the AgentSpeak interpreter.

Although the extended meta-interpreters that we presented were very simple, not all extensions are easy to do with the meta-interpreter. The meta-interpreter that we presented focuses on the interpretation of individual intentions. Consequently, it is difficult to make changes that cut across intentions, such as changing the mechanism for selecting which intention to work on next ($\mathcal{S}_\mathcal{I}$). This doesn't mean that such changes cannot be made using a meta-interpreter, just that a different meta-interpreter is required which explicitly captures the top-level agent processing cycle including intention selection.

Another issue is that although the meta-interpreter has been presented as "an Agent-Speak meta-interpreter", in fact it won't work with the Jason or with the AgentTalk

---

[13] The AgentSpeak interpreter was run under B-Prolog (http://www.probp.com) version 5.0b on a SPARC machine running SunOS 5.9. Timings are the average of ten runs.

implementations of AgentSpeak! The reason for this is that due to the incompleteness of the semantics originally presented for AgentSpeak, different implementations of "AgentSpeak" actually implement quite different languages (some of these differences were discussed in section 2.3). There are a number of approaches to addressing this issue. One approach is for the authors of different AgentSpeak implementations to agree on a common semantics for the language. Another, less ambitious, approach to addressing this issue is to develop a more detailed meta-interpreter that explicitly handles areas where there are differences between implementations. For example, the meta-interpreter in section 4.3 explicitly handles alternative plans rather than delegating this to the underlying interpreter, and so should work with the AgentTalk implementation. A third approach is to use a different agent programming language such as CAN [21] or 3APL [9].

Both these areas are left for future work. An additional area for future work is extending the semantics given in section 2.2 to include variables and unification. In AgentSpeak unifying the triggering event with a clause head doesn't bind variables in the triggering event, because the clause could fail. Instead, when the clause succeeds the unification is applied to the triggering event [7]. This is a relatively subtle issue which only affects non-ground events, and if handled incorrectly causes the meta-interpreter clause $solve(?C) \leftarrow ?C$ to work incorrectly. Since this issue is both subtle and causes problems if done incorrectly, we feel that it is valuable to specify it formally.

Acknowledgements

I would like to thank James Harland for comments on a draft of this paper and to acknowledge the support of Agent Oriented Software Pty. Ltd. and of the Australian Research Council (ARC) under grant LP0453486. I would also like to thank the anonymous reviewers for their comments which helped improve this paper.

References

1. McCarthy, J.: Recursive functions of symbolic expressions and their computation by machine, part i. Communications of the ACM (1960) 184–195
2. Armstrong, J., Virding, S., Williams, M.: Use of prolog for developing a new programming language. In: The Practical Application of Prolog. (1992)
3. Shapiro, E.: A Subset of Concurrent Prolog and Its Interpreter. In: Concurrent Prolog: Collected Papers (Volume 1). MIT Press (1987) 27–83
4. Thangarajah, J., Winikoff, M., Padgham, L., Fischer, K.: Avoiding resource conflicts in intelligent agents. In van Harmelen, F., ed.: Proceedings of the 15th European Conference on Artificial Intelligence, IOS Press (2002)
5. Poutakidis, D., Padgham, L., Winikoff, M.: Debugging multi-agent systems using design artifacts: The case of interaction protocols. In: Proceedings of the First International Joint Conference on Autonomous Agents and Multi Agent Systems (AAMAS'02), ACM Press (2002) 960–967
6. Jones, N.D., Gomard, C.K., Sestoft, P.: Partial Evaluation and Automatic Program Generation. Prentice Hall International (1993) ISBN 0-13-020249-5.

7. Rao, A.S.: AgentSpeak(L): BDI agents speak out in a logical computable language. In de Velde, W.V., Perrame, J., eds.: Agents Breaking Away: Proceedings of the Seventh European Workshop on Modelling Autonomous Agents in a Multi-Agent World (MAAMAW'96), Springer Verlag (1996) 42–55 LNAI, Volume 1038.
8. Ashri, R., Luck, M., d'Inverno, M.: Infrastructure support for agent-based development. In: Foundations and Applications of Multi-Agent Systems, Springer-Verlag LNAI 2333 (2002) 73–88
9. Dastani, M., de Boer, F., Dignum, F., Meyer, J.J.: Programming agent deliberation: An approach illustrating the 3APL language. In Rosenschein, J.S., Sandholm, T., Wooldridge, M., Yokoo, M., eds.: Second International Joint Conference on Autonomous Agents and Multiagent Systems (AAMAS'03), Melbourne, Australia, ACM Press (2003) 97–104
10. d'Inverno, M., Kinny, D., Luck, M., Wooldridge, M.: A formal specification of dMARS. In Singh, M., Rao, A., Wooldridge, M., eds.: Intelligent Agents IV: Proceedings of the Fourth International Workshop on Agent Theories, Architectures, and Languages, Springer-Verlag LNAI 1365 (1998) 155–176
11. Huber, M.J.: JAM: A BDI-theoretic mobile agent architecture. In: Proceedings of the Third International Conference on Autonomous Agents (Agents'99). (1999) 236–243
12. Georgeff, M.P., Lansky, A.L.: Procedural knowledge. Proceedings of the IEEE Special Issue on Knowledge Representation **74** (1986) 1383–1398
13. Ingrand, F.F., Georgeff, M.P., Rao, A.S.: An architecture for real-time reasoning and system control. IEEE Expert **7** (1992)
14. Lee, J., Huber, M.J., Kenny, P.G., Durfee, E.H.: UM-PRS: An implementation of the procedural reasoning system for multirobot applications. In: Proceedings of the Conference on Intelligent Robotics in Field, Factory, Service, and Space (CIRFFSS'94). (1994) 842–849
15. Busetta, P., Rönnquist, R., Hodgson, A., Lucas, A.: JACK Intelligent Agents - Components for Intelligent Agents in Java. Technical report, Agent Oriented Software Pty. Ltd, Melbourne, Australia (1998) Available from http://www.agent-software.com.
16. Machado, R., Bordini, R.: Running AgentSpeak(L) agents on SIM_AGENT. In Meyer, J.J., Tambe, M., eds.: Intelligent Agents VIII - Proceedings of the Eighth International Workshop on Agent Theories, Architectures, and Languages (ATAL-2001), Springer-Verlag LNAI 2333 (2001)
17. Rahwan, T., Rahwan, T., Rahwan, I., Ashri, R.: Agent-based support for mobile users using AgentSpeak(L). In Giorgini, P., Henderson-Sellers, B., Winikoff, M., eds.: Agent-Oriented Information Systems (AOIS 2003): Revised Selected Papers, Springer LNAI 3030 (2004) 45–60
18. d'Inverno, M., Luck, M.: Understanding Agent Systems. Springer-Verlag (2001)
19. Moreira, A., Bordini, R.: An operational semantics for a BDI agent-oriented programming language. In Meyer, J.J.C., Wooldridge, M.J., eds.: Proceedings of the Workshop on Logics for Agent-Based Systems (LABS-02). (2002) 45–59
20. Plotkin, G.: Structural operational semantics (lecture notes). Technical Report DAIMI FN-19, Aarhus University (1981 (reprinted 1991))
21. Winikoff, M., Padgham, L., Harland, J., Thangarajah, J.: Declarative & procedural goals in intelligent agent systems. In: Proceedings of the Eighth International Conference on Principles of Knowledge Representation and Reasoning (KR2002), Toulouse, France (2002)
22. Hindriks, K.V., Boer, F.S.D., van der Hoek, W., Meyer, J.J.C.: A formal embedding of AgentSpeak(L) in 3APL. In Antoniou, G., Slaney, J., eds.: Advanced Topics in Artificial Intelligence, Springer Verlag LNAI 1502 (1998) 155–166
23. Sterling, L., Shapiro, E.: The Art of Prolog. Second edn. MIT Press (1994)
24. Winikoff, M.: Logic Programming with Linear Logic. PhD thesis, Melbourne University (1997)

25. Padgham, L., Winikoff, M., Poutakidis, D.: Adding debugging support to the prometheus methodology. EAAI special issue on "Agent-oriented software development" **18/2** (2005)
26. Ancona, D., Mascardi, V., Hübner, J.F., Bordini, R.H.: Coo-agentspeak: Cooperation in agentspeak through plan exchange. In Jennings, N.R., Sierra, C., Sonenberg, L., Tambe, M., eds.: Proceedings of the Third International Joint Conference on Autonomous Agents and Multiagent Systems, ACM Press (2004) 698–705
27. O'Keefe, R.A.: The Craft of Prolog. MIT Press (1990)

A   A Failed Attempt

In order to show that the meta-interpreter isn't obvious, here we briefly present an alternative meta-interpreter that was considered and explain why it doesn't work. The intention of this meta-interpreter was that by evaluating the context condition as part of the body, rather than the context condition, we could obtain lazy context conditions regardless of the implementation's semantics.

1. solve(Act) : isAction(Act) $\leftarrow$ do(Act).
2. solve(true) $\leftarrow$ true.
3. solve(fail) $\leftarrow$ fail.
4. solve($-B$) $\leftarrow -B$.
5. solve($+B$) $\leftarrow +B$.
6. solve($?C$) $\leftarrow ?C$.
7. solve(P_1 ; P_2) $\leftarrow$ solve(P_1) ; solve(P_2).
8. **solve(!E) : clause(+!E,G,P) $\leftarrow$?isTrue(G) ; solve(P).**

Unfortunately this meta-interpreter does not give correct semantics. The reason is that in order to determine that a clause is not applicable it must be selected and tried, after which it is discarded. This means that if another plan is tried and fails, preceding clauses are no longer available. To see this, consider the following program[14]:

1. g : p $\leftarrow$ print('lazy.').
2. g : true $\leftarrow$ +p ; fail.
3. g : p $\leftarrow$ print('clause 3').
4. g : true $\leftarrow$ print('eager.').

If this program is run with a lazy implementation then the following occurs:

1. Clause 2 is selected (since clause 1 isn't applicable)
2. The belief p is added and clause 2 then fails
3. Clause 1 is now applicable and is selected, printing `lazy` before succeeding.

If the program is run with an eager implementation then the following occurs:

1. Clauses 2 and 4 are applicable, whereas clauses 1 and 3 are discarded.
2. Clause 2 is selected

---

[14] We assume that $\mathcal{S}_\mathcal{O}$ selects clause in the order in which they are written.

3. The belief p is added and clause 2 then fails
4. Clause 4 now runs printing `eager` before succeeding.

However, if the program is run with the incorrect meta-interpreter above then the following occurs:

1. Clause 1 is selected and its guard evaluated. Since the guard is false, the clause instance fails, and it is discarded.
2. Clause 2 is selected, its guard succeeds and it runs, adding p and then failing.
3. Clause 3 is now considered, its guard succeeds and it runs, printing `clause 3` before succeeding.

It should be noted that although this interpreter doesn't work, it is certainly possible to write an interpreter that gives lazy context conditions even when run under an eager implementation. This can be done by making selection explicit (see section 4.3).

Extending the Capability Concept for Flexible BDI Agent Modularization

Lars Braubach, Alexander Pokahr, and Winfried Lamersdorf

Distributed Systems and Information Systems,
Computer Science Department, University of Hamburg,
Vogt-Kölln-Str. 30, 22527 Hamburg, Germany
{braubach, pokahr, lamersd}@informatik.uni-hamburg.de

Abstract. Multi-agent systems are a natural way of decomposing complex systems into more manageable and decentralized units. Nevertheless, as single agents can represent complex subsystems themselves, software engineering principles for the design and implementation of coherent parts of single agents are necessary for producing modular and reusable software artifacts. This paper picks up the formerly proposed capability concept for structuring BDI agents in functional clusters, and generalizes and extends it to support a higher degree of reusability. The resulting mechanism allows for designing and implementing BDI agents as a composition of configurable agent modules (capabilities). It is based on a black-box approach with export interfaces that is in line with object-oriented engineering principles.

1 Introduction

One important traditional software-engineering principle is *modularization* [12], which means that functionality is packaged into delimited units. Thereby, referring to [6] a module is seen as "[...] a well-defined component of a software system that provides a set of services to other modules. Services are computational elements that other modules may use."

For example, in the imperative paradigm modules represent collections of procedures, data types and constants from which only a small subset is made accessible through the module's export interface. For other paradigms such as functional programming or object-orientation adapted forms of modularization have been developed as well. Generally, modularization achieves inter alia the following three advantages: First and most importantly, it enables reuse and extensibility of software artifacts as modules form separate units of functionality. Secondly, modules enhance flexibility through encapsulation, because changes inside a module should not affect other modules. Thirdly, modularization increases the effectiveness of software development and the comprehensibility of the applications as separate modules represent abstractions that can be considered independently for understanding cutouts of the system.

To achieve those advantages in practice, fundamental design principles have to be taken into account for module creation. On the one hand the *coupling*

R.H. Bordini et al. (Eds.): ProMAS 2005, LNAI 3862, pp. 139–155, 2006.
© Springer-Verlag Berlin Heidelberg 2006

of different modules (interrelationships) should be minimized, whereas on the other hand the *cohesion* of the elements contained in a module should be maximized [18]. The basic idea of modules is to abstract from implementation details through *information hiding* [12], which means that the internals of a module are encapsulated and can therefore be changed without affecting other modules. Adhering to these principles ensures that modules represent self-contained, reusable entities for some well-defined functionality.

For the agent paradigm modularization is also an important topic. Even though multi-agent systems are a natural technique for decomposing complex scenarios into autonomous actors, the resulting agents can still be fairly complex. Breaking down such complex agents into teams of smaller ones is not always an appropriate solution, because splitting up a self-contained entity requires a connection between those smaller agents to be established at the communication level, leading to possibly inefficient solutions.

Hence, specifically adapted concepts for structuring the internals of an agent are necessary. Such a structuring technique depends in turn on the considered agent architecture determining the high-level elements and processes which may or may not be suitable for modularization. Cognitive architectures such as 3APL[4], BDI [16] or SOAR [11] propose different high-level abstractions leading to possibly different modularization approaches. In this paper Busetta et al.'s capability concept [3] for modularization of BDI agents is taken up and extended to support more flexible agent configuration.

In the next section the original capability concept is shortly sketched and its limitations are described. In section 3 the extended capability concept is proposed and its implementation within the Jadex BDI reasoning engine is described in section 4. The concepts are further clarified by an example application in section 5. A summary and an outlook of future work conclude the paper.

2   Capabilities Revisited

The capability concept for structuring BDI agents in modules and its implementation within the JACK agent framework [8] was first described in [3]. The main idea of the original proposal is to define beliefs, goals and plans that functionally belong together in a common namespace called capability. In addition, scoping rules allow for an exact specification of the parts of a capability that should be visible from the outside. According to [3] a capability is defined as:

1. an identifier (that is, a name);
2. a set of plans;
3. a fragment of the knowledge base concerning the beliefs manipulated by the plans of the capability;
4. the visibility rules for those beliefs, that is, which ones are restricted to the plans of the capability and which ones can be seen from the outside;
5. which types of events, generated as a consequence of the activity of the capability are visible outside its scope, and their processing algorithm;

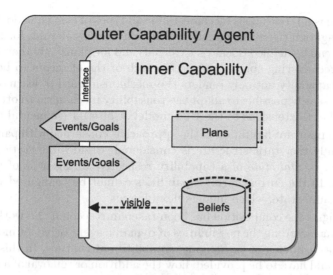

Fig. 1. Original capability concept

6. which types of events, generated outside the capability, are relevant to the capability (that is, to one or more of its plans);
7. finally, recursive inclusion of other capabilities.

Each capability type specified in this way can be included in another capability or in the agent. For this inclusion an additional symbolic name has to be provided to allow multiple usages of one capability type within the same context. This is similar to the usage of a class in an object-oriented language, i.e. the symbolic name identifies a specific instance. In Fig. 1 the main ideas of the original capability concept are also illustrated graphically. The interface of the inner capability is defined by means of the (different kinds of) external events the inner capability can process and also by those exported events that could be handled in the outside capability. In addition beliefs of the inner capability can be made visible for the outer capability, while plans are only visible locally.

As an example, in [3] negotiation functionalities for two types of agents participating in a negotiation are described (initiator and bidder). These functionalities can be encapsulated in two capabilities and reused by all agents which like to take part in a negotiation.

2.1   Limitations

The original capability concept as outlined above allows for grouping mental attitudes according to their functional purpose and therefore is an effective technique for modularization. Nevertheless, this approach exposes some conceptual limitations that are discussed next:

– Concerning the export interface, the approach distinguishes explicitly between mental attitudes and treats them in a different manner. This means that there is no continuous mechanism for all types of elements. So, for events the propagation (from the outside/to the outside) is relevant, for beliefs the visibility can be defined (local vs. external) and for plans only their usage can be declared. Having specific means for each of the elements to be grouped inside a capability not only renders the mechanism hard to learn and use, it is also not easily possible to adapt the reusability mechanism to other mental notions, be it extensions to the BDI model or alternative mental models.

- Another important limitation of the approach is concerned with parametrization as only the static structure is considered. Besides the static structure the *initial mental state* of a capability respective an agent is of major importance. In the current form, capabilities cannot be configured with some initial mental state, which hinders flexible reuse.
- Only design-time composition has been taken into account. No work has been done so far regarding the possibilities of dynamic agent behavior modification by adding/removing or exchanging capabilities at runtime. In this respect a model would have to be provided, how the addition or removal of a capability influences the functionality of other capabilities.
- The concept does not allow for refinement of parts of a capability specification. E.g. it is not possible to provide an extended context condition for a plan. Elements have to be used in exactly the way they are defined in the inner capability, which hinders flexible reuse.

3   Extending the Notion of Capabilities

This section presents a capability concept, suitable to address the aforementioned shortcomings. It follows the general idea of a capability being "[...] a cluster of plans, beliefs, events and scoping rules over them" [3], but differs from the original capability concept in several important ways.

1. The *locality principle* assures that all elements of a capability are part of exactly one capability.
2. A general *import/export mechanism* is introduced to define which elements are part of the capability's interface and are visible from the outside. Elements contained in the interface can be used in the containing capability by defining local proxy elements.
3. A *creation semantics* determines which element instances of a static structure (composed of a single concrete element type and arbitrarily many proxies) are created at runtime.
4. The explicit specification of *initial configurations* separately to the static structure of a capability is supported.
5. The foundations of *dynamic capability modifications* are layed down.

These extensions are discussed in the following sections.

3.1   Locality Principle

The original capability concept assumes a global repository of mental elements (i.e. event or plan type specifications) which are then just referenced in a capability definition. Therefore the same type of element can be used in different capabilities or even agents (i.e. for sending and receiving message events).

In our model we follow the locality principle of elements which means that a capability itself defines the available types (e.g. of beliefs), and forms the namespace for these types. These element types are not globally available, but only inside the capability. As a consequence e.g. from within plans only locally defined beliefs are accessible, which means that it is not sufficient to know that a belief of a contained capability is exported. To be able to use such a belief a local reference has to be declared.

Following the locality principle has the main advantage of increasing the *transparency*. This is because e.g. a plan only depends on local elements and not on elements defined in a subcapability. Changes with respect to a subcapability are therefore hidden from the plan. Another advantage concerns the *openness* of agent applications. As no global elements such as message events are specified, each agent can interpret a received message in its own respect, not depending on message representation details of other agents.

3.2   Import/Export Mechanism

The locality principle requires a newly designed import/export concept. For usability, all mental notions and their interrelations across capability borders should be defined using the same mechanism. The main idea is to cleanly distinguish relationships between different mental elements (such as a certain goal being handled by a certain plan) from the import and export specifications that relate elements from different capabilities. Relationships between mental elements follow the locality principle, and therefore are only allowed inside a capability. Import and export specifications permit a single logical element to be present in several connected capabilities using a proxy model (see Fig. 2). The figure shows how a capability (*outer*) can reuse functionality from another (*inner*) capability. Concrete elements (which may be beliefs, goals, etc.) are presented as white rectangles. Proxy elements (i.e. placeholders for beliefs or goals of another capability) are shown as grey rectangles.

Per default, any concrete element is *internal*, meaning that it is only visible locally in its enclosing capability. E.g. internal beliefs can only be accessed by plans of the same capability. If an element should be accessible to the outer capability it can be marked as *exported*. To be used from the outside, a placeholder (called *reference*) for the original element has to be defined in the outer capability. The reference element specification includes the relative name of the inner element it refers to (e.g. in the form "subcapability.elementname"). Note that references to exported inner elements are optional. An outer capability is only required to provide a reference, when the element is accessed from other elements of the outer capability. For example when a plan of the outer capability wants to access a belief defined in the inner capability, the outer capability

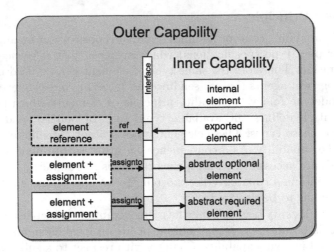

Fig. 2. Reference concept

defines a belief reference, which acts as a proxy for the inner belief. The plan accesses the proxy like it would access a locally defined belief. Therefore, it is transparent to the plan that the belief is actually defined in the inner capability.

A capability may also include *abstract* elements, i.e. proxies which are not assigned to any concrete element by themselves. An abstract *optional* element is an element, which does not require an assignment, what means that the functionality of the capability can also be used, when this element is not present. For example, an abstract belief provides an extension point, where the outer capability can add knowledge to the inner capability. A plan in the inner capability can then check if the belief is available and proceed in different ways according to the information from the belief. An abstract *required* element is an element, which is required for proper operation of the capability.

Both required and optional abstract elements are assigned from the outside, by adding "assignto" specifications to concrete elements of the outer capability. An outer element may be assigned to many different abstract elements, but an abstract element must be assigned from (at most) a single concrete element. In addition, it is also possible to define proxies for proxies, i.e. to define a reference to an element which is itself a reference, or to assign an abstract element to another abstract element of a child capability. This allows building up reference structures through multiple levels of capabilities. E.g. in the figure, the outer capability might choose to re-export elements referenced from the inner capability.

3.3   Creation Semantics

The proxy concept introduced in the last section shows how an element can be visible in a different capability. The definition of proxies only specifies a static structure of references for element visibility. It depends on the creation context, if an instance of a proxy is created for a specific element instance.

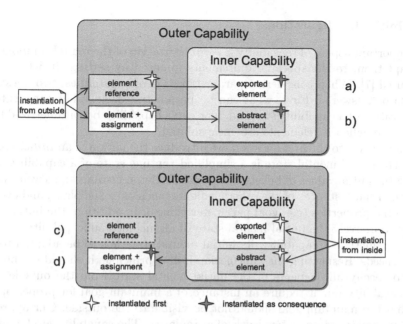

Fig. 3. Element creation cases: a) instantiation of a reference, b) instantiation of an element, when an abstract element exists inside, c) instantiation of an element, when a reference exists outside, d) instantiation of an abstract element assigned from the outside

It has to be assured that changes outside of a capability do not affect the internal functionality, as this would violate the information hiding principle.

To solve these issues semantics is associated to the creation process of elements and proxies in all possible cases. On the one hand, a proxy might be in the outer capability (i.e. a reference) or in the inner capability (i.e. an abstract element). On the other hand, creation of an element might be issued on the original element itself, or the proxy. This leads to four different cases (cf. Fig. 3):

In the first two cases (a and b) the creation is triggered inside the outer capability. It is safe to create elements in the inner capability, because they are an explicit part of the interface. In the last case (d) the initially created element in the inner capability is just a proxy. Therefore it is necessary to subsequently create the original element in the outer capability. As can be seen in the figure, it is only in case c, that a proxy element is not instantiated. In this case the original element is part of the inner capability and creation is triggered from the inside. Creating the outer element would lead to problems, because the element (e.g. an event) might inadvertently be handled in the outside capability, thereby breaking functionality of the inner capability. The export / reference concept assures that an element can be used from the outside (e.g. a goal created outside), but the local functionality (e.g. the goal processing) remains unchanged. Abstract elements provide a way for the inner capability to connect to functionality of an outer capability.

3.4 Initial Configurations

One important aspect of reusability is *parametrization* of the reused components, to adapt them to the special requirements imposed by settings in which they get reused [7]. When considering parametrization of capabilities, two questions have to be answered: First, what can be parametrized, i.e. what constitutes a configuration of a capability? Second, how can a capability be parametrized from the outside, when its elements are encapsulated?

As an answer to the first question, we introduce the notion of an *initial mental state*. The initial mental state is a simplified runtime state of a capability, containing the initial values of beliefs (which are singleton instances), as well as zero or more initial instances of the other elements (such as goals, plans, and events) with initial properties (e.g. goal parameter values). In addition, the initial state defines recursively the initial mental state of all included subcapabilities.

To parametrize a capability, its initial mental state has to be adapted to the current needs. Respecting the information hiding principle, it should not be possible to specify all elements of the initial mental state from the outside. E.g. some capability might require an instance of a maintain goal for proper operation, but the maintain goal should not be visible to the outside. Our approach allows parametrization at two levels of granularity: The capability level, and the level of individual elements. A capability itself can provide one or more initial configurations, which can be referenced by a given name. In this way, common use cases can be captured as a whole, allowing easy out-of-the-box reuse. These configurations are part of the capability, and therefore can contain exported and internal elements. Parametrization at the level of individual elements is only possible when these elements are exported. For example for exported beliefs, the outer capability can override the initial value by defining a reference and locally assigning a new value to this referenced belief.

3.5 Dynamic Runtime Composition

The new improved capability concept is also capable of handling various issues concerning runtime modification of agent behaviour. For that purpose generally two distinct kinds of operations can be performed.

On the one hand complete capabilities could be plugged into or removed from an agent at runtime. The addition of a capability at runtime is conceptually not difficult as it requires only information about the capability type, its initial state, the target capability within the agent and some connection data such as the instance name of the new capability. Given that all information is provided the capability can be linked with the target capability using the connection data and can subsequently be started meaning that its initial state will be executed. The removal of a capability at runtime is far more intricate as the agent's execution state must be considered before a capability can be removed safely. This means the agent e.g. could currently utilize plans or goals from the capability to remove and it needs to be determined if these plans or goals should be executed completely before removal.

On the other hand the modification of a capability at runtime should be possible. Prerequisite for these kinds of modifications is that each capability relies on its personal copy of the underlying capability model, so that changes can be performed without affecting other capability instances of the same type. The creation process for a new model element (regardless if it is an element or an element reference) consists basically of two steps. First, the element has to be created in the capability model. In a second step the elements has to be registered at the runtime layer, making the agent aware of its new element. For the deletion of an element at runtime a similar process can be used. The element has to be deregistered at the capability instance and can afterwards be deleted from the model. In this respect it has again to be considered if existing elements of the removed type should be discarded at once.

For the complete freedom of removing or exchanging a capability at runtime it is a necessary prerequisite that a capability instance is a self-contained entity with well-defined connection points. In the proposed capability approach this is supported by the locality principle which is also valid for capabilities at runtime. Elements from other capabilities are not accessed directly but through local proxies. When a capability or element of a capability is removed, proxies in other capabilities can be preserved, and later be reconnected when an alternative capability or element is available. Further elaborating and implementing the details of this mechanism is planned for future work.

3.6   Discussion

Capabilities are a decomposition concept for agents allowing to reuse functionality captured in a self-contained module with clearly defined import and export interface. This form of reuse is termed blackbox-reuse as only the interface and no details about the internals are known. In contrast to (more flexible) whitebox-reuse changing the internals of a blackbox-component does not break existing usages, leading to application designs that are easier to maintain [17].

Furthermore, the capability concept addresses most of the five fundamental criteria of modularization from [12]: decomposability, composability, understandability, continuity and protection. The concept naturally supports decomposability and composability as functional coherent units can be built and connected in flexible ways. The understandability for BDI agents is increased because capabilities represent encapsulated functionalities that normally have few connections to other capabilities. Additionally, the understandability for a single capability is supported by the locality principle which makes them self-contained. The continuity criterion requires that a small change of the problem specification leads to limited changes in only few concerned modules. This is achieved by extensively using the information hiding principle using small and simple interfaces through the general import / export mechanism. Finally, protection is attained when the effect of an abnormal condition occurring at runtime is confined to the originating module. Capabilities do not add a new level of protection to the development of BDI agents. Nevertheless, failure of plans is already covered by the normal BDI mechanism.

Another decomposition method for BDI agents inspired directly from object-oriented ideas was proposed in [10]. It is based mainly on the inheritance mechanism for agent classes explicitly allowing also multiple inheritance relationships between agent classes. In order to control the exact semantics of inheritance relationships an agent class consists of individual submodels for beliefs, plans and goals respecting the specifics of the individual mentalistic concepts. Similar to capabilities, this approach decomposes agents at the detailed design and implementation level. Other decomposition approaches consider high-level concepts such as roles. E.g. in [9] an experimental system based on the Zeus [13] toolkit is described, which uses roles to group primitive and rule-based tasks as well as external code into a reusable module. Role constraints and a role algebra are introduced to describe how agents can be statically composed of predefined roles. Dastani et al. describe in [5] a formal model of roles composed of beliefs, goals, plans and rules. The approach focuses on an operational semantics for dynamic enacting and deacting of roles. It does not cover interfaces between different roles of the same agent, but assumes that only one role is active at each moment in time.

4   Realization of Capabilities

The extended capability concept as presented in the last section has been implemented within the Jadex BDI reasoning engine [1,15]. In Jadex agents are specified in two different kinds of files. The static structure of an agent or capability including its initial mental state is defined within an XML-file that adheres to the Jadex BDI metamodel specified in XML-schema. The behavior of Jadex agents is encoded within plan bodies that are programmed with plain Java. From within user programmed plans the BDI facilities such as modifying beliefs or creating goals are accessible through an API.

In Fig. 4 the condensed Jadex capability metamodel is depicted. All entities share the same abstract base class "element". Furthermore an agent is modeled as an extended capability. This reflects the fact that agent specifications are very

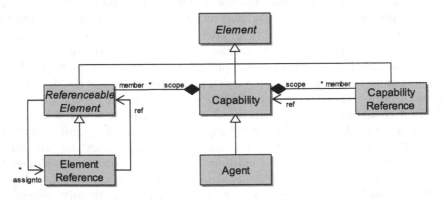

Fig. 4. Capability metamodel

similar to capabilities and additionally may support entities composed of agents such as groups sharing e.g. some beliefs or goals.

A capability is composed of two different kinds of elements. On the one hand it is a container for "referenceable elements", which form the abstract base class for mental attitudes such as beliefs, goals, plans and events (not illustrated). Their common property is that they can be referenced by a proxy termed "element reference" from another capability. Element references, which are used to represent abstract elements as well, are themselves also "referenceable elements" as references to references are explicitly allowed in the model. On the other hand capabilities can contain subcapabilities, which is expressed by the relationship to "capability references". This indirection is used, because a capability includes a subcapability under a symbolic name allowing for inclusion of more than one instance of the same capability type.

5   Example Application

To illustrate the aforementioned concepts in this section an example application for a hunter-prey scenario is detailed. Even though the hunter-prey domain is a well-known and extensively studied AI playing field, various different interpretations exist making it necessary to outline our settings. The environment is inhabited by two different species of creatures (hunters and preys) and various obstacles (trees) which hinder them in their movements. The creature's main objective is to survive by looking for food. Hence, hunters are exploring the terrain in search of prey which they will try to chase and eat. Contrarily, preys look for plants growing in the environment and try to flee if chased by some hunter.

5.1   Scenario Design Details

This scenario is designed as (possibly distributed) agent-based simulation in which the creatures as well as the environment are represented as autonomous entities. The environment agent is responsible not only for holding a representation of the environment which is set up as a discrete grid world, but also for controlling the advancement of time. For simplicity reasons a time-driven scheme is employed, which requires the creatures to announce their next intended action within an adjustable timeframe.

Initially, creatures are placed at random locations in the world and are only able to perceive a cutout of the world according to their vision (automatically sent from the environment to the creatures at the beginning of each round). In each round the creatures have to decide which action they would like to perform. Possible actions are moving to an adjacent field (up, down, left or right) or trying to eat some object resp. creature near to it. The actions have to be communicated to the environment as messages following a hunter-prey domain ontology. If a creature fails to provide its intended action within the round time (e.g. because it reasons too slowly or a network error occurred) the simulation proceeds executing no action in that round for the creature.

As all creatures need basic abilities for sensing and acting in their environment it is natural and advantageous to develop a basic module for handling this fundamental aspect of creature behavior in a reusable way.

5.2 Defining a Capability

In Fig. 5 the capability specification for basic sensing and acting in the environment is depicted. It has two main purposes: The first one is to automatically process "inform vision" messages (lines 51-65) which contain the current vision of the creature sent from the environment. Whenever such a message event is received the "update vision" plan (lines 44-47) is triggered. This plan will extract the information contained in the vision and update the creature's belief sets about known hunters, preys, obstacles and food (lines 13-16) accordingly. Note that all of these belief sets are exported to be accessible from an outer capability and the creature agent itself.

The second purpose is to provide high-level abstractions for performing actions in the environment. Therefore, the capability defines exported goal types for moving and eating (lines 24-29). To initiate an action, a creature has to create and dispatch a new move or eat goal. Such goal instances will subsequently be handled within the act/sense capability by triggering corresponding move or eat plans (lines 36-43) which encode the action into a message and communicate with the environment agent (defined as belief in line 17).

To locate the environment agent the act/sense capability itself relies on an included directory facilitator (DF) capability (lines 8-10) which offers goals for (de)registering and searching at a DF. For being able to access the DF functionality the act/sense capability defines a concrete goal reference to the "df search" goal (lines 30-32). Hence, from within plans of the act/sense capability "df search" goals can be created and dispatched.

For the communication with the environment agent it is necessary for the creature to identify itself which is done by including information available in the "my self" belief. As the act/sense capability should be usable by hunters as well as preys the value depends on the concrete usage of the capability. Thus, the belief is specified as abstract and required (which is the default for abstract beliefs) and needs to be assigned from the outer capability respective the agent that uses the act/sense capability.

5.3 Capability Parametrization

To exhibit reasonable behavior it is necessary for creatures to describe their high-level objectives and the means for achieving them. In this section a "basic behavior" capability (Fig. 6) for preys is described, which enables preys to explore their environment, eat food and flee from near hunters. Three goal types are designed for this purpose. An instance of a "keep alone" maintain goal (lines 27-29) has the task to monitor if the prey is currently in danger. It becomes active whenever a hunter is nearby and will trigger plans for fleeing from the hunter. "Eat food" achieve goals (lines 30-35) are created automatically for every piece

```
01 <capability xmlns="http://jadex.sourceforge.net/jadex"
02   xmlns:xsi="http://www.w3.org/2001/XMLSchema-instance"
03   xsi:schemaLocation="http://jadex.sourceforge.net/jadex
04   http://jadex.sourceforge.net/jadex-0.94.xsd"
05   package="jadex.examples.hunterprey.creature.actsense"
06   name="ActSense">
07
08   <capabilities>
09     <capability name="dfcap" file="jadex.planlib.DF"/>
10   </capabilities>
11
12   <beliefs>
13     <beliefset name="hunters" class="Hunter" exported="true"/>
14     <beliefset name="preys" class="Preys" exported="true"/>
15     <beliefset name="obstacles" class="Obstacle" exported="true"/>
16     <beliefset name="food" class="Food" exported="true"/>
17     <belief name="environmentagent" class="jadex.adapter.fipa.AgentIdentifier"/>
18     <beliefref name="my_self" class="Creature" exported="true">
19       <abstract/>
20     </beliefref>
21   </beliefs>
22
23   <goals>
24     <achievegoal name="move" exported="true">
25       <parameter name="direction" class="String"/>
26     </achievegoal>
27     <achievegoal name="eat" exported="true">
28       <parameter name="object" class="WorldObject"/>
29     </achievegoal>
30     <achievegoalref name="df_search">
31       <concrete ref="dfcap.df_search"/>
32     </achievegoalref>
33   </goals>
34
35   <plans>
36     <plan name="move">
37       <body>new MovePlan()</body>
38       <trigger><goal ref="move"/></trigger>
39     </plan>
40     <plan name="eat">
41       <body>new EatPlan()</body>
42       <trigger><goal ref="eat"/></trigger>
43     </plan>
44     <plan name="updatevision">
45       <body>new UpdateVisionPlan()</body>
46       <trigger><messageevent ref="inform_vision"/></trigger>
47     </plan>
48   </plans>
49
50   <events>
51     <messageevent name="inform_vision" type="fipa" direction="receive">
52       <parameter name="performative" class="String" direction="fixed">
53         <value>jadex.adapter.fipa.SFipa.INFORM</value>
54       </parameter>
55       <parameter name="language" class="String" direction="fixed">
56         <value>jadex.adapter.fipa.SFipa.JAVA_XML</value>
57       </parameter>
58       <parameter name="ontology" class="String" direction="fixed">
59         <value>HunterPreyOntology.ONTOLOGY_NAME</value>
60       </parameter>
61       <parameter name="content-class" class="Class" direction="fixed">
62         <value>CurrentVision.class</value>
63       </parameter>
64       <parameter name="content" class="CurrentVision"/>
65     </messageevent>
66   </events>
67 </capability>
```

Fig. 5. Act/sense capability

```
01 <capability xmlns="http://jadex.sourceforge.net/jadex"
02   xmlns:xsi="http://www.w3.org/2001/XMLSchema-instance"
03   xsi:schemaLocation="http://jadex.sourceforge.net/jadex
04   http://jadex.sourceforge.net/jadex-0.94.xsd"
05   package="jadex.examples.hunterprey.creature.preys.basicbehaviour"
06   name="BasicBehaviour">
07
08   <capabilities>
09     <capability name="actsensecap" class="ActSense"/>
10   </capabilities>
11
12   <beliefs>
13     <beliefsetref name="hunters" class="Hunter" exported="true">
14       <concrete ref="actsensecap.hunters" />
15     <beliefsetref>
16     <!– similar declarations for obstacles and food omitted for brevity. –>
17     <beliefref name="my_self" class="Creature" exported="true">
18       <assignto ref="actsensecap.my_self"/>
19       <abstract/>
20     </beliefref>
21     <belief name="eating_allowed" class="boolean">
22       <fact>true</fact>
23     </belief>
24   </beliefs>
25
26   <goals>
27     <maintaingoal name="keep_alone" exclude="never">
28     <!– details omitted for brevity. –>
29     </maintaingoal>
30     <achievegoal name="eat_food">
31       <creationcondition>
32         $beliefbase.eating_allowed && $beliefbase.food.length>0
33       </creationcondition>
34       <!– further details omitted for brevity. –>
35     </achievegoal>
36     <performgoal name="wander_around" retry="true" exclude="never"/>
37     <achievegoalref name="move">
38       <concrete ref="actsensecap.move"/>
39     </achievegoalref>
40     <achievegoalref name="eat">
41       <concrete ref="actsensecap.eat"/>
42     </achievegoalref>
43   </goals>
44
45   <plans><!– omitted for brevity. –></plans>
46
47   <initialstates>
48     <initialstate name="flee">
49       <beliefs>
50         <initialbelief ref="eating_allowed">
51           <fact>false</fact>
52         </initialbelief>
53       </beliefs>
54       <goals>
55         <initialgoal name="escapegoal" ref="keep_alone"/>
56       </goals>
57     </initialstate>
58     <initialstate name="wander_flee_eat">
59       <goals>
60         <initialgoal name="wandergoal" ref="wander_around"/>
61         <initialgoal name="escapegoal" ref="keep_alone"/>
62       </goals>
63     </initialstate>
64   </initialstates>
65 </capability>
```

Fig. 6. Basic prey behavior capability

of food the creature discovers. They will lead to plan executions for reaching the food's location and eating it. The third goal type is called "wander around" (line 36) and initiates random walking on the map. In this paper the details of goal declarations are out of scope, for an extensive description the reader can refer to [2,14].

For proper operation the basic behavior capability needs access to the environmental beliefs made available by the included act/sense capability (lines 8-10). Therefore concrete belief set references are defined for hunters, obstacles and food (lines 13-16). These belief set references are also exported allowing an outer capability or the creature itself to access these values. An abstract and exported belief reference is assigned for "my self", as the basic behavior capability still does not know in which exact kind of prey it will be used.

To illustrate the parametrization of capabilities it is assumed that two different kinds of preys need to be created from the basic behavior capability. The first labeled "LazyPrey" should only flee from nearby hunters and otherwise just sit and wait where it is. On the contrary a "CleverPrey" should wander around to explore the map, eat food and flee from hunters. For each kind of prey a separate initial mental state has been specified (lines 48-57 and lines 58-63).

For the operation of a LazyPrey it is necessary to have an instance of a "keep alone" goal to flee from hunters. This is achieved by creating an initial goal of that type (line 55). Additionally, it is required to turn off the reactive creation of "eat food" goals which cannot be done directly. Hence, a belief "eating allowed" is introduced as some kind of goal creation switch and used in the creation condition of the "eat food" goal. In the initial state this belief is negated which ensures that no "eat food" goals will be instantiated at runtime.

A CleverPrey needs to exploit the whole functionality of the basic behavior capability. Thus, initial goals for exploring the map (line 60) and for escaping from nearby hunters (line 61) are created. Nothing has to be declared in the initial state for "eat food" goals, because these are created automatically at runtime whenever a new piece of food is discovered as mentioned earlier.

6   Summary and Outlook

This paper revisits the capability concept introduced by Busetta et al. for modularizing BDI agents, in which several conceptual limitations have been identified:

- No generic mechanism for importing / exporting arbitrary mental elements such as beliefs and goals is available leading to a decreased usability.
- The parametrization of capabilities is not supported which hinders flexible reuse of capabilities.
- Only design time composition is supported.
- Refinements of mental elements are not addressed.

In turn a new capability concept based on the main ideas of the original proposal is introduced to address most of these shortcomings. Regarding the usability and generality a new import / export mechanism is presented, allowing to treat all elements (e.g. beliefs or goals) in a similar fashion and hence simplifying the way in which a capability interface is defined. Furthermore, parametrization is supported through the definition of an initial mental state, which is defined as a part of the capability itself. This allows for easy capability configuration as only the state names need to be known in the including capability.

In addition to the aforementioned issues the new capability concept is also prepared to handle the dynamic composition of capabilities at runtime to flexibly adopt agent behavior. The extension points to add functionality at runtime are already present in the new capability concept and have been tested in the current implementation. The process of removing capabilities and their elements at any time during the agent execution has only been sketched and is left for future work.

Another area of future work which is also facilitated through the locality principle is the refinement of elements from subcapabilities. Properties of an element might be redefined on a proxy element. In our vision such an element refinement has similarities with the inheritance relationship from object-orientation. E.g. a goal reference type could be used to inherit all the properties of the concrete goal and add new properties such as additional parameters. At runtime the proposed creation semantics could help in deciding in which cases the redefined or the original specification should be used.

Finally, an interesting topic for future research regards bringing together the role-based decomposition approaches with the component-based capability approach. A capability might provide an implementation entity for a role identified in an abstract design. Building agents capable of playing certain roles could then be easily done by composing the agent from capabilities for each role.

References

1. L. Braubach, A. Pokahr, and W. Lamersdorf. Jadex: A BDI Agent System Combining Middleware and Reasoning. In R. Unland, M. Calisti, and M. Klusch, editors, *Software Agent-Based Applications, Platforms and Development Kits*. Birkhäuser, 2005.
2. L. Braubach, A. Pokahr, D. Moldt, and W. Lamersdorf. Goal Representation for BDI Agent Systems. In *Proc. of the 2nd Workshop on Programming Multiagent Systems: Languages, frameworks, techniques, and tools (ProMAS04)*, 2004.
3. P. Busetta, N. Howden, R. Rönnquist, and A. Hodgson. Structuring BDI Agents in Functional Clusters. In *Proc. of the 6th Int. Workshop, Agent Theories, Architectures, and Languages (ATAL) '99*, pages 277–289. Springer, 2000.
4. M. Dastani, B. van Riemsdijk, F. Dignum, and J.-J. Meyer. A Programming Language for Cognitive Agents: Goal Directed 3APL. In *Proceedings of the first Workshop on Programming Multiagent Systems (ProMAS03)*, 2003.
5. M. Dastani, B. van Riemsdijk, J. Hulstijn, F. Dignum, and J.-J. Meyer. Enacting and deacting roles in agent programming. In *Proceedings of the 5th International Workshop on Agent-Oriented Software Engineering (AOSE'04)*, 2004.
6. C. Ghezzi, M. Jazayeri, and D. Mandrioli. *Fundamentals of software engineering*. Prentice-Hall, Inc., 2003.
7. D. Heimbigner and A. Wolf. Post-deployment configuration management. In *System Configuration Management, ICSE'96 SCM-6 Workshop*, pages 272–276. Springer, 1996.

8. N. Howden, R. Rönnquist, A. Hodgson, and A. Lucas. JACK Intelligent Agents - Summary of an Agent Infrastructure. In *Proceedings of the 5th ACM International Conference on Autonomous Agents*, 2001.
9. A. Karageorgos, S. Thompson, and N. Mehandjiev. Specifying reuse concerns in agent system design using a role algebra. In *Agent Technologies, Infrastructures, Tools, and Applications for e-Services*, 2003.
10. D. Kinny and M. Georgeff. Modelling and Design of Multi-Agent Systems. In *Intelligent Agents III: Third International Workshop on Agent Theories, Architectures, and Languages (ATAL-96)*. Springer-Verlag, 1996.
11. J. F. Lehman, J. E. Laird, and P. S. Rosenbloom. A gentle introduction to Soar, an architecture for human cognition. *Invitation to Cognitive Science*, 4, 1996.
12. B. Meyer. *Object-Oriented Software Construction*. Prentice Hall PTR, 1997.
13. H. Nwana, D. Ndumu, L. Lee, and J. Collis. Zeus: a toolkit and approach for building distributed multi-agent systems. In *Proceedings of the third annual conference on Autonomous Agents*, pages 360–361. ACM Press, 1999.
14. A. Pokahr, L. Braubach, and W. Lamersdorf. A Goal Deliberation Strategy for BDI Agent Systems. In T. Eymann, F. Klügl, W. Lamersdorf, M. Klusch, and M. Huhns, editors, *Third German Conference on Multi-Agent Technologies and Systems (MATES 2005)*. Springer, 2005.
15. A. Pokahr, L. Braubach, and W. Lamersdorf. Jadex: A BDI Reasoning Engine. In R. Bordini, M. Dastani, J. Dix, and A. El Fallah Seghrouchni, editors, *Multi-Agent Programming*. Kluwer, 2005.
16. A. Rao and M. Georgeff. BDI Agents: from theory to practice. In *Proceedings of the First International Conference on Multi-Agent Systems (ICMAS'95)*, pages 312–319. The MIT Press: Cambridge, MA, USA, 1995.
17. C. Szyperski, D. Gruntz, and S. Murer. *Component Software: Beyond Object-Oriented Programming*. ACM Press and Addison-Wesley, 2002.
18. E. Yourdon and L. Constantine. *Structured Design: Fundamentals of a Discipline of Computer Program and Systems Design*. Prentice-Hall, Inc., 1979.

A Model-Based Executive for Commanding Robot Teams

Anthony Barrett

Jet Propulsion Laboratory, California Institute of Technology, M/S 126-347,
4800 Oak Grove Drive, Pasadena, CA 91109-8099, USA
anthony.barrett@jpl.nasa.gov

Abstract. The paper presents a way to robustly command a system of systems as a single entity. Instead of modeling each component system in isolation and then manually crafting interaction protocols, this approach starts with a model of the collective population as a single system. By compiling the model into separate elements for each component system and utilizing a teamwork model for coordination, it circumvents the complexities of manually crafting robust interaction protocols. The resulting systems are both globally responsive by virtue of a team oriented interaction model and locally responsive by virtue of a distributed approach to model-based fault detection, isolation, and recovery.

1 Introduction

Over the next decades NASA mission concepts are expected to involve growing teams of tightly coordinated spacecraft in dynamic, partially understood environments. In order to maintain team coherence, each spacecraft must robustly respond to global coordination anomalies as well as local events. Currently techniques for implementing such teams are extremely difficult. They involve either having one spacecraft tightly control the team or giving each spacecraft separate commands with explicit communication actions to coordinate with others. While both approaches can handle two or three simple spacecraft, neither scales well to larger populations or more complex spacecraft. New techniques are needed to facilitate managing populations of three or more complex spacecraft.

Flexible teamwork is a technique developed in the multi-agent community for teams of agents that achieve joint goals in the face of uncertainties arising from complex dynamic domains that obstruct coherent teamwork. Flexible teamwork involves giving the agents a shared team plan and a general model of teamwork. Agents exploit this model and team plan to autonomously reason about coordination and communication, providing the requisite flexibility. While this framework has been implemented in the context of real-world synthetic environments like robotic soccer and helicopter-combat simulation, these systems take an ad hoc rule-based approach toward failure diagnosis and response.

Our system takes a model-based approach toward representing teams and encoding their group activities. As Figure 1 shows, a user models a team as if one member tightly controls the others, but a compiler takes that model and distributes it across the team to move all reasoning as close as possible to the components being reasoned about. The result is a team with elements that are both locally and globally responsive, without having a user explicitly reason about the distribution.

R. H. Bordini et al. (Eds.): ProMAS 2005, LNAI 3862, pp. 156–167, 2006.

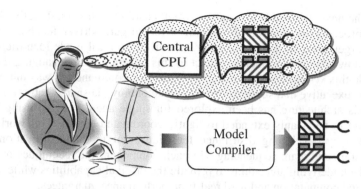

Fig. 1. User models system assuming a central controller, and a compiler handles the underlying distribution and coordination

Defining the approach starts with an explanation of the system architecture that resides on each component and how the components interact. Sections 3 and 4 then discuss the team sequencing and distributed mode management aspects of the system respectively. Section 5 subsequently discusses related work followed by conclusions in section 6.

2 System Architecture

The system architecture involves three distinct distributed components: mode identifier, mode reconfigurer, and team sequencer. As illustrated in Figure 2, the mode identifier combines sensory information from the hardware with past commands from the reconfigurer to determine the mode of the system. The mode reconfigurer in turn takes the current state estimate with a target mode from the team sequencer to

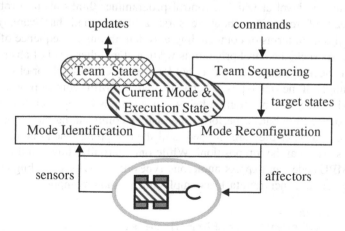

Fig. 2. The component architecture of executive on each robotic element consists of three elements that current state information – some of which is identified as team state information and has to be kept consistent among all robotic elements

determine the next commands to pass to a robot's hardware drivers. Finally, the team sequencer procedurally controls the identifier-reconfigurer-driver feedback loop by providing target states to the reconfigurer. At all times local mode identifiers maintain state knowledge, and sequencers react to this information by changing the target state. While this system can take manually generated commands, it was initially motivated as an executive that supports distributed autonomy via shared activities [1].

While this architecture has been explored for single agent systems using TITAN [2], it has yet to be cleanly extended to tightly coordinated teams. This work makes the extension by developing distributed techniques for mode identification, mode reconfiguration, and team sequencing. In each component the techniques motivated replacing the underlying algorithms to provide the original capabilities while supporting distributed computation and hard real-time performance guarantees.

3   Team Sequencing

The distributed onboard sequencer is based both on the Reactive Model-based Programming Language (RMPL) [3] and a model of flexible teamwork [4] developed within the distributed artificial intelligence community. This teamwork is more than a union of agents' simultaneous execution of individual plans, even if such plans have explicit coordination actions. Uncertainties often obstruct pre-planned coordination, resulting in a corresponding breakdown in teamwork. Flexible teamwork involves giving agents a shared team plan and a general model of teamwork. Agents then exploit this model and plan to autonomously handle coordination and communication, providing the flexibility needed to overcome the emergence of unexpected interactions caused either by slight timing delays or anomalies.

3.1 Procedural Control

RMPL elevates the level at which a control programmer thinks about a robotic systems. Instead of reasoning about sensors, actuators, and hardware, a RMPL programmer thinks in terms of commanding a system through a sequence of configuration states. As such, a control program is written at a higher level of abstraction, by asserting and checking states which may not be directly controllable or observable.

As an example of the rich types of behavior that an RMPL control programmer can encode, consider the control program below for a simplistic approach toward getting to rovers to jointly lift a bar. It performs the task by commanding the robot arms into a rising mode whenever they are stopped, and then stopping when one of the robots senses that its arm is at the top position. While only partially shown in this simplistic example, RMPL code can express numerous types of behavior including conditional branching, iteration, concurrent task accomplishment, and preemption.

```
(do (parallel
        (whenever (= RArm.Mode stopped)
            donext (= RArm.Mode rising))
        (whenever (= LArm.Mode stopped)
            donext (= LArm.Mode rising)))
    watching (:or (= LArmAtTop T) (= RArmAtTop T)))
```

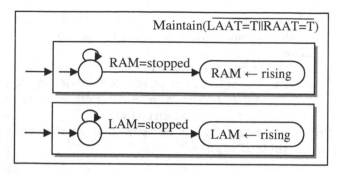

Fig. 3. Hierarchical constraint automaton (HCA) for two rovers lifting a bar consist of four locations inside nested automata, where LAAT, RAAT, LAM, and RAM respectively denote LArmAtTop, RArmAtTop, LArm.Mode, and RArm.Mode

The formal semantics of RMPL has been defined in terms of Hierarchical Constraint Automata (HCA) [2], where the nesting of automata directly corresponds to the nesting of RMPL constructs. For instance, Figure 3 has the HCA for our example, where the outer and two inner boxes respectively correspond to the do-watching and the two whenever-donext constructs.

Unlike standard automata, multiple locations in an HCA can be marked. When marked a location stays marked until its target state (if any) has been reached. At which point the mark gets replicated zero or more times over arcs that have true conditions. For instance, the two left locations lack target states, but stay marked by virtue of the loop arcs. Whenever a robot arm stops, the appropriate arc is enabled and the arm's target state becomes 'rising'. This continues until the Maintain() fails and erases the entire automaton, reflecting the do-watching construct.

In general, an HCA corresponds to a tree of parallel processes whose execution follows the algorithm below. As this algorithm shows, a location is a simple process that asserts a target state and exits upon reaching that state or being aborted from above. Higher level HCAs manage their child components and cannot be restarted until exiting. This algorithm differs from the one presented in [2] due to maintaining a more hierarchical agent focus, which facilitates subsequent distribution. Cycling through all of the processes on each state change and recording the exits at the end of a cycle to subsequently enable transitions on the next cycle would make the two become identical. This divergence was made to facilitate distributed execution of an HCA.

```
Process Execute(HCA)
    If HCA is a location then
        Assert target state until target reached
    Else
        For each initial child component M
            Start Execute(M)
        Repeat
            Wait for a change to the local/team state
```

```
If the Maintain() condition fails then
    Abort each active child component
Else
    For each child component M that just exited
        For each transition M ──C──>N in HCA
            If C holds and N is not executing then
                Start Execute(N)
Until no more child components are executing
Exit on end of cycle.
```

3.2 Teamwork Extensions

From a representational standpoint, team plans are similar to any other hierarchical plan. The only syntactic addition to turn a hierarchical plan into a team plan involves defining teams to perform activities and assigning roles to teammates. More precisely, injecting teamwork modeling into an existing hierarchical plan execution system involves adding three features [4]:

- generalization of activities to represent team activities with role assignments;
- representation of team and/or sub-team states; and
- restrictions to only let a teammate modify a team state.

The key observation underlying the use of RMPL is how the language's approach to defining a control program as an HCA naturally matches the approach to defining a team plan with a model of flexible teamwork. Team plans are hierarchically defined in terms of sub-plans and primitive actions, where each teammate is assigned a role consisting of a subset of the sub-plans and actions. Returning to the our example, the Maintain() is a team HCA with components that are local HCAs for each rover. Thus the right hand rover need only address the components of Figure 4, and the two rovers need only communicate to be consistent over the team's Maintain() condition. The condition tells the rovers when to collectively abort their HCAs. In general, agents only need to communicate when a team level automaton changes its active components or some property of its Maintain() condition changes. Changes in a local HCA's components can be hidden.

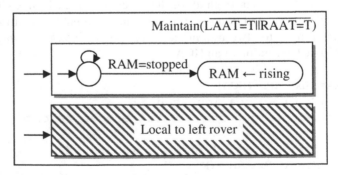

Fig. 4. The right rover executes an HCA that ignores local information regarding the left rover

As the example illustrates, all an RMPL programmer has to do to facilitate distributed sequencing is associate state variables with teammates to determine local and team HCAs. He does not have to worry about synchronization issues across multiple agents. The underlying model of flexible teamwork will robustly manage these issues by keeping team state information consistent among the closely coordinated population of agents.

4 Distributed Mode Management

By building off of the model-based device description language developed for DS-1's Mode Identification & Recovery (MIR) executive [5], we acquire a representation for explicitly defining the interrelationships between an agent team's complete set of software and hardware components. This facilitates reasoning about how one component's status affects others' and ultimately sensor observations, which facilitates taking a set of observations and inferring the team's status. While there are a number of constructs in the language, they all support defining a network of typed components. These component types are defined in terms of how a component's modes define constraints among its port variables, and these constraints are encode using *variable logic equations* – Boolean equations where the literals are simply variable equality constraints. For instance, the following defines a simplistic system with two components for its robot arms using the language defined in [6].

```
(defvalues ArmCmd (raise lower none))
(defvalues bool (T F))
(defcomponent Arm
  :ports ((ArmCmd cmd)(bool stress))
  :modes ((stalled)(stopped)(rising)(falling))
  :transitions
  ((* -> rising  (:and (= stress F)(= cmd raise)))
   (* -> falling (:and (= stress F)(= cmd lower)))
   (* -> stalled (= stress T))
   (stalled -> stopped (= stress F))))
(defsystem rovers
  :sensors    ((bool LArmAtTop)(bool LArmStress)
               (bool RArmAtTop)(bool RArmStress))
  :affectors ((ArmCmd LArmCmd)(ArmCmd RArmCmd))
  :structure
  ((Arm RArm (RArmCmd RArmStress))
   (Arm LArm (LArmCmd LArmStress))))
```

Current model-based diagnosis techniques use some variant of truth maintenance [7], where components are translated into Boolean equations. In both cases the systems require collecting all observations into a central place and then invoking heuristic algorithms to find the most probable mode that agrees with the observations. While some work has been done to distribute these systems, their underlying algorithms cannot support hard real-time guarantees by virtue of having to solve an NP-Complete problem for each collection of observations. While heuristics can make these algorithms fast on average, the point is that they cannot easily guarantee performance in all cases.

Instead of trying to prove the problem dependent speed of heuristics, we will take an approach suggested by knowledge compilation research. This approach involves moving as much of the computation into the off board compilation phase as possible to simplify the onboard computation. Where previous systems take linear time to compile a model and then possibly exponential time to use the compilation to perform mode estimation, our approach takes possibly exponential time to compile a model into a decomposable negation normal form representation and then linear time to perform mode estimation with the equation.

Definition 1. A variable logic equation is in <u>Decomposable Negation Normal Form</u> (DNNF) if (1) it contains no negations and (2) the subexpressions under each conjunct refer to disjoint sets of variables.

For instance, the two robot arm example compiles into a tree-like structure with two subtrees like Figures 6 and 7 for the two robot arms, and these subtrees are combined with an "and" node. In general, the compilation results look like Figure 5 with a substructure for each agent, and these substructures are combined in the team state.

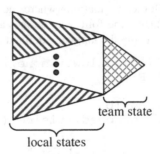

Fig. 5. The global structure of compiled model consists of substructures local to each team member that are connected through a structure in a shared team state

4.1 Mode Estimation

Given that conjuncts have a disjoint branch variables property, the minimal cost of a satisfying variable assignment is just the cost of a variable assignment with single assignment equations, the minimum of the subexpression costs for a disjunct, and the sum of the subexpression costs for a conjunct. With this observation, finding the optimal satisfying variable assignments becomes a simple three-step process:

1. associate costs with variable assignments in leaves;
2. propagate node costs up through the tree by either assigning the min or sum of the descendents' costs to an OR or AND node respectively; and
3. if the root's cost is 0, infinity, or some other value then respectively return default assignments, failure, or descend from the root to determine and return the variable assignments that contribute to its cost.

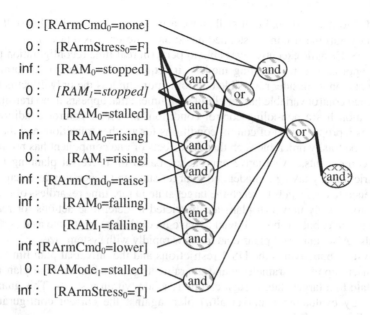

Fig. 6. Utilizing local reasoning on its local and team model, the right-hand rover can determine that it has transitioned to a stopped mode

For instance, Figure 6 illustrates the process of determining that the right arm is stopped. First observing that RArmStress is false results in assigning values to the RArmStress leaves, and the mode and command leaves get costs related to the last known modes and commands. Second, costs are propagated to the tree root. Third, the root node's cost of zero is used to drill down to find the lowest cost tree with the mode assignment (i.e. RAM_1=stopped).

Distributing the DNNF equations across a population is a simple matter of assigning sensors to agent and then assigning each node to an agent depending on the locations of sensors that contribute to that node's computation. If all contributers are on a single agent, then the node can be locally computed. Other nodes contribute to the team state. While all of the higher level nodes can be managed in the team state, it is more efficient to minimize the nodes in the team state. One way to reduce the number of nodes is to exclude nodes whose costs can be computed from other nodes in the team state. This results in only including the leftmost nodes of Figure 5's the team state structure. In any case, given the team state component of the structure, any agent can drill down to determine its local modes.

4.2 Mode Reconfiguration

It turns out that not only do components have modes to estimate, but they also accept commands to change modes to a target configuration once an estimate is determined. For instance, the simplistic robot arm model has four modes. In general, each component is modeled as a state machine that takes commands to transition between states and each state determines interactions among variables. In the example the robot arm can be commanded to rise or drop, but it stalls once arm stress is detected. This stalled mode subsequently puts the arm into a stopped mode once the stress is relieved.

While DS-1's MIR executive was able to perform real-time reconfiguration planning with this approach to representing models, it required a modeler to conform to four requirements: only consider reversible control actions, unless the only effect is to repair failures; each control variable has an idling assignment that appears in no transitions and each transition has a non-idling control condition; no set of control conditions for a transition is a proper subset of control conditions for another transition; and the components must be totally orderable such that the effects of one component has no impact on previous components. Alternative approaches based on universal planning [8] avoid these restrictions by taking a model and a target state and generating a structure that is used to generate commands to reach the target state in real-time regardless of the current state. Unfortunately universal plans are restricted to determine actions for reaching a single target state, but a robot will tend to have an evolving target state as it performs its commands. Also, universal plans tend to grow rapidly with system size.

This system both avoids the DS-1 restrictions and the universal plan limitations by taking a user supplied parameter n and guaranteeing to find an optimal plan from the current state to a target state if such can be reached within n steps. This guarantee is facilitated by evaluating a universal(n) plan against the current configuration and target configuration [9].

Definition 2. A <u>universal(n)</u> plan is a structure that can be evaluated in linear time to generate an optimal n level plan to reach any target configuration from any current configuration if such a plan exists.

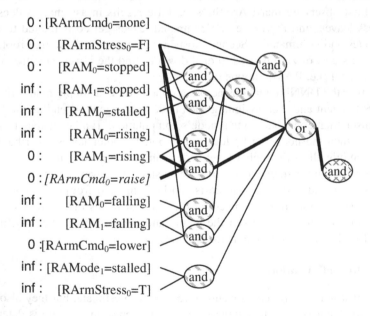

Fig. 7. Utilizing local reasoning on its local and team model, the right-hand rover can determine how to make the arm rise

Universal(n) plans are more general than universal plans by virtue of their not being tied down to a specific target configuration. They are more restricted than universal plans by virtue of the n level requirement, where a level is any number of simultaneous non-interacting actions. When increasing n, the universal(n) plan becomes less restrictive until reaching some model dependent value M – where there is a guarantee that target configuration can be reached from any configuration within M steps. In practice n is kept relatively small because universal(n) plans tend to grow rapidly with n.

To provide an example, Figure 7 uses a DNNF equation to represent a universal(1) plan for the two robot arm example. Just as in mode estimation, using the DNNF to determine the next command is a three-step process. First the current and target modes are used to assign costs to the RAM_0 and RAM_1 leaves respectively, and the $RArmCmd_0$ command leaves get user supplied command costs. Second, costs are propagated to the tree root. Third, the root node's cost of 0 is used to drill down to find the actual command to perform. In this simplistic case the current right arm mode was stopped and, the target mode was rising, and the found command to pass to the right arm was raise.

5 Related Work

The closest related work on distributed sequencing comes from STEAM [4], MONAD [10], and TPOT-RL [11]. These two systems address teams of tightly coordinated agents that can fail, but they are based on rule-based approaches that lack system models to facilitate principled approaches to mode estimation and failure response. Work by Stolzenburg and Arai [12] takes a more model-based approach by using Statecharts to specify a multiagent system, but they focus on communication via events as opposed to maintaining team state information. Still, the constructs of RMPL can be defined in terms of compilation to Statechart fragments instead of HCAs to facilitate formal analysis.

While others have made the leap to applying compilation techniques to both simplify and accelerate embedded computation to determine a system's current mode of operation, they are more restricted than this system. First, DNNF equation creation and evaluation was initially developed in a diagnosis application [13], but the resulting system restricted a component to only have one output and that there cannot be directed cycles between components. Our system makes neither of these restrictions. The Mimi-ME system [14] similarly avoided making these restrictions, but it can neither support distributed reasoning nor provide real-time guarantees by virtue of having to collect all information in one place and then solve an NP-complete problem, called MIN-SAT, when converting observations into mode estimates. Our approach both supports distribution and real-time guarantees.

The closest related work on real-time reconfiguration planning comes from the Burton reconfiguration planner used on DS-1 [5] and other research on planning via symbolic model checking [15]. In the case of Burton our system improves on that work by relaxing a number of restricting assumptions. For instance, Burton required the absence of causal cycles, but our system has no problem with them. On the other hand, our system can only plan n steps ahead where Burton did not have that limitation. Similarly, the work using symbolic model checking lacked the n-step restriction, but it compiled out a universal plan for a particular target state. Our system uses the same compiled structure to determine how to reach any target state within n steps of the current state.

Finally, distribute behavioral systems like CAMPOUT [16] solve similar problems, but lack mechanisms for error handling. Such systems form a natural layer below the system presented here for teams with joint activities that are too tightly interacting to allow reasoning about mode management.

6 Conclusions

This paper presents a model-based executive for commanding teams of agents. It works by letting an operator define and command the team as a single entity with a single controlling CPU. A compiler then distributes the control functions guided by a specification assigning system components (sensors and actuators) to team members.

As the example suggests, there are several ways to improve the system. From a representational perspective, the assignment of an agent to a role in a group activity is hardwired. For instance, there is no way to represent the possibility that LArm and RArm are interchangeable. The multi-agent community has explored multiple techniques for role assignment, but work needs to be done to include them in the team sequencer.

Also, knowledge compilation approaches like those used in mode management are not perfect. While onboard computation has linear complexity, that complexity is in terms of compiled DNNF equation size. Some problems are inherently intractable and lead to equations that are exponentially larger than the source model, but in practice that should never happen with engineered designs. Designs that result in inherently intractable mode estimation problems would be too uncontrollable to use in practice. As a rule of thumb, a system's mode estimation difficulty rises with the number of unobserved component interactions. Thus the number of interactions increases the size of the DNNF equation, but the number of sensors decreases it. Since engineers currently simplify estimation difficulty by adding sensors to a design, DNNF compilation results can be used to guide sensor placement if desired.

Finally, the system has only been tested in toy scenarios like this paper's running example. The main evaluation metrics are the size of the DNNF equation generated by the compiler and the size of the computed team state. Initial experiments in toy domains as well as a domain for a formation flying interferometer [17] show that the size of the teamstate component of the DNNF equation depends on the complexity of the robot interactions and not on the complexity of the entire system. This bodes well for scaling issues.

Acknowledgements

This work was performed at the Jet Propulsion Laboratory, California Institute of Technology, under a contract with the National Aeronautics and Space Administration. The author would also like to thank Alan Oursland, Seung Chung, Adnan Darwiche, Milind Tambe, Daniel Dvorak, and Mitch Ingham for discussions contributing to this effort.

References

1. Clement, B., Barrett, A.: "Continual Coordination through Shared Activities." In *Proceedings of the Second International Conference on Autonomous Agents and Multi-Agent Systems*, 2003.
2. Ingham, M., Ragno, R., and Williams, B. C.: "A Reactive Model-based Programming Language for Robotic Space Explorers." In *Proceeding of the International Symposium on Artificial Intelligence, Robotics and Automation in Space*, June 2001.
3. Williams, B. C., Chung, S., and Gupta, V.: "Mode Estimation of Model-based Programs: Monitoring Systems with Complex Behavior." In *Proceedings of the Seventeenth International Joint Conference on Artificial Intelligence*. August 2001.
4. Tambe, M., "Towards Flexible Teamwork." In Journal of Artificial Intelligence Research, Volume 7. 1997
5. Williams, B. C., Nayak, P. "A Model-based Approach to Reactive Self-Configuring Systems." In *Proceedings of the Thirteenth National Conference on Artificial Intelligence*. August 1996.
6. Barrett, A. "Model Compilation for Real-Time Planning and Diagnosis with Feedback." In *Prodeedings of the Nineteenth Interantional Joint Conference on Artificial Intelligence*. July 2005
7. Nayak, P., Williams, B. C. "Fast Context Switching in Real-time Propositional Reasoning," In *Proceedings of the Fourteenth National Conference on Artificial Intelligence*, July 1997.
8. Schoppers, M. "The use of dynamics in an intelligent controller for a space faring rescue robot." *Artificial Intelligence* 73:175-230. 1995.
9. Barrett, A. "Domain Compilation for Embedded Real-Time Planning." In *Proceedings of the Fourteenth International Conference on Automated Planning & Scheduling*, June 2004.
10. Vu, T., Go, J., Kaminka, G., Veloso, M., Browning, B. "MONAD: A Flexible Architecture for Multi-Agent Control." In *Proceedings of the Second International Joint Conference on Autonomous Agents and Multi-Agent Systems*. July 2003.
11. Stone, P. *Layered Learning in Multi-Agent Systems: A Winning Approach to Robotic Soccer*, MIT Press, Cambridge, MA 1998.
12. Stolzenburg, F., Arai, T. "From the Specificatio of Multiagent Systems by Statecharts to Their Formal Analysis by Model Checking: Towards Safety-Critical Applications." In: Schillo, M. et al. (Eds.): MATES 2003, Lecture Notes in Computer Science, Vol. 2831. Springer-Verlag Berlin Heidelberg (2003). 131-143.
13. Darwiche, A. "Compiling Devices: A Structure-Based Approach," In *Proceedings of the Sixth International Conference on Knowledge Representation and Reasoning (KR)*. June 1998.
14. Chung, S., Van Eepoel, J., Williams, B. C. "Improving Model-based Mode Estimation through Offline Compilation," In *Proceedings of the International Symposium on Artificial Intelligence, Robotics and Automation in Space*, June 2001.
15. Cimatti, A., Roveri, M. "Conformant Planning via Model Checking." In: Biunido, S., Fox, M. (eds.): Recent Advances in AI Planning, 5th European Conference on Planning. Lecture Notes in Computer Science, Vol. 1809. Springer-Verlag, Berlin Heidelberg (2000). 21-34.
16. Pirjanian, P., Huntsberger, T., Barrett, A. "Representing and Executing Plan Sequences for Distributed Multi-Agent Systems." In *Proceedings of the IEEE/RSJ International Conference on Intelligent Robots and Systems*, November 2001.
17. Chung, S., Barrett, A. "Distributed Real-time Model-based Diagnosis." In *Proceedings of the 2003 IEEE Aerospace Conference*, March 2003.

Hermes: Implementing Goal-Oriented Agent Interactions

Christopher Cheong and Michael Winikoff

RMIT University, Melbourne, Australia
{chris, winikoff}@cs.rmit.edu.au

Abstract. Traditional approaches to designing agent interactions focus on defining agent interaction in terms of legal sequences of messages. These message-centric approaches are not a good match with autonomous proactive agents since they unnecessarily limit the agents' autonomy and flexibility. The Hermes methodology proposes an approach for designing agent interactions in terms of *interaction goals*. In this paper we focus on how Hermes designs can be implemented by mapping the design artefacts to collections of plans.

1 Introduction

Existing approaches to designing agent interactions are *message-centric*. These approaches, such as using Petri nets, AUML interaction protocols [1], or finite state machines, are not a good fit with autonomous proactive agents. For instance, they do not support goals, and legal message sequences are explicitly defined in terms of messages and combining forms such as sequencing, alternatives, and loops. One consequence is that autonomous agents are forced to follow these prescribed message sequences, thus limiting the flexibility of interactions. Furthermore, due to the limited flexibility, interactions are also less robust since there are limited recovery options.

The *Hermes*[1] methodology [2, 3] aims to address this by designing interactions in terms of goals, and allowing agents to achieve these goals flexibly and robustly. Hermes uses *Interaction Goals* (IGs) as a basis for designing interactions, along with available actions and timing dependency constraints. Possible message sequences are determined by the agents in accordance with these interaction goals, actions and constraints, allowing message sequences to *emerge* from the interaction. Whereas traditional approaches to interaction design specify message sequences directly, with Hermes the sequences of messages that are possible are specified *implicitly*: the possible sequences are, roughly speaking, the solutions to the constraints specified by the interaction goal hierarchy and the action maps.

The Hermes approach results in a greater degree of flexibility and robustness, and consequently, Hermes is better suited for proactive autonomous agents than current message-centric approaches.

The Hermes methodology aims to be a complete and *practical* approach to developing agents that interact flexibly and robustly. The design aspects of Hermes, including

---

[1] In Greek mythology, Hermes was an Olympian god who acted as the herald of the gods and served as their messenger (http://www.pantheon.org).

R.H. Bordini et al. (Eds.): ProMAS 2005, LNAI 3862, pp. 168–183, 2006.

a design process, notations, techniques, and failure handling mechanisms, have been described elsewhere [3].

In this paper we focus on the *implementation* of goal-oriented agent interactions that have been designed using the Hermes methodology. We present a set of guidelines which can be used to implement a Hermean design, and apply them to implement a sample design in Jadex [4]. The guidelines produce a set of goals and plans that are suitable for implementation using any of a number of goal-plan agent platforms, such as JACK, JAM, Jason, and many others.

To illustrate our work we use an e-commerce protocol based on the NetBill [5] protocol in which a Customer purchases goods online from a Merchant. The NetBill protocol was chosen since a number of other non-message-centric approaches have used it [6–8], and by using the same example it becomes easier to compare our approach to existing approaches.

In section 2 we briefly describe the Hermes methodology, including the design artefacts that are used in the implementation phase. Section 3, which is the central contribution of this paper, describes how a Hermean design can be systematically implemented by mapping design artefacts to a collection of plans. We then conclude in section 4.

2 Background: Hermes

In this section, we briefly explain the Hermes methodology. Since Hermes has been described elsewhere [2, 3] we only describe here the notations and outcomes of the design process, as these are needed in order to understand the implementation described in section 3. The aspects of Hermes which are not necessary in order to present the implementation, including the design process, are not presented here and we refer the reader to [3] for a more detailed description of the Hermes methodology.

Figure 1 provides an overview of the Hermes design process. The process is shown as an incremental mini-waterfall model in which each step is derived from the previous step. However, as is typical of design, the process is applied in an iterative fashion where developing the design may suggest changes to previously developed aspects. Steps marked as *Final Design Artefacts* are used directly in implementing the design, and these artefacts are described in the following sections. Other artefacts, such as *Action Sequence* and *Action Message* diagrams, are used to validate that the implementation matches the design. Although these intermediate design artefacts can be useful in generating test cases for the implementation, they are not discussed further in this paper.

2.1 Interaction Goal Hierarchy Diagram

An *Interaction Goal* (IG) is a goal of the interaction, for example to agree on a price, or to make a trade. Note that it is *not* a goal of an individual agent, but of the interaction as a whole. The interaction goals and their relationships are captured using an *Interaction Goal Hierarchy Diagram* which is effectively a goal-tree, similar to those used in agent-oriented methodologies such as MaSE [9] or Prometheus [10]. This represents IGs as circles containing the name of the IG, the *initiator* role which initiates trying to achieve

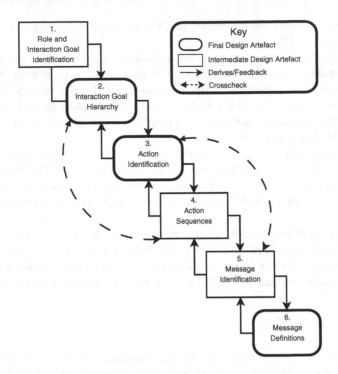

Fig. 1. Hermes Methodology Overview Diagram

the given IG[2], and the roles which are involved in achieving the IG. Interaction Goals can be decomposed into sub-goals, where achieving an IG's sub-goals will achieve that interaction goal. For example (refer to Figure 2), the *Trade* IG can be decomposed into the IGs *Agree* and *Exchange*. Sub-goal decomposition is indicated on the diagram by (undirected) lines. In addition to capturing sub-goal relationships, the Interaction Goal Hierarchy Diagram also captures *temporal dependencies*, depicted as directed arrows between IGs. For example, *Exchange* is dependent on *Agree* and thus, *Agree* must be completed before *Exchange* can be started.

2.2 Action Maps

An *action* is a step, taken by a single agent, that moves the interaction closer to achieving its goal. The actions that can be used to achieve a given interaction goal and their relationships are captured using an *action map* for that (leaf[3]) interaction goal. Action maps are divided into "swim lanes"; one per role involved in the interaction goal. Each swim lane contains different types of actions (see next paragraph) that can be performed by that role.

---

[2] An upward arrow, ↑, is used to indicate that the initiator for the IG is the same role that initiated the parent IG.

[3] There is no need to identify actions for non-leaf-level goals, since they are completed when their sub-goals are completed.

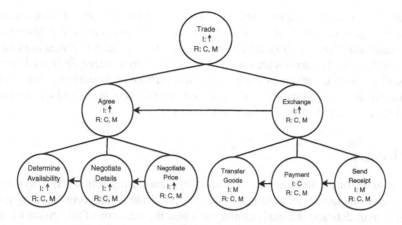

Fig. 2. Interaction Goal (IG) Hierarchy Diagram

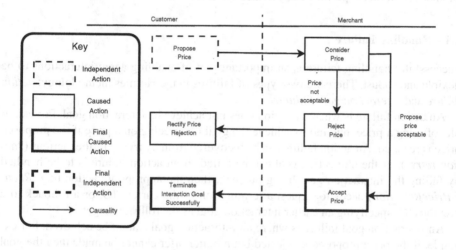

Fig. 3. Action Map for the *NegotiatePrice* IG

The key in Figure 3 illustrates four different action types, each of which has a different meaning and use[4]. An *Independent Action* is one that can start independently from other actions, i.e. it is not necessarily caused by another action, but it *may* be caused by another action. *Independent Actions* are entry points into interaction goals. A *Caused Action* is one which cannot start independently and *must* be triggered by another action. A *Final Caused Action* is a *Caused Action* which terminates the interaction goal for a particular role. Note that performing a final action does not necessarily mean the interaction goal is successfully achieved, only that it is completed. For example, the interaction designer may wish to end the *NegotiatePrice* IG with failure when a price offer is rejected by the Merchant (but this is not the case in Figure 3).

---

[4] The fourth type, *Final Independent Action* is not used in the example, and so is not explained here.

Causality constraints (depicted in Figure 3 as directed arrows) specify that certain actions cannot take place until other actions have occurred. For example, the *ProposePrice* action causes the *ConsiderPrice* action. Where an action is causally linked to more than one action the causality arrows are intended to depict alternative possibilities. For example, the *ConsiderPrice* action either triggers *AcceptPrice* or *RejectPrice*, but not both. Which action is triggered will depend on certain conditions or states and it can be useful to label the causality arrows with the condition or state.

2.3   Messages

When using Hermes, messages are identified by considering action sequences and action message diagrams (not described in this paper). What is important to know in order to be able to understand the implementation is that the outcome of this process is a collection of messages. A message is defined whenever an action in the action map triggers another action that is performed by a different role.

2.4   Handling Failure

Successfully handling failure is an important part of enabling agent interactions to be flexible and robust. There are two types of failures in the Hermes methodology: *action failure* and *interaction goal failure*.

An action failure is where an action does not achieve its interaction goal. For example, offering a price may fail to achieve the goal of agreeing on a price if the proposed price is rejected. An action failure can be recovered from by trying further actions ("*action retry*"), or the interaction goal can be failed. If an action failure is to be handled by failing the interaction goal being pursued, then the appropriate action (e.g. *RectifyPriceRejection*) needs to request a termination of the current IG, or a rollback to a previous IG, specifying an earlier interaction goal as the rollback target.

An interaction goal failure is where an interaction goal cannot be achieved. For example, if the price proposed is rejected but a better offer cannot be made then the goal of agreeing on a price cannot be achieved. Interaction goal failure can be handled either by failing the entire interaction, or by rolling back to an earlier interaction goal ("*rollback*").

Rollback is a failure recovery mechanism based on the idea that if a previous interaction goal is re-achieved in a different manner, the failed interaction goal may be successfully achieved. For example, if the Merchant and Customer have agreed on a product and its details (*NegotiateDetails*) but cannot agree on a price (*NegotiatePrice*) then going back and agreeing on different product details may enable agreement on a price to be reached.

Terminating the interaction and rolling back may not be appropriate for all IGs. For example, if goods have already been transferred then neither rollback nor termination should be permitted. Therefore, for each IG the designer indicates whether termination is permitted, whether rollback is permitted, and if rollback is permitted, to which (earlier) IGs should rollback be allowed. For example, the *NegotiatePrice* IG allows termination, and allows rollback to the *DetermineAvailability* and *NegotiateDetails* IGs.

3   Implementing the Design

In this section we discuss how the Hermean design can be systematically mapped to an implementation. Goal-oriented interactions are implemented by mapping design artefacts, such as the *Interaction Goal Hierarchy* and the *Action Map*s, to collections of plans which can be used by agent platforms. Since the design is in terms of interaction goals, we have chosen to develop an implementation scheme which targets agent platforms where the behaviour of agents is defined using plans and goals. Such platforms include those based on the Belief Desire Intention (BDI) model, such as JACK[5], Jadex[6], JAM[7], and Jason[8]. For the purposes of our work, we have implemented our design using the Jadex agent platform [4], however a Hermean design can be implemented using any of the aforementioned agent platforms.

Figure 4 shows an overview of the implementation, including different plan types and their inter-connections. Coordination plans are derived from interaction goals and are used to coordinate the participating agents through the interaction. Achievement plans are directly derived from actions and are steps which agents take towards completing an interaction goal. Interface plans are not derived from any design artefacts, but are used to transform inter-agent messages into goals and events for intra-agent processing. For example, when a Merchant receives a *NegotiateDetails* message from a Customer, the message is handled by the Merchant's *HandleProposals* Interface plan, which converts the message to a *proposeDetails* goal event and dispatches it for internal agent processing.

In the following sub-sections, we further describe the different components of the implementation, giving pseudo-code for the different plan types. As is typical for descriptions of implementation techniques and algorithms, the description is necessarily somewhat detailed.

3.1   Agent Beliefs and Interaction Goal State Representation

Agents are able to coordinate through the interaction goals via the use of a beliefset that is shared between the different types of plans within a given agent (refer to Figure 4). One important use of the beliefs is to represent the state of the interaction goals. This is done with a combination of three Boolean beliefs for each interaction goal: *in*, *finished*, and *success*. The *in* belief indicates that the IG is currently active. The *finished* belief is used to indicate whether the IG has been completed, whilst *success* indicates whether the IG has been successful.

The states of the IG and valid transitions between states are shown in Figure 5. The dashed circles represent intermediate states that have no conceptual meaning, but are required to change state from *active* to either *succeeded* or *failed*. The Boolean string in parentheses show the values of the three beliefs, *in*, *finished*, and *success*, respectively.

The general structure for an agent's beliefset, along with a brief summary of its use, is shown in Table 1.

[5] http://www.agent-software.com/
[6] http://vsis-www.informatik.uni-hamburg.de/projects/jadex/
[7] http://www.marcush.net/IRS/irs_downloads.html
[8] http://jason.sourceforge.net/

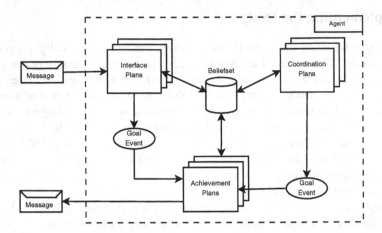

Fig. 4. Implementation Overview

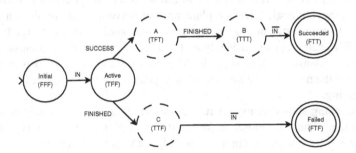

Fig. 5. Interaction Goals States

Table 1. Belief structure and use

Belief	Use
role	Identifies the agent's role in the interaction.
initiator	Identifies the interaction's initiator.
Interaction Goal Initiators	A series of beliefs which identifies the initiator of each IG, e.g. *tradeIGInitiator* (one per IG).
Interaction Goal States	A series of beliefs used to represent the state of IGs, i.e. *in*, *finished*, and *success*. Used for Coordination-Achievement Plan connections.
Interaction Goal Retries	A series of beliefs for retrying IGs. One for each IG that is allowed to be retried (refer to Section 3.4), e.g. *retryNegDetails*.
Interaction Specific Beliefs	Beliefs which are specific to the given interaction, e.g. *merchantName*, *product*, etc.

3.2   Coordination Plans

Coordination plans are directly derived from interaction goals from the *Interaction Goal Hierarchy* diagram. There are two flavours of Coordination plans: *leaf-node* and *non-*

Algorithm 1. Coordination Plan for *Trade* (Non-leaf-node Coordination Plan)

Require: inTrade == true
1: // **Coordination**
2:   inAgree = true
3:   waitFor(finishedAgree **and not** inAgree)
4:
5: **if** agreeSuccessful **then**
6:     inExchange = true
7:     waitFor(finishedExchange **and not** inExchange)
8:     **if** exchangeSuccessful **then**
9:         tradeSuccessful = true
10:     **end if**
11: **end if**
12:
13: // **Synchronization** (with other Coordination plans)
14: finishedTrade = true
15: inTrade = false

---

leaf-node. The *non-leaf-node* variety are obtained from IGs which have at least one sub-IG. These types of Coordination plans deal with coordination between themselves and other Coordination plans. *Leaf-node* Coordination plans are derived from IGs which have no sub-IGs. These plans deal with coordination between themselves and actions.

All non-leaf-node Coordination plans follow the same structure as the *Trade Coordination* plan, shown in Algorithm 1. The coordination rules, obtained from the sub-goal and temporal dependencies in Figure 2, are shown in the *Coordination* section of the plan (lines 1 – 11).

The *require* statement in Algorithm 1 specifies the trigger condition for the *Trade Coordination* plan. Thus when *inTrade* becomes *true*, i.e. the Trade IG is *active*, the plan begins execution. The initial step of the plan (line 2) is to set the Agree IG to the *active* state which triggers the *Agree Coordination* plan. The *waitFor()* statement blocks until the *Agree interaction goal* enters a final state (i.e. *succeeded* or *failed*), which is set by the *Agree coordination* plan.

When the Agree IG is achieved, the *Agree Coordination* plan sets the appropriate beliefs to move the Agree IG from *active* to either *succeeded* or *failed*, depending on the outcome. The condition in the *Trade Coordination* plan's *waitFor()* (line 3) is then satisfied and the plan continues executing.

If the *Agree* IG is successful, the interaction proceeds onto the *Exchange* goal, otherwise it is terminated. This is based on the temporal dependency link between the *Agree* and *Exchange* goals in Figure 2.

The *Synchronisation* section (lines 13 – 15 in Algorithm 1) is used to set the *finished* and *in* beliefs to move the IGs into a final state (either *succeeded* or *failed*).

The sub-goal relationships between the *Trade, Agree,* and *Exchange* interactions goals (refer to Figure 2) are implemented by the *Trade* Coordination plan waiting for completion of the *Agree* and *Exchange* IGs (lines 3 and 7 in Algorithm 1). The dependency between *Agree* and *Exchange* is achieved by triggering the *Exchange* coordination plan after the *Agree* IG has been successfully completed (lines 5 and 6).

Algorithm 2. Coordination Plan for *NegotiatePrice* (Leaf-node Coordination Plan)

Require: inNegPrice == true
 1: **if** not negPriceSuccess **then**
 2:     **if** role == initiator **then**
 3:         dispatch(new proposePriceGoal())
 4:     **end if**
 5: **end if**
 6:
 7: // **Synchronisation** (with Achievement plans)
 8: waitFor(finishedNegPrice)
 9: inNegPrice = false

The leaf-node Coordination plans follow the same structure as the *NegotiatePrice* Coordination plan, shown in Algorithm 2 and are slightly different to non-leaf-node Coordination plans. The main difference lies in lines 1 – 5 of the leaf-node Coordination plan. These lines dispatch a *proposePriceGoal* if the agent's role is the initiator of this IG. Every agent has a set of common beliefs which list the *initiator* of every IG and also a *role* belief which indicates their role in the interaction (e.g. *customer* or *merchant* in this particular scenario, refer to Table 1). In our e-commerce example, the Customer is the initiator for the *NegotiatePrice* IG, thus it takes the initiative and proposes a price to the Merchant.

Although both leaf and non-leaf plans have a Synchronisation section at the end, they serve different purposes. In the non-leaf-node plans, the Synchronisation section synchronises Coordination plans with other Coordination plans, whereas in the leaf-node plans, it is used to synchronise Coordination plans with Achievement plans. The *waitFor()* statement (line 8 of Algorithm 2) allows an arbitrary number of Achievement plans to run. When the final Achievement plan (derived from a final action) has completed its execution, the IG is in either the *B* or *C* state, shown in Figure 5 (i.e. the *finished* belief is set to *true*). This in turn un-blocks the *waitFor()* method and allows the Coordination plan to change the IG state to either *Succeeded* or *Failed*.

3.3   Achievement Plans

Achievement plans are derived directly from actions in the *Action Maps*. There are some slight variations to the Achievement plans depending on which type of action they are implementing, however, Achievement plans all follow the same structure as the *PriceAccepted* Achievement plan, shown in Algorithm 3.

Achievement plans are triggered via goal events that are usually dispatched from Interface or Coordination plans (refer to the first line of Algorithm 3). They have two distinct sections: *Synchronisation* and *Achieve*. The Synchronisation section is similar to that of the Coordination plans and synchronises the Achievement plan with its respective Coordination plan.

All Achievement plans begin with a Synchronisation section (lines 1 and 2), which acts as a guard condition and allows them to execute only when the interaction is achieving the correct interaction goal. Some achievement plans are only applicable in certain

---

Algorithm 3. Achievement Plan for the *PriceAccepted* Action

Require: priceAcceptedGoalEvent **and** priceAcceptable()
  1: // **Synchronisation** (with Coordination plan)
  2: waitFor(inNegPrice)
  3:
  4: // **Achieve IG** (application specific)
  5: price = priceAcceptedGoalEvent.getPrice()
  6: **if** action achieves IG **then**
  7:    negPriceSuccess = true // Action achieves IG
  8: **end if**
  9:
 10: // Finish IG, only done if action is final
 11: // **Synchronisation** (with Coordination plan)
 12: **if** action is final **then**
 13:    finishedNegPrice = true
 14: **end if**

---

situations, and the additional condition, for example only agreeing to a price if it is acceptable, is included in the required condition for the plan to run (first line of Algorithm 3). Whether an action is only applicable in certain situations can be seen in the action map as labels on the causality links. The definition of the condition (e.g. *priceAcceptable()*) is provided by the agent in question. The following section, Achieve IG (lines 4 and 5), contains application-specific code for the action. Furthermore, if an Achievement plan successfully achieves an IG (determined by application-specific conditions), it sets the *success* belief to *true* (lines 6 – 8).

Achievement plans implemented from a *final* action have an additional Synchronisation section at the end (lines 10 – 14) which signals the end of the Achievement plans' execution and returns processing control back to the appropriate Coordination plan for the given IG.

Note that unlike Coordination plans the synchronisation between actions is implicitly handled by having actions trigger other actions with internal events (within a role) and messages (between roles).

3.4 Implementing Failure Handling Mechanisms

This section details how the failure handling mechanisms described in Section 2.4 are implemented. An action failure can be addressed by either terminating the interaction or by attempting to recover from the failure (by using *action retry* or *rollback*).

Termination is implemented by adding three actions to each interaction goal that permits termination: *RequestTermination*, *TerminateOnRequest* and *Terminate*. For example, when the Customer wants to terminate the interaction, it uses the *RequestTermination* action (which is only available in particular IGs as defined by the interaction designer). The Merchant responds by using the *TerminateOnRequest* action. Once the Merchant has terminated the interaction, it replies to the Customer, which then performs the *Terminate* action. The interaction is then ended.

The *RequestTermination* plan is an achievement plan that simply requests a termination of the interaction from the current interaction goal. The *TerminateOnRequest* plan, also an achievement plan, contains IG specific details to terminate the interaction at that point. This may include matters such as re-setting beliefs or general clean up of the interaction and agent state.

Action retry can be implemented by incorporating an action which loops through the interaction again. For example, in Figure 3, the *RectifyPriceRejection* could be used to loop through the interaction again. This will involve *RectifyPriceRejection* triggering *ProposePrice* to send a new proposal with a higher price to the Merchant (not shown in Figure 3). Of course, an upper limit would have to be placed on the price to ensure that the Customer and Merchant do not haggle over the price endlessly.

The implementation of *rollback* is the most complicated of the three failure handling mechanisms. It is implemented by adding the following actions to every interaction goal which permits rollback: *ProposeRollback* and *Rollback* (one for each role). For example, if the Customer and Merchant cannot agree on a price, it is possible for them to rollback to re-negotiate the details and then try to negotiate on the price again. The Customer will perform *ProposeRollback* and the Merchant will use *Rollback* to roll back to the *NegotiateDetails* IG, after which the Merchant will send a message to let the Customer know that it has rolled back. The Customer will then use *Rollback* to roll back to the *NegotiateDetails* IG.

The *ProposeRollback* achievement plan simply sends a request to roll back. The *Rollback* achievement plan is the plan that does the actual rolling back. Rollback plans follow the same structure as Algorithm 4, an example of the Customer's rollback plan for rolling back from the *NegotiatePrice* IG to the *NegotiateDetails* IG.

Rollback is achieved by re-starting the interaction from a specific interaction goal. Therefore, when the *rollbackGoalEvent* is received and the interaction is in the correct IG (lines 1 and 2), the first step is to terminate the current IG, which will terminate the entire interaction. This is achieved by setting its three state representation beliefs to *false* (lines 4–6). Once the interaction is terminated (line 8), the appropriate beliefs are set to flag at which IG the interaction should re-start from (lines 9–17). This includes setting a Boolean belief (*retryNegDetails*) to notify that a rollback has been issued (line 17). The *retryNegDetails* belief is used when the interaction re-starts so that the *ProposeDetails* achievement plan will request a different solution (i.e. colour) to the previous one in order to achieve a different result so that the *NegotiateDetails* IG may succeed. The remainder of the *rollback* plan simply re-starts the interaction and notifies any relevant agents. In the case of the Customer, it does not have to notify any agents that it has rolled back.

3.5 Sample Execution

In this section, we provide an example trace of the implementation in which the Customer is attempting to purchase a monitor at the maximum price of $100 with the following colour preferences: red, blue, yellow, and green and the Merchant is selling blue and yellow monitors at the minimum prices of $110 and $100 respectively. In this situation, for a successful sale to occur, the Merchant must sell a yellow monitor to the Customer at $100. We demonstrate how such an interaction executes on an implemen-

---

Algorithm 4. Customer Rollback Plan (from *NegotiatePrice* to *NegotiateDetails*)

Require: rollbackGoalEvent
  1: // **Synchronise** (with Coordination plan)
  2: waitFor(inNegPrice)
  3: // **1. Terminate current IG**
  4: negPriceSuccessful = false
  5: finishedNegPrice = true
  6: inNegPrice = false
  7: // **2. Wait for apex IG to terminate**
  8: waitFor(finishedTrade **and not** inTrade)
  9: // **3. Set appropriate beliefs to re-start interaction and to begin at desired IG (shortcut)**
 10: // **3.1. Reset current IG beliefs**
 11: finishedNegPrice = false
 12: // **3.2. Set beliefs of IG to begin next interaction from (shortcut)**
 13: negDetailsSuccessful = false
 14: finishedNegDetails = false
 15: inNegDetails = true
 16: // **3.3. Set beliefs for "retry" attempt**
 17: retryNegDetails = true
 18: // **4. Re-start interaction, set "in" belief of apex stage to "true"**
 19: inTrade = true
 20: // **5. Notify relevant agents**

---

tation based on a goal-oriented Hermean design. Figure 6 presents the initial execution steps graphically.

The interaction begins with the Customer receiving a request to start the interaction. This is handled by its Interface plan, *HandleRequests*, which flags a Boolean belief (*inTrade*) to start the interaction. The Customer then enters the *Trade* IG, then the *Agree* IG, and then *DetermineAvailability* IG (based on the Interaction Goal Hierarchy and the Coordination plans, refer to Figure 2 and Algorithm 1 respectively).

The *DetermineAvailability* Coordination plan executes and triggers its achievement plan, *RequestAvailability*, which executes and sends a message to the Merchant, enquiring about the availability of a monitor.

The message is received by the Merchant's Interface plan and is converted into a *checkAvailablity* goal which triggers the Merchant's *GoodsAvailable* plan (since it does sell monitors). Although the *GoodsAvailable* plan is triggered, it does not execute as it is waiting for the Merchant to enter the *DetermineAvailability* IG. Since the Merchant has not started the *Trade* interaction, when it receives the message from the Customer, it starts the interaction (at the *Trade* IG) and moves into the *DetermineAvailability* IG. The *GoodsAvailable* plan then executes and sends a message to the Customer, informing it that there are monitors available. The *DetermineAvailability* IG is then successfully achieved for the Merchant.

The Customer's Interface plan, *HandleRequests*, handles the message and converts it into a goal for internal agent processing. The *DetermineAvailability* IG is successfully achieved for the Customer, it moves into the *NegotiateDetails* IG and its *ProposeDetails* achievement plan is triggered. The *ProposeDetails* plan sends a message to the

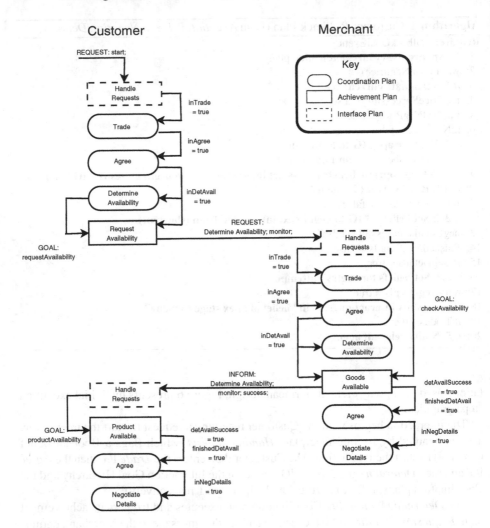

Fig. 6. Sample execution

Merchant to request a red monitor. As the Merchant does not have red monitors, it sends a rejection message to the Customer. The Customer's *DetailsRejected* plan is triggered (after the message is converted to a goal by the Customer's Interface plan). The *DetailsRejected* plan then creates a new goal to trigger the *ProposeDetails* plan to send a message requesting a blue monitor.

As the Merchant sells blue monitors, it returns a positive reply to the Customer and moves into the *NegotiatePrice* IG. The Customer receives the message and also moves into the *NegotiatePrice* IG.

The negotiations over the price of the monitor proceed similarly to the negotiation of the colour of the monitor. When the Merchant rejects the Customer's highest price of $100 (as the Merchant's minimum is $110), the Customer's *RectifyPriceRejection* plan triggers the *ProposeRollback* plan, which sends a rollback request to the Merchant. The

Merchant then uses its *Rollback* plan to return to the *NegotiateDetails* IG and notifies the Customer that it has successfully rolled back. The Customer then executes its *Rollback* to roll back to the *NegotiateDetails* IG.

The Customer and the Merchant re-negotiate the colour of the monitor and settle on yellow. The interaction then proceeds to the negotiation of the price and is able to terminate successfully.

4 Conclusion

We have (briefly) outlined the Hermes design process, focussing on its notations and outcomes, and then presented a mapping from Hermes designs to plans that realise the designed interaction. This mapping produces collections of plans that can be implemented using a goal-plan agent architecture.

A Hermean design for a trading scenario based on the NetBill protocol has been implemented by following this mapping. We have also implemented a Hermean design for a brokering scenario based on [11]. These implementations have shown that the mapping works and that the implementations are capable of realising flexible and robust interactions.

4.1 Related Work

There are other approaches which aim to provide more flexible agent interaction by moving away from a message-centric approach. These include approaches based on *social commitments* [7, 8, 12], Kumar *et al.*'s *landmark-based* approach [13], and Hutchison and Winikoff's *goal-plan* approach [6].

Approaches based on social commitments such as Yolum and Singh's commitment machines [7, 8] or the work of Flores and Kremer [12] captures the meanings of agents' actions in terms of their effects on social commitments. A social commitment is made from one agent to another and represents a condition which an agent will endeavour to bring about for another agent[9]. Commitments are attained and manipulated through inter-agent communicative acts. Therefore, in the course of interacting, agents create and manipulate commitments. Although both approaches allow for complex interactions which would be difficult to implement with message-centric protocols, their design aspects are not well defined. It is not obvious how to determine what commitments are required for a given interaction.

In Kumar *et al.*'s work [13], it is argued that the state of affairs brought about by a communicative act is more important than the communicative act itself. As such, the focus of the work is on the states of affairs, which are represented as landmarks. Thus, an interaction involves navigating through landmarks to reach a desired final state of affairs. Their work is theoretical in nature, and requires significant expertise in modal and temporal logics. Although an implementation ("STAPLE") has been mentioned, no details have been published beyond two posters [14, 15].

Hutchison and Winikoff's approach [6], involves modelling protocols as goals and plans. This involves determining the goals of the protocol and defining plans which are

---

[9] Flores and Kremer define commitments as being to perform actions, rather than to bring about conditions.

able to achieve the goals. Their work can be seen as a predecessor to our work: it gives neither a detailed design process, nor a mapping from design to implementation.

Although the *SODA* methodology [16] — like Hermes — deals with inter-agent design and treats interactions as first class entities, their aims are different. SODA is firstly intended for the analysis and design of Internet-based systems, whilst Hermes is more generic in that it is not specifically intended for Internet-based systems. Furthermore, SODA aims at a broader design methodology in that it is for the design of agent societies whereas Hermes is for the design of agent interactions only (agent interaction design can be seen as a subset of agent society design). Finally and perhaps most importantly, the interaction design in SODA appears to be message-centric as they seem to be focused on passing appropriate information between entities.

4.2   Future Work

One area for future work is to develop a mapping for non-goal-plan agents. In addition there are a number of areas where the Hermes methodology can be further developed including the provision of tool support for the design process. One possibility that we are considering is to develop this by extending the Prometheus Design Tool[10]. We envisage that this tool support will encompass the generation of skeleton code in accordance with the mapping described in this paper.

The mapping described in this paper targets plan-goal agent platforms. One area for future work is to target other platforms that do not define agents in terms of goal-triggered plans. One approach is to compile down to interaction protocols using some representation such as finite state machines, Petri nets, or AUML.

Agent interactions are only one part of creating an agent system. As such, we intend to integrate Hermes with an agent methodology, such as Prometheus [10]. The design methodology and notation will also require further refinement as we undertake research into adapting Hermes to function with protocols which involve many agents. Other, longer term, areas for future work include looking at the verification of goal-oriented interactions, and an experimental evaluation of the approach.

Acknowledgements

We would like to acknowledge the support of Agent Oriented Software Pty. Ltd. and of the Australian Research Council (ARC) under grant LP0453486.

References

1. Huget, M.P., Odell, J.: Representing agent interaction protocols with agent UML. In: Proceedings of the Fifth International Workshop on Agent Oriented Software Engineering (AOSE). (2004)
2. Cheong, C., Winikoff, M.: Hermes: A Methodology for Goal-Oriented Agent Interactions (Poster). In: The Fourth International Joint Conference on Autonomous Agents and Multi-Agents Systems. To appear. (2005)

---

[10] http://www.cs.rmit.edu.au/agents/pdt

3. Cheong, C., Winikoff, M.: Hermes: Designing goal-oriented agent interactions. In: Proceedings of the 6th International Workshop on Agent-Oriented Software Engineering (AOSE-2005). (2005)
4. Pokahr, A., Braubach, L., Lamersdorf, W.: Jadex: Implementing a BDI-Infrastructure for JADE Agents. EXP - In Search of Innovation (Special Issue on JADE) **3** (2003) 76 – 85
5. Sirbu, M., Tygar, J.D.: NetBill: An Internet Commerce System Optimized for Network-Delivered Services. IEEE Personal Communications **2** (1995) 34 – 39
6. Hutchison, J., Winikoff, M.: Flexibility and Robustness in Agent Interaction Protocols. In: Workshop on Challenges in Open Agent Systems at the First International Joint Conference on Autonomous Agents and Multi-Agents Systems. (2002)
7. Yolum, P., Singh, M.P.: Reasoning about commitments in the event calculus: An approach for specifying and executing protocols. Annals of Mathematics and Artificial Intelligence (AMAI), Special Issue on Computational Logic in Multi-Agent Systems **42** (2004) 227–253
8. Yolum, P., Singh, M.P.: Flexible protocol specification and execution: Applying event calculus planning using commitments. In: Proceedings of the 1st Joint Conference on Autonomous Agents and MultiAgent Systems (AAMAS). (2002) 527–534
9. DeLoach, S.A., Wood, M.F., Sparkman, C.H.: Multiagent systems engineering. International Journal of Software Engineering and Knowledge Engineering **11** (2001) 231–258
10. Padgham, L., Winikoff, M.: Developing Intelligent Agent Systems: A Practical Guide. John Wiley and Sons (2004) ISBN 0-470-86120-7.
11. Mbala, A., Padgham, L., Winikoff, M.: Design options for subscription managers. In: Proceedings of the Seventh International Bi-Conference Workshop on Agent-Oriented Information Systems (AOIS). (2005)
12. Flores, R.A., Kremer, R.C.: A principled modular approach to construct flexible conversation protocols. In Tawfik, A., Goodwin, S., eds.: Advances in Artificial Intelligence, Springer-Verlag, LNCS 3060 (2004) 1–15
13. Kumar, S., Huber, M.J., Cohen, P.R.: Representing and executing protocols as joint actions. In: Proceedings of the First International Joint Conference on Autonomous Agents and Multi-Agent Systems, Bologna, Italy, ACM Press (2002) 543 – 550
14. Kumar, S., Cohen, P.R., Huber, M.J.: Direct execution of team specifications in STAPLE. In: Proceedings of the First International Joint Conference on Autonomous Agents & Multi-Agent Systems (AAMAS 2002), ACM Press (2002) 567–568
15. Kumar, S., Cohen, P.R.: STAPLE: An agent programming language based on the joint intention theory. In: Proceedings of the Third International Joint Conference on Autonomous Agents & Multi-Agent Systems (AAMAS 2004), ACM Press (2004) 1390–1391
16. Omicini, A.: SODA: Societies and infrastructures in the analysis and design of agent-based systems. In: Proceedings of the 1st International Workshop on Agent-Oriented Software Engineering (AOSE-2000). (2000) 185–193

Part IV

Multi-agent Platforms and Organisation

Part IV

Multi-agent Platforms and Organisation

Organization and Mobility in Mobile Agent Computing

Ichiro Satoh

National Institute of Informatics,
2-1-2 Hitotsubashi, Chiyoda-ku, Tokyo 101-8430, Japan
ichiro@nii.ac.jp

Abstract. A mobile agent system for organizing multiple mobile agents is presented. It provides two unique two mechanisms for dynamically organizing mobile agents, which may be running on single or multiple computers. The first enables a mobile agent to contain other mobile agents inside it and migrate to another mobile agent or computer with its inner agents. It provides an approach to composing large-scale mobile software from a collection of mobile agents and using mobile agents as deployable software components. The second enables a mobile agent to be deployed at computers according to the movements of other mobile agents. It can move a federation of agents running on different computers, over a distributed system. It can build and aggregate distributed applications from one or more mobile components that can be dynamically deployed at mobile or stationary computers during the execution of the application. This paper also presents a prototype implementation of the system and its application.

1 Introduction

Distributed computing systems are composed of a number of software components running on different computers and interacting with one another via a network. The complexity of modern distributed systems impairs our ability to deploy components at appropriate computers using traditional approaches, such as those that are centralized and top-down Moreover, the requirements of applications in a distributed system tend to vary and change dynamically. Applications must adapt to such changes. Software components, which an application consists of, need to be adapted and deployed at computers in a distributed system according to changes in the requirements of the applications and the structure and computational resources of the system. Mobile agents can provide a solution to this problem, because they are autotomous programs that can travel from computer to computer in a network, at times and to places of their own choosing. Unfortunately, existing mobile agent systems lack the mechanisms for structurally assembling and relocating multiple mobile agents, which may run on different computers.

To solve this problem, a few attempts to organize mobile agents have been proposed, e.g., MobileSpaces [11], CLAIM [5], and FarGo [7]. MobileSpaces and CLAIM enable each mobile agent to be organized within a tree structure and to migrate to other mobile agents, which may run on different computers, with its inner agents. FarGo [7] introduces the notion of a dynamic layout for distributed applications. It explicitly binds more than one mobile agent to a single mobile agent and, when the latter migrates to another location, it relocates the latter agent at the same destination to follow the former agent. This paper proposes a framework for structurally and dynamically federating

R.H. Bordini et al. (Eds.): ProMAS 2005, LNAI 3862, pp. 187–205, 2006.

multiple mobile agent-based components running on either the same computer or different computers. The framework makes two contributions to distributed systems. The first enables large-scale mobile software to be composed from a collection of mobile agents and the second enables a mobile agent to be deployed at computers according to the movements of other mobile agents in a self-organizing manner. The system provides a general test-bed for bio-inspired approaches over real distributed systems.

In this paper, we describe our design goals (Section 2), the design of our framework, and a prototype implementation (Section 3). We outline programs in the system and applications running on it (Section 4), and explain the current status of the implementation (Section 5). We also describe our experience with the framework (Section 6). We then briefly review related work (Section 7), provide a summary, and discuss some future issues (Section 8).

2 Approach

Mobile agents within this framework are computational entities like other mobile agents. When an agent migrates, not only its code but also its state can be transferred to the destination.[1]

2.1 Mobile Agent Composition

Our framework enabled us to construct a distributed computing system as a federation of mobile agent-based software components running on the same or different computers. It provides two approaches for composing mobile agents.

Strong Composition. The framework enables a large-scale mobile agent to be organized within a tree structure according to the following notions.

- **Agent Hierarchy:** Each mobile agent can be contained within at most one mobile agent.
- **Inter-agent Migration:** Each mobile agent can migrate between mobile agents as a whole with all its inner agents.

When an agent contains other agents, we call the former agent a *parent* and the latter agents *children*. Agents that nested by an agent are called *descendent* agents of the agent, and conversely agents that are nesting an agent are called *ancestral* agents of the agent. Parent agents are responsible for providing their own services and resources to their children, and can directly access the services and resources offered by their children. These concepts themselves were discussed in our previous paper [11].

Weak Composition. The framework builds partitioned applications as mobile agent-based software components, enabling them to run on different computers and move to other computers while running. The movement of one agent may affect other agents. For example, two components may be required to be on the same computer when the first is a program that controls the keyboard and the second is a program that displays

---

[1] The framework treats the mobile code approach as a subset of the mobile agent approach.

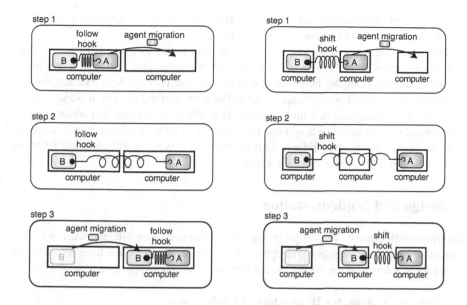

Fig. 1. Component migration with relocation policy

content on the screen. The framework enables each agent to explicitly specify a policy, called a *hook*, for agent migration. The current implementation provides two types of hooks, as shown in Fig. 1. The first enables an agent to follow another component and the second enables an agent to migrate to the source location of another agent.

2.2 Prototype-Based Agent-Creation

Object-oriented languages, which most existing mobile agents are defined in, are classified into two types: class-based and prototype-based. About twenty years ago, researchers discussed the advantages and disadvantages of these two languages.[2] Although the former has swept over almost the entire-field of object orientation, the latter still has several distinct advantages. Existing mobile agents are defined with class-based oriented languages, e.g., Java. Nevertheless, mobile agents can also be viewed as prototype-based objects. When a mobile agent migrates to another computer, the state of the agent's running program is marshaled into data and is then transmitted to the destination as passive data with its program code. Mobile agents can easily and naturally make replicas of themselves by duplicating their marshaled agents. As a result, mobile agents can be created by cloning existing agents as well as instantiating them from classes to define their behaviors. Mobile agents, on the other hand, cannot control the process of cloning themselves at program-level, because their cloning mechanisms are supported by their runtime systems or libraries, instead of their programs. Cloning

---

[2] There have been numerous discussions on the notions of prototype-based paradigms and delegation. However, we do not intend to discuss the definitions of these notions again. We will only introduce the notions as an approach to programming mobile agents.

facilities for object-creation provided by prototype-based languages are useful in enabling mobile agents to customize their cloning.

Class-based languages provide the notion of inheritance as a mechanism for sharing the behavior of objects, whereas prototype-based languages provide the notion of delegation-sharing both the behavior and state of objects. Although existing mobile agents have no mechanisms corresponding to the notion of delegation, it makes agents extensible. For example, each mobile agent is defined by classes that already know everything about the agent so that it cannot adapt its behavior to changes in its requirements or its execution environment. This problem is solved by allowing agents to be created by extending or sharing other agents.

3   Design and Implementation

This framework consists of two parts: runtime systems and mobile agents. It was implemented with Java language and operated on the Java virtual machine. We tried to contain the implementation within the framework as much as possible.

3.1   Runtime Systems for Hierarchical Mobile Agents

Each runtime system runs on a computer and executes and migrates mobile agents. Each also establishes at most one TCP connection with each of its neighboring systems and exchanges control messages, agents, and inter-component communications with these through the connection. Fig. 2 outlines the basic structure of a runtime system, which is similar to the micro-kernel architecture in several operating systems. That is, the system itself only offers minimal functions and other functions are implemented in mobile agents running on the system.

Agent Hierarchy Management. Each runtime system manages an agent hierarchy as a tree structure in which each node contains a mobile agent and its attributes. Also, each runtime system corresponds to the root node in its own tree structure. This framework

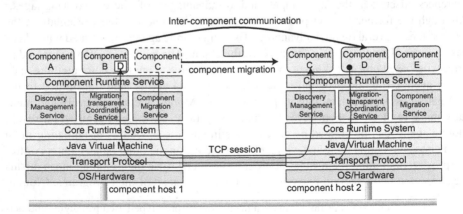

Fig. 2. Architecture for runtime system

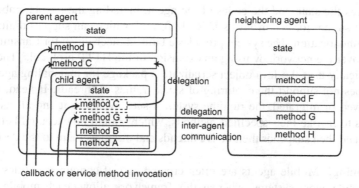

Fig. 3. Delegation between mobile agents

assumes that each agent is active but subordinate to its container agent. Therefore, each agent has direct control of its descendent agents. That is, an agent can instruct its descendent agents to move to other agents, and serialize and destroy them. No agent has direct control over its ancestral agents.

Agent Execution Management.   The runtime system can control all agents in its agent hierarchy, under the protection of Java's security manager. Each agent can have one or more activities, which are implemented by using the Java thread library. Furthermore, the runtime system maintains the life-cycle of agents: initialization, execution, suspension, and termination. When the life-cycle state of an agent is changed, the runtime system issues certain events to the agent and its descendent agents. The system can impose specified time constraints on all method invocations between agents to avoid being blocked forever.

Agent Delegation Management.   Agent hierarchy not only defines the structure of mobile agents but also their functions. Each agent can explicitly provide a set of service methods, which can be accessed by its children, instead of descendent agents. That is, a child agent can share the behavior and state of its parent agent like the notion of delegation in prototype-based languages. Fig. 3 has an example of delegation between mobile agents. The parent agent provides a method, called `writeOnDisk`, to save data in secondary storage but the child agent has no methods of saving its state. However, the child can access the parent's method to save its state in storage. As a result, the semantics and properties of an agent are partially provided by its parent agent. It is worth mentioning why we imposed the restriction that a mobile agent could not access any services supported by ancestral agents other than their parent and stationary agents. This restriction is the key idea in allowing successful migration to occur. If it were not imposed, then migrating an agent could mean that the descendants of that agent might suddenly find they could no longer delegate services upon which they relied.

Agent Migration.   When an agent is moved inside a computer, the agent and its inner agents can still be running. When an agent is transferred over a network, the runtime system stores the state and the codes of the agent, including the agents embedded in it, into a bit-stream formed in Java's JAR file format, which can support digital signatures for authentication. The system provides a built-in mechanism for transmitting the bit-stream over the network by using an extension of the HTTP protocol.[3] The current system basically uses the Java object serialization package for marshaling agents. The package does not support the capturing of stack frames of threads. Instead, when an agent is saved or migrated, the runtime system issues events to it and all its descendent agents to invoke their specified methods, which should be executed before their migration, and then suspends their active threads and migrates them to the destination.

Agent Cloning. Mobile agents are often created as self-contained entities in other existing mobile agent systems, whereas this framework allows each mobile agent to share the behaviors of its ancestral agents. Therefore, if a clone had been created from an agent, which relies on the services of its parent, it could no longer access these services. Object-oriented languages, on the other hand, provide two mechanisms for cloning objects: shallow-copy and deep-copy. The former creates a clone of the state of an agent and shares the behaviors with the agent from which it was cloned by means of delegation. The latter creates a clone of both the state and behavior of the agent. Each runtime system provides two approaches corresponding to the two mechanisms.

- The first creates a clone of only the target agent and provides the forwarder agents of its ancestral agents to the clone so that the clone agent can access the services provided by the ancestral agents.
- The second not only creates a clone of the agent but also the clones of ancestral agents whose services the agent may access.

The current implementation does not support a mechanism for analyzing which ancestral agents the clone shares services with. Therefore, when an agent creates a clone, it specifies which ancestral agents should be cloned with it. Since the framework assumes that a component and its clone are independent, it does not support any mechanism for sharing their updating states with them.

3.2   Mobile Agent Model

Each agent in the current implementation of the framework is a collection of Java objects in the standard JAR file format.

Interagent Communication. Each agent can offer a meeting place for its inner agents. It initially supports basic types of inter-agent communication, e.g., asynchronous one-way message passing, synchronous method call, and future communication. However, runtime systems do not offer mechanisms for communicating between agents, which may be contained in different parents, in a computer. Instead, the system provides two agents, called forwarder agents, to support inter-agent communications between agents contained in different agents. Each agent has its own proxy agent, called a *forwarder*

---

[3] Section 5 describes how the system enables agent migration protocols to be implemented in mobile agents.

agent. When it receives messages, it automatically redirects these to its or their specified destinations. An agent permits other agents to communicate with it and it thus deploys its forwarder agents at their parent agents. As a result, the agents can send messages to the agent via its forwarder agent. When they want replies from the agent, they deploy their forwarder agents at it via its forwarder agent.

Forwarder agents are used for tracking the current locations of moving agents. When an agent wants to interact with another agent, it must know where the target agent is currently located. Immediately before an agent moves into another agent, it creates and leaves a forwarder agent behind. The forwarder agent inherits the name of the moving agent and transfers the visiting agent to the new location of the moving agent. Therefore, when an agent wants to migrate itself to or send a message to another agent that has moved elsewhere, it can migrate into the forwarder agent instead of the target agent. The forwarder agent then automatically transfers the visiting agent or message to the current location of the target agent.

Several schemes for efficiently forwarding messages or agents to and locating moving agents have been explored in the field of process/object migration in distributed operating systems. Such forwarder agents can easily support most of these schemes because they are programmable entities that can flexibly negotiate with one another. Moreover, since forwarder agents are still mobile agents, they can be dynamically deployed at remote computers.

Agent Relocation. When multiple mobile agents coordinate with one another, if one of them migrates to another computer, the others may be required to migrate to other computers. This framework provides a mechanism for enabling mobile agents to be dynamically deployed at computers according to the movement of other agents. The mechanism itself provides *carrier* agents, which convey their inner agents over a network. It enables each carrier agent to specify at most one target container agent. The former agent also carries its inner agents to a suitable computer according to its own policy, when the latter agent carries its inner agents to another computer or agent. We assumed that a carrier agent would have a policy for another carrier agent. That is, when the former agent migrated to another agent or computer, the framework would provide carriers agents based on several basic policies. For example, the latter (or its clone) migrates to the former's destination through the *follow* policy (or *dispatch* policy), and the latter (or its clone) would migrate to the former's source through the *shift* policy (or *fill* policy).

Each carrier agent can contain at most one mobile agent. It can inherit its inner agent and forward its received messages and visiting agent to this inner agent. Therefore, it can be viewed as its inner agent by external agents, which interact with this inner agent, and it can explicitly restrict the mobility of the inner agent. The carrier agent carries the inner agent according to its own policy. Although each carrier agent can have at most one policy, agents can be contained in one or more carrier agents.[4] We can easily define more advanced or complicated policies by combining these policies.

Since carrier agents are just programmable entities, we can easily customize their policies. The current implementation assumes that the carrier agents comprising a group

---

[4] When carrier agents are nested, a parent carrier agent's policy proceeds to its descendent carrier agents' policy.

will be deployed to computers within a localized space smaller than the domain of a sub-network for UDP multicasting. Therefore, the deployment of carrier agents is managed by exchanging control messages through UDP-multicasting. When a carrier agent migrates to another computer, the destination computers ask the source computer (or the previous source computer) to multicast a query message about carrier agents whose policies contain the moving carrier agent.

3.3   Mobile Agent Programming Model

Each agent is defined as a collection of Java objects. It has its own name based on the agent hierarchy and a message queue for incoming messages. It has to be an instance of the Agent interface, the ContainerAgent interface, the DuplicatableAgent interface, and/or the MobileAgent interface. The first defines the callback methods of a stationary agent, the second defines the callback methods of a container agent, the third defines the callback methods of a duplicatable agent, and the fourth defines the callback methods of a mobile agent. The callback methods are invoked by the runtime system when the life-cycle of a mobile agent changes. Parts of these interfaces are as follows:

```
public interface Agent {
    public void create(AgentEvent evt, Context ctxt);
    public void destroy(AgentEvent evt, Context ctxt);
}
```

where create() and destroy() are invoked after the agent is created and before it is terminated. This framework uses interfaces for agents as declarations about their basic functions, e.g., mobility and duplicatability.

```
public interface ContainerAgent extends Agent {
    public void add(AgentEvent evt, Context ctxt);
    public void remove(AgentEvent evt, Context ctxt);
}
```

The above program is the definition of the ContainerAgent interface, where add() is invoked after the agent has received another agent and remove() is invoked after it has sent the visiting agent.

```
public interface DuplicatableAgent extends Serializable, Agent {
    public void duplicate(AgentEvent evt, Context ctxt);
    public void parent(AgentEvent evt, Context ctxt);
    public void child(AgentEvent evt, Context ctxt);
}
```

Each agent must implement the above interface so that it can be cloned. duplicate() is invoked before the agent is duplicated. parent() is invoked at the original agent and child() is invoked at a clone of the agent after it is duplicated.

```
public interface MobileAgent extends Serializable, Agent {
    public void arrive(AgentEvent evt, Context ctxt);
    public void leave(AgentEvent evt, Context ctxt);
}
```

Each mobile agent must be an instance of the above interface. `arrive()` is invoked before the agent has migrated to another location `leave()` is invoked after it has migrated. The `AgentEvent` class in these programs defines information about the agent, e.g., its current location, source, and destination. The `Context` class defines service methods for agents as follows:

```
class Context {
  void go(URL url) throws NoSuchHostException { ... }
  void go(URL url, String methodName) throws NoSuchHostException,
    throws NoSuchMethodException { ... }
  AgentID shallowCopy() throws IllegalAccessException { ... }
  AgentID deepCopy(AgentID aid) throws IllegalAccessException { ... }
  ServiceID getService(Message msg)} throws NoServiceException { ... }
  Object execService(ServiceID sid)} throws IllegalAcceessException { ... }
  setPolicy(AgentProfile cref, MigrationPolicy mpolicy) { ... }
  setTTL(int lifespan) { ... }
  .....
}
```

We will now explain the main methods defined in the `Context` class.

- When an agent performs go (url, methodName, it migrates itself to the destination agent specified as the `url` and executes the method specified in the second argument. This url specifies the destination agent for agent migration based on the containment relationships of an agent hierarchy on a local or remote computer as follows:

  MATP://some.where.com/application-name/function-name

  where `MATP` specifies the protocol for agent migration.
- By invoking shallowCopy(), an agent creates a clone of itself, including its code and instance variables and its inner agents. When an agent invokes deepCopy() with the identifier of its ancestral agent, it creates a clone of its code and instance variables and its inner agents, and clones of the specified ancestral agent and the agents that are contained in the ancestral agent.
- An agent can access service methods provided by its parent agent by invoking getService() with an instance of the `Message` class, which can specify the kind of message, arbitrary objects as arguments, and the deadline for timeout exceptions.
- The framework provides APIs for invoking the methods of other agents. Our programming interface for method invocation is similar to CORBA's dynamic invocation interface and does not have to statically define any stub or skeleton interfaces through a precompiler approach because distributed computing environments are dynamic.
- The setTTL() specifies the life span, called time-to-live (TTL), of the agent. The span decrements TTL over time. When the TTL of an agent reaches zero, the agent automatically removes itself.

While each agent is running, it can declare at most one deployment policy and one or more message policies by invoking setPolicy of the `Context` class. Although policies are open for developers to define their own policies, the current implementation provides the following deployment policies.

- If an agent declares a *follow* policy for another agent, when the latter migrates to another computer, the former migrates to the latter's destination computer.
- If an agent declares a *dispatch* policy for another agent, when the latter migrates to another computer, a copy of the former is created and deployed at the latter's destination computer.
- If an agent declares a *shift* policy for another agent, when the latter migrates to another computer, the former migrates to the latter's source computer.
- If an agent declares a *fill* policy for another agent, when the latter migrates to another computer, a copy of the former is created and deployed at the latter's source computer.

When an agent is created, the dispatch and fill policies can explicitly control whether the newly created agent can inherit the state of its original agent. The following message policies forward messages to agents when messages are specified in the policies.

- If an agent declares a *forward* policy for another agent, when specified messages are sent to other agents, the messages are forwarded to the latter as well as the former.
- If an agent declares a *delegate* policy for another agent, when specified messages are send to the former, the messages are forwarded to the latter but not to the former.

Fig. 4 outlines four deployment policies, which are related to phenomena in biological processes. For example, a `follow` policy enables an agent to approach another agent. For example, when multiple agents declare a policy for a leader agent, they can swarm around it. A *shift* policy enables an agent to follow the movement of another agent. The former agent can track the latter as it moves. The policy thus corresponds to the

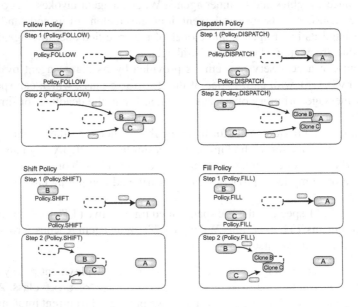

Fig. 4. Basic migration policies

buttons for operating mobile agents

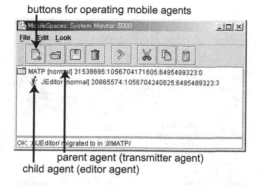

parent agent (transmitter agent)
child agent (editor agent)

Fig. 5. Control window for runtime system

phenomenon of cytoplasmic streaming. A `dispatch`) policy enables an agent to stay in the current location and then deploy its clone at the destination of another moving agent. It can model the footprint of a motile cell. We have assumed that an agent can declare the policy for another agent and specify the TTLs of its clones as their life-spans. As the latter agent moves, cloned former agents are deployed at its footmark and these clones are automatically volatilized after their life-spans are over. Therefore, the clone agents can be viewed as a pheromone that is left behind after the latter agent has moved on. A *fill* policy corresponds to the phenomenon of cell division. The framework is open to define policies as long as they are subclasses of the `MigrationPolicy` so that we can easily define new policies, including bio-inspired ones. A *forward* policy is useful when two agents share the same information and a *delegate* policy provides a master-slave relation between agents.

4   Current Status

A prototype implementation of this framework was constructed with Sun's Java Developer Kit version 1.4. The implementation provided graphical user interfaces for operating the mobile agents shown in Fig. 5. These interfaces allowed us to easily load and migrate mobile agents via full drag-and-drop operations.

Basic Performance. Although the current implementation was not constructed for performance, we evaluated that of several basic operations in a distributed system where eight computers (Pentium-M 1.4 MHz with Windows XP Professional and J2SE 1.4.2) were connected through a fast ethernet. The cost of agent migration in an agent hierarchy was measured to be 4 ms, including the cost of checking whether the visiting agent was permitted to enter the destination agent or not. The cost of agent migration between agents allocated on two computers was measured to be 30 ms. The moving agent was simple and consisted of basic callback methods and contained two child agents. Its data capacity was about 7 Kbytes (zip-compressed). The cost of agent migration included that of opening TCP-transmission, marshaling the agents, migrating the agents from their source hosts to their destination hosts, unmarshaling the agents, and verifying security.

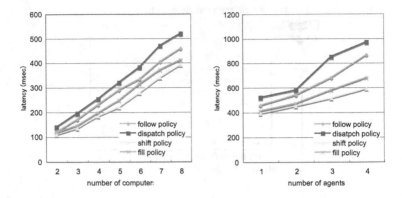

Fig. 6. Cost of multiple-hops for two agents between two to eight computers (left) and cost of multiple-hops for multiple agents between eight computers (right)

The left of Fig. 6 illustrates the cost of multiple-hops for two agents between two to eight computers, where the first agent declares a follow, dispatch, shift, or fill policy for the second and the second migrates between these computers sequentially without synchronizing the migration of the first. The latency between two computers is measured as the half-time of the round-trip time between the source and destination computers. To accurately measure the latency between more than three computers, these computers were connected through a ring topology. That is, the start and and goal of the second agent are assigned to the same computer and we measured the difference between the timing for the first agent to start and the second to arrive at the computer. Each cost at the left of Fig. 6 is the latency for the first agent arriving after the second has begun to migrate to another computer. The cost of agent migration according the dispatch (or fill) policy is larger than that of the the follow (or shift) policy, because the former needs to create a copy of the first agent that has the policy. The cost of agent migration according to follow (or dispatch) is larger than that for dispatch (or shift), because the former and latter agents are deployed at different computers.

The right of Fig. 6 shows the cost of multiple-hops for multiple agents between eight computers, when agents (from one to four) have follow, dispatch, shift, or fill policies for a moving agent. Unfortunately, the cost with many hops is large because the follow and dispatch policies vary due to congestion at several computers. That is, two or more agents may attempt to have their own active threads in a single processor and to simultaneously transmit themselves to the destinations of their target agent in a TCP network connection. Once agents experience congestion at a computer, they tend to migrate as a chunk to further destinations rather than as individuals and this often engulfs other newly arrival agents. Congestion does not always reappear, since computers are not synchronized and congestion often causes more congestion in agent routes. We expect that there will be large fluctuations in the cost of agent migration in large-scale, heterogenous, distributed systems.

Security. The current implementation can encrypt agents before migrating them over the network and can then decrypt them after they arrive at their destinations. Moreover, since each agent is simply a programmable entity, it can explicitly encrypt its particular fields and migrate itself with these fields and its own cryptographic procedure. The Java virtual machine could explicitly restrict agents so that they can only access specified resources to protect hosts from malicious agents. Although the current implementation cannot protect agents from malicious hosts, the runtime system supports authentication mechanisms for agent migration so that each agent host can only send agents to, and only receive from, trusted hosts.

5   Initial Experience

This section presents several example applications that illustrate how the framework works.

5.1   Point-to-Point Channels for Agent Migration

The first example is mobile agent-based active networking for mobile agents. It enables point-to-point agent migration to be provided by mobile agents, called *transmitters*. Transmitter agents correspond to a data-link layer or a network layer and are responsible for establishing point-to-point channels for agent migration between the source host and destination host through a (single-hop or multiple-hops) data transmission infrastructure, such as TCP/IP, as shown in Fig. 7. They abstract away the variety in the underlying network infrastructure and exchange their inner agents with coexisting agents running at remote computers through their favorite communication protocols. Furthermore, transmitter agents are implemented as mobile agents so that they can be dynamically added to and removed from the system by migrating and replacing corresponding agents, enabling them to keep up with changes in the network environment. After an agent arrives at a transmitter agent from the upper layer, the arriving agent indicates its final destination. The transmitter suspends the arriving agent (including its inner agents), then requests the core system to serialize the state and code of the arriving agent. It next sends the serialized agent to a coexisting transmitter agent located at the destination. The transmitter agent at the destination receives the data and then reconstructs the agent (including its inner agents) and migrates it to the destination or to specified agents that offer upper-layer protocols.

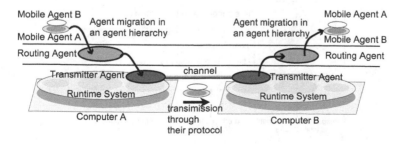

Fig. 7. Transmitter mobile agents for establishing channels between nodes

Several transmitter agents have already been implemented based on data communication protocols widely used on the Internet, such as TCP, HTTP, and SMTP. The authentication services normally available in a secure communications infrastructure include this functionality. Therefore, our secure transmitter agents, which can exchange agents, are implemented with a secure socket layer (SSL), which is one of the most popular secure communication protocols on the Internet. A virtual class is provided in Java that can be specialized to create transmitter agents for various protocols. Therefore, point-to-point channels can easily be implemented based on other secure communication protocols for data transmission.

5.2 Autonomic Electronic-Mail System

The second example is an electronic mail system based on the framework, consisting of two main components: an inbox document and letter documents (Fig. 8). The inbox document provides a window component that can contain two components. The first of these is the history of received mail and the second offers a visual space for displaying content selected from the history. A letter document corresponds to a letter. Since it is implemented as a compound document, it can contain various components for accessing text, graphics, and animation, in addition to a mobility-control component that defines an itinerary for more than one destination. It also has a window for displaying its content. It can migrate itself to its destination, but it is not a complete GUI application because it cannot display its content without the collaboration of its container, i.e., the inbox document. For example, to edit the text in a letter component, one simply clicks on it, and an editor program is invoked by the in-place editing mechanism of the framework. The component can deliver itself and its inner components to an inbox document at the receiver. After a moving letter has been accepted by the inbox document, if a letter in the list of received mail is clicked, the selected letter creates a frame object of itself and requests the document to display the frame object within its frame. Since the inbox document is the root of the letter component, when the document is stored

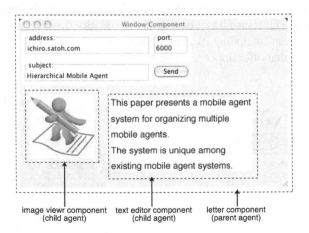

Fig. 8. Window for Compound Letter Agent

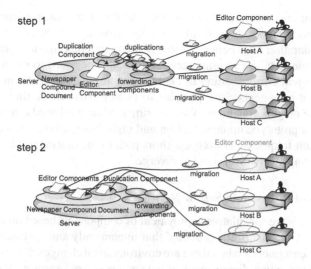

Fig. 9. Newsletter editing system

and moved, all the components embedded in the document are stored and moved with the document.

5.3   Application-Specific Document Distribution

One of the most illustrative examples of the framework presented in this paper is in providing documents to workflow management systems. A second example is an editing system for an in-house newsletter. Each newsletter is edited by automatically compiling one or more text parts, which are written by different people, as can be seen in Fig. 9. A newsletter is implemented as a compound document that can contain the text component inside it and each text part is a mobile agent including a viewer/editor program and its own text data. When the newsletter is being edited, each text part moves from the document to the computer on which it was written, and displays a window for its editor program on the computer's desktop to assist the writer, as shown in Fig. 9. Each editor goes back to the original document after the writer has finished writing it and then the document arranges the arriving components as a bound set. The document is still a mobile agent and can thus be easily duplicated and distributed to multiple locations.

5.4   Ant-Based Routing Mechanisms

Ants are able to locate a path to a food source using trails of chemical substances called pheromones deposited by other ants. Several researchers have attempted to use the notion of ant pheromones for network-routing mechanisms [1,4]. Our framework allows moving components to leave traces on trails that are automatically volatilized after their life-spans are over. A mobile agent corresponding to an ant corresponding to a pheromone is attached to another mobile agent corresponding to another ant based on the fill policy. When the latter agent randomly selects its destination and migrates there, the former agent creates a clone and migrates to the source host of the latter. Since each of the cloned agents defines its life-span by invoking setTTL(), they are active for a specified duration after being created. If there are other agents corresponding to pheromones in the host, the visiting agent adds their time spans to its own time span. When another agent corresponding to another ant migrates over the network, it can select a host that has agents corresponding to pheromones whose time-spans are the longest from the neighboring hosts. We experimented on ant-based routing for mobile agents using this prototype implementation and eight hosts. However, we knew that it would be difficult to quickly converge a short-path to the destination in real systems, because the routing mechanisms tend to diverge.[5]

5.5   Component Diffusion in Sensor Networks

The last example is the speculative deployment of components based on changes in the physical world. A mechanism is provided that dynamically and speculatively deploys components at sensor nodes when there are environmental changes. It was assumed that the sensor field was a two-dimensional surface composed of sensor nodes that monitor environmental changes, such as motion in objects and variations in temperature. It is well known that after a sensor node detects environmental changes within its coverage area, geographically neighboring nodes tend to detect similar changes after a short time. This diffusion occurs as follows in our framework. When a component on a sensor node detects changes in its environment, the component duplicates itself and deploys the clone at neighboring nodes as long as the nodes have the same kinds of components (Fig. 10). Each component is associated with a resource limit that functions as a generalized time-to-live field. Although a node can monitor changes in environments, it sets the TTLs of its components to their own initial value. It otherwise decrements TTLs over time. When the TTL of a component reaches zero, the component automatically removes itself. This example is still in the early stages of experimentation but we have developed mobile agent-based middleware for sensor networks [17] and plan to extend this framework to the middleware.

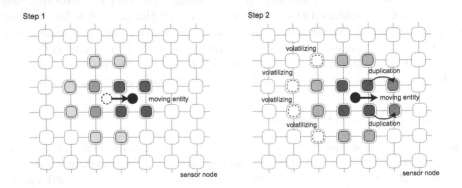

Fig. 10. Component diffusion with moving entities

---

[5] This problem is common in Ant-based routing mechanisms.

6   Related Work

Numerous mobile agent systems have been released, e.g., Aglets [9], Mole [16], Telescript [18], and Voyager [10]. Mole introduces the notion of agent groups to encourage coordination among mobile agents [2]. Its agent groups can consist of agents working together on a common task, but they are not mobile. The FarGo system introduces the notion of a dynamic layout for distributed applications [7] in a decentralized manner. This is similar to our relocation policy in the sense that it allows each agent to have its own policy, but it is aimed at allowing one or more agents to control a single agent, whereas ours aims at allowing one agent to describe its own migration. This is because our framework treats agents as autonomous entities that travel from computer to computer under their own control. This difference is important, because FarGo's policies may conflict if two agents can declare different relocation policies for one single agent. Our framework is free of conflict because each agent can only declare a policy to relocate itself but not for other agents.

There have been a few agent systems based on the concept of agent hierarchy. To our knowledge, the first attempt at introducing hierarchically mobile agents was the MobileSpaces mobile agent system. It proposed two concepts, agent hierarchy and inter-agent migration like the framework presented in this paper, and allowed more than one mobile agent to be dynamically assembled into a single mobile agent. It could provide a practical framework for mobile agent-based applications that were large and complex. Although the framework presented with this paper is based on experience with the MobileSpaces system, it not only offers hierarchical agent compositions but also horizontal agent compositions in the sense that agents can define their relocations according to the locations of other agents.

The notion of agent hierarchy presented in this paper is similar to a process calculus for modeling process migration, called *mobile ambients* [3]. The calculus can formalize a mobile process including other mobile processes like ours, but it is just a theoretical framework. Therefore, to develop a practical implementation of the calculus, we must entirely change its semantics. El Fallah-Seghrouchni and Suna. proposed the CLAIM system [5] that provides hierarchical mobile agents based on the concept of mobile ambients. The system aimed at implementing basic operations of mobile ambients to support intelligent agents, whereas the system presented in this paper uses agent hierarchy as a (meta) mechanism for providing agents with various services, including agent organization over a distributed system.

Several mobile agent systems, e.g., Telescript, have introduced the concept of places in addition to mobile agents. Places are agents that can contain mobile agents and places inside them, but they are not mobile. Our mobile agent system, on the other hand, allows one or more mobile agents to be dynamically organized into a single mobile agent, and thus we do not have to distinguish between mobile agents and places. Therefore, a distributed application, in particular a mobile application that is complex and large in scale, can be easily constructed by combining more than one agent.

There have been several attempts to construct an application from software components running on different computers. Most of these have aimed at dynamically configuring interactions between components or objects running on different computers (e.g., see [6,8]), whereas the framework presented in the paper aims at dynamically deploying components to different computers. Since it supports the typical communication primitives that existing approaches to configuring interactions between components need for coordinating and configuring distributed components, it can naturally use these approaches as configuration mechanisms for deployable components. That is, it can complement existing dynamic configuration approaches to distributed objects or components.

There have been several attempts to develop infrastructures to dynamically deploy components between computers in large-scale computing environments, e.g., workstation-clusters and grid computing. Most of these have aimed at dynamically deploying partitioned applications to different computers in distributed systems to balance the computational load or network traffic. However, they have explicitly or implicitly assumed centralized management approaches to deploy partitioned applications to different computers, so that they have not allowed each partitioned application to have its own deployment approach.

7   Conclusion

This paper described a framework for dynamically organizing multiple mobile agents in distributed computing environments. It is unique to existing systems because it provides two mechanisms for organizing multiple mobile agents. The first enables a mobile agent to contain other mobile agent inside it and migrate to another mobile agent or computer with its inner agents. It is useful in developing large-scale mobile software from a collection of mobile agents. The second enables a mobile agent to be deployed at computers according to the movements of other mobile agents. It can move a federation of agents, running on different computers, over a distributed system in a self-organizing manner. We designed and implemented a prototype system for the framework and demonstrated its effectiveness in several practical applications. We believe that the framework provides a general and practical infrastructure for building deployable applications over a distributed system.

In concluding, we would like to identify further issues that need to be resolved. We are interested in security mechanisms that would enable interactions between people and agents. We developed an approach to test context-aware applications on mobile computers [13], but need to develop a methodology for it. We are further interested in developing a methodology for testing distributed applications that are based on this new framework by using the approach. We also proposed a specification language for the itinerary of mobile software for hierarchical mobile agents [12,14,15]. The language enables more flexible and varied policies to be defined for deploying agents.

References

1. O. Babaoglu and H. Meling and A. Montresor, Anthill: A Framework for the Development of Agent-Based Peer-to-Peer Systems, Proceeding of 22th IEEE International Conference on Distributed Computing Systems, July 2002.
2. J. Baumann and N. Radounklis, Agent Groups in Mobile Agent Systems, Proceedings of Conference on Distributed Applications and Interoperable Systems, 1997.

3. L. Cardelli and A. D. Gordon, Mobile Ambients, Proceedings on Foundations of Software Science and Computational Structures, LNCS, vol. 1378, pp. 140–155, Springer 1998.
4. G. Di Caro and M. Dorigo, AntNet: A Mobile Agents Approach to Adaptive Routing, Proceedings of Hawaii International Conference on Systems, pp.74-83, Computer Society Press, January 1998.
5. A. El Fallah-Seghrouchni, A. Suna CLAIM: A Computational Language for Autonomous, Intelligent and Mobile Agents, Proceedings of ProMAS'03, 2003.
6. K. J. Goldman, B. Swaminathan, T. P. McCartney, M. D. Anderson and R. Sethuraman, The Programmers Playground: I/O Abstractions for User-Configurable Distributed Applications, IEEE Transactions on Software Engineering, Vol.21, No.9, pp. 735-746, 1995.
7. O. Holder, I. Ben-Shaul, and H. Gazit, System Support for Dynamic Layout of Distributed Applications, Proceedings of International Conference on Distributed Computing Systems (ICDCS'99), pp 403-411, IEEE Computer Soceity, 1999.
8. Jeff Kramer and Jeff Magee, Dynamic configuration for distributed systems, IEEE Transactions on Software Engineering, Vol. 11, No. 4, pp.424-436, April 1985.
9. B. D. Lange and M. Oshima, Programming and Deploying Java Mobile Agents with Aglets, Addison-Wesley, 1998.
10. ObjectSpace Inc., ObjectSpace Voyager Technical Overview, ObjectSpace, Inc. 1997.
11. I. Satoh, MobileSpaces: A Framework for Building Adaptive Distributed Applications Using a Hierarchical Mobile Agent System, Proceedings of IEEE International Conference on Distributed Computing Systems (ICDCS'2000), pp.161-168, April 2000.
12. I. Satoh, Building Reusable Mobile Agents for Network Management, IEEE Transactions on Systems, Man and Cybernetics, vol.33, no. 3, part-C, pp.350-357, August 2003.
13. I. Satoh, A Testing Framework for Mobile Computing Software, IEEE Transactions on Software Engineering, vol. 29, no. 12, pp.1112-1121, December 2003.
14. I. Satoh, Configurable Network Processing for Mobile Agents on the Internet, Cluster Computing (The Journal of Networks, Software Tools and Applications), vol. 7, no.1, pp.73-83, Kluwer, January 2004.
15. I. Satoh, Selection of Mobile Agents, Proceedings of IEEE International Conference on Distributed Computing Systems (ICDCS'2004), pp.484-493, IEEE Computer Society, March 2004.
16. M. Strasser and J. Baumann, and F. Hole, Mole: A Java Based Mobile Agent System, Proceeding of ECOOP Workshop on Mobile Objects (MOS'96), 1996.
17. T. Umezawa, I. Satoh, and Y. Anzai, A Mobile Agent-based Framework for Configurable Sensor Networks, Proceedings of International Workshop on Mobile Agents for Telecommunication Applications (MATA'2002), LNCS, Vol. 2521, pp.128-140, Springer, 2002.
18. J. E. White, Telescript Technology: Mobile Agents, General Magic, 1995.

Programming MAS with Artifacts

Alessandro Ricci, Mirko Viroli, and Andrea Omicini

DEIS, Alma Mater Studiorum, Università di Bologna,
via Venezia 52, 47023 Cesena, Italy
`a.ricci@unibo.it`, `mirko.viroli@unibo.it`, `andrea.omicini@unibo.it`

Abstract. This paper introduces the notion of artifact as a first-class abstraction in MASs (multi-agent systems) and focuses on its impact on MAS programming. Artifacts are runtime devices providing some kind of function or service which agents can fruitfully use – both individually and collectively – to achieve their individual as well as social objectives. Artifacts can be conceived (and programmed) as basic building blocks to model and build agent (working) environments. Besides introducing a conceptual and modelling framework, the paper discusses the impact of this new notion on MAS programming, focussing in particular on MAS composed by cognitive agents. To make the discussion more concrete, we provide an example scenario featuring 3APL agents whose coordination activity is supported by TuCSoN tuple centres – an existing coordination model providing some of the basic properties of artifacts for MASs.

1 Introduction

Research on agent programming has been mainly focused so far on issues concerning *individual agents*, from theories to architectures, and programming languages. In particular, in the research contexts where a notion of strong agency is adopted, this attitude results in facing the basic systemic issues concerning MAS (Multi-Agent Systems) – such as coordination and organisation – mainly from the *subjective* perspective, i.e. exclusively relying on agent computational and communicative abilities. Such an approach has indeed some benefits in terms of uniformity, but has also some strong limits in scaling up with complexity, in particular when coordination activities are concerned [14]. On the one side, programming the glue – even the simple glue – still remains a challenging and complex task. Typically, simple coordination problems result in agents with high complexity, either in terms of the communication protocols or the reasoning capabilities that they must exhibit. On the other side, wrapping (and programming) any kind of useful environmental resource as an agent does not scale up with software systems complexity, in particular in MAS composed of cognitive agents.

A naive observation is that not every entity or abstraction in a MAS is suitably modelled as a goal-governed or goal-oriented system. They can of course be wrapped within an agent, but such a solution is more like a trick than a well-defined engineering choice. This point is simple and old: modelling and programming aspects of a system with abstractions that have not been conceived for this purpose has a dramatically negative impact, in particular as far as the

R.H. Bordini et al. (Eds.): ProMAS 2005, LNAI 3862, pp. 206–221, 2006.

system becomes complex and when the application domain requires forms of dynamic control and evolution.

In this paper we aim at tackling the problem at the foundation level. For this purpose, we introduce the notion of *artifact*, as a first-class abstraction used to design / program / build those aspects of a MAS for which the agent abstraction is not suitable for, i.e. everything that is not suitably modelled as a goal- or task-oriented system. In this paper we will focus in particular on the programming aspect – even though this issue affects every aspect of the agent paradigm, from theories to engineering methodologies.

By abstracting from specific mechanisms, artifacts are meant to be basic building blocks – along with agents – that MAS designers and programmers can design and program to build systems: agents and artifacts are meant to be first-class abstractions from design to runtime, supported by suitable infrastructures.

Generally speaking, artifacts can be used to program and build suitable agent *workspaces*, i.e. working environments populated by the set of objects (in the wide sense) and tools that agents can share and use to support their individual as well as social activities. Examples range from simple artifacts providing communication functionality, such as mail boxes and blackboards, to artifacts providing coordination services, such as workflow engines or auction-engines, or again artifacts representing general purpose shared resources, such as a shared memories.

Actually, artifacts and tools have been the focus of important theories studying the development of activities in human society. Main examples are Activity Theory and Distributed Cognition [11,8]. According to such theories, most of the human activities are mediated by some kind of artifacts, and the design and use of such tools play a key role in activities development, heavily influencing their performance and their scalability with problem complexity. Also, the development of human societies itself is strictly related to the development of the tools constructed and used in such societies.

In this paper, we first briefly introduce the conceptual framework characterising the artifact abstraction and the relationships between agents and artifacts – generalising over previous works on coordination artifacts [19,15] –, and then focus on the impact of using artifacts for programming MASs.

The rest of the paper is organised as follows: first we frame the artifact notion from a conceptual and theoretical point of view, providing a first model as well as some examples of artifacts (Section 2). Then, we introduce some issues related to artifact programming, providing some concrete examples using an existing coordination model – the tuple centre model [13] – which have some of the main properties of artifacts (Section 3). As an important point of the contribution, we consider then the impact of artifacts in agent programming, providing some basic examples using 3APL extended to deal with artifacts (Section 4). Related works (Section 5), conclusions and future works (Section 6) complete the paper.

2   A First Theory of Artifacts

By considering the conceptual framework described in [1], agents can be generally conceived as *goal-governed* or *goal-oriented* system. Goal-governed systems refer to the strong notion of agency, i.e. agents with some forms of cognitive capabilities, which make it possible to explicitly represent their goals, driving the selection of agents' actions. Goal-oriented systems refer to the weak notion of agency, i.e. agents whose behaviour is directly designed and programmed to achieve some goal, which is not to be explicitly represented. In both goal-governed and goal-oriented systems, goals are *internal*. *External goals* instead refer to goals which typically belong to the social context or environment where the agents are situated. External goals are sort of regulatory states that condition agent behaviour: a goal-governed system follows external goals by adjusting internal ones [1].

Then, there are systems or parts of a system that are better characterised as resources or tools that are *used* to achieve some goals, having neither internal goals nor a pro-active behaviour, but more simply some kind of functionality that can be suitably exploited, as a service. Here we refer to such basic entities as *artifacts*. Artifacts are computational devices explicitly designed to embody and provide a certain function, which can exploited by agents to achieve their individual as well as social goals – in other words, to support the execution of their individual as well as social tasks. By taking the human society as a reference, the distinction between agents and artifacts mirrors the distinctions between humans as autonomous entities and the artificial, non-autonomous tools they exploit everyday in their activities.

So, while the notions of goal and task are central for agents, the notion of *use* and *function*[1] – which is used here, quite roughly, as a synonym of service – are central for artifacts. As for the devices in human society, artifacts are used by means of a basic well-defined set of operations which define artifacts' interface. From a philosophical and conceptual point of view, there is a neat distinction between communication and use: more precisely, agents communicate with other agents but not with artifacts, which are instead *used* though their interface.

As for artifacts in human society, external goals can be attached to an artifact by its users, in spite of its designed function: in this case, the *destination* of the artifact is different from the purposes for which it has been built.

As remarked in Activity Theory and Distributed Cognition, despite their specific function, artifacts are always kind of *mediators* between agents and their objectives, i.e. instruments to transform agent objectives in outcomes. As discussed in next sections, such a mediation has different concrete forms: we can e.g. have mediation of agents interaction, as in the case of *coordination artifacts*, which are shared and used by multiple agents with the purpose of providing some kind of coordination service; or we can have mediation of an agent with respect to its organisational environment, as in the case of *boundary artifacts*, which are used by a single agent with the purpose of constraining its action space according to some organisational rules.

An important distinction characterising agents / artifacts relationships concerns *use* and *use value* [1]. *Use value* corresponds to the evaluation of artifact

---

[1] The term function here refers to a functionality or service, and should not be confused with the term function as used e.g. in functional languages.

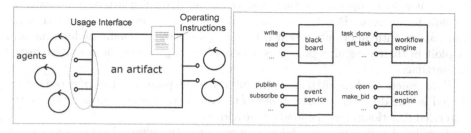

Fig. 1. An abstract representation of an artifact, along with some specific instances

characteristics and function, in order to *select* it for a (future) *use*. This distinction actually corresponds to two different kinds of external goals attached to an artifact by a user agent: *(i)* the *use value goal*, according to which the artifact should have the power of making its user agent achieve its objective by exploiting the artifact itself – such an external goal drives the agent actions concerning the selection of the artifact –; *(ii)* the *use goal*, which directly corresponds to the agent goal, which drives the usage of the artifact. From the agent point of view, when an artifact is selected and used it has then a *use value* goal which corresponds to its internal goal.

Finally, besides users, artifact *designers* and *programmers* play an important role in the picture, acting as the agents (either artificial or not) with the power of constructing, manipulating, adapting artifact behaviour, either for changing / expanding artifact function or for improving current behaviour without changing its function or interface.

2.1 A Model

From the conceptual framework discussed above, we can devise out a first model for the artifact abstraction. As mentioned previously, an artifact can be defined as

> a computational device populating agents' environment, designed to provide some kind of function or service, to be used by agents –either individually or collectively—to achieve their goals and to support their tasks.

An abstract representation of an artifact is depicted in Fig.1. We identified four basic elements to describe an artifact: the *usage interface*, the *operating instructions*, the *function*, and the *structure and behaviour*.

The *Usage Interface (UI)* is the set of the *operations* which agents can invoke to use the artifact and exploit its functionality. The invocation of an operation – as an agent external action – can result in the occurrence of events at some point(s) in the future, typically bringing some information about the result of the operation. Such events are perceived by the agent as external events (perceptions).

Operating instructions (OI) are a description of *how* to use the artifact to get its functionality. Operating instructions describe the possible *usage protocols*, i.e. sequences of operations that can be invoked on the artifact, in order to exploit its function. Besides a syntactic information, they can embed also some kind of semantic information that rational agents can eventually understand and exploit in their reasoning processes, to enable and promote the cognitive use of the artifact.

The *function* of an artifact is its intended purpose, i.e. the purpose established by the designer / programmer of the artifact, in other words *what* are the intended functionalities the artifact provides.

Finally, the *structure and behaviour* concerns the internal aspects of the artifact, that is how the artifact is implemented in order to provide its function. Such an aspect is typically hidden to users and resides in the domain of artifact designers and programmers.

Differently from agents, artifacts are not meant to be autonomous or exhibit a pro-active behaviour, neither to have social capabilities. Among the main properties, that are useful according to artifacts' purpose and nature, we have: *(i)* *inspectability and controllability*, i.e. the capability of observing and controlling artifacts structure (state) and behaviour at runtime, and of supporting their on-line management, in terms of diagnosing, debugging, testing; *(ii)* *malleability*, i.e. the capability of changing / adapting artifacts function at runtime (on-the-fly) according to new requirements or unpredictable events occurring in the open environment; and *(iii)* *linkability*, i.e. the capability of linking together at runtime distinct artifacts, for scaling up with complexity of the function to provide and as a mean to support dynamic reuse.

Also, differently from agents, artifacts can have a *spatial extension*, i.e. given a MAS with a topology, the same artifact can cover different nodes: in other words a single artifact can be both conceptually and physically distributed. For instance, a blackboard artifact can cover different Internet nodes, where agents use it by exploiting a local interface.

Given such a conceptual model of artifacts, three main aspects can be identified for characterising their relationships with agents: *(i)* use, *(ii)* selection and *(iii)* construction and manipulation. Such aspects are quite orthogonal, and involve different aspects of the artifacts on the one side, and different kinds of abilities of the agents on the other side. The usage interface and, possibly, the operating instructions are typically the only things an agent needs for using the artifact. Function is important, instead, for selecting what artifacts to use. Finally, construction and manipulation mainly touches the structure and behaviour of the artifacts. In Section 4 these aspects will be connected to different kinds of abilities requested to the agents to exploit artifacts at different levels.

2.2 Examples of Artifacts

In order to make the discussion more concrete, we provide some basic examples of artifacts which frequently recur in MAS design and programming, here classified according to their purpose (see Fig.2). It is worth remarking that these examples are not meant to be a rigorous taxonomy to partition artifacts: as happen for tools in our society, the same artifact can be classified in different ways according

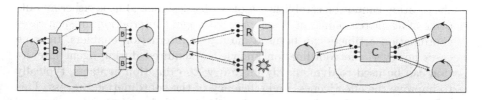

Fig. 2. Some basic types of artifacts: boundary artifacts (B), resource artifact (R), coordination artifacts (C)

to the point of view. However, the following list is useful for pointing out some basic kinds of artifacts that frequently appear when engineering MAS.

Coordination artifacts – artifacts designed to provide a coordination service. Several mechanisms introduced in other computer science fields – concurrent system and software engineering in particular – and in foreign fields such as management science, can be understood as coordination artifacts. Examples at different levels of abstraction range from artifacts with communication functions (message boxes, blackboards, event services), to artifacts with a specific synchronisation function (schedulers, semaphores), up to general high-level coordination capabilities (workflow engines, auction-engines, normative systems, pheromone infrastructures). The notion of coordination artifact is similar to the concept of *coordination medium* developed in the context of coordination models and languages [17]: however, while in general coordination media have been conceived more for processes in concurrent / distributed systems, coordination artifacts (as kind of artifacts) have some basic features – such as Operating Instructions – that make them suitable for agents as a higher level of abstraction, in particular for goal-governed agents with cognitive capabilities. Also, coordination artifacts have properties which are not generally defined for coordination media, such as malleability, linkability, inspectability, controllability.

Any coordination artifact is a mediator of agent interaction, with both a constructive and normative aim: on the one side it is an enabler of agent interaction, as *the* place where the interaction occurs; on the other side, it constrains the agent interaction space to only the subspace which is correct according to the coordinating function it provides.

In management sciences a set of basic categories concerning coordination problems have been identified [9], classifying them according to the dependencies to be managed and then identifying for each category a set of possible mechanisms useful for this purpose [10]. Such a handbook of coordination knowledge can be ported to MASs, and the corresponding mechanisms implemented as coordination artifacts.

It is worth noting that coordination artifacts represent an *engineered* approach to coordination, which basically works when it is possible and useful to design *a priori* the solution to a coordination problem, and then to reify such a knowledge in suitable artifacts. Conversely, there are cases in which

the solution cannot be established a priori by designers, but is either an outcome of agent reasoning, or it *emerges* with agent interaction: in such cases
coordination artifacts can be used mainly as interaction enablers. In some
cases however, the coordination knowledge acquired during agent interaction can be used to dynamically forge new coordination artifacts, typically
to improve the effectiveness and efficiency of the coordination process. This
reflects the role of artifacts in reifying the knowledge coming from agents'
experience and history.

Boundary artifacts – a particular case of organisation artifacts – with an organisation and security function. They take inspiration from the Agent Coordination Context notion introduced in the context of coordination models
and infrastructures [12]. A boundary artifact (BA) is an artifact used to
characterise and control the presence (in its most abstract sense) of an agent
inside an organisation context, reifying and enacting a *contract* between the
agent and the organisation. In role-based environments, a BA embeds the
contract for the role(s) the agent plays inside the organisation.

A BA is released to an agent when starting a working session inside an
organisation, and then it constraints what the agent can do inside the organisation, in terms of the actions on other artifacts belonging to the the
organisation and the communications to other agents. In other words, a BA
can be conceived as the embodiment of a (boundary) ruled interface between
the agent and the environment.

Resource artifacts – artifacts designed either to mediate access to a specific
existing resource or to directly represent and embody a resource part of
the MAS environment. An example is a database. This kind of artifact is
important to bring at the agent level of abstraction all the computational
(and physical) entities which can be useful for agents, from objects (in the
OO sense) to services, such as a Web Service.

Currently, wrapper agents are typically used as a solution for this problem: such an approach, however, is useful and conceptually correct when the
resource can be suitably and effectively represented and programmed as a
goal-oriented or goal-governed system. In all the other cases, resources can
be naturally represented as artifacts, as entities providing some kind of service that can be exploited by means of well-defined operations listed in the
artifact interface. It is worth remarking that, from an implementation point
of view, artifacts are generally much more light-weight than agents, they
more resemble objects (in the OO acceptation): they are typically passive
entities managed by the infrastructure, with no structures – for instance –
for dealing with task scheduling or reasoning. When engineering complex
systems, with many agents and artifacts, this is clearly an issue affecting
performance and scalability.

3   Programming Artifacts for MAS

In the following, we consider *tuple centres* as an example of an existing coordination model for MAS exhibiting some of the main features described for

(coordination) artifacts. Actually, the design and development of models / infrastructures fully supporting the conceptual framework based on the general notion of artifact is part of our future works (Section 6).

3.1 The Tuple Centre Example

A tuple centre is a programmable tuple space, i.e. a tuple space enhanced with the capability of programming its reacting behaviour to communication events in order to define any kind of coordination laws shaping agent interaction space [13]. TuCSoN is a coordination infrastructure providing tuple centres as runtime coordination services distributed among Internet nodes [16]. In the case of TuCSoN, the communication language adopted is based on logic tuples and the reactive behaviour can be specified as a set of reactions – always encoded as logic tuples – in the ReSpecT language. If the reaction specification is empty, a tuple centre behaves like a tuple space: coordination can be realised by suitably composing the basic coordination primitives to insert, retrieve, and read tuples. By programming the tuple centre with a reaction specification, a specific coordinating behaviour (and then the artifact function) is injected in the tuple centre. The detailed description of tuple centres, ReSpecT and TuCSoN are beyond the scope of the article: interested readers can read to reference articles listed in the bibliography.

So, tuple centres can be framed here as general purpose programmable coordination artifacts, whose coordinating behaviour can be programmed dynamically according to the coordination problem. More precisely, a tuple centre can be framed as a coordination artifact where:

- the usage interface is composed by the coordination primitives to insert (out), retrieve (in), read (rd) tuples, and to inspect (get_spec) and set (set_spec) tuple centre coordinating behaviour;
- the coordinating behaviour is expressed as a ReSpecT program;
- the operating instructions and the function description are not explicitly supported: they are implicitly described in ReSpecT programs defining specific artifact behaviour.

As for any other artifact operation, invocations are not blocking (the blocking behaviour has no meaning when dealing with artifacts and agents): after invoking an in operation on a tuple centre, the invoker agent continues to act according to its plan (which can include of course also waiting for the completion of the operation). When the in is satisfied, the operation completes and a completion event is notified to the agent, as a perception.

To exemplify the approach, here we consider a classic coordination problem: the dining philosopher [5]. The problem regards a number of philosophers eating at the same round table, sharing chopsticks. Each philosopher alternates thinking with eating. In order to eat, a philosopher needs two chopsticks, which are shared with other two philosophers, sitting one at his left and one at his right. Coordination here is mostly needed to avoid deadlock, which can happen if each

Table 1. ReSpecT specification for coordinating dining philosophers

```
reaction(in(chops(C1,C2)), (pre, out_r(required(C1,C2)))).
reaction(out_r(required(C1,C2)),(
    in_r(chop(C1)),in_r(chop(C2)),out_r(chops(C1,C2)))).
reaction(in(chops(C1,C2)), (post, in_r(required(C1,C2)))).
reaction(out(chops(C1,C2)), (out_r(chop(C1)),out_r(chop(C2)))).
reaction(out(chops(C1,C2)), (in_r(chops(C1,C2)))).
reaction(out_r(chop(C1)), (
    rd_r(required(C1,C)),in_r(chop(C1)),in_r(chop(C)),out_r(chops(C1,C)))).
reaction(out_r(chop(C2)), (
    rd_r(required(C,C2)), in_r(chop(C)),in_r(chop(C2)),out_r(chops(C,C2)))).
```

philosopher has taken a chopstick and is waiting for the other one, which is in turn taken by a waiting philosopher. In spite of its almost trivial formulation, the dining philosophers problem is generally used as an archetype for non-trivial resource access policies.

A solution to the problem according to our framework consists in using a suitable coordination artifact playing the role of the table, used by the philosopher agents to access the resources (chopsticks). The coordination artifact is here implemented with a tuple centre – called `table` – programmed to provide the coordinating behaviour which avoids deadlock. As an artifact, the table is characterised by:

- a usage interface, composed by the operation `acquireChops(C1,C2)` and `releaseChops(C1,C2)`. Using a tuple centre, the former operation is realised by an `in(chops(C1,C2))`, while the latter with an `out(chops(C1,C2))`;
- a function, informally described as to dine, which matches the the dining goal of the philosopher agent;
- operating instructions, which can be informally described as follows: "let C1 and C2 be the chopsticks you need, then first invoke `acquireChops(C1,C2)` operation. When the operation is completed, dining task can be scheduled. When the dining task finished, invoke `release(C1,C2)` operation". Such an informal description can be described more rigorously adopting a formal framework based on operational semantics, as discussed in [20].
- a coordinating behaviour to avoid deadlock. Using a tuple centre, the behaviour is provided by the ReSpecT specification described in Table 1 (for details concerning how the specification works refer to [13]).

Philosopher agents can be realised in any programming language: in Section 4 we show an implementation using 3APL. Basically, the philosopher agents' goal is to survive, interleaving thinking and dining behaviour. For the latter one, following the operating instructions, they need to get the chopsticks from the table and to give them back when dining has finished.

The main point here is that philosophers do not need to worry about how to coordinate themselves, or how the resources are represented: they simply need to know which chopstick pair to ask for, and then they can focus on their main tasks (thinking and eating).

4   Impact on Agent Programming and Reasoning

An important issue of our approach concerns how artifacts could be effectively exploited to improve agents' ability to execute individual as well as social tasks. Which reasoning models could be adopted by agents to use artifacts in the best way, simplifying their job? How could operating instructions be used in agent reasoning processes, in order to help them using artifacts and finally achieving their goal(s)? Or rather: how could an agent reason to select which artifacts to use? How could artifact function description be exploited for this purpose? And finally: how could agents reason to construct or adapt artifacts behaviour in order to be useful for their goals? All the above questions are strictly related to some of the main *foci* in the research in service-oriented (agent-based) architectures, i.e the description and discovery / brokerage of artifacts (services).

On the one side, the simplest case concerns agents directly programmed to use specific artifacts, with usage protocols directly defined by the programmer either as part of the procedural knowledge / plans of the agent for goal-governed systems, or as part of agent behaviour in goal-oriented systems. In spite of its simplicity, this case can bring several advantages for MAS engineers, exploiting separation of concerns when programming light-weight agents, without the burden – e.g. coordination burden – which is instead upon artifacts designed for this purpose. On the other side, in the case of fully open systems, the intuition is that operating instructions and function description can be the key for building MAS where intelligent agents dynamically look for and select which artifacts to use, and then exploit them accordingly, simplifying the reasoning required to achieve the goals with respect to the case in which artifacts are not available.

Actually, the conceptual framework discussed in Section 2 makes it possible to frame such abilities progressively, scaling with the openness and complexity of the domain context. Some levels can be identified, involving different kinds of artifact aspects and agents' abilities:

- *unaware use* – at this level, agents and agent programmers exploit artifacts without being aware of them. In other words, agents' actions never refer explicitly to the execution of operations on some kinds of artifacts.
- *programmed use* – at this level agents use some artifacts according to what has been explicitly programmed by the developer. In the case of cognitive agents, for instance, agent programmers can specify usage protocols directly as part of the agent plan. For the agent point of view, there is no need to understand explicitly artifacts' operating instructions or function: the only requirement is that the agent model adopted could be expressive enough to model in some way the execution of external actions and the perception of external events.
- *cognitive use* – at this level, the agent programmer directly specifies in the agent program some knowledge about what artifacts to use. However, how to exploit the artifacts is dynamically discovered by the agent, by reading the operating instructions. So, generally speaking the agent must be able to embed the procedural knowledge given by the operating instructions in

the procedural knowledge defined in its plans. In this case the adoption of shared ontologies for operating instructions description / goal description is necessary.

Focussing on this point, an interesting note comes from the studies on human behaviour using artifacts. According to Activity Theory, a hierarchy can be identified among activities, actions, and operations:

- *Operations* – Operations are defined as routinised (interactive) behaviour of individuals, that require little conscious attention (e.g. rapid typing). Responsive of actual conditions, operations provide an adjustment of actions to current situations;
- *Actions* – Actions are defined as behaviour that is characterised by conscious planning. There may be many different operations capable of fulfilling an action. Actions are directed toward *goals*, which are the objects of actions. Usually, goals are functionally subordinated to other goals, which may still subordinated to other goals and so forth. Actions must be understood within the frame of reference created by the activity;
- *Activity* – Activity can be defined as the minimum meaningful context for understanding individual actions. An activity is directed toward a *motive*, which is the object which motivates the whole activity.

Such a remark can be useful in our case for exploring two different ways to use an artifact:

- *Conscious* – in this case any interaction with the artifact is under the direct control of the main reasoning process of the agent (e.g. main deliberation cycle), where the operating instructions have been embedded;
- *Unconscious* – in this case the interaction with the artifact is not governed by the deliberation cycle of the agent, but realised by some automated procedure which executes directly – on the background of agent main reasoning – the operating instructions. Only in the case of a breakdown, the reasoning focus of the agent is shifted on the interaction with the artifact, by properly reacting to perceptions which represent the problems.

The last case can be very interesting in order to devise out agents that very efficiently exploit artifacts in the background, while keeping the reasoning focus on other issues;

- *cognitive selection and use* – this case extends the previous one by conceiving agents that autonomously select artifacts to use, get operating instructions and use them. With respect to the previous case, agents must be able both to understand and embed the operating instructions, and also understand artifacts function / service description, in order to possibly decide to use the artifacts for their own goal(s). It is worth noting that such a selection process can concern also set of cooperative agents, interested in using a coordination artifact for their social activities. As in the previous case, shared ontologies are necessary, in this case both for operating instructions and function description;
- *construction and manipulation* – in this case the point of view is changed, considering agents playing the role of programmers of the artifacts. At this

level agents are supposed to understand how artifacts work, and to adapt their behaviour (or build new ones from scratch) in order to make it more effective or efficient for other agents' goals. For its complexity, this level generally concerns humans. However, agents can e.g. be adopted to change artifact behaviour according to schema explicitly defined by the agent programmer.

4.1   An Example Using 3APL

In order to help the reader's intuition, in the following we describe a first example of MAS composed by a set of cognitive agents using a tuple centre as a simple kind of coordination artifact. Agents are implemented in 3APL [3], which is taken here as a reference example of agent-oriented programming language for goal-governed agents.

Actually, the basic 3APL model is extended to support the artifact framework. In particular the extension introduces external actions and perceptions (external events), as in the case of dMARS [6]. The extension is a generalisation of the work described in [4], where 3APL is extended to support communicative actions to send and receive FIPA ACL message, and to react to external events concerning the reception of messages. There, the authors define a message base as a new part of a 3APL agent state: communicative actions and external events alter the content of the message base. Practical rules with a guard are introduced for reacting to the presence in the message base of events related to the arrival of new messages.

Our extension consists first in modelling the execution of an operation on a specific artifact as a 3APL (external) action. For this purpose, we extend the set of possible 3APL goals with the action

$$\texttt{invoke\_op}(O, A)$$

where O is a term representing the signature of the operation to be invoked, and A is a term used as identifier of the artifact. As an example, the action `invoke_op(get_token, synchroniser)` invokes the `get_token` operation on the `synchroniser` artifact. Another case is action `invoke_op(in(age('Bob',X))`, `dbase)`, which invokes the `in` operation on the tuple centre `dbase` in order to retrieve a tuple matching the template `age('Bob',X)`.

Second, the extension also models the perception of events generated by artifacts. To this end, the practical rule on message reception is generalised to consider also external events concerning the completion of an operation executed on an artifact. A new guard is introduced:

$$\texttt{op\_completed}(O, A, R)$$

where O represents the signature of an operation previously invoked, A the source artifact, and R a result term carrying information related to the completion of the operation. An examples of rule is:

```
<- op_completed(get_token, synchroniser, _) | do_critical_task()
```

Table 2. A dining philosopher implemented in 3APL, using the tuple centre **table** as a coordination artifact

```
 1 PROGRAM "philosopher"
 2
 3 CAPABILITIES:
 4   { not hungry } think { hungry },
 5   { hungry } eat {not hungry },
 6   { not holding_chops } update_chop_belief(acquired) { holding_chops },
 7   { holding_chops } update_chop_belief(released) { not holding_chops },
 8   { left_chop(C1),right_chop(C2) } invoke_op(in(chops(C1,C2)),table) {},
 9   { left_chop(C1),right_chop(C2) } invoke_op(out(chops(C1,C2)),table) {}
10
11 BELIEFBASE:
12   left_chop(...),
13   right_chop(...)
14
15 GOALBASE:
16   survive()
17
18 RULEBASE
19   survive() <- not hungry | think,
20   survive() <- hungry | dine,
21   dine() <- not holding_chops | invoke_op(in(chops(C1,C2)),table),
22   dine() <- holding_chops | eat ; invoke_op(out(chops(C1,C2)),table),
23   <- op_completed(in(chops(C1,C2)),table,_) | update_chop_belief(acquired),
24   <- op_completed(out(chops(C1,C2)),table,_) | update_chop_belief(released)
```

This practical rule executes the goal do_critical_task() when the completion of the operation acquire_lock is perceived. The following rule executes the goal update_info when the in operation completes, retrieving a tuple from the tuple centre dbase:

```
<- op_completed(in(age('Bob',X)),dbase?in(age(_,Y)))|update_info(Y)
```

As an application example, we consider a solution to the dining philosopher problem, using 3APL agents as philosophers and exploiting the table as a coordination artifact. This is a a case of programmed use of artifacts, since the knowledge about how to use the artifact is directly encoded by the agent programmer among the practical rules of the agent. As a coordination artifact, we consider the tuple centre described in Section 3: in the overall we build up a solution with 3APL agents exploiting a TuCSoN tuple centre. The source code of the 3APL philosopher is shown in Table 2.

The agent goal is to survive. The plan to survive is described in the rule base, and involves thinking and dining activities. If the philosopher is not hungry, he can think: thinking activity is simplified into a simple action in the capabilities (line 4), whose effect is to make the philosopher hungry (hungry is inserted in the belief base). If the philosopher is hungry, then he plans to dine (line 20). In order to dine, the philosopher needs to have the chopsticks. If he believes to hold them (holding_chops is his belief base, line 22), then he can start the eating activity, again simplified into a simple action (line 5), whose effect is to make the agent not hungry. Instead, if the philosopher believes not to hold the chopsticks, then he interacts with the artifact table to get the chopsticks. In particular, he executes an external action to invoke an **in** operation on the tuple centre **table** to get a tuple **chops(C1,C2)** representing the chopsticks (line 21, 8). The information about the specific chopsticks to request are stored in the belief base in the form of the **left_chop** and **right_chop** beliefs. When the philosopher perceives the completion of the operation to get the chopsticks (line 23), the belief base is updated by means of an internal action asserting the **holding_chops** fact (line 6). Then, the plan of the agent is to release the chopsticks after eating. For this purpose an external action is executed (line 22, 9), which invokes an **out** operation on the same tuple centre, inserting back the tuple **chops(C1,C2)**. When the philosopher perceives that the operation to release the chopsticks has completed (line 24), the belief base is updated by means of an internal action asserting the **not holding_chops**.

5   Related Work

This work generalises and extends previous works on coordination artifacts [15].

The artifact abstraction brings in MAS ideas and concepts that have played a central role in other (un)related fields. From concurrent and distributed systems, coordination artifacts in particular can be considered the generalisation of traditional coordination abstractions, from low level ones such as semaphores, monitors, to high-level ones, such as tuple spaces and, more generally, coordination media as found in coordination models and languages [17]. Blackboards as defined in Distributed Artificial Intelligence context can be framed and modelled in MAS as coordination artifacts, toward the integration of the two different points of view (traditional multi-agent and blackboard systems) in designing collaborating-software engineering space [2].

Actually, artifacts can be exploited as an analytical tool for describing existing approaches based on some form of mediated / environment-based interaction. For instance, the environment provided by the pheromone infrastructure in [18] supporting stigmergy coordination can be interpreted as a coordination artifact exploited by ants to coordinate: as such, it provides operations for depositing and sensing pheromones, and the coordinating behaviour is given by the environmental laws ruling the diffusion, aggregation and evaporation of pheromones.

Also some coordination and organisation approaches developed in the context of intelligent / cognitive agents can be framed in terms of artifacts. A main example is is given by electronic institutions ([7] is an example), where agent societies live upon an infrastructure (middleware) which governs agent interaction according to the norms established for the specific organisation, representing both organisation and coordination rules. The institution then can be framed as a kind of shared artifact, characterised by an interface with operations that agents use to communicate, and providing a normative function on the overall set of agents.

6   Conclusion and Future Works

In the paper we introduced the notion of artifact as first-class abstraction for MAS engineering. Artifacts are meant to be used as basic bricks to program

MAS working environments, supporting agents in their individual and social activities. After providing some glances about artifact programming, in the paper we focused on the impact on agent programming, framing some levels related to artifact adoption.

Several directions characterise future works. An important one is devoted to deepen the investigation on how the artifact abstraction and its basic properties can be effective in supporting agent reasoning in achieving individual as well as collective goals. Another direction concerns the development of infrastructures and tools fully supporting the artifact abstraction and the basic kind of artifacts discussed in the paper, in particular integrating such infrastructures with existing MAS platforms for cognitive agents (3APL is an example). In particular, as in the case of service-oriented architectures, the infrastructure should provide services that agents can exploit for registering, discovering, locating artifacts, for retrieving their description and operating instructions (for agent using artifacts) and for their inspection and control (for human and agents managing artifacts). For this purpose, existing research literature on service description and discovery / brokerage will be considered among the reference sources.

Finally, our intuition is that the separation of concerns obtained by introducing artifacts could be important to make more tractable the verification / validation of formal properties of (open) MAS; accordingly, research studies will be devoted to define formal frameworks to specify artifacts function / behaviour semantics, and to explore how to use them for verification problems, both offline and on-line.

References

1. R. Conte and C. Castelfranchi, editors. *Cognitive and Social Action*. University College London, 1995.
2. D. D. Corkill. Collaborating software: Blackboard and multi-agent systems & the future. In *International Lisp Conference*, 2003.
3. M. Dastani, F. de Boer, F. Dignum, and J.-J. Meyer. Programming agent deliberation: an approach illustrated using the 3APL language. In *Proceedings of AAMAS '03*, pages 97–104. ACM Press, 2003.
4. M. Dastani, J. van der Ham, and F. Dignum. Communication for goal directed agents. In M.-P. Huget, editor, *Communication in Multiagent Systems, Agent Communication Languages and Conversation Polocies.*, volume 2650 of *Lecture Notes in Computer Science*, pages 239–252. Springer, 2003.
5. E. Dijkstra. *Co-operating Sequential Processes*. Academic Press, London, 1965.
6. M. d'Inverno, M. Luck, M. Georgeff, D. Kinny, and M. Wooldridge. The dMARS architecture: A specification of the distributed multi-agent reasoning system. *Autonomous Agents and Multi-Agent Systems*, 1:5–53, 2004.
7. M. Esteva, B. Rosell, J. A. Rodríguez-Aguilar, and J. L. Arcos. AMELI: An agent-based middleware for electronic institutions. In *Proceedings of AAMAS '04*, volume 1, pages 236–243, New York, USA, 19–23 July 2004. ACM.
8. D. Kirsh. Distributed cognition, coordination and environment design. In *Proceedings of the European conference on Cognitive Science*, pages 1–11, 1999.
9. T. Malone and K. Crowston. The interdisciplinary study of coordination. *ACM Computing Surveys*, 26(1):87–119, 1994.

10. T. W. Malone, K. Crowston, J. Lee, B. Pentland, C. Dellarocas, G. Wyner, J. Quimby, C. S. Osborn, A. Bernstein, G. Herman, M. Klein, and E. O'Donnell. Tools for inventing organizations: Toward a handbook of organizational processes. *Management Science*, 45(3):425–443, 1999.

11. B. Nardi, editor. *Context and Consciousness: Activity Theory and Human-Computer Interaction*. MIT Press, 1996.

12. A. Omicini. Towards a notion of agent coordination context. In D. Marinescu and C. Lee, editors, *Process Coordination and Ubiquitous Computing*, pages 187–200. CRC Press, 2002.

13. A. Omicini and E. Denti. From tuple spaces to tuple centres. *Science of Computer Programming*, 41(3):277–294, Nov. 2001.

14. A. Omicini and S. Ossowski. Objective versus subjective coordination in the engineering of agent systems. In M. Klusch, S. Bergamaschi, P. Edwards, and P. Petta, editors, *Intelligent Information Agents: An AgentLink Perspective*, volume 2586 of *LNAI: State-of-the-Art Survey*, pages 179–202. Springer-Verlag, Mar. 2003.

15. A. Omicini, A. Ricci, M. Viroli, C. Castelfranchi, and L. Tummolini. Coordination artifacts: Environment-based coordination for intelligent agents. In *Proceedings of AAMAS '04*, volume 1, pages 286–293, New York, USA, 19–23 July 2004. ACM.

16. A. Omicini and F. Zambonelli. Coordination for Internet application development. *Autonomous Agents and Multi-Agent Systems*, 2(3):251–269, Sept. 1999. Special Issue: Coordination Mechanisms for Web Agents.

17. G. A. Papadopoulos and F. Arbab. Coordination models and languages. *Advances in Computers*, 46:329–400, 1998.

18. H. V. D. Parunak, S. Brueckner, and J. Sauter. Digital pheromone mechanisms for coordination of unmanned vehicles. In *Proceedings of AAMAS '02*, pages 449–450. ACM Press, 2002.

19. A. Ricci, A. Omicini, and E. Denti. Activity Theory as a framework for MAS coordination. In *Engineering Societies in the Agents World III*, volume 2577 of *LNCS*, pages 96–110. Springer-Verlag, Apr. 2003.

20. M. Viroli and A. Ricci. Instructions-based semantics of agent mediated interaction. In *Proceedings of AAMAS '04*, volume 1, pages 102–109, New York, USA, 19–23 July 2004. ACM.

Programming Deliberative Agents for Mobile Services: The 3APL-M Platform

Fernando Koch[1], John-Jules C. Meyer[1], Frank Dignum[1], and Iyad Rahwan[2]

[1] Institute of Information and Computing Sciences,
Utrecht University, Utrecht, The Netherlands
fkoch@acm.org, {jj, dignum}@cs.uu.nl
[2] Institute of Informatics, The British University in Dubai,
P.O. Box 502216, Dubai, UAE
iyad.rahwan@buid.ac.ae

Abstract. 3APL-M is a platform for building deliberative multi-agent systems whose components execute on handheld and embedded computational devices. The solution takes advantage of the 3APL language and definitions, delivers a methodology for building Belief-Desire-Intention inference systems and provides an interface to integrate the applications to the external world. The library is distributed for the Java 2 Micro Edition (J2ME) programming platform, which is widely adopted by the hardware manufactures and available for a myriad of mobile computing devices. The role of agent-based computing for mobile services is explained, the architecture and programming structures are presented and proof-of-concept applications are demonstrated.

1 Introduction

The promise of mobile technologies is to remove the bindings between a fixed space and a person's information and communication resources. Intelligent mobile services should make use of local processing to reason about the user's context and predict user's intents, actions and location. However, mobile computing introduces issues of resource limitations, security, connectivity and, limited power supply, which are inherent to the environment [26]. These characteristics call for the optimal use of local resources, communications and connectivity. Therefore, the problem is how to create intelligent mobile applications that execute on mobile computing devices.

Agent-based computing [16] seems to offer a set of features that are very closely aligned with the requirements of service delivery challenge in mobile computing [18]. For the purpose of this paper, agents are computer systems capable of flexible autonomous action in dynamic, unpredictable and open environments.

This paper presents the 3APL-M (Triple-A-P-L-M) platform for implementing deliberative autonomous agents that execute on mobile computing devices. It works as a scaled down implementation of the 3APL language interpreter [14] re-designed for the requirements of mobile computing applications. The inference system implements the Belief-Desire-Intention paradigm [25], which intrinsically provides the solutions for designing systems capable to creating mental

R.H. Bordini et al. (Eds.): ProMAS 2005, LNAI 3862, pp. 222–235, 2006.

models. Moreover, it supplies the programming structures to implement *sensors* for context-sensitiveness [12] and *actuators* for pervasive content delivery.

The paper is organized as follows. Section 2 **analyses** the use agent-based computing for the development of mobile service applications. Next, section 3 presents our **approach** for building the scaled down version of the 3APL platform. Section 4 presents the **solution** for the 3APL-M system architecture. Finally, section 5 presents the **results**, as two proof-of-concept applications implemented using the platform and their running parameters. The paper concludes by presenting the achieved results and pointing to further works.

2   Motivation and Related Work

In this section, we introduce the role of agent-based computing in delivering mobile services and present the related works that deliver a platform to build those applications.

The role of agents in mobile services is to provide the support to the requirements of the future generation of software applications [27]. The support provided by agents are in the realms of:

- *situatedness*, as the mobile service must be aware of the environmental conditions surrounding the mobile user;
- *openness*, as the mobile service's components must be able to integrate and adapt to the presence of new modules being integrated to or removed from the system's environment;
- *local interaction*, as the mobile service's applications and components must be able to interact to other modules and interact with the environment, and;
- *local control*, related to the problem of implementing mobile applications able to run autonomously.

For the sake of demonstration, let us consider the scenario shown in Figure 1:

- (I) the user enters his shopping list at home, in front of his fridge when running out of a product.
- (II) when the user is walking by a grocery store, the location-based service detects the user's position and notifies the local processing application. This application holds the user data and has the capability of negotiating

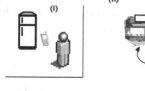

(I) user learns about the need of purchasing more soft-drinks while grabbing the last can from the refrigerator at home;
(II) that information will be most useful when passing by a food store.

Fig. 1. Mobile Commerce Scenario

the stored shopping list. Several aspects of the context could be taken into consideration during the deliberation. For example, the user's agenda (the negotiation should be avoided if the user has an appointment set up for the next minutes); the user's preferred stores (the application should be able to collect the quote from the stores where the user normally does its shopping); availability of computing resource (avoid the negotiation if the device is running low in power supply), and connectivity.

The requirements to implement this mobile solution are: the structures for knowledge representation (shopping list, preferred stores, calendar and device information); the interface to a location detection system; an inference system that cross relate the internal and context information; a negotiation system, and; a content delivery interface.

Agent-based software engineering provides the tools to implement these requirements, as presented in [18]. The solutions provided by the agent-paradigm are:

- *Structures for knowledge representation*: existing agent systems can provide an answer to the situadedness requirement. This ability is an intrinsic problem in multi-agent systems, and hence inherent in agent architectures, especially in the belief-desire-intention paradigm. In the demonstration, it provides the structures to represent the shopping list, preferred stores, device information and calendar.
- *Responsiveness and adaptivity*: as pointed out in [16], these are inherent features provided by agent systems; agents should be able to adapt to constantly changing execution environment. In the demonstration, it provides the features to either dropping or adapting the negotiation process in answer to the computing resource availability information.
- *Sociability and locality of interaction*: also described in [16], agents are able to interact with other agents or humans when needed. In the demonstration, this feature would provide the support for the negotiation process.
- *Autonomy*: as argued in [17], the agent paradigm offers mechanisms that address varying degrees of autonomy, from basic reactive architectures based on a set of pre-determined rules, to mechanisms for proactive behaviour [11] considering the context and user preferences. In the demonstration, the local processing agent must be able to act autonomously for adapting the application execution in face to possible computing or connectivity problems.

Moreover, agent-based software engineering incorporates support for *decomposition*, *modularity* and *abstraction* [15], which are essential features considering the distributed nature of mobile computing applications.

2.1   Related Work

Here we introduce the related works that deliver platforms to build agents-based applications in mobile computing devices. In [21] it is argued that making agents to run in resource-constrained devices is still not an obvious task. We have selected a number of available platforms, which we considered to be representative of what is available.

In [8] it is presented a model of agent construction for ubiquitous computing which is conceptually grounded and architecture neutral and makes use of a component based approach for agent design. The project uses *S.M.A.R.T.* (Structural, Modular agent Relationship and Types) framework and *actSMART*[9] for the implementation in a Java 2 Micro Edition [13] platform. Although the work presents a support to generic services in ubiquitous computing environment, it does not focus on the problem of supporting the development of intelligent personal assistants.

The Lightweight Extensible Agent Platform (LEAP) [10],is the first attempt to implement a FIPA [3] agent platform that runs seamlessly on both mobile and fixed devices over both wireless and wired networks. It uses a set of profiles that allows one to configure it for execution on various machines, OS and Java VM. This platform has many strengths and satisfies the requirements for intelligent support (B.D.I. based), collaboration and personal assistance. Although the platform can be adapted to integrate to, e.g., context-awareness and device interface support, this feature is not clearly defined in the product.

The MobiAgent platform [22] delivers a solution where neither the platform nor the agents run locally in the device. In this solution, when the user wants to delegate a task to an agent, the mobile device connects to the Agent Gateway and downloads an interface that configures it. The agent performs its task and, later, reports the results via the same mechanism. The shortcoming of this solution is the dependency of a reliable connectivity mechanism between the device and the Agent Gateway.

The kSACI platform [5] is a smaller version of the SACI platform [6]. SACI is an infrastructure for creating agents that are able to communicate using KQML [19][20] messages and use a mailbox structure to exchange messages. Although kSACI platform is usable on small devices running the Java 2 Micro Edition, the platform is not entirely situated on the small device. Moreover the kSACI is oriented to communication aspects of multi-agent system and does not provision for enhanced inference systems.

Finally, the *AbIMA* platform [23] delivers agent-based intelligent mobile assistant that runs on a handheld device and assists the user through the execution of individual tasks. It makes use of the abstract agent programming language AgentSpeak(L) [24]. Nevertheless, AbIMA offers support to single-user environments only.

Table 1 summarises support provided by the aforementioned platforms to the components in intelligent mobile service solutions: (i) *Local Processing* is the support to local execution for personal assistant applications; (ii) *Context Awareness* is the support to the component for context awareness in mobile applications; (iii) *Inference* is the support to the component for "enhanced deliberation" in intelligent applications; (iv) *Collaboration* is the support to the component for collaboration in multi-user environment, and; (v) *Device Interface* is the support to interfacing in mobile computing.

Table 1. Classification of Platforms for Agent-Based Applications in Mobile Computing

Classification of Agent-based Platforms for Mobile Computing and Mobile Personal Assistant Solutions

Platform	(i) Local Processing	(ii) Ctx. Awareness	(iii) Infer.	(iv) Collab.	(v) Dev. Interface
JADE/LEAP	Yes (various)	Not Explicit	Yes (BDI)	Yes (FIPA)	Not Explicit
MobiAgent	No	No	No	Yes	Partial
kSACI	Yes (J2ME)	No	No	Yes	Not Explicit
AbIMA/ AgentSpeak(L)	Yes	Not Explicit	Yes (BDI)	No	Not Configurable

Hence, based on the analysis of the related work, we conclude that there is a unaddressed opportunity to deliver a platform that supports the components required for in intelligent mobile service solutions. In the next sections, we move towards the specifications for a platform to build B.D.I. architecture, agent-based applications in mobile computing devices.

3   Approach

A platform for building agents in mobile devices must provide solutions for the problems inherent to the environment, such as computing resource availability, networking, security, interfacing and compatibility. For example, how to execute the deliberation cycle in the limited computing resources environment?; how to implement the structures for context awareness and content delivery?; what agent-oriented language to use for the development of the application knowledge structures?; which programming language to choose for the application development?

The requirements for the development of 3APL-M are to be:

- compatible with 3APL language and programming environment;
- lightweight enough to be deployed on small devices with as few as 20Mhz CPU and 512Kb RAM.
- developed in the Java 2 Micro Edition (J2ME) [4][13] programming platform. J2ME is a reduced version of the Java programming platform tailored to fit in low profile mobile computing devices. It provides a programming and runtime environment for Java coded applications. This environment is widely adopted by the hardware manufactures and available for a myriad of mobile computing devices;
- optimized for processing, reducing the number of operations per deliberation, thus ensuring performance and minimum battery utilization, and;
- provide the application programming interface (API) for the integration of the 3APL application to context-awareness and content-provider structures.

The resulting 3APL-M implementation is fully compatible with the 3APL language and syntax. It is a "cut down" version of 3APL, with the structures optimized for the creation of mobile service applications and deployment in mobile computing devices. Nevertheless, the platform delivers a solution as powerful as the original 3APL implementations. In fact, when executed in the desktop environment, this platform can be an alternative for 3APL solution implementations.

In the next sub-sections, we will introduce the 3APL programming language and then present the system architecture for 3APL-M platform.

3.1 About 3APL

3APL is a logic-based agent programming language that provides constructs for implementing agents' beliefs, plans and capabilities as explicit run-time entities. It uses practical reasoning rules in order to generate plans (i.e., sequence of actions) for achieving the applications goals. Each 3APL program is executed by means of an interpreter that deliberates on the cognitive attitudes of that agent. More information about the 3APL language, syntax and logic fundament is available at the 3APL project's web-site at [2].

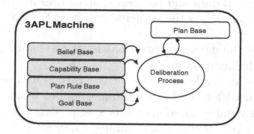

Fig. 2. 3APL Architecture

Figure 2 presents the abstract architecture of 3APL. Each agent has the explicit representations of its goals in the *goal base*. For example, the goal to finish an assignment may be represented with the predicate *finish(assignment)*. In order to achieve its goals, the agent decomposes these into *sub-goals* using planning rules from the *plan rule base*. The sub-goals can be further decomposed until *basic actions* are reached (i.e., physical actions agents may execute directly in the world).

During plan generation, the agent takes into account its *belief base*, which stores the contextual information in form of predicates. For example, the predicate *near(fernando, storeA)* denotes that the agent believes *Fernando* is currently located near the *storeA*. The *capability base* describes basic actions by the agent and user. A planning rule takes the form *head ← guard|body*, and means that if the agent has goal *g* that unifies to the head of the plan *head* and the condition declared in *guard* is satisfied (i.e., it unifies to the contents of the belief base), then goal *g* can be achieved by executing the sequence of actions (or set of sub-goals) listed in *body*.

As it will be presented in the next section, the application architecture is influenced by the features of the 3APL language and the platform requirements.

4   System Architecture

The 3APL-M platform architecture is presented in Figure 3. The main features are: sensor and actuator modules, which provide the interface to integrate to context-awareness and content delivery solutions; the 3APL machinery, which includes the infrastructures for the B.D.I. based inference systems, and; the communicator module, which provides the support for communication in a multi-agent system.

The modules in the 3APL-M architecture are explained below:

- the *3APL machine* encapsulates the 3APL language components and provides the programming interface for the integration of the logic structures to the Java programming language. This module provides a runtime interpreter for the complete semantics of the 3APL language;
- the *belief, capabilities, goal* and *plan rules* modules are implementations of the 3APL structures. These elements are part of the 3APL machinery and provide the internal data and processing structures for the platform;
- the *deliberation process* is the implementation of the executive module (deliberation cycle);
- the *plan base* is the data structure that holds the list of current plans generated by the deliberation process;
- the *m-prolog* is an implementation of the PROLOG language engine, optimized to be used for the low-level inference processing in 3APL-M. The m-prolog programming interface holds special structures to make it more compatible to 3APL engine programming. However, it is a fully compatible PROLOG language implementation and, in fact, PROLOG applications can be executed in this environment.

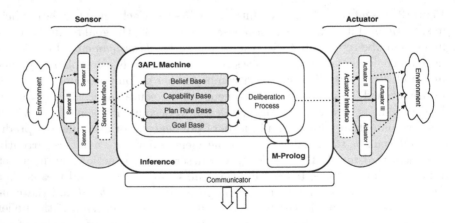

Fig. 3. 3APL-M Architecture

- the *sensor* and *actuator* are the programming interfaces for the integration of the 3APL-M machinery to the external world. The *sensor* module provides the infrastructure for the creation of context-aware application (i.e. environmental sensors) and system input (i.e., device's keyboard). The *actuator* module provides the means for content delivery (i.e., integration to the device's display interface) and acting upon the environment.
- the *communicator* module provides the is the generic interface for the data exchange infrastructure, required for multi-agent system module integration and communication to external services. The module provides internal support for FIPA communication [7][10], however any other protocol or data representation can be plugged in the system through the programming interface.

The 3APL-M architecture emphasizes the *sensor module* as the input interface for data from the external world. Popular BDI models have neglected "perceptions" as the mental state component that is the basis of communication and interaction. In the classic BDI architecture data is collected by some interface structure and inserted into the BDI belief base. In some BDI approaches, perceptions are indeed treated as beliefs. However, this is clearly unsatisfactory, both conceptually and technically. Conceptually, perceptions are transient, while beliefs are persistent. Hence, the introduction of a *sensor* module provides the technical support to map the perception of an event can into a corresponding event has happened belief, thus avoiding a irrelevant perceptions that would lead to an overflow of the belief/knowledge base of an agent.

Moreover, for the *deliberation process*, the 3APL-M platform provides the Java programming class *Agent*, which implements the *basic deliberation cycle* [14]. Due to space limitation, this work shall not discuss the deliberation process in detail but introduce the general idea. For detailed information, we refer to Hindriks et al [14] and Dastani et al [11].

The *basic deliberation cycle* is depicted in Figure 4. In this case, the agents generate their plans by choosing the first applicable rule that matches a par-

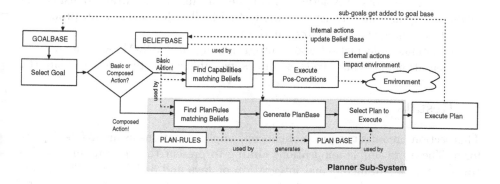

Fig. 4. Basic Deliberation Cycle

ticular goal/desire. This means that an agent generates only one plan for each achievable goal, and only generates other plans if the initial plan fails.

4.1   Programming

The 3APL-M platform works as a library loaded in the distribution package. This library supplies the application-programming interface (API) for the 3APL machine modules. The Java application makes calls to the library's modules for loading information, configuring the deliberation engine and executing the applications. Figure 5 presents: (A) the 3APL-M programming interface for the *Agent* class (simplified view), and; (B) a simple Hello World Java-3APL-M code example.

(A) Agent class programming interface (simplified view)

```
void addBelief (String beliefStr )  // Add a belief.
void addCapability (String capabilityStr )  // Add a capability
void addGoal (String goalStr )  // Add a goal
void addPlanRule (String planRuleStr )  // Add a plan
void addProlog (String prologStr )  // Add Prolog knowledge
void addActuator (String actionStr ,
            ActuatorInterface   actuator)   // Add actuator
void addSensor (String id, Sensor sensor,   int interval,
                boolean  addGoalNotification )  // Add Sensor
void deliberate()   // Starts deliberation cycle
void destroy()   // Terminate agent
String sendMessage (String  msgId , String to,
            String  performative , String data)   // Send a message
void setFipaCommunication (boolean enabled)
```

(B) HelloWorldsource code

```
public class HelloWorldExample {
  public void startApp () {
    Agent  ag = new Agent("hello");

    // load knowledge
    ag.addCapability ("{} Print(X) {  GUI(print, X)}");
    ag.addPlanRule (" <- TRUE | Print('hello world')");
    ag.addGoal ("print");

    // add  J2ME display actuator
    ag.addActuator  ("GUI(Type,Message)",
        new J2MEGUI(this));

    // deliberate
    ag.deliberate ();
  }
}
```

Fig. 5. Programming with 3APL-M

Figure 5(B) presents an example for the programming steps. The code must instantiate a new *Agent* object and to load the 3APL information (i.e., beliefs capabilities, goals, plan rules) using the Agent methods (presented in Figure 5(A)). Next, sensors and actuators can be initialized and attached using the *addSensor(.)* and *addActuator(.)* methods. Finally, the deliberation process is started by calling the *deliberate()* method.

For detailed information about programming in 3APL-M, we refer to the documentation and source code examples available at the project's web-site [1].

5   Results

This section presents two proof-of-concept implementations using 3APL-M platform. These are simple applications aiming to present the programming structures, running parameters and integration of Java and 3APL code. The source code for these and other demonstration applications can be found at the project's web-site [1].

5.1   Block World Demonstration Application

The Block world demonstration is presented to show the compatibility between the 3APL-M and the 3APL standard specifications. This is the example provided at the 3APL web-site [2].

The application is composed by a robot that needs to arrive to a base in a grid world. The robot knows where are the bases and the rules for the decision process. The knowledge representation and deliberation process is implemented in 3APL and the GUI manipulation is done in Java. Figure 6 presents: (A) the application running on a HP iPaq hardware; (B) the 3APL code; and; (C) the 3APL-M and Java code integration.

In this example, the Java code initializes the agent (new *Agent(.)*), loads the knowledge (3APL code) from an input stream (*ag.consult(.)*) and attaches the Block World interface actuator (*ag.addActuator(.)*). Next, the application triggers the deliberation process (*ag.deliberate()*). The 3APL machinery will load the intention from the goal base (*goBase*). From the deliberation, the 3APL code will end up calling the Block world actuator passing the argument "west". The Java coded *BlockWorldActuator.actuator(["west"])* will be executed to update the interface.

The test was executed using 3APL-M version 1.3. On the HP iPaq device, this application executes using 142.7 Kbytes of RAM memory and takes approximately eight seconds to find a solution (including interface update time). In

(A) BlockWorldon HP iPaq

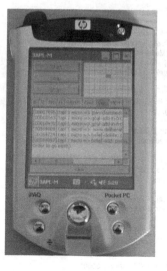

(B) 3APL code for robot deliberation

```
CAPABILITIES:
{pos(X, Y)} West { NOT  pos(X, Y), pos(X - 1, Y), BlockMove(west)}.
{pos(X, Y)} East { NOT pos(X, Y), pos(X + 1, Y), BlockMove(east)}.
{pos(X, Y)} North { NOT  pos(X, Y), pos(X, Y + 1), BlockMove(north)}.
{pos(X, Y)} South { NOT  pos(X, Y), pos(X, Y - 1), BlockMove(south)}.
{} BlockMove(X) {EXTERNAL}.

RULEBASE
goBase <- pos(X, Y) AND base(X, Y) | SKIP.
goBase <- pos(X, Y) AND base(A, B) AND X > A | West,   goBase.
goBase <- pos(X, Y) AND base(A, B) AND X < A | East,   goBase.
goBase <- pos(X, Y) AND base(A, B) AND  Y > B | South,  goBase.
goBase <- pos(X, Y) AND base(A, B) AND  Y < B | North,  goBase.

BELIEFBASE
pos(9, 9).
base(0, 0).

GOALBASE
goBase.
```

(C) 3APL-M and Java integration

```
/**
 * Midlet Interface
 */
public void startApp () {
  // create agent
  Agent ag = new Agent("robot");
  // load knowledge bases
  ag.consult (System.getResourceAsStream ("robotAgent.tapl "));
  // attach actuator
  ag.addActuator ("BlockMove(X)", new BlockWorldActuator (this.blockWorld ));
  // deliberate
  ag.deliberate ();
}
```

Fig. 6. BlockWorld demonstration interface and code

total, it process 38 deliberation steps and requires 539 unifications operations on the PROLOG engine.

5.2   Mobile Commerce Demonstration Application

This demonstration presents the 3APL-M based implementation for the mobile commerce problem from Figure 1. For simplicity, the demonstration will concentrate on the 3APL code and Java integration and overlook technical details about the location-based service and connectivity. It is assumed that there is a location-based service feeding the agent's belief base with landmark proximity information and there is stable connectivity.

The 3APL code for this solution is presented in Figure 7(B) and the screenshots from the running application in a mobile phone simulator are depicted in Figure 7(A).

Basically, when a landmark proximity is detected (near grocery store), the location service provider adds the context information to the agent's belief base (*location(near, storeA)*), the goal resolve to the goal base and starts the deliberation process. The sequence of actions will be created by processing the plan rule named *resolve* if there is a *location(.)* and *shoppingList(.)* available in the belief base. The sequence of actions are: to ask the confirmation on the negotiation process to the user (*AskConfirmation(.)*); in case of positive answer, to request the quote from the store (*getQuote(.)*); once the quote is received, to assert that information in the belief base (*Assert(receivedQuote(.))*, and; finally, to display the received quote in the devices interface (*displayQuote(.)*).

(A) Screen shots

(B) 3APL code

```
CAPABILITIES:
{ shoppingList (List)}  AddItemToList (Item)
{ NOT shoppingList (List),  shoppingList (List + Item)}.
{} AskConfirmation (Message) {  GUI(promptYesNo , Message)}.
{} Display(Message) {   GUI(promptOk , Message)}.
{} GUI(Type, Message) {EXTERNAL}.

RULEBASE
addItemToList (Item) <- TRUE |
AddItemToList (Item).

displayQuote (Shopping, Quote) <- TRUE |
Display([Quote received from , Shopping,  is $, Quote]).

getQuote (Shopping, List, Result) <- TRUE |
Send( MsgId , Shopping, query- ref , quote(List)),
Receive( MsgId , Shopping,  Performative , Result, 4).

resolve <- location(near, Shopping) AND     shoppingList (List) |
AskConfirmation ([Near , Shopping, . Request for quote?]),
getQuote (Shopping, List, Result),
Assert( receivedQuote (Shopping, List, Result)),
displayQuote (Shopping, Result).

BELIEFBASE
addressBook (storeA , http:// localhost :50001).
shoppingList ([ productA , productB ]).
location(near,  storeA ).
```

Fig. 7. Mobile Commerce Solution: (A) Conceptual Model and (B) 3APL code

From the sequence of actions above, some will be decomposed in sub-goals and added to the goal base while others will trigger capabilities. The capabilities are executed based on the definition in the capability base, built-in capabilities (e.g., *Assert(.)*, *Send(.)*, *Receive(.)*) or through attached actuators (e.g., *GUI(.)*). For a complete list of the built-in capabilities, we refer to the documentation available in the project's web-site [1].

Once again, this is a simplified demonstration application and several improvements are possible. The test was executed using 3APL-M version 1.3 and run on the phone simulator supplied in the J2ME Wireless Toolkit 2.1, from Sun Corporation. The execution utilized 163.8 Kbytes of RAM memory and processed eight deliberation steps.

6   Conclusion

3APL-M provides the support technology to develop deliberative multi-agent systems to be executed in mobile computing devices. The main features are the *sensor* and *actuator* modules, which provide the interface to integrate to context-awareness and content delivery solutions; the 3APL machinery, which includes the infrastructures for the B.D.I. based inference systems, and; the communicator module, which provides the support for communication in a multi-agent system. Hence, the platform provides the infrastructures for the technologies required by the new generation of mobile applications: context-sensitiveness, mental modelling, local processing, and pervasive content delivery. The B.D.I.-based inference module provides the solutions for applications capable of creating mental models and to represent the human thought structures.

The platform delivers a development environment compatible with the 3APL language structures. The demonstration applications proved that the resulting applications are small enough to be deployed on small devices with 20Mhz CPU and less than 512Kb RAM. The platform is compatible with Java 2 Micro Edition (J2ME) development and running environment, which has a large development community. Consequently, several development environments, platforms and programming libraries are commercially available. The strength of J2ME is industry adoption and to be Java-compatible, thus this running environment is present in a myriad of commercially available mobile computing devices.

There are several possible enhancements and optimizations for the platform. A future line of work is to better position the project against *FIPA standards* [3] especially for communication and community management. Moreover, *security* is a major area of research to be explored by this project. While there are limitations already imposed by the running environment – e.g., Java 2 Micro Edition sandbox security – the high-level security must be implemented by means of platform structures and logic operations.

For detailed information about programming in 3APL-M, downloads, demonstration codes and documentation, we refer to the project's web-site [1].

Acknowledgments

This work was conducted while Fernando Koch and Iyad Rahwan were working at the Department of Information Systems, University of Melbourne. The authors are thankful to the folks in that department for the discussions surrounding the paper topic.

References

1. 3APL-M web-site, http://www.cs.uu.nl/3apl-m.
2. 3APL web-site, http://www.cs.uu.nl/3apl.
3. Foundation for Intelligent Physical Agents (FIPA) web-site, http://www.fipa.org.
4. Java 2 Micro Edition (J2ME) web-site, sun corporation, http://java.sun.com/j2me.
5. kSACI web-site, http://www.cesar.org.br/ rla2/ksaci/.
6. Simple Agent Communication Infrastructure (SACI) web-site, http://www.lti.pcs.usp.br/.
7. M. Aparicio, L. Chiariglione, E. Mamdani, F. McCabe, R. Nicol, D. Steiner, and H. Suguri. FIPA - intelligent agents from theory to practice. *Telecom 99*, October 1999.
8. R. Ashri and M. Luck. An agent construction model for ubiquitous computing devices. In *Proceedings of AAMAS Workshop in Agent Oriented Software Engineering*, New York, USA, 2004.
9. R. Ashri, M. Luck, and M. d'Inverno. actsmart - building a smart system. In M. d'Inverno and M. Luck, editors, *Understanding Agent Systems*. Springer-Verlag, 2nd edition edition, 2003.
10. F. Bergenti, A. Poggi, B. Burg, and G. Claire. Deploying FIPA-compliant systems on handheld devices. *IEEE Internet Computing*, 5(4):20–25, 2001.
11. M. Dastani, F. Dignum, and J.-J. Meyer. Autonomy and agent deliberation. In M. Rovatsos and M. Nickles, editors, *The First International Workshop on Computatinal Autonomy - Potential, Risks, Solutions (Autonomous 2003)*, pages 23–35, Melbourne, Australia, July 2003.
12. A. K. Dey. *Providing Architectural Support for Building Context-Aware Applications*. PhD thesis, Georgia Institute of Technology, November 2000.
13. E. Guigere. *Java 2 Micro edition: The ultimate guide on programming handheld and embedded devices*. John Wiley and Sons, Inc., USA, 2001.
14. K. V. Hindriks, F. S. De Boer, W. Van Der Hoek, and J.-J. Ch. Meyer. Agent programming in 3APL. *Autonomous Agents and Multi-Agent Systems*, 2(4):357–401, 1999.
15. N. R. Jennings. An agent-based approach for building complex software systems. *Communications ACM*, 44(4):35–41, 2001.
16. N. R. Jennings and M. Wooldridge. Applications of intelligent agents. *Agent technology: foundations, applications, and markets*, pages 3–28, 1998.
17. F. Koch and I. Rahwan. Classification of agents-based mobile assistants. In *Proceedings of the AAMAS Workshop on Agents for Ubiquitous Computing (UbiAgents)*, New York, USA, Jul 2004.
18. F. Koch and I. Rahwan. The role of agents in mobile services. In *Proceedings of the Pacific Rim International Workshop on Multi-Agents (PRIMA2004)*, Auckland, NZ, August 2004.

19. Y. Labrou and T. Finin. A semantics approach for kqml a general purpose communication language for software agents. In *Proceedings of International Conference on Information and Knowledge Management*, 1994.
20. Y. Labrou, T. Finin, and Y. Peng. Agent communication languages: The current landscape. *Intelligent Systems*, 14(2):45–52, 1999.
21. Z. Maamar, W. Binder, and B. Benatallah. *Agent for Ubiquitous Computing*, chapter 19, pages 395–412. Kluwer Academic Publishers, 2004.
22. Q. Mahmoud. Mobiagent: An agent-based approach to wireless information systems. In *Proceeding of the 3rd International Bi-Conference Workshop on Agent-Oriented Information Systems*, Montreal,Canada, 2001.
23. T. Rahwan, T. Rahwan, I. Rahwan, and R. Ashri. Agent-based support for mobile users using agentspeak(l). In P. Giorgini, B. Henderson-Sellers, and M. Winikoff, editors, *Agent Oriented Information Systems*, Lecture Notes in Artificial Intelligence. Springer Verlag, Berlin, Germany, 2004.
24. A. Rao. Agentspeak(l): Bdi agents speak out in a logical computable language. In W. V. de Velde and J. W. Perram, editors, *Proceedings of the Seventh European Workshop on Modelling Autonomous Agents in a Multi-Agent World*, volume 1038 of *LNAI*. Springer, 1996.
25. A. S. Rao and M. P. Georgeff. BDI-agents: from theory to practice. In *Proceedings of the First International Conference on Multiagent Systems*, San Francisco, USA, 1995.
26. M. Satyanarayanan. Pervasive computing: vision and challenges. *IEEE Personal Communications*, 8(4):10–17, 2001.
27. F. Zambonelli and H. V. D. Parunak. Towards a paradigm change in computer science and software engineering: a synthesis. *The Knowledge Engineering Review*, 2004. (to appear).

Implementing Multi-agent Systems Organizations with INGENIAS

Jorge J. Gómez-Sanz and Juan Pavón

Dep. Sistemas Informáticos y Programación,
Universidad Complutense de Madrid
{jjgomez, jpavon}@sip.ucm.es

Abstract. In a multi-agent system, the organization determines the architecture of the whole system, and the way and policies for agent collaboration and interactions. Although this is a key element in the development process of this kind of systems, existing efforts in modeling organizations have not yet been integrated into common bodies of knowledge, neither into existing standards. This paper provides a study of general requirements for organization modeling during the analysis phase, and describes how this can be applied in the design and implementation of multi-agent systems. This is illustrated with a real example that has been developed with the INGENIAS methodology and tools, and implemented on the JADE agent platform.

1 Introduction

The description of a Multi-Agent System (MAS) should always consider different aspects, such as agent types, goals, tasks, interactions, environment, etc. Among these, the organization plays a key role as it determines the general purpose of the system, the global structure of the MAS, the context in which agents play specific roles, the policies and interactions for collaboration among agents. Since the beginning, many research works in the agent field have been concerned with organizational issues, just to cite some:

- What is an organization and the elements to describe it have been formalized by using meta-models [8]. This work is supported by the implementation of MADKIT [18]. This work has been extended in [9] and [16].
- Organization related concepts such as dependence and resource in order to enable social reasoning [24]. This work has been implemented in the DEPINT [23] and DEPNET [4] frameworks.
- Electronic institutions [7] focus on the definition of norms accepted by a set of agents. This work has been the basis for the EIDE integrated environment [6].

These works represent some of many contributions to the concept of organization. However, these approaches do not address all the problems that concern the organization in the development of a MAS. Developers need to know how an organization influences different MAS aspects, for instance, which elements are required in an agent architecture to deal with its role in an organization, special behaviors demanded in order to successfully participate in organizations, mandatory changes in the agents internal state due to the participation in a organization, and so

R.H. Bordini et al. (Eds.): ProMAS 2005, LNAI 3862, pp. 236–251, 2006.
© Springer-Verlag Berlin Heidelberg 2006

on. These questions are answered partially by previous works, but still, a global approach is needed.

Agent oriented methodologies provide a suitable framework where the complete MAS is described, and, in this way, the influence of an organization in the whole MAS can be described more precisely. There are efforts in this sense in most agent oriented methodologies, such as GAIA [25], Vowel Engineering[5], or MESSAGE [3]. However, these methodologies have not yet answered the questions presented before, since they do not describe agent architectures and they address the organization design with *ad-hoc* concepts whose implementation is not further described. SODA [20] is closer to what this proposal intends. It bases on the concept of coordination model and specifies the MAS in terms of tasks, roles, resources, interaction protocols, and interaction rules. The Group concept is part of SODA and it represents the result of grouping social tasks, permission to access resources, involved roles, and interaction rules. Besides, SODA is oriented towards an implementation based on artefacts, which are objects and tools agents use to achieve their purpose [19]. The main difference of SODA and this proposal can be summarised in three points: this proposal provides finer grain descriptions of agents including their mental state, a higher specific concept for the management of MAS (i.e., the organization concept), and a generic implementation procedure by means of code generation techniques.

With respect to standards, FIPA [10] does not propose a special infrastructure towards organization implementation nor organization modeling. It could be said that protocols and services described by FIPA induce organizational structures. Perhaps, if a MAS would respect strictly the semantics of speech acts [11], which are specified using modal logic, their behavior would be closer to the ideal of many researchers and would show many of the features associated with organizations. However, the semantics of ACL speech acts does not appear into existing FIPA implementations. So organizations do not appear explicitly nor implicitly.

This paper contributes with a generic description of concepts and components that are needed to explicitly describe organizations in FIPA compliant platforms, and this is applied to design and implementation on a popular FIPA compliant platform, JADE [2]. It is a preliminary work in the sense that it does not integrate all of the research works mentioned here, only a part, but provides hints about how organizational concepts influence agents. Our starting point is Ferber's work [8] and the goal is to integrate gradually other approaches. To do so, we needed a generic way of incorporating the different elements needed to implement the dynamics of an organization. The work can be seen from an analysis and from a design point of view.

In the analysis, we will use explicit organizational concepts in order to better understand the MAS. In the design, all the organization dynamics will be captured within three elements: goals, tasks and protocols. Hence, we reduce the organization problem to an interaction problem and the satisfaction of a set of goals. We will see along the paper what resources are needed in order to execute each task and what consequences do result. At the end, the organization concept will reify into agents playing organizational roles.

Results presented here are illustrated with an extensive case study about business processes that appear in the modeling of a bookstore company. This case study has been used to validate our approach for the definition and implementation of organizations. The notation and tools used for modeling and code generation are those provided by the INGENIAS Development Kit (IDK, available as free software [17]).

Section 2 presents the case study that will illustrate how to implement organization management functionality. After a brief review of this example, Section 3 analyzes the requirements, from the case study, that an organization implementation should meet. Section 4 shows how to satisfy these requirements by sketching organization dynamics, which would be the design part. Section 5 provides further details about one of the dynamic aspects of the organization: how to subscribe new agents. Afterwards, section 6 presents implementation details of the dynamics, including modeling and implementation on the JADE platform. The last section presents the conclusions, pointing out open issues.

2   The Bookstore Case Study

We have selected as case study the Juul Møller Bokhandel A/S problem which is described in [1]. It deals with some interesting agent research areas, such as supply chain management, workflows, enterprise modeling, and user modeling. It describes a

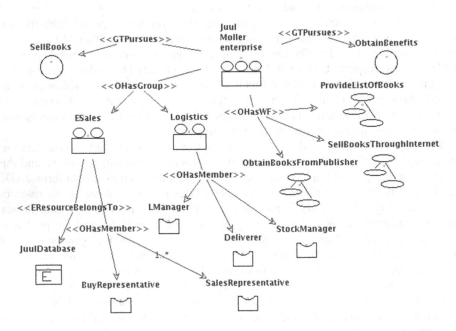

Fig. 1. Bookstore organization. This figure uses INGENIAS notation to represent organizations (rectangles with three circles above), groups (rectangles with two circles), goals (circles), workflows (linked ovals) and roles (the hollowed squares). In this example, the organization, *JuulMoller enterprise,* pursues two goals: *SellBooooks* and *ObtainBenefits.* This organization is structured in two groups, the *Esales* and *Logistics* departments, each one with a structured set of roles. Some worflows (e.g., *SellBooksThroughInternet, ProvideListOfBooks,* and *ObtainBooksFromPublishers*) are defined in the context of the organization.

bookstore that sells books to, mainly, the students of one university. The bookstore has an agreement with professors and students to obtain a list of the books that will be used in their courses and to sell them at special prices. The bookstore is considered an organization in which there are departments in charge of sales and departments in charge of logistics. This organization has to negotiate with other organizations, the publishers, for acquiring books at the best prices and with specific timing constraints. It can also negotiate for special arrangements for certain books that are demanded in concrete courses. Sales can be conventional or via web.

In this case study, the goal is to define an electronic sales system. Fig. 1 shows a draft of the initial organization for the bookstore. The *Juul Møller* bookstore is initially structured in two departments: *Logistics* and *ESales*. The first is responsible of delivering goods to customers and from publishers. The second is responsible of interacting with customers and providing representatives that interact with other editorials.

3 Studying General Requirements

This initial presentation of the main organization for the case study is rather simple. It is expressed with a language whose semantics are basically an extension of Ferber's work [8]. This extension was published first in [12] and then reviewed in [13]. The extension integrates the organization and group concepts into a more detailed model of MAS. Organization here is considered as a first order entity that pursues goals and cannot exist by itself. It depends on a set of agents that perform the tasks that will satisfy organizational goals. Internals of organizations are detailed using goals, workflows, group structures, and resources.

A developer may realize that this concept is not useful unless some additional concepts are added. Since agents are autonomous, they may not always execute the tasks required by the organization. Also, agents are adaptative and they may potentially change its behavior. Therefore, an organization should be aware that agents that fulfilled compromises in the past, may not in the future.

Organizational goals require agents to execute tasks and produce results. In an open environment, an organization may find different agents that are able to perform similar tasks. The quality of results, in some cases, depends on many variables, like CPU time or available memory. This is the case of automatic document clustering tasks or planning tasks. Also, in that environment, an agent may disappear and appear several times during the lifetime of the organization. An organization should keep a record of agents so that it always incorporates the most effective.

We could model these requirements by means of trust and effectivity. Both concepts can be modeled, in part, with INGENIAS:

- *Trust.* Trust can be represented with a history of the activity of an agent and a utility function. This function would generate an estimation of the trust that deserves an agent according to its past history. The history would contain records about whether an agent satisfies all of its compromises or not. For instance, if an agent was responsible of executing a concrete critical task and it failed to execute it on time, a wise action would be to remember this failure and locate another agent with better statistics, to reassign responsibilities.

- *Effectivity.* Effectivity could be represented in terms of the account of performed tasks, quality of results produced, and execution conditions. Quality would be computed with another utility function. Execution conditions should be determined when defining the organization in order to consider parameters related with its goals. This way, the organization executes tasks adapted to each situation.

These are the concepts we want to incorporate in order to complement the static definition of the organization we gave in Fig. 1, but, first, they need to be translated into some modeling constructs. Following INGENIAS, at the modeling level, these aspects are synthesized in the form of a single goal: *organizational health* (see figure 2). Satisfying this goal means having agents that deserve trustiness and execute the required tasks with certain effectivity. At the end, the organization, in order to achieve this goal, has to ensure that:

- There are no members that do not collaborate when requested.
- There are no members with low productivity.
- Existing members do not abuse organizational resources, avoiding other agents to perform other tasks.
- Conflictive agents are expulsed and never admitted again.

So it could be said that achieving organizational health implies defining management functions for adding, removing, and monitoring agents in a organization. The situation is similar to a previous work published in [14][15] about community based collaborative filtering. In that system, agents were admitted in communities provided that they suggested good information to other agents. The goodness of a piece of information was measured with a voting scheme and a comparison with previous known interesting documents. Here, the situation is similar in the sense that the members of the organizations help to detect these annoying agents with a low computational cost.

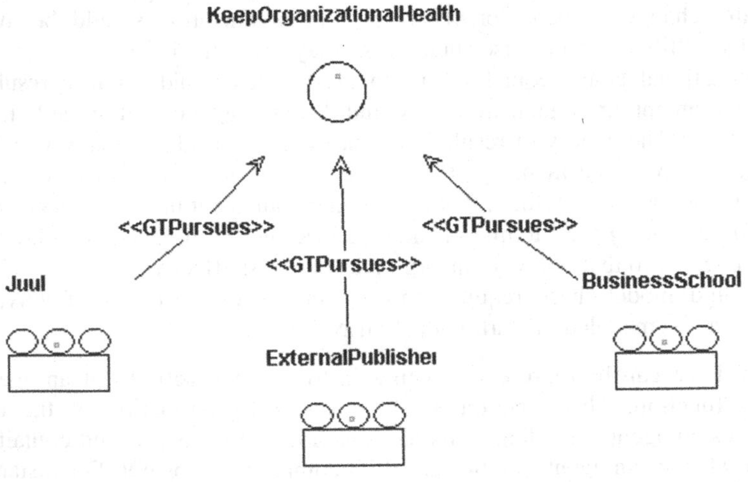

Fig. 2. The intention of achieving organizational health in the organizations involved in the case study is represented as a goal that is pursued by the organizations

This solution is adapted to this case study in the form of *Organizational Health*, that stands for: everything goes fine if most of its members think it goes fine. As a first step towards including organization management capabilities into the case study, the original specification is modified to associate this new goal to current organizations (see Fig. 2). In order to implement this goal, new roles (functionality) appear for organization management, as it is described in figure 3.

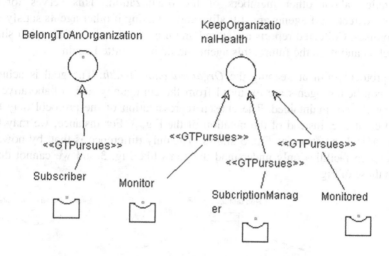

Fig. 3. Organizational Roles required to manage an organization

4 Designing the Dynamics of the Organization

Trust and effectivity can be used as criteria for deciding whether an organization benefits when an agent belongs to it. But, it should be also established under which criteria an organization should decide to find a new member or accepting a new one. Altogether, these aspects define the organization management framework. This is represented here as four basic workflows:

1. **Subscribing into an organization.** Deciding to admit a new member into the organization depends on two factors:
   - **Organizational needs.** If existing goals can be satisfied in many ways, the organization may accept agents with new skills or new implementations for existing tasks that increase performance.
   - **Trust and effectivity.** Admitting an agent that belonged to the organization in the past is safe whenever this agent behaved satisfactorily. For instance, if an agent has demonstrated that it does not fulfill a compromise, it should not be admitted anymore. If it is an unknown agent, the organization should evaluate the benefits of introducing this new agent against the benefits that have being obtained up to the moment.
2. **Leaving an organization.** This process is started by a member of the organization. This member, first, finishes compromises acquired with other members of the

organization. Once its compromises are carried out, it can leave the organization safely.

3. **Expulsion.** The organization expels those members whose behaviour does not stick to what was expected. Deciding whether a member has to be rejected or not is based on a set of reports collected during the life of the agent within the organization.

4. **Monitoring the organization.** Monitoring means asking each member of the organization about other members of the organization. This serves for two purposes: detecting if agents are still alive and detecting if other agents satisfy their compromises. Collected reports are stored and used for deciding if an agent should be expelled and if, in the future, this agent should be admitted again.

These protocols aim at keeping the *Organizational Health*. The goal is achieved whenever conflicting agents are expulsed from the community and collaborative and effective agents are maintained. The chosen representation of the protocol may have been a different one, instead of the notation of the Fig. 3. For instance, we may have chosen an AUML notation, as Fig. 5 shows. The only difference is that, by now, our code generation facilities only understand diagrams like Fig. 3 and we cannot do the same with those of Fig. 5.

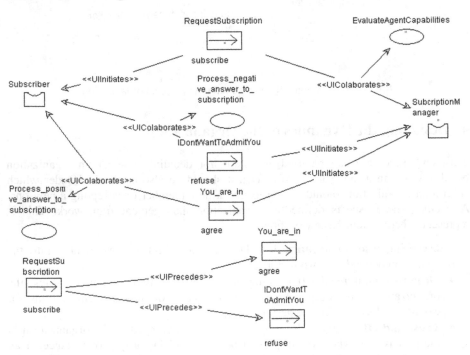

Fig. 4. Subscribing Interaction between a subscriber and a *subscription manager*. Squares with arrows represent interaction units. An interaction unit stands for a message passing, a shared tuple space writing/reading, or any other communicative act. *UIInitiates* means that a role sends a message. *UIColaborates* means that a role receives a message. *UIPrecedes* means that a communication act precedes in time another.

5 Designing Subscription Interactions

As an example of what detail level to achieve, this example considers detailed design elements for a concrete interaction, the one responsible of subscribing new agents to the organization which was introduced in Fig. 4.

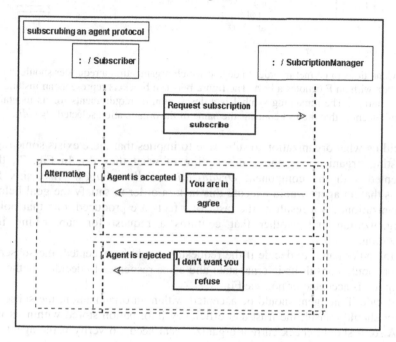

Fig. 5. Representation in AUML of the protocol presented in Fig. 4

This is an important part of the dynamics of an organization, since it gathers elements from subscription and reuses results from the monitoring stage. The roles depicted in Fig. 3 are involved in the functionality required from an organization. Agents that want to become members of an organization have to play Subscriber and Monitored roles. Agents in charge of managing the organization will play Monitor and Subscription Manager roles. One of these protocols is the subscription protocol, shown in Fig. 4. In this protocol, the *subscription manager* executes the task *evaluate agent capabilities* if it decides to participate in the interaction. In response, the *subscriber* will execute internal changes to register that now it belongs to the organization (task process positive answer), or to register that it has been removed (task process negative answer). These tasks are associated within the interaction in the initiator or collaborator of each interaction unit.

The initiator of the protocol knows that it must start then interaction when the condition from Fig. 6 is satisfied. This condition means that a running instance of an agent has an Organization Compatible fact pointing at an organization, and that an agent subscribes to a concrete organization. This fact is produced by an internal task of the agent that plays the role subscriber. The task is shown in Fig. 7.

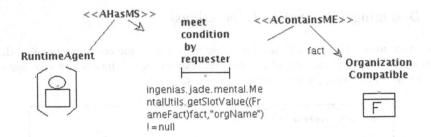

Fig. 6. Conditions to be met in order to decide which organization a requester should subscribe to. The box with an F denotes a Fact. The figure between brackets represents an instance of an agent in runtime. The remaining symbol is a description of requirements for its mental state. The requirement is that the fact contains the name of the organization selected (*!=null*).

Deciding what organization to subscribe to implies that there exists some registry of existing organizations and a description of what they do. In Fig. 7., this is represented with the component *Organization Yellow Pages*. Also, this figure explains that an agent would execute this task in order to satisfy the goal belong to an organization. As a result of the task, two facts are produced, one that points at the organization and another that contains a request for subscribing in the organization.

On the other hand, to decide if the requester should be accepted, the subscription manager should consult its internal state and some resources to decide whether if the subscription is accepted or not, see Fig. 8.

To decide if an agent should be accepted within an organization, the subscription manager should consult the trust and efficiency information stored within its mental state. Also, it should check current organizational needs to verify if the agent would be needed at all. As a product of the task, the agent produces a negative or positive evaluation. And why the subscription manager would like to execute this task, because it wants to achieve a good level of organizational health.

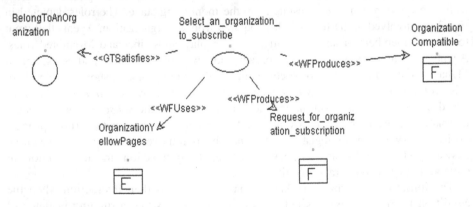

Fig. 7. Task that decides what organization an agent should subscribe to. The oval denote a task. Boxes with an F denote a Fact. Boxes with an E denote applications that already exists in the environment.

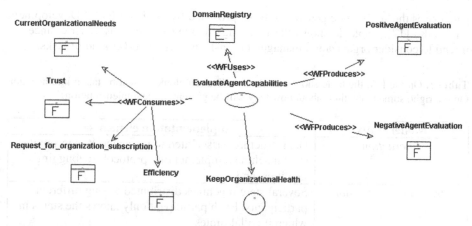

Fig. 8. Description of the task responsible of deciding whether a requester is accepted or not

6   Linking the Case Study with Organization Management and Implementation Issues

Using the models shown in Fig.4, Fig. 6, Fig. 7, and Fig. 8 the developer identifies components that have to be present in the design of the MAS. Concretely, these elements are:

- A responsible of managing the organization (Fig. 4)
- Elements for storing information about trust and efficiency as described in section 3.
- Implementation of the protocols from section 4.

So far, what we have are models that specify these elements within a BDI framework. These models explain what changes are expected in an agent by detailing which are the outputs of the tasks it performs. In figure 6, the diagram establishes that there is a procedure to select an organization to subscribe to, that there should exist a yellow pages service for organizations, and that the mental state of the agent should be changed to incorporate two new facts after the task execution.

Original case study is modified to take into account these aspects, but the modifications are simple. First, the goal keep organizational health is associated with existing organizations (Fig. 2 (A)). Then, organizational roles from Fig. 2 (B) are associated with existing agents in the original case study. With these slight modifications, the case study would incorporate functionality able to behave as it has been specified here.

There is one open issue, yet: how it is possible to ensure that this new functionality appears in the final development. Modeling is not enough. Diagrams presented before are useful only to indicate what entities exist and what relationships connect them. So far, what we have is an analysis and design work, but in the detailed design and implementation these entities should map to computational entities and code. This goal is achieved by defining methods to map the specifications (see Table 1), diagrams in this case, to code. This is addressed following. To perform this task, this paper uses the set of code generation tools provided by the INGENIAS Development Kit (IDK) [17]. Table 1 shows the mappings applied so far. It is generic since we intend to consider organization management tasks just as any other kind of tasks.

Table 1. On the left, the table shows which specification elements will be taken into account. On the right, some indications about how they will be present in the implementation.

Model entity	Implementation elements
Interaction	Data structures associated to the agent. It incorporates state machines implementing protocols, debugging facilities, and
Protocol specification	Several state machines distributed among different participants. Each participant only knows the states in which it collaborates
Agent	A JADE agent with infrastructure for conversation management.
Role	An entry in the yellow pages of JADE. Functionality associated to the role is directly migrated to each agent playing it.
Organization	Information within data structures of agents
Organization Group	Information within data structures of agents
Tasks	Components encapsulating agent actions
Goals	Information within data structures of agents
OrganizationYellowPages	A specialized use of the yellow pages of JADE. We represent each organization by special roles in the yellow pages directory
Effectivity	A fact in the mental state of the agent playing the Monitor role
Trust	A fact in the mental state of the agent playing the Monitor role

As an example of how it works, we will centre in the implementation of the interactions needed to implement the protocols from section 4 as well as tasks and the role of facts in the final prototype. The target platform is JADE, which, in principle, does not provide facilities for representing organization management functionality. The basic JADE agent is extended by associating it a mental state and methods to handle different conversations on demand. An agent in this initial prototype has a mental state implemented as a blackboard. The agent runs different instances of state machines, each one representing a concrete conversation. Each state machine has a control that decides which state is next. Next state is decided by reading the blackboard and checking if certain conditions hold.

We have built these elements with the help of IDK libraries and frameworks. These elements are described within *templates* which are linked with the specification. The prototype is the result of instantiating these templates with the specification data. The role of the IDK is to instantiate a framework made up with templates and conventional source code with pieces of information extracted from the specification.

```
<?xml version="1.0" encoding="UTF-8"?>
<!ELEMENT file (#PCDATA I v)*>
<!ATTLIST file
    overwrite (yeslno) #REQUIRED>
<!ELEMENT program
(#PCDATAlrepeatlsavetolv)*>
<!ELEMENT repeat (#PCDATA I saveto I v)*>
<!ATTLIST repeat
    id CDATA #REQUIRED>
<!ELEMENT saveto (file, text)>
<!ELEMENT text (#PCDATA I repeat I v I
saveto)*>
<!ELEMENT v (#PCDATA)>
```

Fig. 9. DTD for templates to be filled with the information extracted from the specification

```
...
@repeat id="condfacts"@
Fact @v@label@/v@=
  getAgent().getFact("@v@type@/v@");
@/repeat@
if (@v@condition@/v@){
  sb.setState(options[0]);
}
...
```

```
...
Fact
fact=getAgent().getFact("Request_for_organizat
ion_subscription");
    if (fact.get("orgName")!=null){
       sb.setState(options[0]);
    }
...
```

(A)   (B)

Fig. 10. (A)Excerpt of a template of code that represents a change of state according to the presence of some facts in the mental state of an agent and the satisfaction of a boolean expression. (B) Result of instantiating the previous template with information from the diagram of Fig. 6.

Templates are described in XML with a custom language based on a simple set of tags which are presented in Fig. 9. These tags are used to describe where the specification data is going to be inserted. Informally, the different entities of the template language could be defined as follows:

- **Program.** The root node of the document. It declares a template of a program.
- **Saveto.** It says that some text has to be saved into a file determined by the *file* tag. Text to be saved is the one wrapped by the *text* tag.
- **Repeat.** It declares that the enclosing text should be repeated as many times as needed. Repeating a text means creating duplicates and placing them one after another. The number of duplicates depends on the data extracted from the specification
- **V.** It represents a single piece of data and it is supposed to be replaced by data coming from a data source.

More information about templates in the IDK and how to produce code can be found in [17]. As an example of the kind of templates a developer could find, and to give an idea of how it works, readers can check Fig. 10. That figure shows part of more complex templates which are used for this case study.

```
...
Fact expectedInput=null;
Fact expectedOutput=null;
Resource expectedResource=null;

@repeat id="expectedInput"@
expectedInput=(Fact)this.getFact("@v@factName@/v@");
tobject.addExpectedInput(new ExpectedItem("@v@factName@/v@",expectedInput));
@/repeat@

@repeat id="expectedResource"@
expectedResource=(Fact)this.getFact("@v@resourceName@/v@");
tobject.addExpectedResource(new
ExpectedItem("@v@resourceName@/v@",expectedResource));
@/repeat@

tobject.execute();

@repeat id="expectedOutput"@
expectedOutput = (Fact)tobject.getOutput("@v@factName@/v@").getValue();
this.addFact(expectedOutput); //Adds a new fact to the agent mental state
/repeat@
...
```

Fig. 11. Part of the template of code that represents the execution of a task

Some templates are simple, like the one shown in Fig. 10 (A). Parts of the original prototype that relate with diagrams are marked up with XML tags like the ones shown in Fig. 10 (A). That piece of code is part of the control code of the state machine. It is supposed to depend on the information of diagrams like the one from Fig. 6. To facilitate codification of programming constructs in templates, the < and > symbols of XML tags were replaced by the @ symbol. This way, a developer can edit the source of the template and codify with characters proper of a programming language (like the *greater than* symbol or the *ampersand*) without converting these symbols to their corresponding codes in XML. Afterwards, a conversion program will transform all the compromising symbols to a valid XML representation, and the @ symbols to their original form (< and >). Taking the piece of code from figure 8 and replacing the bold text with the data from Fig. 6, it results a piece of code such as the one shown in Fig. 10 (B). The process is performed automatically by the IDK.

The implementation of other aspects such as task execution, modification of mental state, initial mental state of the agents, initial organizations, and others, are translated in a similar way. Fig. 11 shows another piece of code that shows how task execution is translated taking into account its inputs, outputs, and required resources.

```
public class @v@agentid@/v@JADEAgent
                extends JADEAgent {
...
        /**
         * Agent initialization
         */
        public void setup() {
                super.setup();
                @repeat id="interactions"@
                  knownProtocols.add("@v@interactionid@/v@");
                @/repeat@
                  boolean continueInit=false;
                @repeat id="interactionsColaborated"@
                  knownProtocols.add("@v@interactionid@/v@");
                @/repeat@
...
```

Fig. 12. Piece of code of the template that implements the JADE agent. Shown code is the responsible of assigning an agent the interactions it knows in the specification.

Note that in the code template, after the task execution, task results are added to the mental state of the agent. There is also code to deal with task failures and more templates that define what is a task, a goal, a resource, and other implicated elements, but they have been omitted here. Anyway, readers can see that this way the IDK is forcing the analyst to define inputs and outputs of tasks and the developer to take into account these aspects.

Finally, Fig. 12 presents part of the code of the JADE Agents that we use. The code shown is part of the standard JADE initialization method. In this method, the agent is assigned the different behaviors detailed in the specification. The **repeat id="interactions"** refers to the interactions initiated by the agent. The **repeat id="interactionsColaborated"** refers to the interactions where the agent participates as collaborator, following the terminology of FIPA. There are similar sections for tasks, roles, registration into JADE directory facilities, and mental state initialization.

7 Conclusions

This paper has presented an example of how to model an organization using the IDK and how a part of the generated specification is realized into generic computational elements using a deterministic method. Organization elements have been first modeled using INGENIAS notation. Organizational concepts have been added to the original case study by linking case study entities with roles and goals required by the organization management elements.

Their implementation has been introduced by means of the IDK code generation framework and simple components. Concretely, the paper has introduced briefly the elements required for the implementation, and presented details about the implementation of protocols and tasks.

The interest of this work is that we success in defining dynamics in terms of simple elements. The paper works at two levels, an analysis high level which deals with theoretical concepts, and a design level, where these concepts are translated into more simple elements: tasks, interactions, and mental entities, such as goals and facts.

Organizational health goal concept, protocols, and tasks proposed in this paper should be applicable into other kinds of organizations where membership is not predetermined. In those systems, there has to be a registration mechanism and criteria to decide if expulsion makes sense or not. We defined these criteria for a concrete development in terms of the opinion that each agent had about other agents in the same organization. Nevertheless, other domain problems would find other different criteria.

In this line of research, there are pending tasks, like providing concrete algorithms for selecting which agent to admit and to expulse. The criteria will determine the dynamics of the population within the organization and designers should be aware of their effect.

This work has used tools that are available to the research community on [17]. Researchers can download the tool and the initial specification of the case study, included in the distribution, though the final version of the templates presented here are not part of it. However, there are other functional versions of protocol code generators for JADE and JADE Leap, which has been the main topic considered in the implementation. It is possible to make experiments with these, and others, code generation facilities. Also, readers are invited to try the JADE Leap code generation module which is able to execute tasks appearing in the specification diagrams. Details about how to run these use cases are available in the INGENIAS Development Manual, which can be downloaded also from [17].

Acknowledgements

This work has been developed in the project INGENIAS, which is funded by the Spanish Council for Science and Technology, reference TIC2002-04516-C03-03.

References

[1] Andersen, E (2005). *Juul Møller Bokhandel A/S case study*. http://www.espen.com

[2] Bellifemine, F., Poggi, A., and Rimassa, G. (2001). *JADE: a FIPA2000 compliant agent development environment*. In Proceedings of the Fifth international Conference on Autonomous Agents. ACM Press, pp. 216-217.

[3] Caire, G., Coulier, W., Garijo, F. J., Gomez, J., Pavón, J., Leal, F., Chainho, P., Kearney, P. E., Stark, J., Evans, R., and Massonet, P. (2002). *Agent Oriented Analysis Using Message/UML*. In Proceedings of the Second international Workshop on Agent-Oriented Software Engineerins. Lecture Notes In Computer Science, vol. 2222. Springer-Verlag, pp. 119-135.

[4] Conte, R, Sichman, J S. *DEPNET: How to benefit from social dependence*. Journal of Mathematical Sociology, 1995

[5] Demazeau, Y. (1996). *Vowels*. Invited lecture, In the First Ibero-American Workshop on Distributed AI and Multi-Agent Systems (IWDAIMAS`96), Xalapa, Mexico.

[6] EIDE (2005). *Electronic Institutions Development Environment* (EIDE). http://e-institutor.iiia.csic.es/islander/pub/

[7] Esteva, M, de la Cruz, D, and Sierra, C (2003). *ISLANDER: an electronic institutions editor*. In Proceedings of the First international Joint Conference on Autonomous Agents and Multiagent Systems. ACM Press, pp. 1045-1052

[8] Ferber, J, Gutknecht. O (1998). *A Meta-Model for the Analysis and Design of Organizations in Multi-Agent Systems.* In Proceedings of Third International Conference on Multi Agent Systems (ICMAS'98), 1998

[9] Ferber, J (1999). *Multi-Agent Systems.* Addison-Wesley

[10] FIPA (2002). *FIPA Abstract Architecture Specification.* http://www.fipa.org/specs/ fipa00001

[11] FIPA (2002). *FIPA ACL Message Structure Specification,* http://www.fipa.org/specs/ fipa00061/index.html

[12] Garijo, F, Gómez-Sanz, J J, Pavón, J, Massonet, P (2001). *Multi-Agent System Organization. An Engineering Perspective.* In Proceedings of Modelling Autonomous Agents in a Multi-Agent World.

[13] Gómez-Sanz, J J, Pavón, J, and Garijo, F (2002). *Meta-models for building multi-agent systems.* In Proceedings of the 2002 ACM Symposium on Applied Computing. ACM Press, pp. 37-41.

[14] Gómez-Sanz, J J, Pavón, J (2003). *Personalized Information Dissemination using Agent Organizations.* In Proceedings of the Ninth IEEE Workshop on Future Trends of Distributed Computing Systems. IEEE Press, pp. 38-44 .

[15] Gómez-Sanz, J J, Pavón, P, Díaz, A (2003). *The PSI3 Agent Recommender System.* I Proceedings of the Third International Conference on Web Engineering, Lecture Notes in Computer Science, Volume 2722, pp. 30 - 39

[16] Gutknecht, F, Ferber, O, Michel, J (2001). *Integrating Tools and Infrastructures for Generic Multi-Agent Systems.* In Proceedings of the Fifth international conference on Autonomous agents. ACM Press, pp. 441 - 448

[17] INGENIAS Development Kit (IDK). http://ingenias.sourceforge.net

[18] MADKIT (2005). *Multi-Agent Development KIT,* http://www.madkit.org

[19] Molesini, A, Omicini, A, Denti, E, Ricci, A (2005). SODA: A Roadmap to Artefacts. In Proceedings of the Sixth International Workshop Engineering Societies in the Agents World.

[20] Omicini, A. (2001). *SODA: Societies and Infrastructures in the Analysis and Design of Agent-Based Systems.* In Proceedings of the First Agent Oriented Software Engineering workshop, Lecture Notes in Computer Science, Volume 1957, pp. 185-193

[21] Pavón, J, Gómez-Sanz, J (2003). *Agent Oriented Software Engineering with INGENIAS.* In Multi-Agent Systems and Applications III, Lecture Notes in Computer Science, Volume 2691, pp. 394-403

[22] Picard, G, Bernon, C, Gleizes, M, Peyruqueou, S (2003). *ADELFE: A Methodology for Adaptive Multi-agent Systems Engineering,* Lecture Notes in Computer Science, Volume 2577, 2003, pp. 156 – 169

[23] Sichman, J S (1998). *DEPINT: Dependence-Based Coalition Formation in an Open Multi-Agent Scenario.* Journal of Artificial Societies and Social Simulation, volume 8

[24] Sichman, J S, and Demazeau Y (2001). *On Social Reasoning in Multi-Agent Systems.* Inteligencia Artificial. Volume 13, pp. 68-84

[25] Zambonelli, F, Jennings, N R, and Wooldridge, M (2003). *Developing multiagent systems: The Gaia methodology.* ACM Transactions on Software Engineering and Methodology, 12 (3), 317-370.

Declarative Agent Programming Support for a FIPA-Compliant Agent Platform

Mengqiu Wang, Mariusz Nowostawski, and Martin Purvis

University of Otago, Dunedin, New Zealand
{mwang, mnowostawski, mpurvis}@infoscience.otago.ac.nz

Abstract. Multi-agent system(MAS) is a blooming research area, which exhibits a new paradigm for the design, modeling and implementation of complex systems. A significant amount of effort has been made in establishing standards for agent communication and MAS platforms. However, communication is not the only difficulty faced by agent researchers. Research is also directed towards the formal aspects of agents and declarative approaches to model agents. This paper explores the bonding between high-level reasoning engines and low-level agent platforms in the practical setting of using three formal agent reasoning implementations together with an existing agent platform, OPAL, that supports the FIPA standards. We focus our discussion in this paper on our approach to provide declarative agent programming support in connection with the OPAL platform, and show how declarative goals can be used to glue the internal micro agents together to form the hierarchical architecture of the platform.

1 Introduction

Multi-agent system(MAS) research is an important and rapidly growing area in distributed systems and artificial intelligence. The agent notion has evolved from a monolithic artifact of software to a new and exciting computing paradigm, and it is now recognized that MAS, as a conceptual model, has the advantages of high flexibility, modularity, scalability and robustness [16]. Proprietary MASs have existed for years, but the lack of agent communication standards hindered the convergence of individual research efforts and restricted further growth until the emergence of the current set of standards, the FIPA[1] specifications and the JAS[2] standards, which afford agents the ability to communicate with each other without requiring them to gain inside knowledge of each other.

However, communication is not the only difficulty faced by agent researchers. There exists a gap between the semantics of an agent and its practical implementation. For example, if an agent is specified to have a BDI[3][19] architecture but is

---

[1] FIPA, Foundation for Intelligent Physical Agents, has developed specifications supporting interoperability among agents and agent-based applications[3].

[2] The Java Agent Services (JAS) project defines a standard specification for an implementation of the FIPA Abstract Architecture within the Java Community Process initiative[10].

[3] BDI stands for Belief, Desire and Intention.

R.H. Bordini et al. (Eds.): ProMAS 2005, LNAI 3862, pp. 252–266, 2006.
© Springer-Verlag Berlin Heidelberg 2006

implemented with a conventional programming language, it is difficult to verify whether the agent satisfies the specifications [1,18]. This problem has been addressed by various research groups around the world, and the result is a set of agent programming languages, e.g. 3APL, Agent-0, AgentSpeak. [7,15,17]. We are particularly interested in the 3APL language developed at University of Utrecht, which allows the programmer to design an agent in a declarative way, by specifying the rules, goals, beliefs and capabilities of the agent. The declarative nature of 3APL helps bridge the semantic gap, and allows flexibility in agent development.

As the number of agent platforms grows, a gap remains in-between these two building blocks. That is, though an intelligent agent can be built in isolation, one may find it difficult to migrate such an agent onto a platform which hosts other types of agents that it needs to cooperate with. On the other hand, only few agent platforms provide facilities to ease the development of complex agents, or provide a unified approach for integrating such agents onto the platform [16]. Many platforms that exist today only provide the basic services that are required by the standard, such as agent management, directory service, and naming service. [4] Agents on such platforms are developed primarily in some arbitrary imperative programming language, such as Java, but the semantic gap remains.

One of the few platforms that do attempt to treat this problem and provide declarative support is the 3APL Platform developed at the University of Utrecht [8], the same group that invented the 3APL language. But the 3APL Platform has a few limitations. In particular, it has a closed architecture as opposed to an open architecture: only 3APL agents can be hosted on the platform. Consequently, the platform is subject to whatever drawbacks the language itself may have.

This paper explores the bonding between high-level reasoning engines and low-level agent platforms in the practical setting of using the 3APL language, the OPAL platform[12], the ROK system and the ROK scripting language[11] and the JPRS reasoning engines[11]. We focus our interest in this paper on our approach to provide declarative agent programming support in the OPAL platform, and show how declarative goals can be used to glue the internal micro agents in OPAL to form the hierarchical architecture of the platform.

The theoretical extension discussed in this paper is accompanied by a practical implementation. The extended OPAL platform is now equipped with three powerful high-level declarative agent language and reasoning engines, as well as with a graphical IDE for constructing complex agents with a hierarchical structure.

2   The 3APL Language

3APL[4] is a programming language for implementing cognitive agents, and was developed at the University of Utrecht, the Netherlands. The 3APL language incorporates the classical elements of BDI logic and also embraces first-order logic features. It provides programming constructs for implementing agent beliefs, declarative goals, basic capabilities, such as belief updates or motor actions,

---

[4] 3APL stands for An Abstract Agent Programming Language, and is pronounced "triple A P L".

and practical reasoning rules through which an agent's goals can be updated or revised [1]. In this section we give a very brief introduction to the main constructs of the language; the formal syntax and the semantics of the 3APL language can be found in Dastani et al. [1].

2.1 Beliefs

An agent's beliefs are represented in 3APL as prolog-like well-formed-formula (wff). An example of using beliefs to represent information about the environment is an agent with the task of going to a lecture class at a certain time. The agent will have beliefs such as *class_starts_at(X)* and *NOT in_class(self)*. If the agent attends the class, the agent's mental state and the state of the environment change. The belief *NOT in_class(self)* denotes that the agent believes he is not attending a class, so this has to be updated to be *in_class(self)*. The beliefs *NOT in_class(self)* need to be removed from the belief-base(knowledge database) in order to make sure the agent's view of the world is consistent.

2.2 Actions

The most primitive action that an agent is capable of performing is called a basic action, which is also referred to as a capability. In general, an agent uses basic actions to manipulate its mental state and the environment. Before performing a basic action, certain beliefs should hold and after the execution of the action the beliefs of the agent will be updated. Basic actions are the only constructs in 3APL that can be used to update the beliefs of an agent.

An action can only be performed if certain beliefs hold. These are called the pre-conditions of an action. Take for example an agent that wants to attend a meeting, using the basic action *AttendMeeting(Room1)*. Before this action can be executed, there should be a meeting pending at room *(Room1)*, and the agent should also be at another location but not already engaged in a meeting. The precondition of *AttendingMeeting(Room1)* is represented as:

$$\{ meeting(Room1), position(Room2), NOT in\_a\_meeting(self) \}$$

After performing the action, the post-condition will become true, and the agent's beliefs will be updated. For example, after the *AttendingMeeting* action took place, the following beliefs will hold:

$$\{ in\_a\_meeting(self), position(Room1) \}$$

2.3 Goals

A 3APL agent has basic and composite goals. There are three different types of basic goals: basic action, test goal, and the predicate goal. A test goal allows the agent to evaluate its beliefs (a test goal checks whether a belief formula is true of false). For example, a test goal for testing if the agent is carrying a box looks like *carrybox(self)?* This type of goal is also used to bind values to variables, like variable assignment in ordinary programming languages. When a test goal is used with a variable as a parameter, the variable is instantiated with a value from a belief formula in the belief-base. The third type of goal is a predicate goal. It can be used as a label for a procedure call. The procedure itself is defined by a practical reasoning rule (practical reasoning rules are introduced in the next subsection). From these three types of basic goals, we can construct composite goals by using the sequence operator, the conditional choice operator and the 'while' operator. A special type of goal that has been recently added is JavaGoal. This type of goal enables the programmer to load an external Java class and invoke method calls on it. Each method is assumed to return a list (possibly empty) of well formed formula.

2.4   Practical Reasoning Rules

Practical reasoning rules are at the heart of the way 3PAL agents operate. They can be used to generate reactive behavior, to optimize the agent's goals, or to revise the agent's goals to get rid of unreachable goals or blocked basic-actions. They can also be used to define predicate goals (i.e. procedure calls). To allow for the dynamic matching of rules, goal variables are used as place-holders. Unification mechanisms are used when performing goal-matching.

3   Rule-Driven Object-Oriented Knowledgebase System

ROK, Rule-driven Object-oriented Knowledge base system, is a forward chaining production rule system derived from JEOPS. JEOPS was developed by Carlos Figueira Filho and Carlos Cordeiro [2]. ROK provides a library and API written in Java, with a mechanism for embedding first-order, forward-chaining production rules into Java applications. It was created to provide the declarative expressiveness of production rules, which is useful for the development of large or complex systems [11]. ROK production rules can be described as condition-action patterns. Any Java object can be matched in a ROK rule, and any Java expression can be used in the condition and action part of ROK rules. There are two major modes of operation for a ROK system: native and interpreted. In the native mode the programmer declares the rules using the provided Java API. In the interpreted mode, users prepare the rules as a text script file to be parsed and interpreted by the ROK interpreter. In the interpreted mode, the programmer is freed from writing Java code and only has to write declarative pseudo-Java scripts. But there is a performance trade-off: native mode is faster in execution and is the optimal method of operation.

3.1   An Example ROK Program

Here we present a simple ROK program as an example. The rules in this program say that "If a salesman is selling a product the customer needs, for a price the customer can afford, then the deal is made". Supposing that Salesman, Customer and Product are Java classes, previously defined by the programmer (or even by third-parties), the rule should be stated as the following:

```
import example.Salesman;
import example.Customer;
import example.Product;
rule: trade {
  declarations:
    Salesman s;
    Customer c;
    Product p;
  conditions:
    c.needs(p);
    s.owns(p);
    s.priceAskedFor(p) <= c.getMoney();
  actions:
    s.sell(p);
    c.buy(p);
}
```

In this example, if there is an object for each of the Salesman, Customer and Product classes, and all the expressions in the condition part evaluate to be true, then the action part of the rule will be executed. The formal syntax description of ROK and more examples can be found in [11].

3.2   Internal Structure of ROK

The heart of the ROK system is the knowledge-base. It is composed primarily of three main blocks: the object-base, the rule-base and the conflict set. The object-base is the working memory, where the facts that the agent knows are stored. The rules written by the programmer or compiled from rule scripts are placed (installed) inside the rule-base. The rule-base is the place where all the information about the rules is stored, such as their declarations, conditions, actions, and several other items of control information. The RETE network [6] is used to store the partial matches between rules and objects, and to increase the performance of the matching process. Finally, the conflict set is the component in which the rules that can be fired at a certain moment are stored, as well as the objects that have been matched to the rule declarations.

The object-base is simply a collection of objects. It could be simply implemented as a Java vector, but we decided to store the objects in a structure from where we could retrieve the objects of a given class in a more efficient way. Hence, the object base is implemented with a hashtable that maps fully-qualified names of the classes to the set of objects belonging to that class. With that arrangement, we can efficiently retrieve all objects that belong to a given class, which is a necessary operation in the matching stage of the inference engine. The object-base is also responsible for storing the inheritance relationships between the class of the objects stored in it, so that when the inference engine asks for all objects of some class, it will return both the direct instances of this class and the instances of its subclasses (i.e., its indirect instances).

RETE is a classical algorithm used in production systems to minimize the number of tests required in the matching process [6]. Partial matchings are stored in a RETE, and they do not have to be re-tested. New objects that arrive in the network are tested only where necessary.

The conflict set of the knowledge-base is the area where rules ready to be fired are stored. The user has the ability of choosing the conflict resolution policy to be used in the knowledge-base. In most of the cases, the user will not need to use any complex policy, and the predefined classes will be sufficient. ROK has some predefined classes that implement different policies for choosing which rule is to be fired at any given moment. The predefined classes are the following:

1. DefaultConflictSet: The conflict set used when none is specified. Its conflict resolution policy is not specified. In other words, any of the instantiations can be returned, and it was implemented to be as efficient as possible.
2. LRUConflictSet: A conflict set that will choose the least recently used rule. If there is more than one rule in the conflict set, it will choose one that was fired before the remaining ones.
3. MRUConflictSet: A conflict set that will choose the most recently used rule. If there is more than one rule in the conflict set, it will choose one that was fired after the remaining ones.
4. NaturalConflictSet: A conflict set that will not allow a rule to be fired more than once with the same objects. This conflict set requires a large amount of memory to store the history of rule firing, so it must be used with care. It also tends to get inefficient when the history grows.
5. OneShotConflictSet: A conflict set that will not allow a rule to be fired more than once.
6. PriorityConflictSet: A conflict set that will give priorities to the rules. Rules defined first in the rule base file will have higher priorities than rules defined later.

3.3   The Reasoning

The current implementation of ROK enables the user to operate in two modes on the knowledge-base: one-shot mode and continuous mode. When the user calls the run() method on the knowledge-base, the inference engine is triggered to operate. It will perform reasoning on the objects of its working memory until the conflict set is empty. Then it will return the control (return from the method call). Another possible method is to call runInLoop() method. This method will block the current thread and perform reasoning of the knowledge-base continuously, i.e. until the halt() method is called. In the continuous mode, the reasoning will not stop when the conflict set is empty, but will be triggered on every change of the knowledge-base state, i.e. on addition/removal of rules or facts. To get information from the knowledge-base, the agent (user) can use the objects() methods to retrieve all the objects of a given class that are stored there. Another way of retrieving the information gathered during the execution of the run() method is to store the information needed in the internal state of some fact object.

4   The Java Procedural Reasoning System

JPRS, Java Procedural Reasoning System, is a Java library and API written for performing goal-driven procedural reasoning. Its ancestors can be traced back to the architecture of the PRS system proposed by Georgeff [5], as well as UMPRS and JAM [9]. The notion of procedural reasoning is derived from the idea that some of human knowledge can be best represented as a set of procedure/steps performed in order to achieve a particular goal. A simple example of procedural reasoning can be the planning of a trip from Dunedin to Beijing. The goal is to start off from an apartment in Dunedin, and end up in Beijing International Airport. One of the possible plans is: make a booking, then pay for a economic class ticket from Dunedin to Beijing, take a shuttle to the Dunedin Airport, transit at Sydney Airport, and finally get off the plane at Beijing Airport. An alternative plan would be to take a taxi to Dunedin Airport, pay for a first class direct flight, and then get off at Beijing Airport. We may decide to choose a plan based on how much money or time we have, or the level of service we are seeking. Those represent part of our knowledge about the external world, in other words, our beliefs. Each JPRS agent is composed of four primary components: a world model, a plan library, a plan executor, and a set of goals. The world model is a database that represents the beliefs of the agent. In the previous example, the agent may store information, such as a bank balance, travel departure date, etc. The plan library is a collection of plans that the agent can use to achieve its goals. The plan executor is the agent's "brain" that reasons about what the agent should do and when it should do it. An agent finishes its tasks when there are no more goals to be achieved. JPRS uses a framework-like model for declaring the plans and goals, which provides the specific conventions for declaring goals and plans. The formal syntax and semantics of JPRS are available at [11].

5   Hierarchical Agent Architecture Using Micro-agents

Before we discuss how the reasoning engines are incorporated into OPAL, it is necessary to describe the system architecture. The notion of agency is used at all abstraction levels in modeling OPAL agent systems. At the lowest abstraction level *micro agents*, which are the closest agent entities to the machine platform, are used. In order to be efficient at this fine-grained level, they do not have all of the qualities often attributed to typical, more coarsely-grained agents. In contrast to higher abstraction level agents, such as those based on FIPA specifications [3], micro agents are more concerned with efficiency and thus do not have all of the qualities and flexibility of FIPA-compliant agents. For instance, micro agents employ a simpler form of agent communication (they communicate via method calls) and are implemented by extending predefined Java classes and interfaces [13].

There are two kinds of micro-agent: primitive and non-primitive. Primitive agents use native services, in particular native micro-kernel libraries, and directly interact with the underlying virtual machine (in our case the Java Virtual Machine). Non-primitive micro-agents, which are typically more sophisticated and exist at a higher abstraction level, are composed only of micro-agents and do not use any native services.

Because the smallest building block in OPAL is an agent, the system designer can apply agent-oriented modeling approaches throughout the development process. There are two basic constructs in the micro agent system, namely agents and roles. Agents represent actors in a system that can play one or more roles. A role represents a cohesive set of services that may be provided by some agent. Agents that perform the same role are not restricted in the way that they provide the services as prescribed by the role.

There is a special type of role called a group role. When an agent performs a group role, it acts as the group owner and creates a group environment in which other agents could register as group members. By registering with a group, an agent is associated with the group owner and can collaborate with the owner agent. For example, upon receiving a task to solve or a goal to achieve, the group owner can choose to disseminate the goal to its group members and request the members to achieve the goal. And alternatively, if a group member performs a role that the owner, itself, doesn't perform, the owner may still advertise itself as an actor of the role. When the set of services of the role are subsequently requested, it can request its group members to provide the services for him. The group membership can be dynamically modified according to the needs of individual agents. For example, if an agent is managing a group with too many members, and the action for searching for the right member becomes a lengthy operation, it may decide to get rid of some not frequently used group members. Also, an agent may decide to deregister itself from a group because it is more often needed in another agent group.

Although the group concept can be effectively used for organizing agents into hierarchies, one is still faced with the problem of providing ways for the agents to exchange information and cooperate at semantics level. One way for micro agents to talk to each other and share their capability is to use role-matching. When an agent needs other agents to perform certain services for it, it will need to know what type of role provides such services and then will need to recursively search through other agents and their groups for that role. If roles and services could be specified declaratively, this approach would suffice for systems in which agents would be requesting new services dynamically. But because roles and services are such generic concepts, difficulties arise in defining formal semantics specifying the services. And also, since OPAL is written in Java, a complete high level language built on top of Java is needed to support specifying services declaratively at runtime . In the current OPAL implementation, roles and services are not declarative constructs. The role-matching approach would only be suitable for systems in which all services are known before runtime. This poses potential restrictions on the dynamism of the systems.

A second approach, which is the one we are currently taking, relies on using declarative goals to aid in the cooperation among micro agents. The meaning of a goal in OPAL is similar to the meaning of a goal in 3APL. It typically specifies some post-conditions that represent the states after the goal has been achieved, but doesn't enforce how these post-conditions are to be realized. In other words, a goal carries some declarative information of some state, but not the procedural information on how to reach that state. Agents collaborate through goal exchanging. For example, an agent may decide according to its own internal state, what its next goal to be achieved is. And if the agent, itself, is not capable of achieving the goal, or if it wants other agents to provide alternative solutions to achieve the goal, it can send the goal to other agents. Goals in OPAL are self-descriptive, other agents can evaluate the goals and try their own way of achieving the goal. At the end it will inform the initiating agent whether it succeed in achieving the goal or not. Similar to the role-matching approach, the goals can be recursively passed down through the agent hierarchy, or even from the bottom-up. The advantage of using goals instead of roles becomes evident when the system designer can only describe the states of the system declaratively but does not know exactly how the transitions between states take place. In contrast to a service, a goal is a simpler concept and can be formally specified as pre-condition and post-condition clauses, which makes the implementation easier. It allows more dynamic interactions among agents. For example, if the semantics of the pre and post-conditions of the declared goals is commonly understood among agents, an agent can creating a new goal on the spot.

This hierarchical structure of agents allows us to construct more complex agents. And since the agents, even at the lowest level, are completely autonomous, not only systems that operate in dynamic environments can be modeled using this architecture, we can even model intrinsically dynamic systems that are changing or evolving over time.

The hierarchical agent architecture is also highly modular and open. Since micro agents communicate with each other through declarative goals, their internal structure or state is hidden from each other. This important feature allows us to introduce new components into the platform easily. In the next section we describe how we integrate the high level reasoning engines and programming languages into OPAL.

6   Integrating 3APL, ROK and JPRS into OPAL

To integrate the three high level reasoning engines into OPAL, our idea is to introduce them as special micro agent components. It means that apart from having the original Java primitive micro agents, we also have three special kinds of micro agents — 3APL micro agent, ROK micro agent, and JPRS micro agent. The integrating process for the three components are the same in principle, and only differ slightly in implementation. The 3APL micro agent class has a 3APL interpreter and a 3APL engine as its core. It inherits the role playing and group behavior from the primitive micro agent class. The 3APL micro agent loads its source from a prepared 3APL program script and compiles the source using the interpreter. Recall that in Section 2.3, we mentioned a special kind of goal in 3APL language called JavaGoal, which represents a simple Java method invocation. In our implementation, we have modified the JavaGoal construct so that when the 3APL program produces a JavaGoal, an OPAL goal is created to wrap up the contents of the JavaGoal. The 3APL micro agent can then treat it as a normal OPAL goal and decide whether it has the ability to solve this goal using its local capability or not; and in the latter case, it can distribute this goal to other micro agents for assistance. When external information arrives at the 3APL micro agent, whether it is a message or a goal, the 3APL micro agent will insert the information into its belief-base, in the following format:

- if the arriving data is a message, the belief *message(content)* will be added to the belief-base.
- if the arriving data is a goal(which represents a service request), the belief *goal(precondition, postcondition)* will be added to the belief-base.

In both cases, the belief-base is treated as a knowledge-base for holding information. It would be more straightforward to insert the incoming OPAL goal as a 3APL goal instead of inserting it into the belief-base as a belief item. But the problem is that there is a set of eight programming constructs for 3APL goals (BactionGoal, PredGoal, TestGoal, SkipGoal, SequenceGoal, IfGoal, WhileGoal, JavaGoal), and in order to do the goal transformation, one is faced with the problem of interpreting the content of the OPAL goal, and deciding which one of the eight types of 3APL goal to transform to. By inserting the OPAL goal as a belief, we leave the handling of the goal to the programmer. The programmer can write rules coping with the belief change caused by receiving goals. This implementation restricts the dynamism and flexibility we gained from having declarative OPAL goals, because the 3APL programmer needs to know what kind of OPAL goal the program will receive in order to prepare sensible rules for it. But on the other hand, even with 3APL goals, true dynamism is not possible. The 3APL programmer can only specify the plan of achieving goals knowing what goals to expect. In this sense, this implementation compromise is not too severe. Nevertheless, to provide better bridge of this existing semantic gap remains as a future goal for OPAL development.

We take almost identical approaches for integrating ROK and JPRS micro agents. Upon receiving messages or goals, the information is wrapped up as an item of belief and inserted into the knowledge-base of ROK and JPRS agents, respectively.

7 Performance Comparison of the Three Reasoning Engines

The absolute speeds of these reasoning engines are difficult to measure, because implementation bias in the test programs is inevitable. And also in a multi-agent environment, agents that are powered with these reasoning engines spend their processing time not just on local computation, but also on communication. Although precise quantitative figures are difficult to obtain, we believe some computationally intensive test could still give us suggestive evidences on the relative speed of the reasoning engines. We choose to implement mergesort tests using all three engines, because mergesort is a standardized algorithm, which helps to minimize the amount of implementation error or bias introduced.

The tests were run on an Acer machine with a Celeron 2.4 GHz processor and 240MB RAM. We wrote a 3APL program, a ROK program running in native mode, a ROK program running in scripting mode, and a JPRS program, all running mergesort on integer arrays containing random integers.

The average times each program took to sort the arrays are given in Table 1 and are plotted in Figure 1 and Figure 2. When the length of the array to be sorted became larger than 1000, the 3APL program took too long (longer than 15 minutes) to compute and thus the results are omitted.

We plotted the results of the 3APL program separately from the other results, because the scale of the 3APL program's execution time is too large for visual comparison with the other reasoning engines. From Figure 2 we can see that ROK in native mode is the fastest. It is about twice as fast as ROK in scripting mode, and many times faster than JPRS, especially when the the array size becomes greater than 1000. We also observed that both ROK and JPRS are

Table 1. Mergesort Time (in ms.)

No. of int to sort	3APL	ROK Native	ROK Scripting	JPRS
50	12078	361	110	40
100	28632	661	141	80
200	83040	801	200	350
300	178797	841	360	841
400	318919	1072	341	1773
500	519127	1312	390	3265
600	761235	1472	441	6319
1000	...	3565	1402	3004
2000	...	6920	2924	20250
3000	...	10836	4737	68318
4000	...	16854	9374	168853
5000	...	21892	10495	314111

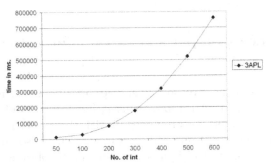

Fig. 1. 3APL Mergesort Program Runtime Plot

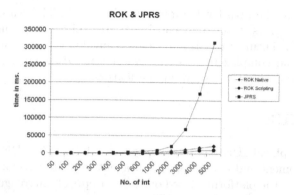

Fig. 2. ROK and JPRS Mergesort Program Runtime Plot

much faster than 3APL. This result is not surprising, because JPRS and ROK are built closely to primitive Java, and the goal-plan matching algorithm is not computationally expensive. On the other hand, 3APL has a more complex internal structure. It uses a JIProlog engine internally to process prolog-like wffs, and its first order logic features (variables) makes the reification process much more complicated than ROK or JPRS. The slower speed of 3APL is a trade-off against its declarative expressiveness, and its first order logic features.

8   The Master Mind™Games

We developed a system for benchmarking, the Master Mind™Game[14], to verify the integration of the high level reasoning engines, and also to demonstrate the two different approaches of agent development in OPAL – declarative and procedural. In the game, the *master mind* holds a key of 4 pegs, each has one of six colors. The *code breaker* tries to deduce the answer by making guesses at it. *master mind* will mark each guess with a *black* or a *white* marker. A *black* marker means one of your pegs is the correct colour and in the correct position. A *white* marker tells you that one of the pegs in the guess is of a colour which is in the solution, but not in the correct position. A full description of the Master Mind game can be found in Nelson [14]. In our implementation, three high level OPAL agents were developed. Each high level agent is composed of two lower-level micro agents. One of them is in charge of FIPA-compliant messaging services, and the other micro agent is the reasoning agent that implements the game logic. The three reasoning micro agents were a 3APL micro agent, a ROK micro agent, and a JPRS micro agent. The high level agents represent *code breakers* and have a common goal of winning the game using as few guesses as possible. They share information and cooperate through exchanging FIPA messages. The real-world Master Mind game is not a multi-player game and therefore adopting it and setting it into a multi-agent scenario is not naturally suited for multi-agent system applications. But our purpose is to demonstrate the usability of the extended OPAL platform by showing an example of how one could use all the high-level components in OPAL. The reasoning power of the high-level engines, albeit under-utilized, are still well-demonstrated in this example system. Future work is expected to involve the development of more sophisticated and complex multi-agent systems in OPAL, using the reasoning engines and the declarative programming feature.

9   OPAL IDE

Recently, a graphical IDE has been added to OPAL. The IDE facilitates the design, development and testing phases of agent software development, without having to reboot the platform. Based on the concepts of micro agents and agent-oriented software development, the IDE provides support for:

- creation of new micro-agents by simply dragging icons and plugging them into the existing hierarchy (currently we support the graphical instantiation of 3APL agents, ROK agents, primitive Java agents, OPAL agents and primitive Java roles);
- grouping and regrouping of agents (we currently support moving, regrouping, copying and deleting micro-agents in a drag-n-drop fashion).

The intuitive graphical operations on agents in the IDE are enabled by the underlying more complex interactions with the platform. For example, when a

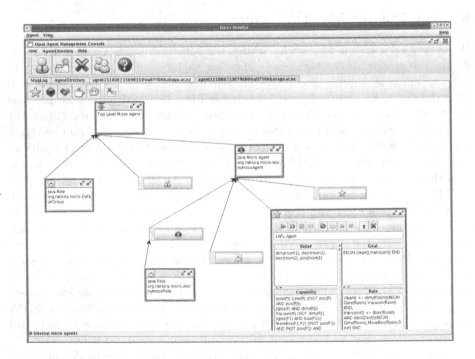

Fig. 3. OPAL Agent Composition Panel Screen-shot

new micro-agent is created, we first determine the agent type and its creator in the agent hierarchy, then we make an instance of the agent, and handle all the necessary registration and association with other agents. Also we show such associations to the developer in the GUI. A full scripting interface is implemented for 3APL micro-agents. The user can load a source file, modify and compile the source file, or create the source file on-the-fly in the text area provided. The IDE is still in the prototyping phase and not yet released. To allow the IDE to support dynamic scripting of general Java agents, we are currently evaluating different approaches of either using our own scripting engine, or relying on customized Java classloaders. This is the next phase of OPAL development. The screen-shots of the IDE are shown in Figure 3.

10   Conclusion

As discussed at the beginning of this paper, declarative agent programming languages and techniques bridge the semantic gap that exists between agent specification and practical implementation. We have presented our approach of incorporating declarative agent programming support into the OPAL multi-agent platform. In particular, we have described in detail how the agent-oriented hierarchical architecture of OPAL can facilitate the easy integration of high-level agent programming languages such as 3APL and ROK. The extended OPAL platform allows developers to use the powerful features of declarative languages in developing complex agent systems, while maintaining agent-oriented architecture.

References

1. Dastani, M., Riemsdijk, B. V., Dignum, F. and Meyer, J. J. C. (2004). "A Programming Language for Cognitive Agents Goal Directed 3APL", *In Proceedings of the First Workshop on Programming Multi-agent Systems: Languages, frameworks, techniques, and tools (ProMAS03)*, Springer-Verlag, Berlin, 2004.
2. Figueira, C. and Ramalho, G. (2000). "JEOPS - The Java Embedded Object Production System", *In M. Monard, J. Sichman (eds.). Proc. of 7th Ibero-American Conference on AI (Atibaia, November 19–22, 2000). Lecture Notes in Artificial Intelligence*, pp.53-62, Vol. 1952. Springer-Verlag, Berlin, 2000.
3. *FIPA Organization.* http://www.fipa.org
4. FIPA. "FIPA Agent Management Specification",
   http://www.fipa.org/specs/fipa00023/sc00023j.html
5. Georgeff, M. P. and Lansky, A. L. (1986). "Procedural Knowledge", *Proceedings of the IEEE Special Issue on Knowledge Representation*, 74(10):1383-1398, October 1986.
6. Forgy, C. (1982). " Rete: a Fast Algorithm for the Many Pattern/Many Objects Pattern Match Problem", *Artificial Intelligence*, 19:177, 1982
7. Hindriks, K., De Boer, F., Van der Hoek, W. and Meyer, J. J. (1999). "Agent programming in 3APL", *Autonomous Agents and Multi-Agent Systems*, 2(4): pp.357-401, 1999.
8. Hoeve, E. C. ten (2003). "3APL Platform", *Master's Thesis, University of Utrecht, The Netherlands*, Oct 2003.

9. Huber, M. J. (2001). "JAM agents in a nutshell", Nov 2001.
10. *Java Agent Service.* http://www.java-agent.org
11. Nowostawski, M. (2001). "Kea Enterprise Agents Documentation", Aug, 2001.
12. Nowostawski, M. (2004). "Otago Agent Platform Developer's Guide", Feb 2004.
13. Nowostawski, M., Purvis, M., and Cranefield, S. (2001). "KEA - Multi-level Agent Infrastructure", *In Proceedings of the Second International Workshop of Central and Eastern Europe on Multi-Agent Systems (CEEMAS 2001)*, pp.355-362, Department of Computer Science, University of Mining and Metallurgy, Krakow, Poland 2001.
14. Nelson, T. (1999). "Investigations into the Master Mind™Board Game", http://www.tnelson.demon.co.uk/mastermind/, 1999.
15. Rao, A. S. (1996). "AgentSpeak(L): BDI Agents Speak Out in a Logical Computable Language", In W. van der Velde and J.W. Perram, editors, *Agents Beaking Away (LNAI 1038)*, pp.42-55, Springer-Verlag, 1996.
16. Ricordel, P. M., and Demazeau, Y. (2000). "From Analysis to Deployment: A Multi-agent Platform Survey", *ESAW*: pp.93-105, 2000.
17. Shoham, Y. (1993). "Agent-oriented Programming", *Artificial Intelligence*, 60: pp.51-92, 1993.
18. Wooldridge, M. J., and Jennings, N. R. (1995). "Intelligent agents: Theory and practice", *Knowledge Engineering Review*, 10(2), 1995.
19. Wooldridge, M. J. (2002). *An Introduction to MultiAgent Systems*, West Sussex, England: Wiley, 2002.

Author Index

Lecture Notes in Artificial Intelligence (LNAI)

Vol. 3662: C. Baral, G. Greco, N. Leone, G. Terracina (Eds.), Logic Programming and Nonmonotonic Reasoning. XIII, 454 pages. 2005.

Vol. 3661: T. Panayiotopoulos, J. Gratch, R.S. Aylett, D. Ballin, P. Olivier, T. Rist (Eds.), Intelligent Virtual Agents. XIII, 506 pages. 2005.

Vol. 3658: V. Matoušek, P. Mautner, T. Pavelka (Eds.), Text, Speech and Dialogue. XV, 460 pages. 2005.

Vol. 3651: R. Dale, K.-F. Wong, J. Su, O.Y. Kwong (Eds.), Natural Language Processing – IJCNLP 2005. XXI, 1031 pages. 2005.

Vol. 3642: D. Ślęzak, J. Yao, J.F. Peters, W. Ziarko, X. Hu (Eds.), Rough Sets, Fuzzy Sets, Data Mining, and Granular Computing, Part II. XXIII, 738 pages. 2005.

Vol. 3641: D. Ślęzak, G. Wang, M. Szczuka, I. Düntsch, Y. Yao (Eds.), Rough Sets, Fuzzy Sets, Data Mining, and Granular Computing, Part I. XXIV, 742 pages. 2005.

Vol. 3635: J.R. Winkler, M. Niranjan, N.D. Lawrence (Eds.), Deterministic and Statistical Methods in Machine Learning. VIII, 341 pages. 2005.

Vol. 3632: R. Nieuwenhuis (Ed.), Automated Deduction – CADE-20. XIII, 459 pages. 2005.

Vol. 3630: M.S. Capcarrère, A.A. Freitas, P.J. Bentley, C.G. Johnson, J. Timmis (Eds.), Advances in Artificial Life. XIX, 949 pages. 2005.

Vol. 3626: B. Ganter, G. Stumme, R. Wille (Eds.), Formal Concept Analysis. X, 349 pages. 2005.

Vol. 3625: S. Kramer, B. Pfahringer (Eds.), Inductive Logic Programming. XIII, 427 pages. 2005.

Vol. 3620: H. Muñoz-Ávila, F. Ricci (Eds.), Case-Based Reasoning Research and Development. XV, 654 pages. 2005.

Vol. 3614: L. Wang, Y. Jin (Eds.), Fuzzy Systems and Knowledge Discovery, Part II. XLI, 1314 pages. 2005.

Vol. 3613: L. Wang, Y. Jin (Eds.), Fuzzy Systems and Knowledge Discovery, Part I. XLI, 1334 pages. 2005.

Vol. 3607: J.-D. Zucker, L. Saitta (Eds.), Abstraction, Reformulation and Approximation. XII, 376 pages. 2005.

Vol. 3601: G. Moro, S. Bergamaschi, K. Aberer (Eds.), Agents and Peer-to-Peer Computing. XII, 245 pages. 2005.

Vol. 3600: F. Wiedijk (Ed.), The Seventeen Provers of the World. XVI, 159 pages. 2006.

Vol. 3596: F. Dau, M.-L. Mugnier, G. Stumme (Eds.), Conceptual Structures: Common Semantics for Sharing Knowledge. XI, 467 pages. 2005.

Vol. 3593: V. Mařík, R. W. Brennan, M. Pěchouček (Eds.), Holonic and Multi-Agent Systems for Manufacturing. XI, 269 pages. 2005.

Vol. 3587: P. Perner, A. Imiya (Eds.), Machine Learning and Data Mining in Pattern Recognition. XVII, 695 pages. 2005.

Vol. 3584: X. Li, S. Wang, Z.Y. Dong (Eds.), Advanced Data Mining and Applications. XIX, 835 pages. 2005.

Vol. 3581: S. Miksch, J. Hunter, E.T. Keravnou (Eds.), Artificial Intelligence in Medicine. XVII, 547 pages. 2005.

Vol. 3577: R. Falcone, S. Barber, J. Sabater-Mir, M.P. Singh (Eds.), Trusting Agents for Trusting Electronic Societies. VIII, 235 pages. 2005.

Vol. 3575: S. Wermter, G. Palm, M. Elshaw (Eds.), Biomimetic Neural Learning for Intelligent Robots. IX, 383 pages. 2005.

Vol. 3571: L. Godo (Ed.), Symbolic and Quantitative Approaches to Reasoning with Uncertainty. XVI, 1028 pages. 2005.

Vol. 3559: P. Auer, R. Meir (Eds.), Learning Theory. XI, 692 pages. 2005.

Vol. 3558: V. Torra, Y. Narukawa, S. Miyamoto (Eds.), Modeling Decisions for Artificial Intelligence. XII, 470 pages. 2005.

Vol. 3554: A.K. Dey, B. Kokinov, D.B. Leake, R. Turner (Eds.), Modeling and Using Context. XIV, 572 pages. 2005.

Vol. 3550: T. Eymann, F. Klügl, W. Lamersdorf, M. Klusch, M.N. Huhns (Eds.), Multiagent System Technologies. XI, 246 pages. 2005.

Vol. 3539: K. Morik, J.-F. Boulicaut, A. Siebes (Eds.), Local Pattern Detection. XI, 233 pages. 2005.

Vol. 3538: L. Ardissono, P. Brna, A. Mitrović (Eds.), User Modeling 2005. XVI, 533 pages. 2005.

Vol. 3533: M. Ali, F. Esposito (Eds.), Innovations in Applied Artificial Intelligence. XX, 858 pages. 2005.

Vol. 3528: P.S. Szczepaniak, J. Kacprzyk, A. Niewiadomski (Eds.), Advances in Web Intelligence. XVII, 513 pages. 2005.

Vol. 3518: T.-B. Ho, D. Cheung, H. Liu (Eds.), Advances in Knowledge Discovery and Data Mining. XXI, 864 pages. 2005.

Vol. 3508: P. Bresciani, P. Giorgini, B. Henderson-Sellers, G. Low, M. Winikoff (Eds.), Agent-Oriented Information Systems II. X, 227 pages. 2005.

Vol. 3505: V. Gorodetsky, J. Liu, V.A. Skormin (Eds.), Autonomous Intelligent Systems: Agents and Data Mining. XIII, 303 pages. 2005.

Vol. 3501: B. Kégl, G. Lapalme (Eds.), Advances in Artificial Intelligence. XV, 458 pages. 2005.

Vol. 3492: P. Blache, E.P. Stabler, J.V. Busquets, R. Moot (Eds.), Logical Aspects of Computational Linguistics. X, 363 pages. 2005.

Vol. 3490: L. Bolc, Z. Michalewicz, T. Nishida (Eds.), Intelligent Media Technology for Communicative Intelligence. X, 259 pages. 2005.

Vol. 3488: M.-S. Hacid, N.V. Murray, Z.W. Raś, S. Tsumoto (Eds.), Foundations of Intelligent Systems. XIII, 700 pages. 2005.

Vol. 3487: J.A. Leite, P. Torroni (Eds.), Computational Logic in Multi-Agent Systems. XII, 281 pages. 2005.

Vol. 3476: J.A. Leite, A. Omicini, P. Torroni, P. Yolum (Eds.), Declarative Agent Languages and Technologies II. XII, 289 pages. 2005.

Vol. 3464: S.A. Brueckner, G.D.M. Serugendo, A. Karageorgos, R. Nagpal (Eds.), Engineering Self-Organising Systems. XIII, 299 pages. 2005.